Crete and James

Crete and James

Personal Letters of
Lucretia and James Garfield

Edited by John Shaw

Michigan State University Press

East Lansing

1994

All Michigan State University Press books are produced on paper which meets the requirements of American National Standard of Information Sciences—Permanance of paper for printed materials ANSI Z39.48-1984.

Michigan State University Press
Esat Lansing, MI 48823-5202

Cover and Frontispiece photo courtesy of The Western Reserve Historical Society, Cleveland, OH

02 01 00 99 98 97 96 95 94 1 2 3 4 5 6 7 8 9

Library of Congress Cataloging-in-Publication Data

Crete and James : personal letters of Lucretia and James Garfield / edited by John Shaw.
    p.   cm.
    Includes bibliographical references and index.
    ISBN 0-87013-338-1
    1. Garfield, James A. (James Abram), 1831-1881—Correspondence. 2. Garfield, Lucretia Rudolph, 1832-1918—Correspondence. 3. Presidents—United States—Correspondence. 4. Presidents' spouses—United States—Correspondence. I. Shaw, John, 1922-
E687.A4 1994
973.84'092—dc20
[B]   94-26661
                                                             CIP

Contents

Preface   vii

Introduction   ix

A Cast of Characters   xvii

Chapter 1.   Courtship: The First Year, 1853-1854   1

Chapter 2.   Courtship: The Second Year, 1855-18565   43

Chapter 3.   Marriage and the Ohio Senate, 1856-1861   80

Chapter 4.   The Civil War, 1861-September 1862   118

Chapter 5.   The Civil War, Washington, Chickamaugua, and Congress, 1862-1863   156

Chapter 6.   "The Shadows Passed," January 1864-December 1865   199

Chapter 7.   Washington and Hiram, 1866-1869   229

Chapter 8.   1870-September 1872   262

Chapter 9.   The Credit Mobilier, thr Salary Grab and the California Trip, 1872-1875   286

Chapter 10.   Spring 1876-June 1879   324

Chapter 11.   The Final Two Years, September 1879-September 1881   360

Bibliography   393

Index   395

Preface

The Garfield personal letters, written between 1853 and 1881, are among the documents in the James A. Garfield Papers, Library of Congress, Washington, D.C. Of the more than twelve-hundred letters in the collection, I have chosen about four hundred for inclusion in this volume. My basis for selection has been the inherent interest in the topics discussed and a regard for the continuity of the marital relationship. I wish the letters, above all, to tell a story of a marriage. Accordingly, while my annotations for the surrounding context of political or military situations have been minimal, I have tried to clarify the domestic situations as much as possible.

Most letters are presented in their entirety. Only when passages of very minor interest to my purposes appear have I omitted any material. In a few cases, also, I have had to omit words or groups of words because of unintelligible handwriting or fading ink. In such cases I have used an underlined space to indicate an omission.

Since both correspondents generally wrote with mechanical correctness, I have made few changes in presenting the text. I have attempted to record spelling exactly as I found it, though I have sometimes taken the liberty of bringing punctuation into line with modern practices, especially when an added comma clarifies meaning.

A very few of James' letters have been printed elsewhere, except in Frederick D. Williams' *The Wild Life of the Army: Civil War Letters of James A. Garfield* (East Lansing: Michigan State University Press, 1964) and in an appendix to Margaret Leech and Harry Brown's *The Garfield Orbit: The Life of President James A. Garfield* (New York: Harper and Row, 1978). None of Lucretia's letters have been published to my knowledge, though brief excerpts from a few have been included in various biographies, notably in Theodore Smith's *James Abram Garfield: The Life and Letters*, 2 vols. (New Haven: Yale University Press, 1925).

Many scholars and teachers have given me encouragement and help during the preparation of this volume. I am grateful to the National Endowment for the Humanities for a year's grant, which provided me with the time to read through the more than twelve-hundred letters, catalogue all and record over half of them. The enthusiasm and advice of my lifelong friend, Mr. James Milholland Jr., an avid history buff, have been a constant inspiration. Dr. David Anderson of Hiram College and Dr. John Strassburger of Knox College have been especially helpful. The librarians of the Hiram College Library, Ms. Lisa Johnson and Mr. Jeff Wanser in particular, have been ready and willing to track down recondite references. Ms. Nora Jones, Librarian at Western Reserve Academy in Hudson, Ohio, brought long sought for information to my attention. And Professor Fred H. Stocking of Williams College provided me with important facts regarding Garfield's attendance at a special ceremony there.

My daughter Clara of Carleton College and her husband, Robert Hardy, both classics scholars, have provided me with translations of Latin or Greek phrases and have made imaginative suggestions regarding Garfield's use of them.

Above all, I wish to mention the crucial aid I received from Dr. Harry Brown at Michigan State University who, both personally as well as with his splendid edition of *The Diary of James A. Garfield*, 4 vols. (East Lansing: Michigan State University, 1967–1981), has helped to make me familiar with the world of the Garfields and their friends. So essential was his edition of the *Diary* to this work that I can only describe him as a "silent partner" in the preparation of these letters, which I hope will light up a domestic corner in the world of Garfield military and political scholarship.

Crete and James I dedicate to my wife, whose steady encouragement and frequent help in preparing the manuscript have given a touch of reality to Lucretia's glowing comment that "many homes have been brightened and blessed by the love we have revealed to them," ours, perhaps, being one of them.

Introduction

James A. Garfield and Lucretia Rudolph Garfield exchanged about twelve hundred letters during their courtship and marriage. The correspondence began in November 1853, when James was on a visit to Niagara Falls, continuing through five years of an uneasy courtship. In 1858 the two were married. But as James rose in the military and political arenas, he and Lucretia were constantly separated. Their emotional life was for months on end held together only by their letters. In 1863, James entered the House of Representatives in Washington after serving with the Union armies. By this time Lucretia could point out to James that during their nearly five years of married life, the two had lived together only twenty weeks. Still, Lucretia and her growing family had to wait until 1869, when James built a home in Washington, before they would live together permanently.

In the 1870s, as James' career neared its apogee, the two corresponded hundreds of times a year, usually because James was on the campaign stump, or at an important trial, or attending Congressional business. Less frequently, Lucretia was the traveling one: back to Ohio to take care of ailing parents, taking the boys to school in the east, or vacationing at their farm near Lake Erie in Ohio.

Finally, James was elected president of the United States and the two, with their family of five children, moved into a dilapidated White House in March 1881. On July 2 of that year, as James was boarding the train for Williams College for his 25th Reunion, Charles Guiteau walked up behind him and shot him twice in the back. Garfield died in September 1881. He was not yet fifty years old.

Though the letters tell of military and political activities, for the most part they are not about public affairs; they are domestic letters. From beginning to end, they reveal with unusual candor a domestic relationship. Lucretia, or Crete, as James called her, is the emotional center of this correspondence. Her complex character grows steadily from a shy, diffident girl of the 1850s, romantic, yet known, too, for her practical common sense to an outstanding woman, guiding her husband's social and political careers with tact and intelligence. In 1880 Mary Clemmer Ames, a newspaper correspondent, could write of her:

> I know her and know that she is her husband's equal not only, but in more than one respect his superior. She has 'the philosophic mind' that Wordsworth sings of; she has a self-poise, a strength of unswerving, absolute rectitude her husband has not and never will have, though her temperament does not give her the capacity for the seasons of moral enthusiasm which are possible to him. Much of the time that other women give to distributing visiting cards, in the frantic effort to make themselves 'leaders of society,' Mrs. Garfield spends in the alcoves of the Congressional Library, searching out books to carry home to study while she nurses her children. You may be sure of one thing: the woman who reads and studies while she rocks her babies will not be left far behind her husband in the march of actual growth.[1]

In some respects, Lucretia represents the typical middle-class woman of the mid-nineteenth century. She follows the trends set by the popular magazines and books like Catharine Beecher's *Treatise on Domestic Economy*, which she undoubtedly read. She assumes a submissive role in relation to her husband, and she sees her mission as that of providing for him a comfortable, pleasant home. But she goes much beyond this vision, too. She may write, on the one hand, that women must exhibit love and gentle deeds, as well as strength: "woman's province is her home, and if she is not fitted to make it a place around which warmest affections cluster, and on whose hearth-stone attractions center, she is not prepared to act her part in life." On the other hand, she can also write: "It is horrible to be a man but the grinding misery of being a woman between the upper and nether millstone of household cares and training children is almost as bad. To be half civilized with some aspirations for enlightenment, and obliged to spend the largest part of the time the victim of young barbarians keeps one in a perpetual ferment!"

About the persistent issue of woman suffrage, Lucretia and James were no doubt in agreement. James thought the claim "that woman should have all the rights of man and still enjoy all the exceptions which a chivalric regard for her physical inferiority has so long conceded her" was absurd. He wrote: "suffrage is not the appropriate remedy for the many evils of which Woman so justly complains." But one senses a more sympathetic attitude on the part of Lucretia. In her earliest letters to James, in 1855, she writes of a remark a rude man made about women's right to education: "I judge he thinks all we are made for is work, and as for accomplishments, it is a sin even to think of them. What an idea of life! Bake bread, wash dishes, scrub, iron and mend, week in week out, month after month, year after year—without a thought of anything else. True, those things must all be attended to, and each one should bear her part, but to make their thorough performances the end and aim of life, and the only object to receive any attention is most intolerable."

When the matter of her own education comes up, Lucretia writes, "True, it has become almost a proverb that when a lady is married, she may as well lay aside her books, still I do not believe it contains very much wisdom after all."

But neither Lucretia nor James supported the woman's rights movement; in fact, they both saw it as antagonistic to the peace and quiet of the household. James felt that certain features of the movement tended to "strike down the sanctity of marriage and break up the foundations of the family." Late in their marriage, when a women's rights advocate had apparently spread some gossip about James, Lucretia and James both suspected the woman was part of a "scheme of alienating all husbands and wives." Lucretia wrote to this woman:"[But how you] could have given credence and currency to such a report and branded with licentiousness the reputation of a man whom you have been able to know so much about, I am utterly unable to explain to my own mind . . . unless in your infatuation over the Rights of Woman you allowed spite to triumph over reason."

The story of the Garfield courtship and marriage, as told by the letters, is clearly Crete's story. That is no doubt why Mrs. Garfield, who lived thirty-seven years after her husband's assassination, preserved the letters so carefully. It may be that she destroyed one or two, but there is little evidence that she did. Rather, she added dates or places when not clear, and she saw to it that even letters having to do with Garfield's infidelity or her own jealous fears, were saved. She had seen a number of biographies written about her husband, during his campaign for the presidency and after his death, but she wanted posterity to know "the inside story," her story, too. The letters tell this story.

John D'Emilio and Estelle Freedman's *Intimate Matters* describes a pattern of courtship in nineteenth-century America typical of middle-class young men and women, against which we may assess the experience of James and

Lucretia. "Courtship," D'Emilio and Freedman write, "involved a delicate ritual, a sharing of hearts that only gradually overcame middle class reticence about sexuality. During courtship and once engaged, couples exchanged personal confidences, baring their souls and exposing their weaknesses to each other."[2]

Early correspondence between James and Lucretia illustrates this pattern fully. "It is my desire to 'know and be known,'" writes James, and he continues, "I long to hear from you . . . to know your heart and open mine to you. . . . Let your heart take the pen and your hand hold it not back." From Lucretia comes the reply immediately: "I in return for that last kind letter of yours surrender my pen to my heart." At which point Lucretia speaks of her concern that she is viewed by "the world" as "cold" and "heartless." "If I can only," she writes, "learn to unbosom my whole soul to you and prove myself worthy of receiving your entire confidence in return."

Later in the correspondence, Lucretia's keen perception tells her that her letters have, in fact, produced a vision of emotional warmth and perfection that her true self cannot sustain. Ellen Rothman, in *Hands and Hearts*, points out that often at this time with such couples as James and Lucretia "lovers were left exposed to the risks of idealization."[3] This is precisely the case, and Lucretia knew it. After the failure of their relationship during 1856–57, Lucretia writes to James that her letters have conveyed "to you impressions and [have] awaken[ed] expectations which my presence fails to make you realize." Is it not true, she asks, "that heretofore almost all you have known of me was gained not from my life or my actions but from my pen?"

Thus, Lucretia and James' courtship was typical of its day in many respects, although it nearly failed to succeed in marriage. Lucretia's expectations for marriage, romantically idealistic at first, gradually assumed more realistic dimensions. In the end, she acquiesced to the thought that James was marrying her because he felt he ought to. "There are hours," she wrote the summer before their marriage, "when my heart almost breaks with the cruel thought that our marriage is based upon the cold stern word *duty*." And it is true, during their first ten years of marriage, 1858–1868, James and Lucretia experienced many stresses, hinted at in their letters and sometimes explicitly discussed.

Perhaps the fundamental problem in their relationship was at first an emotional incompatibility. In a revealing letter, Lucretia wrote: "I do not think I was born for constant caresses, and surely no education of my childhood taught me to need them. Nor am I sorry that life to you means demonstration. . . . I am only sorry that my own quiet and reserve should mean to you a lack of love." Later she wrote, "Before when you were away my heart missed you, now my whole self mourns with it and longs and pines for your presence, my lips for your kisses, my cheek for the warm pressure of yours. In short, I understand what you meant when you used to say, 'I want to be touched!'" Still, such a comment was easier for Lucretia to make in writing than to express in speaking, and the relationship stumbled along uncertainly through half a dozen more years of misunderstanding.

Another more obvious problem the young married couple faced was that of constant separation. Domestic historians have written in detail of two worlds men and women occupied in their daily lives. "Man's sphere is out of doors among men," Emerson declared, "woman's is in the house. Man seeks for power and influence, woman for order and beauty. Man is just; woman is kind."[4] James and Lucretia fully accepted such a concept "in order that the great work of society may be better carried on," in Catharine Beecher's words.[5] Yet, such a separation of gender roles was only cause for anxiety and pain for Lucretia. She concluded, and certainly with justification, that James did not wish to be with her at home any more than he had to be.

Evidently, James sought sexual intimacy outside of the marriage. He had two love affairs that threatened not only the happiness of his marriage, but also the success of his political career. The first affair was with Rebecca Selleck, a vivacious, emotional girl from Lewisboro, New York, whom Garfield met while a student at Williams College. Lucretia, who was introduced to Rebecca at the Williams commencement in 1856, did her best to accept her as a friend. But as she became more aware of the hold Rebecca had on James, she found she could not. At one point in 1856, Lucretia told James she felt "a great wrong" had been done, perhaps a suggestion that James and Rebecca had consummated their relationship. And later Lucretia bitterly suggested that James marry Selleck instead. Moreover, as late as 1869, eleven years after their marriage, Lucretia pleaded with James not to continue visiting Rebecca every time he was in New York. James refused, however, insisting his friendship with Rebecca meant too much to him to give up. Her final dutiful words on this matter were, "The truth, whatever it may be, alone can live. Whatever is false will die of itself and by itself. There is not need of violence to destroy it."

The other woman in Garfield's life is more mysterious, and was infinitely more hazardous to his reputation. He apparently fell deeply in love with a young widow while serving his first term in Congress, sometime in the spring of 1864. Lucia Gilbert Calhoun had been born in North Brookfield, Massachusetts, in 1844 and married in 1862. A writer for the New York *Tribune*, she may well have met Garfield in New York when he was visiting his good friend from Ohio, Whitelaw Reid, the managing editor for the newspaper. At any rate, by May of 1864, Harmon Austin, Garfield's political mentor and great friend from Warren, Ohio, must have told Garfield to break the affair off, both for his own good as well as for the good of the Republican Party. There was gossip. Lucretia heard some in her own home, and James mentioned rumors himself, which he said were "groundless." But he suddenly came home to Hiram and told the truth. He confessed this illicit love to Lucretia and perhaps also to Almeda Booth, a teacher at Hiram whom Garfield much admired and whose advice he had always cherished. He told them he had fallen in love with a certain Lucia Gilbert Calhoun.

Lucretia forgave James on the condition he would immediately return to New York to break off the affair, which James did, though with difficulty. Such extramarital affairs evidently took place, not infrequently, without disrupting marriage. It would seem that a "double standard" for men was something to be tolerated. That Garfield probably told Almeda Booth of this humiliating circumstance would suggest the frequency with which such problems occurred in nineteenth century families.

Mrs. Calhoun went on to marry Cornelius Runkle, a New York lawyer, also connected with the *Tribune*. Her writings in that newspaper on cooking "treated from an artistic standpoint" gained her much adulation.[6]

By the end of 1869, then, with a home, "built as a monument to our love," going up in Washington for Lucretia to move into, the Garfield marriage settled into its best years. Though they returned to Hiram for the summer vacations, James and Lucretia now had a domestic base in Washington. Reading letters exchanged during this period between them, one can only come to the conclusion that James had at last fallen in love with his wife. As James himself put it:

> I will not lie down to sleep till I have told you again that I love you. Surely, 'love is the fulfilling of the law,' and the law of our love is liberty. We no longer love because we ought to, but because we do. The tyranny of our love is sweet. We waited long for his coming, but he has come to stay.

Lucretia's reply is equally rapturous:

> The cool days and falling leaves are bringing to me some very sweet reflections. The years tell me that we have passed the period called 'bright youth,' and that whatever more of life

there is for us belongs to the less enviable time, to the maturity which sobers us for the swift-coming future. But with our love so perfected, the coming years promise me so much that is sweet and beautiful in the loving, trusting gentleness and peace of our united and uniting lives that I look to them with more joy than to all the past.

The mid-nineteenth century view among middle class couples that marriage should be a "romantic union" influenced a "literary" style of writing in these letters. Lucretia and James' heightened style rarely spoke directly or realistically of their emotions. Instead, an imagery from popular fiction of the time, or from the Bible, permeates their writing. They speak of "veils" being lifted, of "dark clouds," of breathing "the fragrance of the alabaster box, which so long sealed has been broken at last," of "valleys of fear" and "mountains of hope," of "crossing the Jordan," of "terrible truth," and of "fire" in the heart. They wrote in the idiom of their day. Yet, in those letters written in 1870, one senses less a self-consciously "literary" style, and more a genuine emotional communication.

Beyond the story of their marriage, Lucretia and James' letters reveal many details of daily life during those years. We gain insight into the kind of household Lucretia managed in Hiram, with several boarders from the village's Eclectic Institute, plus Garfield's mother and the children. We learn about the difficulties of travel and the vagaries of the weather, cockroaches in the new home and the problems of cleaning house or educating the children. Topics of the day are also touched on—the slavery issue and Civil War, of course, the assassination of Lincoln, the debate about women's rights, the Henry Ward Beecher trial, and the impeachment of Andrew Johnson.

But even more interesting, we can sense unstated feelings within this complex relationship. "Any two people," writes A. S. Byatt in a short story, "may be talking to each other, at any moment, in a civilized way about something trivial, or even something complex and delicate. And inside each of the two there runs a kind of dark river of unconnected thought, of secret fear, or violence, or bliss. . . . The pace changes, the weight of the air, though the talk may run smoothly onward without a ripple or quiver."[7] We sense beneath the lines of many of these letters, in Lucretia's particularly, that "the pace changes" and fears and angers and hurts are exposed. What, precisely, may be the reasons behind these subtle alterations we cannot know for sure. Glancing references, like "the severe trial through which you made me pass," left unexplained, cause us to wonder the extent to which such women as Rebecca Selleck and Mrs. Calhoun were, even at the apparently happiest moments of their marriage, present in Lucretia's thoughts. But such intimate tensions must remain in the darkness of privacy.

The letters are written by two educated, literate persons, both intelligent, well-read, articulate correspondents. James' more flamboyant style is scholarly and interesting, while Lucretia's detailed, perceptive, complex manner is impressive for its penetrating insights. Reading the two sides of the correspondence as the years go by, we come to know James and Lucretia intimately, almost as if members of our family or close friends. We see them mature from no more than children into forceful adults. We watch their own children grow; and we never cease to be aware of the shadow of their final separation fast approaching. Phyllis Rose has commented in her book about Victorian marriages, called *Parallel Lives*, that "we are desperate for information about how other people live because we want to know how to live ourselves."[8] We cannot learn *all* of the details of their lives, but the letters of James Garfield and Lucretia Rudolph Garfield tell us much about how they experienced each other and their lives between 1853 and 1881.

❧ NOTES ❧

1. Quoted by Charles Carleton Coffin, *The Life of James A. Garfield* (Boston: James H. Earle, 1880), 337.

2. John D'Emilio and Estelle B. Freedman, *Intimate Matters: A History of Sexuality in America* (New York: Harper and Row, 1988), 75.

3. Ellen K. Rothman, *Hands and Hearts: A History of Courtship in America* (New York: Basic Books, Inc., 1984), 98.

4. Ralph Waldo Emerson, "Love," in *The Early Lectures of Ralph Waldo Emerson, 1835–1842*, vol. 3, edited by R. E. Spiller and Wallace E. Williams (Cambridge: Harvard University Press, 1972), 62.

5. Quoted by Kathryn Kish Sklar, *Catharine Beecher: A Study in American Domesticity* (New York: W. W. Norton, 1976), 156–57.

6. A brief sketch of Lucia Runkle appears in *Appleton's Cyclopaedia of American Biography*, vol. 5 (New York: D. Appleton and Company, 1888).

7. A. S. Byatt, 26 October 1992.

8. Phyllis Rose, *Parallel Lives: Five Victorian Marriages* (New York: Alfred A. Knopf, 1984), 9.

Cast of Characters

James Abram Garfield (1831–1881). Born in a log cabin built by his father in Orange, Ohio, Garfield attended school in Chester, Ohio, and at the Western Reserve Eclectic Institute in Hiram, Ohio, before graduating from Williams College in 1856. Garfield taught at the Eclectic Institute in Hiram; married **Lucretia Rudolph** in 1858; went to the Ohio Senate in 1860; joined the Union army in 1861; was elected to the U.S. Congress as Ohio's 19th District Representative in 1862, where he served until he was elected to the presidency in 1880. On 2 July 1881, Garfield was shot in Washington as he boarded the train for his 25th Reunion at Williams College. He died on 19 September, the anniversary of the Battle of Chickamauga, at which he had distinguished himself.

Lucretia Rudolph Garfield (1832–1918). Lucretia and James Garfield became acquainted when they attended a school at Chester, Ohio, and continued the friendship as students at the Western Reserve Eclectic Institute. Their romance began in 1853 and continued off and on until they married in 1858. Lucretia resided in Hiram while James was in Columbus serving in the Ohio legislature, while he was away during the Civil War, and for the first six years he served in Congress in Washington. She and her children moved to Washington after James built a house there in 1869. She spent most summers in Ohio, but she traveled with James occasionally. A highly intelligent woman, Lucretia read constantly, and in the later years of their marriage was a vital influence on her husband. They had seven children.

Eliz Arabella Garfield, nicknamed "Trot" (1860–1863). Eliz died in December 1863 of diphtheria.

Harry Augustus Garfield, nicknamed "Hal" (1863–1942). Harry attended St. Paul's Preparatory School and Williams College. After teaching at Princeton University and serving in the government during World War I, Harry became President of Williams College.

James Rudolph Garfield (1865–1950). James attended St. Paul's and Williams College. From 1907–1909 he was secretary of the interior; later he practiced law in Cleveland.

Mary Garfield, called "Mollie" (1867–1947). Educated in private schools in Cleveland and Connecticut, Mary married her father's personal secretary, Joseph Stanley-Brown in 1888.

Irvin Garfield (1870–1951). Irvin became a lawyer in Boston.

Abram Garfield, called "Abe" (1872–1958). Named after Garfield's father, Abram was a successful Cleveland architect.

Edward Garfield, called "Neddie" (1874–1876). Edward died after a bout of whooping cough in 1876. He and Eliz are buried in the Hiram cemetery.

Eliza Ballou Garfield, "Grandma" (1801–1888). Domineering, opinionated, and doting, James Garfield's mother directed him in every matter, including his love affairs. For example, when Garfield and his admired teacher and colleague, Almeda Booth, were so intellectually inseparable during Garfield's early days at Hiram, she wrote to James: "[Miss Booth] is old and wily. She will draw you on from one step to another by fawning and flattering…shun her as much as you can." Grandma caused friction in the Garfield home with her sharp tongue and intolerant disposition. Her conflict with Almeda Booth was apparently serious enough, at one time, to force James home from Washington to straighten matters. Unless she is in her childhood home in Hiram, Lucretia's frequent mention of "mother" or "grandma" usually refers to Eliza.

Almeda Booth (1823–1875). Almeda was a teacher and colleague of Garfield's at the Western Reserve Eclectic Insitute at Hiram, who became a close friend of both James and Lucretia, though Lucretia had her moments of rivalry. Miss Booth earned her degree from Oberlin College. She taught at Hiram between

1851 and 1866, exercising a powerful intellectual influence on Garfield. Both Garfield's mother and his wife tended to resent this influence.

Rebecca Selleck (1831–1909). Garfield met Rebecca, a glamorous and emotional woman, while a student at Williams College. From Lewisboro, New York, Rebecca often visited her friends, in Poestenkill, New York, not far from Williamstown. There Garfield became intimately acquainted with her, and perhaps fell in love with her. She, always in love with Garfield, became a haunting name to Lucretia during the early years of the marriage, but James insisted on visiting her whenever in the New York area.

Harry Rhodes (1836–1890). Rhodes was one of Garfield's closest political and academic friends. A student at the Eclectic Institute, like Garfield, Rhodes attended Williams College for his degree (1859) and then returned to Hiram to teach at the Institute. Later Rhodes became a lawyer, practicing in Cleveland.

Burke Hinsdale (1837–1900). A close friend of the Garfields, Hinsdale was associated over the years with Hiram's Eclectic Institute, first as a student, then as a teacher, and finally as its principal. Burke and his wife rented the Garfield home in Hiram for several years before buying it. Burke later became superintendent of the Cleveland schools and then a professor at the University of Michigan.

Dr. John P. Robison (1811–1889). Over the years from Hiram days on, "Doc" or "the doctor" was an intimate friend of the Garfields. Conservative and outspoken, he was often the subject of the correspondence between James and Lucretia, right up until the last days at the farm in Mentor. Robison was one of the first to speak of Garfield as a "dark horse" candidate in 1880.

Symonds Ryder (1792–1870), **Norman Dunshee**, **Harvey Everest** (1831–1900), and **Amos Hayden** (1813–1880) were men associated with the Eclectic Institute. An elder in the Disciples Church, **Ryder** was one of the founders of the Institute. **Dunshee**, a graduate of Western Reserve College in Hudson, Ohio, began teaching at Hiram in 1851; he was a scholar of classics. **Everest** taught at Hiram through the 1850s and was principal in 1862–64. **Hayden**, one of the founders of the Institute, was principal during Garfield's student years and until 1857.

Corydon Fuller (1830–1886) and **Charles Wilber** (1830–1891) were early friends of Garfield during their years at Hiram. Fuller's book, *Reminiscences of*

James A Garfield (Cincinnati: Standard Publishing Company, 1887), tells much about Garfield during the Hiram and Williams years. **Wilber** followed Garfield to Williams where the two roomed together and graduated in 1856.

Mark Hopkins (1802–1887), president of Williams College, became a friend of the Garfields in later years. Profoundly influenced by him during his two years at Williams College, Garfield admired Hopkins as one of America's greatest educators. Hopkins' last action as president of Williams before retiring was to award Garfield an honorary degree.

Harmon Austin (1817–1893) of Warren, Ohio, became Garfield's political mentor, as well as personal friend. He was a businessman and banker and active in the Disciples Church.

Jacob Dolson Cox (1828–1900) and Garfield roomed together in Columbus during their brief career in the Ohio senate. Cox later became a general in the Union armies, governor of Ohio, and finally president of the University of Cincinnati.

Wallace Ford (1832–1916) is mentioned from time to time in the letters of both the Garfields. He attended the Hiram Eclectic, of which his father was a founder, and was Garfield's secretary when James first went to Washington. Though Ford and Garfield were good friends, Lucretia did not think highly of him and once chastised James for allowing such a man to associate with him.

Salmon Chase (1808–1873) was both a governor of Ohio and a U.S. Senator before being made Secretary of the Treasury under Lincoln. Garfield lived at his home while in Washington during the fall of 1862. Chase's daughter, **Kate** (1835–1899), a socialite in the city, introduced Garfield to many fascinating personalities on the Washington scene.

Jeremiah Black (1810–1883) was Attorney General and Secretary of State, under Buchanan and a life-long Democrat, whom Garfield, nevertheless, admired greatly. Garfield conducted several law cases in association with him, and wrote to Lucretia about his unexpected visit to Black's home in Pennsylvania.

Henry Ward Beecher (1813–1887), a preacher from the Plymouth Congregational Church in Brooklyn, was sued by Theodore Tilton in 1874 for alleged adultery with his wife. No verdict was given by the jury; Garfield attended the trial on one occasion and described the courtroom scene to Lucretia.

Colonel Rockwell, a fellow graduate of Williams, returned to Washington in 1874 and was a frequent visitor of the Garfields. The Rockwell boy, Don, was at St. Paul's school when the two older Garfield boys entered in the fall of 1879.

Captain Swaim (1834–1897) was an intimate friend of the Garfields, going back to Civil War days when Swaim served as a staff officer under Garfield. Thanks to Swaim's encouragement and financial assistance, Garfield built his Washington home in 1869. Captain Swaim accompanied Garfield on his Montana trip in 1872.

George Rose, Garfield's part-time secretary, copied much material into Garfield's diaries. Garfield did not appoint Rose his secretary, however, after he became president.

Whitelaw Reid (1837–1912), a longtime friend of Garfield's, was, as managing editor of the *New York Tribune*, a powerful supporter of Garfield during the election of 1880. Reid comes into the correspondence particularly during Lucretia's secret visit to New York to have her inaugural gowns fitted.

CHAPTER 1

Courtship: The First Year, 1853–1854

D URING THEIR FIRST YEAR OF CORRESPONDENCE *James and Lucretia exchanged forty-five letters, of which twenty have been selected for inclusion here. James' first letter to Lucretia, written from Niagara Falls, came as a total surprise to her, for he had not shown any obvious interest in her before. They had known each other as children at the Geauga Academy in Chester, Ohio, and they had been well-acquainted at Hiram, where both were studying at the Western Reserve Eclectic Institute, a newly founded Disciple school, later to become Hiram College.*

But in November 1853 James turned his eye to Lucretia and began a correspondence that was to result in an engagement three months later, and in five years, marriage. The first letters are stilted and stiff; both write in a self-consciously "literary" style. In James' phrasing one can detect echoes from the classical texts he was reading and teaching. In a way he was "showing off" stylistically, impressing Lucretia, who had been one of the pupils in the Virgil class he taught the year before. Now she was herself teaching a class of children at a school in Chagrin Falls, a nearby town, while James was continuing his studies and teaching at Hiram's Eclectic Institute.

Though not quite twenty-two years old, James had traveled from home only as far away as western Pennsylvania and southern Ohio. It is not difficult to imagine his awe at seeing "the greatest waterfall upon the globe." Both Elizabeth McKinsey and John Sears, who have discussed the comments of nineteenth-century visitors to Niagara Falls, speak of the emotional experience recorded by countless travelers to this "preeminent American tourist attraction." "Educated people knew what they ought to feel in the presence of the Falls," writes Sears, "but it was inevitable that many of them did not respond with the full Burkean intensity. This was particularly true once the experience of

Niagara had become a cliché, as it did by the 1830's."[1] But reading James' account one feels he was indeed impressed by what he saw, though it is true that he has organized his impressions carefully in order to build emotion to a climactic moment.

Still, in his exact account of this vacation trip—he calls it a "statistical document"—James reveals a mind of more scholarly tendency than artistic. He does not speak of the development of industry and tourism, though he mentions the usual attractions: Goat Island, Horseshoe Fall, and the staircase to the foot of the Falls. Like most visitors, too, he visited Lundy's Lane, where a battle took place during the War of 1812.

Niagara Falls, Nov 16, 1853

Lucretia My Sister,

Please pardon the liberty I take in *pointing* my pen towards *your name* this evening, for I have taken in so much scenery today I cannot contain it all myself. Finding a necessity of stirring around some before the confinement of another term, and having long cherished a strong desire to see the greatest waterfall upon the globe, I concluded to do so now. Accordingly I went to Cleveland on Tuesday and tried to get a passage on the Lake, but the boat had left a short time before I reached the wharf. Being thus deprived of a passage upon moonlit Erie, I took the cars at 4 1/2 o'clock, and passing across the neck of the Key-Stone State, I arrived in Buffalo at 11 o'clock at night. The city is about three times as large as Cleveland, and contains 10,000 inhabitants.[2] I strolled through the city till 9 o'clock, when I again took the cars, and in less than one hour I came in sight of the hoary monument of mist that stands in the abyss below the Falls, and bathes its head in the clouds. Most of the distance from Buffalo, we were in sight of the St. Lawrence through whose channel flows the water of all the great Western Lakes. It is about two miles in width and is tranquil and smooth as polished silver, till we reach the rapids. First there is seen only a slight ripple. Soon wavelets become waves, which burst into whitecaps and are scattered in foam. Among the "bounding billows" of the rapids are several beautiful islands covered with hemlock and other evergreen trees, and a bridge passing over from the American side to Goat Island, the principal one of these, where there are a few buildings, and walks are elegantly laid out through this forest island. It divides the river and forms the American and Canadian Fall, which last from its Shape is called "The Horse Shoe Fall." It comprises a circle of 2100 feet and is 158 feet high. I stood upon the Canadian shore (having crossed the ferry below the falls) and beheld embattled myriads of hoary billows leaping along the rapids till they reached the awful brink, where they sprang with a furious bound and disappeared in "thunder and in foam." Then clothed in an oilcloth suit, I descended a spiral staircase, and followed a guide behind the falling sheet of table rock to the distance of 230 feet. The scene there presented overwhelms the soul and beggars all description. To look above you and behold a liquid world begirt with rainbows, tumbling from the skies, and thundering as it comes, would seem as though the heavens themselves were molten seas and falling to the earth.... I am stunned and overwhelmed at its immensity and grandeur, and to attempt to describe is only to desecrate it. I leave it—you can never *feel* it till you gaze *yourself.*

I then proceeded a few miles into Her Majesty's Dominions to the "Battle Ground" of\at Lundy's Lane where Gen Scott and his compeers won wreaths of lasting fame by being successful in the slaughter of 1100 human beings. An old soldier who was in the battle was there upon the observatory, and "fought the battle o'er again." I feel like moralizing here upon *war* and *worldly fame.* But I desist. From the Battle Ground by an "equestrian proceedure" I arrived at the suspension bridge. It is 800 feet long and is 230 feet above the water which at that place is 250 feet deep. They are now building a Rail Road Bridge about 40 feet directly above the other. From there I sauntered along the evergreen bank of the river looking down far below me upon the tops of tall trees growing at the water's edge, and thus closed the explorations of the day. I shall visit several other places of interest tomorrow, and in the afternoon return to Buffalo and if possible get an evening passage on the lake to Cleveland. I fear I shall miss it again, *for there are but few boats that venture out now.*

Now, Lucretia, if you have had patience to read thus far, this statistical document, I shall be fully confirmed in the belief that you are a woman of remarkable patience; and would say, I know not why I have written, only just I felt like it and did so. I expect, Deo Volente,[3] to be in Hiram in a few days, perhaps in advance of this. Meantime with the kindest regards, I am, as ever, J. A. Garfield.

Address: J. A. G., Hiram, Portage C., Ohio.

Lucretia's reply to this letter comes from Hiram, where she lived. Her father, a carpenter, had been one of the founders of the Eclectic Institute in 1850 and had moved to Hiram from nearby Garrettsville in order to give his children the salubrious atmosphere of a "college town." At this time, however, Lucretia, who was twenty-one years old, was living a short distance away in Chagrin Falls, teaching at a school there; she visited her family's home on the weekends. She excuses her boldness in answering his letter by pretending that his noun "Address" was an imperative verb, so that James was in fact requesting that she "address" him. Even after she had returned to Hiram from Chagrin Falls, the two corresponded rather than talked, at least three or four weeks more. On one occasion the postmistress received a letter from Lucretia and, as James came in, simply handed it to him.

Hiram, Nov 20, 1853

Very Kind Brother:

Your Niagara offering was not received until last Saturday evening. None the less welcome, however, nor less fraught with interest to me by its delay, for until its reception I was not aware of your visit to the world's greatest wonder, and to receive a line prompted by the inspiration of that mighty torrent's grandeur truly called forth a large amount of gratitude. Often as I have read or listened to descriptions of its inconceivable vastness and sublimity have I desired to stand beside it and "feel" myself the power of its overwhelming might, and as often have I determined that thus it should sometime be—when, however, the future must reveal. At present my attention and my mind with all its energies are directed towards and concentrated upon one little spot of Earth; so that I do not know that even the Great Niagara could attract my notice, only if it might serve to amuse my little dear ones, as to illustrate some wonderful idea I could impress on their minds. A little time, however, each day I devote to Virgil and other reading. Have you ever read a work of Carlyle, "Heros and Hero Worship"?[4] If not, I think you would be interested with it.

I presume you are enjoying yourself and that the school is prospering. This time, though, I know but little more about it than I would a hundred miles distance. I would like to know how many hundred lines the Virgil class are ahead of me, etc. and trust I'll see you before long, as I would like to learn and hear about your trip, and whether you were favored with a night's sail upon Erie's blue waters, and if so whether all or any of your youthful conceptions of a home on the billows were realized.

I have no apology for troubling you with this line since you charged me to "Address J. A. G., Hiram, Portage County, Ohio," and as I know not when an opportunity would permit my so doing personally, concluded to at least acknowledge the reception of your favor and my gratitude for the same, hoping you will receive it with a brother's kindness and forbearance. Truly your sister, Lucretia.

Curiously, James in his next letter repeated some of the descriptive material from his first letter, namely, the process of the build-up of the waters from "placid and smooth as polished silver" to the furious rapids and the "embattled host of billows." He apparently liked these phrases. The psychology of growth or development appealed to him; this emphasis on the process of emotional or intellectual build-up appears frequently in his writing in various guises.

Hiram, Dec 8, 1853

Much Respected Sister:

Many thanks to you for your kind and very welcome letter, which was recieved last Monday morning. I well understand your feelings in reference to your school, that your whole being is absorbed in the work of moulding and giving direction to the plastic minds of the youth placed under your care. To know that we are handling the delicate machinery of mind, and impressing thoughts on the principles that shall remain forever must necessarily impress us with a sense of great responsibility. I think every person should teach at least one school to obtain the true viewing of humanity and human life.

I have never read Carlyle's work, but have heard it spoken well of, and very much desire to read it. I am fully satisfied that textbooks alone will not make the mind rich and overflowing with that fullness of thought that everyone desires, and I know that for my part I am very deficient in general knowledge. I am, however, trying to do something this winter. I am now reading "McCaulay's History of England"[5] and some miscellanies. I have a book called "The Heroines of History" which I like very much, so far as I have read it. Also, a book called "Hurry Graphs" by N. P. Willis, in which there are some fine things. Have you ever read them? There is great beauty in his writings, but it is said that his personal character is rather exceptionable. Should we allow that consideration to influence us in reading an author?[6]

I spent the forenoon of the day after I wrote you in wandering through the beautiful islands above the falls, writing, pondering and admiring. I have no words to describe the emotions inspired by that awfully sublime scene. To see the majestic Niagara two miles in width with its surface placid and smooth as polished silver, first become gently ruffled, and then the sloping channel stirs its crystal depths, and maddens all its waters. An embattled host of billows come leaping down the opposing rocks of the rapids until they reach the awful brink, where all surcharged with frantic fury, leap bellowing down the rocky steeps which thunder back the sullen echoes of their roar, and shout God's praise above the cloudy skies. O that the assembled millions of the earth could once behold that scene, sublime and awful. . . .

I loved to be alone, but still I wished all of my friends were by my side to gaze with me upon that scene. I must sometime see it again—if I live.

That afternoon I took the cars for Buffalo, and at 4 o'clock P.M. was seated in the splendid cabin of the steamer "Ohio," bound for Cleveland. A cloudy night succeeded, and I contented myself with visiting the boat. I went into the hold, where were 40 or 50 Irish and German emigrants. I made some of their acquaintances, listened to the songs and stories of their dear Fatherland, then viewed the complicated machinery of the powerful engine, and then walked, talked and discussed with the passengers in the cabin. Among these were a Canadian scholar and a young Catholic who is educating himself for a priest. With these I spent much time in discussing the comparative merits of England and America, and Protestantism and Catholicism. We were, on account of head winds, all that night, the next day, and next night till nearly midnight upon the lake. The last evening, just as we were leaving Fairport, and as Virgil says, "urbesque terraeque recedebant,"[7] the virgin moon rose in a clear sky. I stood upon the hurricane deck alone. Her blush paved the lake with silver, and she looked down upon her own bright face immersed in its crystal depths. Then I gazed far back towards the receding city, and beheld the swirling waves of the steamer's wake, sparkling in the moonbeams like diamond gems, and then a slight breeze arose, which rippled gently the bosom of the Lake that glittered then with drops of gold and pearl. You ask me, "if any of my youthful conceptions of a home on the billows were realized." I will not trouble you with that long, strange story of my early youth, but only say for years my soul longed for a home upon the deep blue sea, and even yet, when higher aims and objects fill my heart, I love the ocean with its foaming waves, and let me often from the cares of life retire, and listen to its deep toned music and gaze upon its crested waters.

The latter part of that night I spent at the "Forest City House," where lingered other recollections of a former visit, and the next evening I was in Hiram.

The school[8] is going on quite pleasantly, though among the 240 that are here we have some unruly ones. Today, the Virgil class finished the third book and are going about 50 lines per day. Are you ahead? I presume so. Won't you come in to both Greek and Latin in the spring? We miss you very much in these two classes. What are your views now with regard to studying the classics? Have you reconciled yourself to devoting a few more years to them? I would like to hear your reasonings on the subject. I would much rather converse "ore quam calamo,"[9] but it seems that our leisure hours do not synchronize, and will you therefore forgive me for inflicting so long a letter upon you.

I should be much pleased to receive another bundle of thoughts from you, if you deem it worth your time to send them. Have you concluded to keep closed doors or to admit spectators to your school's, your winter's empire? I have some interest in the decision. Hoping that you will overlook these many imperfections, and pardon them, I am

Truly and sincerely
Your Brother,
James.

Hiram, Dec 14, 1853

Brother James:

We seem very artlessly to have commenced a correspondence by letter as a substitute for an occasional personal interview, which the concurrence of circumstances unavoidable appears at present to forbid, and as it is in perfect harmony with my inclinations I shall not be the one to discontinue it at present; indeed, I could with the familiarity of a *Sister* ask rather that it be continued, since by your queries concerning my views now in reference to studying the classics you have paved the way for an investigation of their merits, which I do hope will result in *some kind* of a decision in my mind. Candidly, I will confess that thus far I have prosecuted the study of them without any argument in their favor which appeared to me conclusive. Do you wonder that *conscience* sometimes upbraids me? Doubtless, it is owing to my lack of penetration and ignorance and with this consideration I have quieted the Monitor. But am I never to get wiser, or is it indeed a truth that the time and attention they demand *might* and therefore *should* be devoted to pursuits more worthy? True, it is a rigid discipline for the mind in that *digging* out those Greek and Latin roots, and straightening those crooked sentences; but is it there alone it can receive it? Perhaps it is. Perchance the phrenologist is *right* when he affirms that a certain class of faculties will remain uneducated unless culled out by their pursuit. Strange, however, that the Creator should have endowed man with such faculties, and for over two thousand years left him unprovided for their training. I wish you would convince me of their superior merit if they *really possess it*; for I do not like to give them up—neither do I like to continue in them feeling ever that precious moments are being wasted, moments that should tell of stores of wisdom treasured.

I have laid them aside for the winter, however, as I felt that I could not do justice to my school should I devote the time to them it would be necessary to in order to keep along with the classes.

The first two weeks I read Virgil a little but shall read it no more this winter; consequently, in the spring will be thrown from both my old classes.

I am still reading "Carlyle" and quite captivated by him—a fault with me in reading. I have not read Greek and Latin enough yet to have sufficient judgment to guide me, and am therefore influenced very much by the author whose works I peruse. I have read neither of those works you mention; but am reading now "Grime's History of England."

Am I to admit spectators into *my* "empire"? That depends upon who they are and what their object. I did not *dare* close my gates against President Hayden,[10] but should one of his "cabinet" appear, I *might* have the audacity to attempt it.[11]

You say every person should teach at least one school "to obtain true views of humanity and human life." Surely of all places, there it is to learn that lesson, but I would not have every *one* there. No, no. Its responsibilities are too great, and I feel my incapacity to meet them. The interests of the *mind* and the *soul* are too weighty for every one to experiment with, and was it not for this consideration that a large proportion of the parents are as utterly unfit to manage aright the interests of their children as the teachers they employ and many times more so, it would be my conclusion at once that schools for children should be prohibited. As the world is, however, it is doubtless better they should continue.

Should it harmonize with your feelings to bestow another message, it will most gratefully [be] received by your sister, Lucretia.

In the letters following, the question Lucretia has raised about the value of the classics becomes the central concern. James enters into this subject with complacent authority, grounding his arguments on elaborate analogies.

Lucretia makes some telling points against reading the classics, but, at the same time, she seems to bow to James' opinions. In this tenth letter Lucretia, while allowing James to have won the debate over the value of the classics, now asks for an explanation of "why it was necessary to the development of ideas and the perfection of thought that a diversity of languages should be given" mankind. "Lead on," she writes, clearly desiring the correspondence to continue.

Hiram, Jan 26, 1854

Kind Brother:

Were it on the field of combat I was standing before you, my great powerful brother, I should most surely "Surrender arms" and acknowledge you *Victor* without further contest, but as it is rather with you for a guide and co-seeker after the priceless treasure truth I can appear, I will not yet abandon the friendly path of inquiry.

I have often heard much said upon this subject both pro and con; and have ever felt that those opposing a classical education had the better side but I will candidly confess that I am beginning to see differently and to you I stand indebted for my enlightenment: I know that new energies of my mind have been awakened and that I can think more clearly and accurately than I could previous to my studying the classics, and I have attributed it entirely to the mental effort I have been obliged to make in the pursuit of them. So far I presume my conclusion was correct; but I had supposed that the same effect might have been produced studying something else. There, you will say, has lain my error, and perhaps you are correct; in truth, I begin to believe you are. I will admit also that in order to understand and feel the force of words of another language, we must understand their use in that language, must *see* them in that language. My old Geography told me that "Ge meant the earth and graph to describe," but when I came to find these words in the Greek, they awakened altogether a new feeling, and I could see a beauty in the name at least I never saw before. Still, I do not yet perceive why it was necessary to the development of ideas and the perfection of thought that a diversity of languages should be given. It seems to me that with one language man by its improvement might have expressed every idea as fully and forcibly as with a dozen. Every word would then have been in its native tongue and not needed to be traced out to find its beauty or force. I may be wrong, however. I will now wish you [to] examine this subject from another point of observation. Lead on.

This winter passes with me not unpleasantly; still I shall not be sorry when its hours have all flown. I know it is wrong to feel so but cannot avoid it. I see so much to be done, or that *ought* to be done, and have so little power to do that I cannot help often feeling discouraged. You ask "if my mind ever inclines to chase the tossing bubbles of ambition." I wish it did more than it does. Almeda[12] tells me that I have not enough ambition and I do not know but it is so; at least I feel that I am lacking something or else I should be awake and energetic. There are bright imageries of fancy enough before me, yes too many; for they unfit me for dealing with real—the matter of fact—as I should.

Pardon me for writing so briefly and disconnectedly; for I feel in altogether a bad humor for writing—even to you.

May I not hear again soon and I will try and feel better another time.

Sincerely your Sister:
Lucretia

Hiram, Jan 28, 1854

Lucretia:

Your very welcome message was received from the hands of the Post Mistress who made the remark that "she had just heard it drop," but "did not know who dropped it." I am sincerely glad that our views so nearly coincide upon the important question before us and still more am I pleased if anything I may have written has elicited any truth upon it. I can truly say I have been very much benefitted by this correspondence. Your candid and just stricture upon my reasoning has been beneficial to me. It is a fault with me, as you have doubt-less noticed, to reason too much by comparison or analogy. A good argument is sometimes injured by a poor comparison.

Your remarks concerning "Ge" and "Graph," I fully appreciate for I have often felt the same. When I was told that *Philander* signified a "friendly man" and "Alexander" a "preserver," I did *feel* when read upon the pages of Xenophon and Homer . . . that Philander was a "lover of man" and Alexander was his "protector."

You have introduced a fruitful field for investigation, viz.: "why was a diver-sity of languages given"; "was it necessary to the perfection of thought"?

We know, in the first place, that it was given as a punishment, but the very chastisements of God are turned to good accounts and will bless man. The sluggish minds of men needed some necessity placed upon them, some work which they must perform, and they were placed under the necessity of acquiring other languages, which, it seems to me the Almighty chose as the best means of developing the whole power of the mind. The close and constant application which the acquisition of these languages requires, is to the mind what a grindstone is to a mechanic's tools, making it ready and acute (*Comparison again!*) Infidels have attempted to account for the present diversity of tongues upon natural principles, and though that position cannot be sustained, yet it must be admitted that there are many things that tend to keep up the differences of dialect throughout the world. A man living in the tropical regions, would never, from nature, need to use the terms "glacier," "iceberg," "avalanche," etc., nor would the Scandinavian need to talk of the palm tree or olive or any of the beautiful productions of the sunny south. The Laplander would well understand the use of the hunter's and fisher's terms, but the language of the farmer and herdsman would be like Greek or Latin to him. Hence, to my mind there seems a necessity for a diversity of dialects under the present circumstances of the world. But I consider it by no means necessary that this should always exist, for when there shall be universal knowledge (if that happy day ever arrives) then and not till then can there be a universal language. The great men of our day believe that our own dear Saxon is destined to be that language, and it seems to me to be a reasonable conclusion. Have you read Bro. Campbell's[13] Lecture on the "Origin and Destiny of the Anglo Saxon Language"? It is most a profound and eloquent address and ought to be read by every one. Our vernacular combines the stateliness of the Latin, the beauty and fire of the Greek, and the strength and energy of the pure Saxon, and it [lacks] only the liquidity of the French and Spanish, the metaphorical beauty of the Oriental Asiatic languages, and the philosophical technicality of the grunting Dutch (pardon the expression) to make ours the language that shall girdle the world and be the harbinger of Anglo-Saxon enterprise.

I must be allowed to differ with you as to the correctness of the remark that you "have little power to do." Let me ask you, Did you ever attempt to learn anything that you could not?

You speak of ambition. We all shrink with horror from the effects of [unsecured?] ambition, and some almost conclude that the thing itself is wrong— but it seems to me that it is necessary to success in every department of life. It is to the man what the fire is to the steam engine, and though the fire be made of shavings and trash, yet it will *propel*; so with ambition. It *urges* one to *action*. So, let it burn. Restrain it only by the laws of God.

At times I love to beguile a weary lonely hour in revelling among the golden scenes of a fancied future, yet I will not allow this to blind me to the sober realities of life—Is this right?—

I often think of your quiet situation, away from the noise and bustle of the Institution, that you have a fine opportunity for reading and meditation. I hope your "*bad humor*" will not continue so as to shorten your letters, which I love to read. Being thankful for past favors, may I *hope* for more? I would be pleased to converse with you through more than the "silent medium" if agreeable to yourself. Excuse haste and believe me, affectionately, James.

During February James and Lucretia seem to have seen each other enough (without resorting to the "silent medium") to be prepared for a serious talk about their future. There is a later reference to a sleigh ride on New Year's Eve, and they no doubt saw each other on various other occasions. Sometime during the last days of February the two met in the "lower chapel" at Hiram, kissed for the first time, and declared their love. At least James declared his, while Lucretia did not object; she tells of a kiss "coldly received and not returned," because James had not "reached her heart yet." After the declaration in the chapel, both write letters which recount their feelings about the interview and each confessed to being nervous about the meeting. Nevertheless, an engagement was agreed upon.

Soon after, James had departed with his mother for a visit to southern Ohio, where her brother lived. Before the trip James stops for his mother at Solon, a village near Cleveland and close to his birthplace. He had been born in a home built by his father (he was the last of our presidents to be born in a log cabin), but it had burned and James could only walk about the ruins, which he did with resonant sentimentality. In this correspondence James also refers to an infatuation he had had with Mary Hubbell of Chagrin Falls. He had broken that affair off a few months before he "pointed his pen" at Lucretia.

Virginia Ridge, Ohio, March 2, 1854

Dear Lucretia:

In Muskingum County, fifteen miles below Zanesville, and one and a half miles from the Muskingum river, in a large brick house, on a very high hill in a nice little room in the attic story, alone, I am seated to write to you.

The day after I saw you, I went to where my home formerly was, and visited my folks there (the Boyntons), but finding that my mother had gone to Solon, I went there and visited her and my two sisters. While in Orange, on Saturday morning, I walked over the lonely farm that was once my home, my earliest home. Strange and mingled indeed were my feelings when I stood upon the spot where I was born—that spot which is now covered with dried weeds and dead herbage is meaningless to the eye of a stranger, but not to mine. The old stone back wall to the chimney is still standing, a monument to the dead past, and as I stood there and looked upon those stones, it brought vividly to my mind the days of my childhood, when that wall served as a screen against which the blaze of the log fire was leaping and crackling, in which I traced a thousand fantastic figures of giants on fiery steeds and hosts embattled for war, in all the wild imaginations of a childish fancy. I again seemed tumbling upon the floor with brother and sisters, and the forms of playmates and friends long dead seemed to stand before me. The intervening years seemed to have dropped out, and I was ten again. But the wind came moaning among the old orchard trees, sighing the dirge of departed years, and youth-vision was gone. Early friends stalked away to the graveyard or to distant lands, youth grew hoary, and the hoary died, and I was alone—a young tree among the dead pines. But my heart still clung to the dear old spot and I embraced that old time worn wall almost with affection. Perhaps you consider this a weakness, and probably it is, but I cannot help it.

On Monday my Mother and I went to Cleveland and took the cars for Zanesville via Columbus, at which latter place we arrived in five hours from the time of starting. Staid there with a cousin of mine one day and night, but on account of the bad roads we did not visit the State Institutions, but we intend to do so on our return which will be in about one week from this time. Yesterday we took the cars for Zanesville, and thence to Blue Rock by Steam Boat.

My Cousin Ellis Ballou is at College in Athens, Athens County, about 30 miles from here. I intend to visit him in a few days and for the sake of recruiting my health and seeing the country, I shall go across the country on horse-back. My health is improving every day and my throat, I trust, will get rested sufficiently to carry me through with the next term's labor.

Lucretia, I am very glad we have had the opportunity of conversing and have improved it as we did at our last interview. In my memory, that will ever be a bright spot. There has heretofore been a bar between us that has not given us that freedom that should [suffice?] even between school mates. I hope it is taken away. It is my earnest desire to "know and be known." I fear you do not know me. As you said in your last kind and thrice welcome letter which you handed me, I am terrified when I behold the strange inconsistencies of my nature. And when I behold it leaping and bounding, I scarcely know whither-ward, yearning for something I know not what, filled with high resolves, with holy aspirations, with earnest desires to live for God and Eternal Life, and then coming so infinitely short of living the life, I almost at times doubt my own honesty and even question whether the love of God is in my heart. For if a man is to be judged by his fruit, where shall I stand? It is only those promises of which you spoke that buoys me up.

That evening I sketched to you very briefly the facts concerning my past history in a social point of view, and I wish now to say if I did say it then, that my reasons for breaking off from that intimacy (for it was never any thing more) were not from any consideration that I had another in view, for such was not the case. At that time I felt myself entirely cut loose from the world of womankind and felt like always remaining so. At any rate, I determined from that hour [to] be master of my heart's affections, and let my better judgment be sole arbiter of my heart's empire. For months I struggled against any rising of affection towards you, till I had thought as coolly and candidly as my acquaintance would permit. On this basis I love you with my heart's warmest affections, and it fills me with joy to know that in some degree (I know not what) that love is returned, from a heart purer than mine. Thus stands the case, and in it all I pray God to give us wisdom to do that which is righteous in His sight. I wish to do nothing without due consideration, and whatever be its issue, I desire to take that course which we shall both approve when many years have fled. The stern realities of life must be considered with serious thoughtfulness.

I have wondered that I had the boldness to turn my thoughts toward you. I, whose future is yet so uncertain and whose past is so commingled, and am very feebly battling the world with naked hands and without a home; and though I know your noble heart will not rest down upon any similar considera-tions, yet, what I have said concerning myself is true, and it is also true that a cold, cold world must be looked in the face. But I long to hear from you, and still more to see you, to know your heart and open mine to you, for though you have it now, I fear you do not know its contents.

The whole subject is one of life's most serious problems, and above all things, the heart's affections should be planted upon a basis which neither fancy nor the flight of years will ever destroy, and which will remain when youth with all its charms has gone, and the corroding cares of life press heavily upon the time-worn spirit. Then, when the heart needs solace, there should be a well of pure affection, deep as our beings and lasting as Love itself.

It seems to me that the storms of Life require in man all the cultivation of mind and heart, all the reliance upon God and all the strength and resolution and determination of which our poor natures are capable, to buffet them and make straight our pathway upon its troubled waters. Then let the mind grow, the heart be softened, and the soul turned upward to God for succor.—I hope to find a letter from you in the Blue Rock P.O. today when I carry this. If you should write to Columbus immediately upon the reception of this, I should get it there. I hope you will find it in your heart to do so. With warmest love, I am yours affectionately,

James.

Lucretia's letter regarding the interview in the lower chapel is characteristically more restrained than James'. She, too, had been having a love affair, now ended, with a young man named "Albert," and she tells the reasons why that relationship had not worked out in her letter to James.

Hiram, March 3, 1854

Dear James:

This is a strange, *strange* world, and as I glance over its wide spread field, I notice strange scenes being enacted—actions which I can no way comprehend and occurrences most mysterious. . . . Here, allow me to become a little more *personal* in my reflections, and James pardon me though I speak very plainly. Our last interview was one which I *had hoped* might be further in the future, for I feared that we might be yet ignorant of our *own hearts* and *knew* our acquaintance with each other was scarcely commenced; and as I *believed* you would never marry anyone until you were acquainted with them, and *knew* I would not myself, I wished the entrance to "matrimonial bliss" might remain triple barred until time and circumstances should consummate a due acquaintance. For then, should we find that we could not with united hearts pass its threshold as friends, we might still regard each other while no unpleasant associations would be crowding themselves upon us. But I feel now that perhaps I was wrong; for that confidence which is necessary to forming such an acquaintance could never have been obtained standing as we did merely friends. Therefore, I regret not the position we have taken.

But resolutions I have long since made, and by them I am determined to stand. The first is doubtless one of every *rational* being, viz., That I will never give my hand to one who has not my heart. The second—That I will withhold my hand ever from the one I love should I be convinced that by bestowing it I should in any way lessen the little power I possess of benefiting others, or cause myself to serve less faithfully my Savior. It was this last consideration which induced me finally to discontinue my acquaintance with Albert. I saw no hope of his ever becoming a Christian, and I knew that I could not lead the life I ought bound to one who was not. In the first place I ought never to have loved him, but for some reason—I know not what—I did. I believed his character good, and had it proven so I would still cherish for him a sister's regard, but now I cannot. I can only try and think kindly of him and hope that he may reform. I have written but little though this sheet is nearly covered, and I do not wish to write more until I hear from you.

Circumstances unavoidable have prevented my writing before; consequently, I direct to Columbus, as I fear it would not reach Blue Rock before you leave.

Hoping that I may both see and hear from you soon, I will add no more at present.

Faithfully yours,
Lucretia

Lucretia and James were together through the springtime of their love; but in July they had to separate. James had decided to obtain a college degree from Williams College in Massachusetts. Accordingly, in July 1854, he traveled east toward Williamstown to take placement tests and to enter the College. On his way he met an old Hiram friend, Corydon Fuller, and the two of them went to New York and New Jersey for a visit before James returned to Massachusetts to take up his studies. Lucretia, in the meantime, was back at her home in Hiram. James' first letter from Williamstown tells something of the second part of his journey from Hiram to Massachusetts.

Already James had "done" the greatest American tourist attraction, Niagara Falls. Now he experienced several others: the Hudson river voyage from Albany to New

York City, the Crystal Palace in New York, which had been opened just the year before, Barnum's Museum, and Greenwood Cemetery in Brooklyn.

While the many travelers who recorded impressions of the Hudson would emphasize the diversity of the natural scenery, Garfield seemed more impressed with its historical associations. His remarks about the Crystal Palace and Barnum's Museum are minimal, considering the effects these places had on so many visitors. The Crystal Palace, for example, opened by President Franklin Pierce in July 1853, must have been a compelling sight with its one hundred-foot dome and its great equestrian statues. Barnum sold over thirty-eight million tickets to his museum, this "most popular cultural institution of its day."

According to John Sears, Mount Auburn in Cambridge (1831), Laurel Hill in Philadelphia (1836), and Greenwood in Brooklyn (1837) were especially popular as tourist attractions. Well over one hundred thousand people, it was estimated, visited Greenwood each year in the 1850s. Tourists flocked there because these cemeteries "represented tangible expressions of 'noble sentiments and refined taste.'" Greenwood impressed James particularly because of the prominent names—"poets, orators, statesmen and warriors"—he found there. Sears writes that the great popularity of these burial grounds could be attributed to the way "they intensified and reflected back the emerging fashion-conscious, status-oriented, property-owning culture of the time. The well-to-do wished to display their wealth, the less well off to observe that display."[14]

Williams College, July 15, 1854

Dear Lucretia,

Your most welcome letter is just recieved and I sit down to write in return. How anxiously I have watched each mail to see if it would not bring a welcome word from Ohio. When I reached this place last Tuesday (10th), I found three letters for me which I read with much satisfaction. One was from Almeda, and was laden with sympathy, good wishes and good advice. She has ever been a faithful sister to me. Since then I have been at the office twice a day and have recieved no token of remembrance till this hour. I need not tell that I was thrice glad to recieve your letter.

On Wednesday morning (5th) after I wrote you from Butler, Corydon and I took the cars, and that evening were in Albany, the "Ancient City of the Knickerbockers". . . .

On Wednesday evening we stepped aboard the steamer "Hendrik Hudson" and were soon ploughing the calm bosom of that noble river. It has truly been called the "Rhine of America." Standing upon the upper deck we enjoyed the glories of a sunset scene. The broad river looked like a silver scarf girding the earth between the giant hills. As the sun sank behind those western sentinels, it fringed their tops with gold and stained the skies with crimson. Our boat glided like a queen upon the mirrored waters, while her 1300 passengers were gazing with delight upon the castle-crowned heights, the fields of waving grain, and the scenes of quiet hamlets scattered along the banks. I almost fancied I could see the tall forms of Hamilton and Burr standing up in the shore, as they stood up [on] the orchard platform. . . .[15]

But it is useless in this short space of a letter to attempt a description of that mighty river with its many associations. The next morning we were landed in New York the Metropolis of the Western Continent. We spent that day in visiting the *Famous Crystal Palace*, where are all the species of the productions of nearly every clime under the sun. That immense structure built of cast-iron and glass is certainly a triumph of Art, that our nation may well be proud of. We visited also Barnum's Museum—a little world of curiosities and the Ludburne Printing Press which runs off 10,000 papers per hour. The next day we visited Greenwood Cemetary on Long Island. That is a most delightful spot—a place for serious and sober meditation. There are only two more such cemeteries in America. "Mount Auburn" near Boston, and "Laurel Hill" near Philadelphia. A large forest several miles in circuit laid off in circular walks and interspersed with large artificial fountains and adorned with the richest shrubbery whose branches are continually stirred by the cool breezes of the Atlantic, forms the last resting place of the departed. We lingered several hours among the tombs of the Poets, Orators, Statesmen and Warriors, and thousands of humbler names, and sat beneath the cooling shade of the weeping willows that bend their branches above their marble homes. Would that you could have been there and roamed with us through these halls of the departed. At three o'clock in the afternoon we started again, and in two or three hours were in Corydon's New Jersey home. I staid there till Monday (10th) roaming over the places where Washington lead his patriot army, and getting an inkling of Jersey society till I am sunburnt as a Mohawk. On Sunday I listened to the long drawn but, I suppose, *orthodox* groans of the "Dutch Reformed" (!!) Minister of whom Corydon has written so much. I must certainly commend Corydon's patience in enduring it so long as he has. With an elongated face and a longer sermon, he "fed his flock" upon the wholesome doctrine of "*Original Sin,*" and "*Fore-Ordination.*"

The next morning I went to New York and that evening took a Steamboat for Troy, where I found myself next morning when I awoke 50 miles distant from my supper table. By cars and stage I arrived that afternoon at Williamstown. It is a quiet little village sleeping in the verdant lap of the Green Mountains and girt about on all sides by pine-clad peaks that tower to the skies in their primeval grandeur. I have not yet been around much and hence know but little of the place. Within three hours after my arrival I was examined in the mathematics, Homer, Zenophon's Memorabilia, Livy and Horace, and permitted to enter the junior year, but I am to bring up Mensuration and Conic Sections. I came at an unfavorable time, for they are in the bustle of preparing for Commencement, and it is difficult to get a place to board and room. I regret that I came so soon, for I might have entered the junior class just as well next September, and saved a considerable expense. But it will not pay to go back and then return. When I learn more of the Institution I will particularize. I think they are very thorough.

I am very glad to learn that the people in Hiram are awaking to the subject of *In*temperance as it has been so much an annoyance to the school and destruction to the interests of society. I sincerely hope they will rid themselves of that "*Mercatorial* pest" for he has long been an injury to the community. Your mention of that "Lower Chapel" brings back to my mind a thousand recollections for it has been my home for many months. I would love to see it this calm afternoon.—I must confess that I feel very much alone here. My heart clings so fondly to the friends I have left behind that I can scarce bear the thought that I am separated from them, and cannot enjoy their society. I want you to write *very often.* Any of the proceedings at Hiram will be interesting to me. Follow the example of this in respect to length. I will try to know more of the Institution next time than I do now. Hoping to hear from you again very soon, I am most affectionately

James

July 24, 1854

Hiram, Monday morning 4 o'clock

Dearest James:

Dawn with her rosy fingers has scarce tinged the East with her crimson glow to herald the approach of day's glorious king, as I now treat myself to the pleasant duty of answering your last kind favor. . . .

What shall be my future course I am wholly undecided. I had almost determined that I would go through with a gentleman's full course; but your remark in reference to it at our last interview rather disconcerted my plans. I know it would not be prudence for me to attempt this in the same time that many could. Still by allowing sufficient time I see no reason (unless it be my mental incapacity which I suppose you would say you do not believe) why I may not accomplish it. But it might not be in three or even four years. In reference to that unanswered question, though withdrawn, allow me to say—in confidence which we have promised each other—half jocosely, half in earnest, that should you wish me before that time to become your wife and I willingly should acquiesce, I know not why I might not still study. True, it has become almost a proverb that when a lady is married, she may as well lay aside her books, still I do not believe it contains very much wisdom after all; and even if it did, you know my superior powers would warrant me in being an exception. I trust you will pardon my nonsense. When I report my progress in Virgil for the past week, I presume your advice will be to speak a little more modestly, though it may serve as a partial excuse for my not even opening it for more than a week that we have been in all the confusion of a regular "housecleaning" tearing up carpets, scrubbing, whitewashing, papering, etc. etc. so that I have read only about 150 lines since I wrote before. My success in Music I can scarcely tell. Sometimes I grow almost discouraged—or rather "out of patience" because I cannot advance more rapidly, but that I know is very foolish as I ought to consider that time and a great deal of it too must be spent before much can be accomplished or even a moderate proficiency attained in the performance of instrumental music, especially by one who has not much skill naturally. I practice on the piece I learned last term and have learned a few pieces in the "Melodeon" and "The Young Choir," a little book Mr. Burns brought me. I would have enjoyed much a visit with you at Greenwood Cemetery, also a sail upon the Hudson. When I read of the many places beautified and adorned by the combined efforts of both Nature and Art, I can scarcely content myself to remain so quietly at home. My eye longs to drink in their beauty, and my soul to feel their holy influence. But there is beauty everywhere and not in its most inconsiderable forms does it appear among the rolling hills, towering forests, and verdant fields of our own loved Hiram. . . . I think it quite too bad that you must remain unnecessarily through vacation so far away when your presence in Ohio would make so many glad hearts; but perhaps it may prove for the best. I believe a great deal in providence, and that seeming trifles frequently produce the most weighty results, and often circumstances apparently adverse prove the most favorable. You acknowledge yourself somewhat lonely: remember, James, if it affords you any happiness, that among the many friends whom you have left, there is one whose heart often turns to you in holiest love, and who would gladly cheer a lonely hour with a smile of affection would it be permitted. Trusting that I shall receive soon another long long letter, I add no more at present.

> Unchanged in Heart, I remain
> Lucretia

In the following letter, in which James gives his impressions of Williams College, he refers to the president of the College, Mark Hopkins, one of America's great nineteenth century educators. In the years that followed, Garfield and Hopkins became close friends. James had made his decision to graduate from Williams College, rather than from Bethany—another Disciple institution in West Virginia—Yale, or Brown, mostly because of the cordial letter he had received from Mark Hopkins.

James' fierce ambition is evident in this letter. His diary entry at this time was similar to the words in the letter: "The olden fires that have had no need to blaze for the last two years begin to flame up again and take away my midnight rest. I am now among classmates of vigor and that have had much better advantages than I in most respects. But let it stand recorded on this page thus early; if I am blessed with life and health, I will stand at least among the first in that class. I do not study for honor, no, I trust I have higher, holier motives, but when I am in the class, how can I be behind? No! The bare thought of being far behind makes my flesh crawl on my bones. I must not, I shall not be!"[16]

Williams College, July 30, 1854

Dearest Lucretia:

'Tis a quiet, lovely Lord's-day evening, and I am seated alone in my chamber to respond to your kind favor of the 24th post-marked 26th and received by yesterday's mail. I have listened to two long essays (sermons) read by *Reverend* Gentlemen today, and feel nearly exhausted by the effort. I see I am doomed to two hours of misery weekly while I stay here. But I will not make that remark of President Hopkins, for neither his *written* sermons nor sectarian shackles can fetter his noble soul and I love to hear him, but he only speaks about once in four weeks. The regular minister, a broken down missionary, returned from across the seas and settled here. He is a devoted and earnest Christian, but he possesses very moderate powers of mind and a poorer faculty of expressing his thoughts. In comparison with him, the preaching of our Brother Rider could be music to my ears, and in fact I would like to hear Bro Rider[17] speak to this people. But one thing consoles me. There are very frequently strangers here that speak, and often men of note.

This is a solemn, lonely hour. The leaves of the aspen and locust trees that stand near my window, swayed by the evening breeze, are holding out their trembling hands to the west, and as they beckon thitherward, I wander back, and my heart lingers around those happy scenes, and fondly clings to those dear, dear friends. Dear Lucretia, how I would love to rest this head that throbs with pain tonight upon your own dear bosom, and listen to the beating of your heart. But this cannot be. I have as yet written nothing of my health, for I hardly know what to write. I think this is a most delightfully healthy location, but for some reason the atmosphere is different from that in Ohio, so that notwithstanding the warm weather I have taken cold nearly every night since I came here. For this reason I have had a severe headache incessantly for the last seven days, and my throat is not particularly benefitted by it. But I think I shall get acclimated soon. And then it will all be right. I see I have commenced my letter with a catalogue of complaints which might as well have been left out. Please don't think I'm sick and *mourning*. These thoughts *will* steal out imperceptibly.

I am *well pleased*, very well pleased with the College and its Proffessors, and am very glad I determined to come here instead of Bethany. It is said that the last two years instruction here is not equalled by that of any Institution in America. The President himself has the entire charge of the Senior Classes, and they are rigidly thorough. I am discussing a question in my own mind upon which I would like your assistance. There will be, between this and the close of next College year 13 weeks of vacation. By using that time to the very best advantage, and by carrying on one or two private studies in term time, I believe I could leap a year and thus graduate one year from August. Whether that is best, or not, is the question. If I conclude to stay two years I think I shall get a school and teach this winter. There are six weeks of vacation and by taking three from each adjoining term I can make out a three months' school without materially affecting my College studies. This will give me a taste of New England Society and perhaps of their money.

I do not feel satisfied merely to carry away the skin of a Massachusetts sheep, but I want to know something of the *men*, the *thoughts*, that are here. I feel the necessity of breaking through the shell of local notions and getting mentally free. I mean no disrespect for the influences and teaching that I have had, but I mean to say that to mould one's mind in one place and under one system of things must necessarily give it one particular channel, and not that breadth of field that is desirable. This is to my mind an argument for staying two years, but the question has two strong sides. I have commenced reciting in the "Olynthyacs of Demosthenes" and the "Integral Calculus." These are reviews to the class, but advance for me. So I have double their labor. There are some splendid scholars in the class. Many come from Harvard, Amherst, and Yale to finish here. Lucretia, I must confess that those inner fires come surging up through every nerve and fiber of my being in strong desire and strong determination not to stand—at least, last of all. Whether it is right or not I do not know but they *will* burn and cannot be quenched till the building falls. *Honor* is not the object for which I labor; but when in a class I am miserable if *far* behind. I do not think it is an unholy impulse if only guided; certainly it is one deeply implanted in my nature.

About your own course, allow me to say a few words. I regret that I have ever said anything to thwart your purposes, and I hope you will let no such considerations as I may have presented keep you from any course productive of advantage to you. I felt solicitous for your health, and if that can be secured and retained, the more study the better. I believe that you would be benefitted by breathing another atmosphere after a while—the sooner, however, the better—I know you will understand me that I say nothing against Hiram. This is true of any and every place. No one would be more pleased than I to have you go through a course of study, and I certainly hope, nay I *request* that you do not let *me* stand in the way of that or any of your plans. I presume you could graduate in two or three years. Let me hear from you further on this point. . . .

I would say many things, but the stars are climbing to the zenith ('tis half past eleven) and my letter waxes long and *dull* I fear. Oh, the night, the grand old night—the heavens so calm, the world so still and pulseless. I can almost hear Time's stealthy tread. How I would love to stand upon the mountains now and look down upon the sleeping world below—as Paul Flemming says "On the end of this oily midnight my spirit loves to revel."[18] But I must stop. Dear Lucretia, do let me hear from you often, very often and *long*. Let your heart take the pen and your hand hold it not back—and now at this lone solemn hour I implore our Heavenly Father to keep us in his mercy, and give us hearts to do his will, and not repine at His Providences. Lucretia, Dear Lucretia, my arm is around you now, my cheek is pressed to yours: here is my kiss.

Good night, As ever, James.

Hiram, August 7, 1854

Dearest James:

O, what a treasure is a letter: To receive from absent loved ones lines traced by their own dear hands. To feel that beneath their eyes every word has fallen and more than all to realize that every thought, every expression of kindness is but a part of themselves impressed upon the surface of the fair page, makes the very heart-strings tremble anew with the gush of affectionate gladness, and leads the soul into sweet and holy communion with the dear, the loved, in memory only present; but when a message comes from the one than all others more dear, 'tis better known than told the rapturous thrill of joy that vibrates upon each trembling chord of the fond heart. And now my own dear James shall I in return for that last kind letter of yours, surrender my pen to my heart, and bid my hand obey its dictates? If so it will be for the first time, save to my soul, my earliest friend, Lizzie.[19] And this is why perhaps the world calls me so cold, and thinks me so heartless; and is this why you scarcely yet believe I have a heart other than an iceberg has? James, I have a heart and as warm and true, as ever throbbed beneath woman's gentle breast. I know this though from the world it may ever be concealed, and I would have you know it too; then in secret the silently flowing tear shall no longer tell my sadness at the world's mistake, and my own inability to cover it. No, no, if I can only learn to unbosom my whole soul to you and prove myself worthy of receiving your entire confidence in return, I shall ask no more; my cup of happiness will be filled to overflowing. Then the world may think me what they will; it will matter little if you but know me rightly. True I will not cease striving to unmask my real self to others also, till then I feel I will not mourn if turning to you I can feel that I am truly known. You heart, take this pen and guide it ever and learn to trust your whole self unreservedly to one—at least who is in every way worthy of your freest confidence. Yes, this is my resolve, and may I never disregard it, *never 'till you cease to love me.*

I am glad to learn that you are so well pleased with the College and Proffessors; but I fear for your health. It may be however that it is only the change of climate that affects you now, and as you become accustomed to it will cease to produce any unpleasant results. At least I hope it is so. I would gladly assist you in making a decision as to the time you should spend there if I could, but I am quite uncertain which would be the wiser course. When I first read your letter, although I felt that consulting my own pleasure and that of your other friends, I should certain say "Haste and return," still I thought I should advise you differently; for your argument in favor of staying two years seemed quite conclusive. The more I think of it however the stronger seem the reasons on the other side—providing you can complete the course in one year *without injury* to your health. But by staying and teaching next winter you might get as you say a taste of New England society and perhaps of their money; still if the latter, though it might be a generous slice, you would scarcely get as much in that time, I think, as you could in another year with Diploma in hand. Again, when a person appears in society, a graduate from an Institution of high standing, and especially having merited high honors—as *I know you will*—a position is granted him which will readily gain for him access to whatever society he may wish, and while he may learn something of the men and thoughts of society in general, an opportunity is also afforded of forming an acquaintance with men whose Intellectual greatness and Literary excellence has given them a position far above the medium classes. I acknowledge the School teacher can go deeper into Society and learn more of its secret springs than perhaps any other person, but can he obtain as extensive knowledge, or form as large a circle of acquaintances, as he who spends the same time travelling and visiting whatever places he chooses? I submit these few reflections for your consideration for whatever they are worth. Certainly you will not allow them to have any influence in deciding you to take this course, should your better judgement advise differently. I would say, first of all, act with due reference to your *health*; then take whatever course seems most wise, whatever will result in the most good to yourself and enable you to accomplish the most for mankind so far as you can determine. Heaven has bestowed upon you noble powers, equalled only by a few, surpassed by none, thus placing upon you responsibilities far higher than otherwise would rest upon you; consequently, there is so much the more need that you consider well whatever steps you take. I say not this to flatter. No James I love you too well to say aught but the truth in reference to anything so intimately connected with your own dear self.

And shall you quench ambition's fires? *No*, James, never! *Watch* them well, but *let* them burn, not to consume the building, but to give it the *warmth* and *vigor* of *life*, and light it with high and holy impulses and determination.

I know not what to say in reference to myself. I know what I wish, but whether it can ever be accomplished surely I cannot tell. If health and means were mine, I would—after staying here another year—go to Antioch and graduate. As far as I have been able to learn anything of the Institution there I am better pleased with it than any other where ladies are allowed a privilege. How I should be able to effect this even if my health would permit, I do not know, still if I was sure of that I believe I would make an attempt. I have had a slight cough ever since the close of last session. Still it has not been very troublesome in the last two weeks. I took some more cold than I suppose which with *over-exercise* at housecleaning gave me a severe pain in my right side, and made my cough much worse, but by *Hydropathic* treatment and the magic of *little pills* I am now much better and trust I shall be well entirely when next session commences. I have had a *real nice time*, though, sitting in the *rocking chair* and reading . . . and last week I translated about 500 lines of Virgil in a little more than 4 days; but the Dr. and Mother put a *stop* to that, so I am not to study any more until school commences. . . . James, never say again that you fear your letters [are] long and dull. If you should write forever, I should not weary reading. No, I am always sorry when I finish reading one, and would sooner have it ten sheets longer than one word shorter. Shall I hear from you again, dearest James, one week from next Saturday?

My image shall be forth-coming soon. I am not going to return that sweet little kiss 'till I see you again. Then, sir . . . Am I still fondly your own,

Lucretia.

James replied to the preceding letter as follows: "With regard to Antioch. I am certainly better pleased with that Institution than any other one for Ladies, with which I am acquainted. It has at its head a true Man(n) [Horace Mann, 1796–1859] in a two-fold sense and if your health will permit I presume you will never regret going there. I think there is much of that generous liberal spirit which we all so much admire."

After the Williams Commencement in August and before the beginning of his first term in September, James took a holiday trip to visit relatives in Massachusetts. In the meantime, Lucretia had written concerning her persistent problem of what course of study to pursue: should she go on for a Bachelor of Arts degree studying the classics, or should she consider her academic work complete with her Hiram certificate? She is reluctant to take up classical studies again, and she refers to a book written by Theophilus Fiske, who writes, "Let the modern languages—German and French—be substituted for the languages that are dead. The one contains an inexhaustible stock of useful knowledge, the other not a particle, as all that is useful in Latin and Greek has been translated into English." "Is he not more than half right?" Lucretia asks James.

Williams College, Sept 13, 1854

My Dear Lucretia:

Your welcome letter of the 23rd ultimo was mailed at Hiram the day I left Williamstown for a trip of three weeks and today I have returned, having just made an end of my travels. During that time sixteen letters have found their way hither to bless me with words of kindness and love. This will explain my delay in answering your last—I was glad to hear that you were well again and am also happy to tell you that I return from my wanderings much refreshed, and feel strong and ready to grapple again with the duties of life. . . . Tomorrow the session commences, and every thing seems prosperous and indicative of a good and pleasant session. Tomorrow noon I expect to see Bro Wilber,[20] though I have an intimation in one of my letters that he is sick. Still, I hope it may not be so. It would be so discouraging to him. I certainly hope that there may be the most entire freedom of thoughts and expressions between us, and I will try to speak what my judgment dictates since you request it. Concerning studying the languages apart from other modifying circumstances, you know my views, and you must pardon my lack of reverence for the "Rev. Fiske" when I say that I cannot agree with him when he would substitute the modern languages for the Ancient and declaim against the utility of the classics. If he be a classical scholar I venture that he does not regret that he studied them. But I have never been among those who say that all persons under all circumstances should complete a full course of Latin and Greek. On the contrary, in many instances such a course would be most unwise. I am satisfied that to obtain the rudiments and genius of the Ancient Languages is a very superior and important discipline of the mind, and I know of nothing that will accomplish that work so well; and for those who design to occupy important, influential, and I will also add *lucrative* stations as teachers or preachers, I consider a complete classical course as almost indispensable, considering the way in which Society is now organized.[21] Now concerning yourself. I think that thus far you have pursued the best course you could have done, and whatever your future course may be, the discipline and knowledge you have acquired by studying the classics will be of invaluable service to you. But I must confess that I have felt for some months that it would not be best for you to continue them much longer to the exclusion of other branches, unless you were intending to complete a full course of study, and I am of opinion that your health forbids that. You have now laid a solid foundation, broad and deep, and were I to choose I would much rather that you should now bring up the natural sciences, French and German, music and painting and thus cultivate more the Esthetics, than that you should neglect these, and go farther with the classics.—I know the atmosphere Hiram has, thus far, been somewhat averse to Belleslettres, but I believe the mind, and especially the female mind, should be ornamented, as well as strengthened. Strength without ornament is gloomy and unattractive. Ornament without strength is shallow and insipid. But ornamented strength is lovely and wins the soul. 'Tis like the rock-built tower, whose top is crowned with garlands of flowers. Home joys are made doubly joyful by the attractions which cultivated taste and skillful hands can throw around it, and, Dear one, let me say, if it shall ever be ours to enjoy the same home should we not endeavor to be able to make that a spot around which our affections may cling and where we may find an attractive and happy retreat from the chilling world around us. The sententiousness of Livy, the terseness of Terence, and the abstrusities of Mathematical formulae will fail to accomplish this; and I fear the rugged path that lies before me will not enable me to do so much of that as I should love to do. Yet I could enjoy and prize it—and without it, life would lose much of its enjoyment.

I have written thus freely and fully. Read and reflect and let me hear again. I am glad you are reading the "Novum Graecum Testamentum" for without that, half of the object of Greek would be lost. I think you will be repaid to read Cicero after a while. . . . Do let me hear from you again soon and you shall hear from me sooner than this time. And now farewell for this time. I am most affectionately

James.

Hiram, Sept 20, 1854

My Dear James:

At last the loved and long long looked for letter has reached my waiting hand, and quick I haste to answer. . . .

I thank you a thousand times, dear James, for the kindness and frankness with which you expressed your opinions and wishes in regard to my future course, and am not a little *pleased* with the spirit you manifest in vindicating the claims of your favorites—the Classics—to attention. And you in turn I doubt not would enjoy a bit of *fun* could you witness the *lashings* we classics rebels receive occasionally from Bro Munnell.[22] He has no patience with those who condemn the study of the Ancient languages and will give them credit for nothing but *right down laziness*. He accuses them of dishonesty and I guess of almost everything else bad . . . and as for myself, I am in about the same ridiculous predicament the old Dutch juryman was when he declared it "a clear case" on both sides, and I presume it would be advisable for me to keep quiet hereafter, at least as long as I stay where I am. Your remarks referring to the education of the female mind were in strict accordance with my own views. I plead for strength most surely, and the more the better, both of mind and body; still, woman with *that alone* would differ nothing from her brother, and could never fulfil her mission of love, and gentle deeds which make Earth a *home* for mortals. Woman's province is her home, and if she is not fitted to make it a place around which warmest affections cluster, and on whose hearth-stone strongest attractions center, she is not prepared to act her part in life. And she who would neglect her home to shine in public life I cannot but consider as having altogether lost sight of her true place. Let woman's brightest rays be shed upon her own household, and her words of deepest eloquence fall by her own fireside; for *there* she can exert an influence, as enduring as the everlasting hills. Then should she be educated for that position, which was designed for her by her Maker, and while she must gain strength of intellect as a solid basis on which to build her hopes of usefulness, she must also cultivate those faculties which shall enable her to throw about it charms of beauty; for first she must *win* before she can *bind*. Man may rule by strength alone, and command not only the respect of his fellowman, but even his affections by the stern authority of intellectual greatness; but when woman attempts this, she becomes a monster.—

And so, dearest James, I will frankly acknowledge to *you* that if there is one earthly wish ruling in my head, it is that I may make *our home*, if Heaven ever grants it, truly a loved retreat where our fondest joys may center, and where by its quiet beauty and breath of love our spirits may gain new fitness to baffle the ills of life. . . .

I saw the Programme of your commencement exercises which you sent to Harvey;[23] also read your letter, as he very kindly offered me the pleasure. I was much interested with your account of "Ralph Waldo Emerson's" address, but Wilber told me that he should *give you a whipping* when he got there for falling so deeply in love with him, though he considers him as possessing a great mind, yet he thinks him rather dangerous as a guide.

Now must I wait so very long before I hear from you! Of course, I do not ask a letter only when it is your wish to grant it, still I would like to have you writing *very often*.

With truest affection:
Lucretia.

Williams College, Oct. 28, 1854

My Dear Lucretia:

The labor of the week is done, and your dear good letter has arrived to cheer this quiet evening hour, and you give me the pleasure again of writing down my thoughts to you.

I have just been looking at the stars through their ponderous telescope here. I could see plainly the rings of Saturn, and the moons and belts of Jupiter. We then turned it upon the crescent moon. It was a grand sight. We could see a round dark spot, and in the centre, a red sparkling light. The astronomers here were much entranced at that, which is supposed to be a volcano in a state of eruption. These are pleasing things to contemplate, but I am better pleased to sit here alone, and turn my thoughts toward *The Western Star*.

I have spent the day in preparing an oration for next Wednesday evening in the Philologian Society, where I am to make my "maiden speech" in Williams College. The advantages here in Literary Societies are very fine, and I hope to be benefitted by them. Speaking of College, I will say that I have concluded to remain two years, for I shall never go through College but once. I wish to do it thoroughly. In two years I shall have more time to read, think, and mature my mind, and taking my life time (if it should be many years long) into the account, I think it will be better for me. I hardly dare look forward to the end of two years, for it seems as if something must arise to deter me from finishing the course, but still I will hope for it and labor for it. And if that privilege is granted me of graduating here one year from next August, nothing could please me more than to have *you* here then. Why could not a company of our good Ohio friends take a trip at that time, and breathe for a few days the mountain air of New England? But let me not anticipate too much. There are thousands of blows to be struck, and thousands of heart throbs to be given ere that day arrives. Still such is life the world over. . . .

We are now having lectures and experiments of a very interesting charac-ter, each one of which furnishes enough thought for a whole week. These old Professors have spent their whole lives in arranging and analyzing the great truths of Science. Oh how I wish you could hear them. What a badly arranged world this is, that you cannot be permitted to come here and study, too. Their teachings give one such grand views of nature and all things around us. Such lectures are kept up during the whole course. I will give you a sketch of some of them sometime if you wish. Accompanying this I send you a Catalogue of the College, just published. I would like to see the Eclectic Catalogue when it comes out. Dearest, I know this letter is dull and I will relieve you by stopping soon. But you must pardon for I am weary tonight. I wonder where you are at this moment, doubtless in slumber. Happy dreams Dearest, and so good night. Let me hear soon again and remember me ever as your affectionate,

James

Hiram, Nov 7, 1854

Dearest James:

I would not be selfish but I must confess I am glad you are sometimes *weary*, so that your spirit can find pleasure in turning from ponderous worlds and the majesty of Science to rest awhile in the affections of my heart, and have the communing which lifts *my* soul on an inspired flight, though it be but a rest-ing place on which *your* spirit folds its *drooping* wing. But not always would I have you linger here dear James. Oh no. Turn again to the boundless fields of Science. Track her mysterious paths and through her wonders learn the wis-dom of her Author. And though I cannot accompany you there, slowly I will follow in the track, and thank Heaven that even her outer gates have been thrown open at last for woman's entrance, and though we must yet tarry in the portal, hope for the speedy appearance of that day whose dawning has already begun when side by side brother and sister may tread her inviting paths and together pluck her golden fruit. I thank you for the kind proposal you made of giving me a sketch occasionally of the lectures which you are permitted to hear. Nothing could please me more, and I hope to receive them often; also may I not be favored with a copy of your "maiden speech"? The evening that you deliv- ered it I was at Garrettsville listening to a Temperance Address by Mrs. J. Everett. She is a very young-looking handsome genteel appearing woman pos- sessing a good deal of intellect withal. I should judge however that she is not very thoroughly educated. Her address evinced more reading than study. Like the Doctor she is rather discursive; still I have no particular fault to find and presume her speech was pronounced very good considering she is a *woman*. She read it all which seemed to strip it of half its force especially as her style of read- ing was rather monotonous, and I found it necessary to make quite an exertion of my imaginative power to keep myself in the belief that she was in earnest, it seemed so much like a school girl's essay. . . .

It is true James we know nothing of the chances and changes of an uncer- tain future, still I do believe that trusting all with God, relying on his Omnipotent arm for support you will see the accomplishment of your design. You have struggled nobly, and Heaven never leaves unrewarded those who toil in a good cause.

This week finishes another session of the Eclectic. O. P. Miller and Barbara Fisk are preparing *valedictories* for us. Today I recited alone my last lesson in Greek for this session, read the last 24 verses of the last chapter of Luke and conjugated the verbs in the active voice. I wonder if this week will recall to your mind any of the incidents of a year ago, of the examination, the *preparation* for it. I wonder if in the treasure chest of your memory as in mine there are any *happy hours* which you count as the miser does his gold.

A week from next Thursday (16th) will be the anniversary of our corre- spondence' commencement, when you sat within the sound of Niagara's roar and penned your first lines to me. Will you not celebrate it by writing another letter? Do not wait to answer this 'til then, but write something expressly in *commemoration* of that *wonderful event* if it is nothing but a sermon. I will answer it a year from the day I answered that if you will give me the date.

I thank you for the Catalogue of Williams College you sent, and shall [send] you one of the Eclectic just published. . . .

Hoping to hear again very soon, I remain Dearest James faithfully your own:

Lucretia.

From his early days James had been interested in creation theories and the biblical account. Later he was to debate the question on several occasions. Here he writes Lucretia enthusiastically on his discovery of Hugh Miller's theory. Miller, a stonemason by trade, lived from 1802–1856. He is the author of a number of works of geological interest.

Williams College, Nov 12, 1854

Lucretia Dearest:

I am happy to sit down and answer your ever-welcome messages, and cannot feel that it is wrong for me to spend a part of the quiet Lord's Day afternoon in communing with you.

I am still enjoying good health with the exception of an occasional difficulty with my throat which is quite easily affected by cold weather and exposure to the night air. My studies are still pleasant and interesting. It is indeed a great luxury to me to sit down and feel that all the day and evening are my own, without the necessity of spending most of it in teaching. But still, besides my regular College duties, I find considerable time for Miscellaneous reading. I have today read a Sermon by Hugh Miller of Scotland called "The Two Records" which is the best thing of its kind I have ever seen. The "Records" referred to are the Mosaic and Geological accounts of creation.

He first speaks as a Geologist and proves that there have been three great Geologic periods. First, of great vegetation, from which coal was formed. 2nd of Great Sea Monsters, and 3rd of Great Land Animals. No remains of man are found below these, and there are indubitable testimonies that these occupied a great many thousand years in formation.

In looking at the Bible account, he says, "I find myself called on as a Geologist to account for but the three of the six days, for of the day when light was created—of the day when the firmament was made—and of the day when the two great lights were made, we need expect to find no record in the rocks. Now the 3rd, 5th and 6th days' creations were in the same order and kind as the three Geologic periods—and after those came Man." The "day" he shows does not refer to 24 hours, for in the fourth verse of the second chapter the word "day" means the whole six. Hence it is indefinite and may be any length of time. He then answers an objection made by some, that if these were not natural days, the Institution of the Sabbath could not be observed. He says human actions can only be miniatures of the Divine, just as a map may be a true representation of the world though a million times smaller. So man's days are but miniatures of the days of God, yet still a seventh of his time. He then says, God rested from the work of creating on His Seventh *day*, and the work of His Sabbath is not yet done, for it is the work of Redemption which brings to perfection the last work of his Creation. I did not think of taking so much space in speaking of that book, but I was much interested in it, and I wish you could find it and read it.

I am sure you would not ask me for my Speech if you knew what kind of a thing it is. Please don't require me to send it till I have got reconciled from its nauseating effects. But I will try to do it in a few days. I do get sick of an oration by the time I get it delivered! By the way I am doing considerable in our Literary Society, and we have the best advantages I have ever enjoyed. I should like to have heard the Valedictories of Barbara, and O. P. Doubtless they were very fine. That reminds me of two years ago when there were two valedictories on that stage. "*Do I dwell on the memories of the past?*" My only intimate Society is that of distant Friends, and my little world of joys is in the past, when I am here alone. I am much pleased with your proposition to write on the anniversary of the strange beginning at Niagara, and I will do so. I hope to receive an offering from you written on the 30th of November, the date of your first. I have half a mind not to let you read mine till you have written yours, but just as you please. But you must not wait till the 30th before you write to me at all—will you. . . .

Dearest Lucretia, let me hear from you very soon, *on a large sheet of paper.* As ever,

Your
James.

It is in the following letter that James responds to Lucretia's request to write something about his thoughts on the anniversary of their correspondence. The date, November 16, is close, also, to James' birth date, November 19. Reference in this letter to troubles

before he visited Niagara Falls hearkens to the row raised when he cut off his affair with Mary Hubbell, a girl from Chagrin Falls, Ohio. Mary's family had threatened reprisals against James since he had so far committed himself to Mary as to give her family the impression that he would marry her. The end of the relationship had been traumatic for James, and he felt "as if severed from society."

Williams College, Nov 16, 1854

My Dear Lucretia:

Strange indeed are the thoughts that come thronging upon me as I wander back to one year ago this day. And if I can transcribe even a meagre portion of them correctly, I shall do more than I expect to. What a strange, strange world we live in! Its lights and shadows how varied and changeful! My life especially has seemed to me a continued miracle. Its brightness and darkness, its sorrow and joy have been so strangely mingled, and yet I have had scarcely an inch of existence as yet. Next Sunday, 23 years ago, a man child was born, and they called his name J. A. G.—

But I cannot, at this time, even hint at the little world of incident of Life-History that has been enacted by and around me. I will speak more particularly of one year ago today, when I stood among the wonders of that rushing cataract. But a few months before, my spirit had been involved in a worse commotion than Niagara's, the details of which you know. I had felt for a time as if severed from society, and had no desire to renew my connection with it. But as well may the human heart live and pulsate in an iceberg's bosom as to try to exist and enjoy existence, alone and uncared for by the tender sympathies of human kind and to feel that no heart in all the cold world throbs in unison with it. O how wide the world seems then! My heart had for some time been going out instinctively, as it were, toward you, and yet I felt we were a great distance apart, and when I sat down to write those few first lines I felt as if I might be trespassing on forbidden grounds, but I thought if it should be considered improper I would lay the blame to Niagara!!

I cannot tell you how strangely I felt when I found your first letter, recognizing the receipt of mine, and speaking words of kindness. I cannot trace my heart's history from its first faint beginnings when the first little tendrils of my heart began to cling to yours. How frail were those tendrils then! They might easily have been broken, turned away, and forbidden to twine. But as time rolled on, they grew in strength and numbers till they have intertwined themselves around your whole being. My mind follows along through that correspondence in all its different features and recounts my secret heart-throbbings at those happy little interviews. You remember them all—the midnight return from the New Year's sleigh ride, the visiting Perintha's school,[24] that lower chapel consecrated by the evening farewells of the Eclectic Students, when alternating between hope and doubt, I ventured to tell you what you knew already, and with a soul full of agitation waited to hear from your own lips a response to my affection. Never, while reason sits on the throne of my being, can I forget the fullness of joy that filled my heart, when in that tone of earnestness that spoke all your soul, you told me I was loved. That evening is marked with a "white stone" in my memory. Those words with which you answered me are still ringing in my ears, distinct, as when they were spoken and their tones cheer me in loneliness and tell me I still am loved. Then came the spring, its studies and duties, and its thousand little spots of joy and sunshine, when we watched the opening peach blossoms at your window, while the sun all bright and golden was sinking behind the western forests, read the beauties of Longfellow's genial heart, or walked upon our lengthened shadows as we descended the hill that slopes eastward from your home. I turn over the leaves of my Anabasis, and Kuhner, here, and find on every page mementos of departed scenes, and am led back to that chair by the stove in front of that little love seat, where sat those dear Grecians, oh yes, and their picture is lying before me, which calls to mind the injunction I whispered in the Artist's private ear, in regard to seating the group (did you then suspect I was so wicked?). I seem to be there again with but one to recite, and only one book. Ah, I fear I was not always a faithful *teacher* then. But I *did* try to be! Again when the forenoon labor was done, that sweet music in the Library told me I might while away a moment with the musician and talk of the passing events. But the session passed away swiftly, and left its events only among the things that were. But they all live in my memory clear as sunlight. They form a large share of my life when in loneliness and much of my joy when sad.

The hour of departure came and with beloved friends behind, and the cold world of strangers before, I left the scene of all those happy hours. Since that hour, Dearest One, your loved letters, those Souvenirs of the heart, have cheered and blessed me and here they lie before me with that likeness of your own dear self. And now in the silence of the night, your spirit seems to be with me here, and whisper words of tenderest affection, and I cannot tell you the gratitude of my heart to God, that I have found a treasure so dear to me. Dear loved one, I would not be too hopeful, and expect too much—I trust I *am not.* I have long ago determined to let sober judgement and not impulse rule my head. But I am cheered by the hope that our hearts may someday be united without an intervening distance. Is it too much to hope that we may yet enjoy each other's society in that holiest and closest of unions? I would fain write more—My mind leads on to the days when life advances and to that scene where life broadens and deepens into eternal life, and my Soul rises up in strong desire that we may there meet, freed from this clay of mortality, and drink together of the water of life that flows from the Throne of God. But I must close. Would that I could be but one short hour by your side!—But, Dearest one, I *know* you will write a long long letter to me, so write freely, and tell me your heart's history and emotions. If I have been tedious in this forgive me. My thoughts have [been] multitudinous, and I have penned them as they rose. Dearest I cannot see you tonight, but God has seen you, and I will ask Him to bless you.

May Good Angels guard your slumbers and our Father save you is the prayer of

Your own
James.

Williams College, Nov 30, 1854
Thanksgiving Day

Dearest Lucretia:

Your dear letter was duly received, and now on the day of New England's Thankfulness, I am seated to be with you a short time.

It's a bitter cold day without, and the winter winds howl like demons. The valley is barren and bare, and the mountain tops are shrouded with a garment of snow. It is indeed a dreary day without, but New England's heart is warm within and thousands of homes are made glad by the return of children who gather around the old familiar hearthstone of their childhood home, and thousands of pious hearts are today going up in thankfulness to God for the mercies of the past year, and asking His blessing to rest upon the absent ones who tread the wild forests or ride upon the mountain waves. This is a good old custom in New England of observing this day of public thanksgiving and festivity. I think the West is too irreverent in reference to it. I have no sympathy with that narrowminded fear that some Christians have of defiling the garments of their sanctity if they observe a religious appointment made by the commonwealth. This forenoon at eleven we assembled at the place of worship and the aged minister recounted the history of the Pilgrim Fathers, and their struggles to plant Freedom and Christianity on the cold shores of New England, and told us how "they left unstained what there they found, freedom to Worship God."

He spoke of the Providence of God over our nation and especially this State the past year, and then over individuals. I was more edified than I have been for some time before.

About [the] middle of the afternoon every table will be laden with something special for the Thanksgiving Dinner[25]—for the attending upon which I shall soon be called from my writing, I presume. . . .

I wonder if you are writing to me now! How I would like to look over your shoulder and not have you know it! I hope you will not get tired till you have written a long one.

Five months ago yesterday I left Ohio. The hours are swiftly rolling away. In about ten days the session closes, and a third of the college year is past. . . . I hope to hear from you soon in reference to your course in teaching or indeed anything you please to write. Now this letter isn't a bit dull nor stupid I am sure!

Dearest, I hope to have the privilege of reading your anniversary letter soon. Meantime I am as ever

Your own affectionate
James.

James and Lucretia wrote New Year's Eve letters to each other during the first years of their courtship. Here is Lucretia's to close the first calendar year of their courtship.

Hiram, Dec 31, 1854
My Dear James:
New and strange are the emotions thrilling my soul as I sit down at this still solemn hour to commence writing to you, feeling this assurance that away over many an intervening hill and dale you are also seated at this very hour—moment perchance—with your thoughts to me turning, and your heart

prompting messages of love for your hand to trace, destined for my eyes soon to behold. *Another year gone!* numbered with the years that were but are not—now a part of the mighty Past. And, whither have gone all its hours, its precious moments? So vividly are the scenes of one year ago this time before me, when I sat very near you with my hand clasped in your own, that it seems but yesterday and I can scarcely realize that long months have borne me from them—and you so far from my side. But true it is. Today I have been sitting within the sound of Bro Rider's voice, and trying to be a listener, but my thoughts would not follow. Backward they were wandering over the past year, and I trust the reflections in which I have indulged will in a measure atone for my inattention to the words of the Preacher. Of all my years the last has brought me the most pure and true happiness. Its hours of unalloyed enjoyment have been many, and no small portion of them have been the hours of sweet communion with you. Through the bright spring time daily I had your loving smiles and heard your words of kindness, and though the hour of parting came, and duty called you far away, still I was happy. For oft from your blessed hand came those sweet assurances of your spirit's presence, which told me that still I was loved. The *bell tolls* the departing year—1855: A happy, *happy* New Year to you. Its untried realities are all before us and what they may prove we know not; but to you I trust they may all prove bright and beautiful; for you are deserving it. So, dear James, listen to me. I have said the past year my brightest: but for all its rich gifts what returns have I made? Have I become any better? Have I by any act manifested an increasing devotion to Him from whom all my enjoyments and blessings have come? Spiritually, have I grown and gained new strength? These are queries which come home to me with startling earnestness, and when I think of the response I am compelled to give, I am terrified. When I consider how listlessly I have lived—how unmindful of duty, I tremble for myself, while the tear of penitence falls. What is the best of life if Heaven is not gained?—I am resolved that another year shall not so pass, Heaven helping me, and you my dearest earthly friend I make a witness of this resolution, and ask you that often you may remind me of it. One year from this night if I am spared the precious boon—life—I shall write to you again—unless circumstances unforseen should forbid—and I am determined to have less cause for regret. With you, I believe we should make the chief object of living to be "to make ourselves holy and happy" and for this will strive.—

The old year passed away with sunshine upon its brow. The wintery mists and clouds have departed like the dimness which often falls from the vision of

old age ere it opens upon a new life, and the New Year is ushered in with the holy star light watching over it, and welcomed by the moon's soft beams. So in love and joy may its days all be numbered and peacefully may it die. My heart is full of deep untold love, but my lips are sealed, and my pen cannot reveal it. No more tonight, my love. . . .

With truest affection, I remain your
Lucretia

✥ NOTES ✥

1. John F. Sears, *Sacred Places: American Tourist Attractions in the Nineteenth Century* (New York: Oxford University Press, 1989), 14–15. Elizabeth McKinsey, *Niagara Falls: Icon of the American Sublime* (New York: The Cambridge Press, 1985), 157.
2. According to the Census of 1850, Buffalo had a population of 42,000.
3. "God Willing."
4. Thomas Carlyle (1795–1881) was a British essayist. His *On Heroes, Hero-Worship, and the Heroic in History*, a lecture, was published in England in 1841.
5. Thomas Babington Macaulay (1800–1859) was a British historian. His *The History of England* (5 vols., 1849–1861) is considered one of the great works of the nineteenth century.
6. Nathaniel P. Willis (1806–1867), an American writer of verse, essays and plays, whose works were much admired by both James and Lucretia, was reputed to have led an immoral life.
7. "Urbesque terraeque recedebant" may be translated, "and the cities and land receded." This quotation is from book 3 of *The Aeneid*, which Garfield says his class has been reading.
8. The "school" referred to is, of course, the little college of Hiram, where James was teaching Virgil, a class Lucretia had attended the preceding year. Founded just three years earlier, in 1850, Hiram was described by a fellow student of Garfield's in its first years as a disappointment: "We ascended quite a hill, and on the west side of the road stood the school building; the basement was of yellowish sandstone, with two stories above, of red brick. The cupola or dome was covered with zinc. The building was in an open field; small trees had been planted, but they gave no promise of shade from

the hot sun" (Corydon Fuller, *Reminiscences of James A. Garfield* [Cincinnati: Standard Publishing Co., 1887], 26–27).

9. "By mouth rather than by pen."

10. President Hayden was Head of the Eclectic Institute at Hiram. He evidently visited some of the Hiram students teaching in local schools.

11. "One of his cabinet" refers to James, a member of the Hiram staff while still a student.

12. Almeda Booth was a teacher at the Eclectic Institute who had taken a special interest in James and knew Lucretia well, too. She later became a close friend of James and Lucretia, living in their home on the Hiram campus for a number of years.

13. This is Alexander Campbell, founder of the Disciples of Christ, the religious movement so influential in the early lives of James Garfield and Lucretia. Hiram's Eclectic Institute was established by this denomination and Campbell's thought proved a great influence on the thinking of both James and Lucretia. Campbell's lecture on "The Anglo-Saxon Language," presented in Cincinnati in 1849, had as its main theme the "general adoption" of English as the one "God given" language of the whole earth. "No event in the future," Campbell said, "appears more natural, more probable, more practicable or more morally certain and desirable, than this Anglo-Saxon triumph in the great work of human civilization and redemption."

14. John F. Sears, *Sacred Places*, 15.

15. The Hamilton-Burr duel took place on 11 July 1804 on a ledge overlooking the Hudson at Weehauken, New Jersey, across from New York City. Burr wounded Hamilton mortally.

16. Harry J. Brown and Frederick D. Williams, eds., *The Diary of James A. Garfield,* (East Lansing: Michigan State University Press, 1967), 1: 267–68.

17. This is Symonds Ryder, one of the founders of the Eclectic Institute at Hiram and a local preacher.

18. Paul Flemming is the romantic hero in Longfellow's *Hyperion*, a tale of travel and sentiment much admired by James and Lucretia.

19. Lizzie Atwood, Lucretia's closest friend from childhood, later married Albert Pratt, a Williams graduate from Massachusetts. Lucretia visited Lizzie in the summer of 1858, just before she married Garfield.

20. Charles D. Wilber, like James, was from Hiram. He, too, entered Williams College in the fall of 1855. He was James' roommate during their first year there.

21. James' response to Lucretia's question about the study of the classical languages is in harmony with the general opinion on this topic.
22. Thomas Munnell was an early faculty member of the Eclectic Institute, a graduate of Bethany College.
23. Harvey Everest, a fellow student of James' at the Eclectic Institute, went to teach at Bethany, but left on account of his abolitionist views and returned to teach at Hiram.
24. This evidently refers to a trip James and Lucretia took to visit the school of Parintha Dean, a fellow student at the Eclectic Institute.
25. Thanksgiving Day, except in New England, was celebrated only sporadically in America, and rarely in the Western Reserve. In 1863, however, Lincoln urged the formal establishment of Thanksgiving as a national holiday, and each succeeding president annually proclaimed the day to be the fourth Thursday of November.

CHAPTER 2

Courtship: The Second Year, 1855–1856

F ROM JANUARY 1855 UNTIL AUGUST, *the correspondence of James and Lucretia continued to flow passionately, James in Massachusetts and Lucretia in Ohio. Constructing an intimate relationship out of pure language, the two went on rapturously into the summer, dreaming of future joys together, all unclouded. James returned for a brief vacation in August; the two met for the first time since July of the year before. Lucretia, now teaching a class in nearby Ravenna, the county seat, felt out of tune with James, and he evidently felt the same, for rather than visiting her for any length of time, he left Ravenna immediately for Hiram, where he spent the rest of his holiday. But on his way back to Williamstown, he stopped again to see Lucretia, and this time the two experienced the old feeling of love. More than ever before, they were enamored of one another.*

During the months following, while James was back at Williams College and Lucretia was teaching in Ravenna, the correspondence returns to an even higher pitch of romantic expression, continuing in this vein until August 1856, when James graduated with honors from Williams.

But something else had happened during the months of this chapter. James had become acquainted with Rebecca Selleck and Maria Learned. A curious tangle of relationships ensued with Sister Maria, a happily married woman herself, promoting the affection of James and Rebecca, while both women professed to love Lucretia, when James had described her to them. As Margaret Leech puts it, "It taxes belief that . . . James should have found a respectable woman who sympathized with his artlessly polygamous impulses. But James had done something still more extraordinary; he had found two such women."[1] As time went by, Lucretia became more and more concerned

with whether or not James had consummated his relationship with Rebecca. However,
before she met Maria and Rebecca at the Williams Commencement in the summer of
1856, she was not suspicious of James' behavior.

The letters in this chapter begin, then, after the New Year of 1855 with Lucretia
still in Hiram and James in Williamstown; they end just before August 1856, as the
two writers look forward with impassioned longing to James' graduation, the moment
when they will be reunited.

Hiram, Feb 23, 1855

Dearest James:

After a silence of six long weeks it is again my happy privilege to address
you once more. . . .The winter is called rather hard; for almost five weeks we
have had the best of sleighing, and for four weeks the thermometer stood constantly below freezing point, and the frozen earth is still wrapt in its winding
sheet. But, though the moon's smiling face unveiled with clouds and the snowy
earth would little remind me of one year ago this night, still memory is busy
with those happy hours. I think of the first kiss given—have you forgotten the
icy coldness with which it was received? You had not yet reached the heart.
Then through all the scenes of that day memory follows on, and again I am in
your arms, clasped to your heart, again that wild strange delight of love first
spoken thrills my heart's trembling chords. Then follows that holy calm which
the low music of your voice brought as long you talked to me, resting on your
bosom. My own James, did not Heaven grant that holy hour? Were not angels
hovering near to record its bright revealings? And did not our guardian spirits
meet in the fond embrace of Heaven's holy love, and bending o'er us cast
around our hearts the silken cord which on earth shall nearer and nearer draw
us, and in Heaven bind in a union perfect and entire? . . .

As for myself and what I am doing—I am writing a letter to you just now,
and that is about the only *definite* thing I can say of myself at present. I do not
know whether they will want me in the Institution to teach next session or not.
If not, I may possibly study all the term, but I think not. I have about concluded
to teach somewhere else if I can get a school. I am reading now Mrs. H. B.
Stowe's "Sunny Memories of Foreign Lands."[2] Almeda may have told you of
them as she has been reading them this winter. They are very interesting, and
quite as instructive as books of travel. True, we get only the bright side of the
picture; but why not? she asks. "They are the impressions as they arose of a
most agreeable visit," and she thinks after all, "there are many worse sins than

a disposition to think and speak well of one's neighbors." It is really quite amusing to read with what almost idolatrous enthusiasm she was every where received. I doubt whether "Kissath" or the "Swedish Nightingale" produced a much greater excitement among the Americans.[3] And I think those of the Old Countries who have so much ridiculed young America's enthusiasms at sight of a foreigner might as well spare a dish of their raillery for *home consumption*. I have also commenced reading "Butler's Analogy."[4] I felt a little "out of patience" when I first began, it required such close attention to understand it— so different from anything I had been accustomed to read. But I am getting quite interested in his concise matter of fact course of reasoning. There seems not to be a superfluous sentence, or even word, in it. So directly opposite to most that is written now, whose chief excellence generally is beauty of style. I would not underrate the *flowers* though. I am as fond of them as anyone; still I think this Analogy cannot be too highly prized for the mental discipline which it affords. I do not wonder the Bishop never married. There was not *romance* enough in his nature to love a *woman*.

> . . . Ever and forever, your own Lucretia.

> No. 12, South College
> Williamstown, Mar 6, 1855

Lucretia Dearest:

Your dear letter of the 24th ultimo was duly recieved and though I had written to you but a few days before, I will write again. I was much rejoiced to hear from you , still more after so long a delay. I was fearing that you were sick, or that some one of the ten thousand evils of which the dreaming spirit conceives had befallen you, but the arrival of your long looked for letter dissipated all those phantoms and made my sleep sweet again.

(You will pardon this "grey goose quill" for its unseemly marks, for this is the second letter I have written with a quill pen for many year.)

O Dearest, you do not know the thrilling joys which vibrated through the thousand strings of my being as I read your reminiscences of one year ago. It waked to life all those scenes as vividly as if they occurred but yesterday, and I lived over again that short hour of delirious joy when you told me for the first time that I was loved. How long my heart and lips had trembled on that question before it was asked! and how full and overflowing was my heart's joy when your own dear heart echoed the affections of my own! The recollection of that hour and many that followed it cheer many a desolate hour when Life seems so hollow, so cold and drear. Let the swift months roll, for they bring me nearer to you. If God spares us both, I shall hope to enjoy a few days of happiness in your society in the end of the summer of '55. But I will not hope too much. . . .

They are having a great "Revival" in College now, and though I cannot subscribe to all the ways and means, yet I believe there is much good being done, and I can truly say I have never been among more spiritually minded Christians than those I find in Williams College. I am heartily cooperating with them in arousing the unconcerned to the interests of the Christian Religion, but I let them have their way in reference to doctrine. I do not think I should be doing right to interpose a discordant element at such a time as this, though I can hardly resist my desire to tell them what the Gospel is. . . .

Has Almeda gone to Oberlin?[5] I have not heard one word from her for nearly two months. Well, I did not notice how many queries was collecting on one page. But I must close. Give my love to any that you please to, who inquire for me. . . . Let me hear soon again. With much love, I am your

James.

Lucretia, back in school at Hiram, is now engaged in teaching as well as studying. Despite her conservative views on women's rights, one detects a tendency toward a more liberal position in her remarks about "Uncle Symonds," who is Brother Ryder, an elderly member of the Hiram community.

Hiram, April 1, 1855

My Dear James:

They call this "fools day"; but I will try and not fool you any worse than I always have, which I hope is not very badly, as I am sure you must know something of what I am by this time. Owing to the bad roads yesterday's mail did not reach here till this morning. Consequently, your letter was not received until then, and as my time is so fully occupied through the week that I shall be unable to answer before Friday evening next unless I write tonight, I have concluded so to do, trusting it will not be very wicked. I am engaged in school again, reading Horace, and studying French, also teaching two classes. The same I taught last session, and today Bro Hayden spoke to me about taking a class commencing French. The class in Horace read it all last winter, and are now reading about 100 lines per lesson, which for me is a rather long pull. We will be through with it in a few weeks and then we read "Cicero" the remainder of the term. I am feeling much better than I did two weeks ago, though not entirely well yet, and presume I shall not be until the weather becomes more settled as I must of necessity expose myself a good deal. Your *whisker logic* is *doubtless* very good; but was it not a great blunder in dame Nature to furnish *man* with such a *necessary* protection for his lungs and leave poor frail woman's throat unprotected?

"Uncle Symonds" gave the ladies a terrible dressing a week ago today, so they say. I did not hear it. I judge he thinks all we are made for is to work, and as for the accomplishments, it is a sin even to think of them. What an idea of life! Bake bread, wash dishes, scrub, iron and mend, week in week out, month after month, year after year—without a thought of anything else. True, those things must all be attended to, and each one should bear her part, but to make their thorough performances the end and aim of life, and the only object to receive any attention is most intolerable; and yet she must be an angel in goodness, mild as a summer morning and smiling as a moonbeam. Strange inconsistency! I do think Bro Rider, good as he is, is the most unreasonable man sometimes I ever knew. But I suppose we ought to bear with him patiently as he is getting to be an old man. Why has the God of Nature thrown all about us with such lavish hand beauty and grace if we are not to love it and cultivate it in our hearts and lives? Mrs. Stowe says, "Did not He who made the appetite for food make also that for beauty? and while the former will perish with the body is not the latter immortal?" and is it not as much our *duty* to feed our higher nature with food sufficient for it, as our bodies? And as much, or even more, a sin to let it famish and die than leave our animal bodies to perish for lack of proper nourishment?

I am finished reading "Sunny Memories" and am well pleased with them. Her travels in Germany interested me not a little, as she visited many places, the theaters of those nations which made up the Romance of Paul Flemming[6]—"Interlachen" where he met, loved and parted with crushed hopes from his Mary, "Strasbourg," "Heidelberg" and several other places. . . .

Now, my dear, may I expect another letter in just two weeks? I don't like to wait after I expect one. With truest love, I am faithfully your own,

Lucretia.

In his reply James excuses Brother Ryder because of his advanced age ("It is really a great trial to have him preach as he does sometimes"), and, in response to Lucretia's comments about Stowe's travels in Germany and Longfellow's Hyperion, goes on to speak of his love for the German language. "I hope before I leave College here," he writes, "to have a tolerable knowledge of that sweet tongue, the language of the heart, the repository of such sweet soul stirring thought: I have already made some advancement in it and intend to keep it up."

Lucretia's reference in the letter which follows to Harriet Beecher Stowe's Uncle Tom's Cabin is an early indication of her attitude toward the slavery issue. Though James does not respond to these comments, he mentions reading the work in his Diary in July 1852. It had been published that year.

Hiram, April 14, 1855

My own Dearest James:

True to the appointed hour your dear letter came, and found me just finishing "Uncle Tom's Cabin." With it unsealed beside me, I read to the close of that sad thrilling story, then turned from the dark picture to contemplate the loved revealings of your noble spirit to mine. And as I contrast my happy lot, the sweet pure delight of my life in possessing one so good and true to throw about me the strong affections of his heart, and draw my spirit into such a sacred nearness of holy love and trust, without fear that the powers of earth may ever divide, with the heart-rending fate of my many sisters, not darker than myself, whose very heart strings are rudely severed, and all the warm and gushing affection of their nature trampled in the dust, the very tears blind my eyes, as in thankfulness my heart is raised to God for the mercies I enjoy; and speedily, speedily, may the wrongs of the oppressed be redressed is the prayer my spirit offers.

It is growing late and wearied nature bids me yield to her "sweet restorer— balmy sleep." Still I fancied my dreams would be sweeter, and visions fairer would rise before me if but a few lines only were traced for your dear eyes ere I slept. May Heaven guard us while in slumbers we rest, and the morning's light find us renewed for the work of life—the holy privileges of the Lord's day. One kiss, dearest. Good night.

Sunday afternoon. The bright glad sunshine, the still soft twittering of the southern gales telling us that another spring time in its virgin beauty draweth near, together with the holy quiet the day inspires, are all conspiring to soften down my spirit into that heavenly calmness which it is not for mortals fit to feel. I seem to be living over again one of the many days my childhood knew when Earth seemed heaven, so hauntingly my unfettered spirit yielded to Nature's tranquil voice, and lost its self in her ten thousand harmonies. What would life be without such holy harmony? without this day of sacred rest—so quiet and heavenlike that I have often thought that if from a long sleep I should awake on a Lord's Day morning, I should not need to be told that it was the day commemorating the resurrection of our Lord from dark shades of death; for Nature's hush and sweet calmness would sufficiently proclaim it. . . .

I received a letter from Almeda since I last wrote you. She is almost killing herself I judge but says I must not tell her friends of it; perhaps you have heard from her though and know what she is doing. I heard something so funny a while ago about her that I do believe I must tell you. Mind, you don't say a word to her about it, though. A widower from the West has been spending the win-ter in Mantua [a nearby village], and someone there picked up a letter on the street written by him to our Almeda, making proposals of marriage. Dear little man, I wonder if he thought there was any hope of getting her! Wouldn't you laugh, though, to see her Greek and Latin turned into the kitchen, and her Mathematic called into active exercise over pies and cakes, etc. for a family of step-children! . . .

I wish you might spend a year in Germany, dear James, if you wish it. And perhaps Heaven may yet favor you that you may. I would like to study German, and now intend to sometime. You recollect I commenced Greek under *your* tuition. Perhaps I may wait until you have returned from your German tour and take lessons of you. No, no, that is not what I am going to do. I shall go to Germany with you. I should not allow you to get any farther away from me.

You *laugh* at my "ad mulieren argument." Well, it was just what I expected, therefore did not feel very much disconcerted. But *mind* you—you don't hear what I am about *now*. . . .

May I hear again very soon, Dearest? Knowing that I shall, still fondly I remain yours in truest love.

Lucretia

P.S. I am quite well again.

In her letter of June 25 Lucretia describes the Hiram Commencement, speaking specifically of Dr. Robison's crude behavior whenever a young woman took the platform. She added: "I can't endure that man. I never did like him, and it is less than ever that I esteem him now. You know, James, that I am far from ultra on the question of 'woman's rights'; but I will despise Dr. Robison or any other man of his intelligence who would prevent a lady from the stage, who has stood, as a student, beside her brothers."

Dr. Robison, a prominent Disciple and, later, Trustee of Hiram College, became a friend and political mentor of Garfield. He left medicine for various business enterprises, becoming one of the most influential businessmen in the Cleveland area.

Williams College, July 7, 1855

My Own Dear Crete,

Yours of June 30th reached me July 6th and I will start one back as soon as possible, for it seems as if the mails had declared war against us, and were determined to detain our letters as long as possible. I had just returned from a botanying expedition when I received yours. I have travelled 14 miles of the way on foot to get a view from the top of Greylock, the highest mountain in Massachusetts.

When I reached there it began to rain and I didn't do much else the rest of the day but float! It would tickle you to see me walk. There are blisters on the bottom of both feet so that I can not limp but go waddling along like a little blind man in company. So here I am with my feet bolstered up trying to write a letter to you. I read your account of the Commencement exercises with much interest, and during the day that it was going off I wanted very much to be there and see the many whom I should know. No doubt all the performers acquitted themselves well. . . .

You speak of Dr. Robison's nonchalant in reference to the exhibition. He does sometimes act as if the idea of being pleased never entered his mind. I saw him sit by the side of Bro Campbell and sleep most soundly while Bro C. was preaching. Now, I know you are not ultra in reference to Woman's Rights, and tell me, dearest, do you think it conducive to her best interests to accustom herself to delivering orations before public audiences? I confess I do not and the more exalted views I get of woman's character and capabilities, the more I am inclined to the opinion that her own best interests do not lie in that path. Far be it from me to "frown her away" from haranguing, but I would have her own highest good and hence the good of others, dissuade her from taking that direction. How far she may go or where the line should be drawn is no easy question to decide. We see society taking extreme positions on each side as they do in every thing else.

There seems to be a favorable opening at Ravenna for a school, and it would doubtless be a good place for you. Now, Dearest, what can I say after all your modest talk about your own abilities. Really, I am nearly provoked at you to hear you say, "I doubt very much my capabilities for managing such a school." My only fear is that the care and labor of such a school would be too much for your health and strength. You have not told me for a long time the state of your health. Tell me next time. . . .

How are you spending the vacation? Would I like to walk down east with you some of these lovely evenings to that large stone where we sat over a year ago! Do you ever go there? Do write soon and tell me all about yourself, and your enjoyments.

As ever, your own
James.

Barbara Berg has written of the pervasive ill health of women in nineteenth century America. "Visitors and residents alike expressed astonishment at the extent of ill health among American women." She also quotes Catharine Beecher's remark that "there was a terrible decay of female health all over the land."[7] Lucretia's delicate health is mentioned a number of times in the letters as reason for her caution about hard work or study. Nevertheless, she decided to accept the position in the Ravenna schools. Ravenna, the Portage County seat, was about fourteen miles from Hiram.

James' return to Hiram, with his visits to Lucretia in Ravenna, had been far from satisfactory for the two of them. But in the last minutes, just as he was starting back east, James stopped by to have one last "interview." The result was that the two found their love again, so that the letters from September until the following July continued in the romantic vein of the earlier ones—perhaps even more so.

Hiram, Sept 12, 1855

My Own Loved James:

I can scarcely realize my own existence this evening, all seems so new, so strange. A new leaf in life's book has been turned over, and with what beautifully bright characters are its pages traced. I look, and wonder if it is indeed true that I have opened upon such a bright sort of existence, and almost tremble lest it be an illusion; but again I look and know that it is real, that it is indeed no false fleeting vision. Is it true, dearest, that you did come again? That you were verily beside me again, and that we talked together; and that we looked into each other's eyes and through them down to the very depths of our hearts?[8] Surely it is true; but how strange it seems to me when I had so entirely given up the hope of seeing you before you left. I know not why I should, or did so; but if ever I gave up a loved hope it was that one. True, it sent a chill through my whole being for I felt that if you were what I had thought you were, you would come to give one "good-bye kiss." But I was settling down upon this conviction, that I had before me a false ideal, and began to doubt whether there could be in our fallen state a perfect union of spirits in hopes and desires so that there might be no jarrings; and I had very heroically determined to make the best of it, and though it was a freezing thought, concluded that I could never find that sweet trust and confidence which every throb of my heart was calling for. I saw how others lived—that, what they called wedded love was not truth but a union of earthly interests, and I feared, indeed I had almost decided, that there *was in reality* no love deeper and holier. What an awful conclusion! and yet I was striving to reconcile myself to it. . . . Dearest James, I can see only the guiding of a providential hand in all your visit to Ohio. The darkness, doubt and cold distrust which made us both so miserable formed but the background on which was brought out so clearly, so vividly that beautiful brightness which has thrown around us its halo of glory. And now my own, my loved, my noble James, am I not happy? Did my heart ever know such happiness before? Such a pure deep joy? Never, *never*. But must there ever be one chord that will vibrate with sadness? Even now there is one in my heart, and that because you cannot be near. Another year must now roll its long months between us; but a year, what is it! Days will soon melt into weeks, and weeks roll months around, and dearest I feel in confidence that this will be spared to us both; and that we *shall* meet again, and enjoy that sweet communion which it was ours to know last evening. Heaven grant it!

Thursday evening. Well Jamie, it was not a very dear letter I wrote you last night after all, but I will send it to show you that at least I kept my promise. I felt more like thinking and trying to bring myself into a realization of that happiness which I know was mine, but which seemed so unreal, because so unexpected, than trying to arrange and write down those sweet thoughts and impressions that were floating with fairy like indistinctness through my brain. Did you give my love to your mother? I know I forgot to tell you to. I am such a thoughtless girl; but you certainly know that I intended so to do though I did not say it. I have just been out riding with C. P., and a nice little brotherly and sisterly visit we have had! What a new world I am living in. All my life before has been in a mist, a cloud. I believed there was pure glad sunshine beyond and sometimes I fancied I saw it gleaming through the darkness. But now is it *true?* the shadows have fled; the dark cloud has parted before me, and rolls back its misty form beneath my feet; and the sunlight of Heaven glad, free and pure reveals such a wealth of beauty and gladness all around me. Its warming rays enter my soul, and unseal fountains of love, which before were bound with icy fetters. Oh, how beautiful to live in such a world of light and love, and I cannot—you will not ask me, dearest, will you, so forbid the outgushing of this heart longer. May I not draw near, and discarding all conventionality, throw myself into your arms and call you *all mine*—friend, lover, *husband!* I know not why I ask this; for I know already it is my privilege but the heart is ever asking some new assurance.—

You told me to fill four sheets but should I fill a dozen I could not tell you all, nor can I ever until I am with you every day, every hour, and even then will the fountain of love never be exhausted. Will there not ever be new depths of purer holier love opening up to surprise and gladden us on; on even to eternity? I know that I shall hear from you soon. Your own loving

Lucretia.

Williams College, Sept 18, 1855

My Own Beloved Lucretia:

Did you ever dream in a winter night of the lovely summertime? It is a cold shivery day here, but it is the sweet summer time in my heart. I shrink even from the greetings of warm friends that welcome my return and have hastened away to my desk to bask in the joyous sunlight of love and drink in the refreshing felicity that your dear letter brings me. My soul once cried "Rooms to let!!!" but it is full to overflowing now. From foundation to topstone its halls are alive with joy. My every thought goes westward singing like a golden seraph its song of rejoicing and love. Need I tell you that it is your pure love that thrills me, fills me with emotions I never before felt! God grant they may never grow less! But you will ask a brief history of myself since that sweet but tearful kiss was given.

I reached Mother's that afternoon at five o'clock, and the next day went with her and brother Thomas to Newburgh. On Friday morning I went back to Bedford after some books for the Theological Society here and then went to Cleveland where I found Mother and Thomas and both my sisters. We all sat together for our Daguerreotype and gave it to Mother. There we parted; Thomas for the West, I for the East, and poor Mother went back tearfully and lonely.

At 9 in the evening I stood again on the deck of the "Queen of the West"[9] ... The Lake was still as a mill pond and we had a pleasant passage. I should have preferred a storm.

At 7 in the morning we were in Buffalo and at 8 we were on the cars thundering on towards the Orient. Noon found us in Syracuse ... and in the evening [we] reached Troy. Early this morning I was flying along the foot of the Green Mountains, and at 2 o'clock this afternoon I stood within the halls of "Old Williams." I find a young chaos in my new room, but I have sat down among it all to drop this letter to you that you may know that I yet live, notwithstanding a very narrow escape on the cars in Newburgh, Ohio. One inch and I should have been under the sod ere this, but all right now.

I am six days behind my class, but I'll overhaul them ere long. Darling one, I shall walk in the light this year, yes, in the warm sunlight of your own dear love. I would write a quire to you but I must tell mother I am safe and several others. My only dearest beloved, let there never be a veil between us again. Come to my arms and heart always and I will to yours. There is my home, my only home on earth. Let yours be here. I am wholly your own. I know, may I not ... that you are all, all mine. I know I shall hear often. I would say much more but I must close. Most lovingly,

Your James.

Ravenna, Oct 2, 1855

James, My Loved One:

It is already past ten, but before I can seek my pillow, and visit you in the land of dreams, [I] must answer your treasure of a letter not received until today.

I designed this evening for this my sweetest task, but tomorrow I enter upon the duties of my new situation, and Mr. Collier (our new teacher) has been here making some arrangements and visiting which has detained me until this late hour for commencing. I am very well pleased with the appearance of our new superintendent. He is very friendly and social and I think I shall enjoy very much the society of himself and wife as they are to board with us. I have been visiting the school today that we are going into, and am much pleased with it. I shall teach the classes in French, boy's written Arithmetic, one class in Mental Arithmetic, one in Algebra, also one in written Algebra, and the Reading classes. Such is the material out of which a map of my work for the remainder of the fall term is formed. I closed the [Hiram class] last Thursday, and did not tell the scholars that I was going to leave them, thinking that they would probably be pleased with a change and I would allow them the pleasure of a surprise also. Yesterday noon I went over to see the teacher, and to my surprise found almost all of my girls crying and some of the boys, and flocking around me they begged of me to stay with them. Then I felt that for all my toil I was compensated a thousand times. It is sweet to be loved, is it not? O yes, but what would the love of all the world be, if you had none for me! But with the warm sunshine of your fond love pouring around me its golden light there can be no darkness more, whatever clouds may hang above me their threatening forms. And dearest James, are the heavens indeed all light above you? Has that bright day, for which your soul has so long sighed, at last dawned upon you? and have you found in this love which *my heart* so freely bestows all the demands of your noble nature satisfied? . . .

Somehow you have left me in the rears in our reading. I know not how I am since I have read the amount understood by me every night, viz. whenever there were not 20 verses in a psalm we would read two. Perhaps you intended when there was not twenty in the two we should read three. If so, I will do so most certainly hereafter.[10] Reckoning from those you read last Thursday evening, I read tonight the 35th Psalm—is it that one you read this evening? And that we may be sure and be together we will read the 41st and 42nd next Saturday night.

Now James, I hope I shall not hear that you have been through the streets of New York *bare headed*. Do remember even if you have no care for yourself to take better care of your hat. Now dearest, one fond kiss and then goodnight. I hope this may reach you before you start for N.Y. but I do not know, but do write again very soon. Your paper came yesterday. Thank you for it. Another kiss I do want and another, and another still. Now, I will go and sleep a little while. Good night again, and remember me as *all* your own, Lucretia.

My Own Darling "*Crete*":

Fifteen minutes ago I wrote in my journal as follows: "I am disappointed in not receiving a letter from my own dear Lucretia this evening, but though I should not receive one for a month I should know her love is as true as the Sun in the heavens." I had just written this and closed the book when a classmate came in from the office bringing your sweet letter—a souvenir of the heart. It is most deliciously joyful for my heart to drink all the love your dear letters bring. Just tonight when all the labors of another week are done—and all around is quiet save the distant notes of a flute or guitar—and I alone here in my quiet room—the light from my open stove is dancing out and painting fantastic shapes on the further side of the room and I sitting here indulging in the reveries which their shadowy shapes suggest and yearning to share them and the scene with you—just at this time it is so inexpressibly sweet to hear from your own true heart another fond assurance that your heart is all all mine. It is blissful to [have] recieved a letter from your loved hand at any time, but peculiarly so now. We are revelling in Metaphysics now. I love to flounder in such a sea of strange thoughts as our studies now present. But I never treasured so many jewels of thought in twice the time as I am doing now from our powerful and Beloved President, Dr. Hopkins. I am writing almost all he says and will bring it to you when I am done. Today I have written 13 foolscap pages of his thoughts. Last Lord's Day I was in Poestenkill.[11] I spoke three times—twice in the Brethrens' house and once in a Free Will Baptist House by invitation. I gave them the Division of the Word and the Setting up of the New Kingdom for an hour and a half and the old deacons said it was good Baptist doctrine, but I am afraid they could not adopt it and still hold their places in the F.W.B. fold.

The Brethren at Poestenkill are expecting Bro Streator[12] back there next week. He is going to bring his new wife along with him. She was a daughter of Bro Hubbard of Deerfield [Ohio]; perhaps you knew her. She was at Hiram at the beginning of this term.

I have just received another letter from the Church in Danbury, Ct. soliciting me to spend the coming vacation with them. I think I shall do so, but have not yet decided certainly.

What do you think of the following proposal that has been made to me. I have been offered $1000 per annum to take charge of the High School in the city of Troy, N.Y. The Brethren in Troy, Millville and Poestenkill will between them give me from $400 to $500 per annum to speak for them, thus making from $1400 to $1500 per annum, *minus expenses*. The chief difficulty now is that they want me to begin the first of next March, which would take me away from College the last half of the year. Another reason is that I love the West more than all the Orient—How would you like, Dearest, to become, not exactly a Trojan Helen, but a Trojan Lucretia? Tell me all your thoughts about it. Surely this sheet of paper has done but a little toward telling of those "hundred things" and were not the wee hours close at hand I would take another. Give my love to your Father and Mother. Now Dearest I know I shall hear from you right soon, but one sweet kiss of love before we say goodnight. Heaven bless you Darling. Ever your own loving James.

Ravenna, Nov 30, 1855

My Hearts Sweetest Love:

Now Jamie don't laugh if I say a thousand "sweet" things—equivalent to "silly" with some people you know; for released from the duties of another week, and by your dear letter called away to you, my spirit like an _____ bird fairly dances upon the wing with delight, and away it darts with the swiftness of thought to its home within your bosom where it nestles so quietly beneath your frolicking eye. O, it is such a Heaven of bliss to be loved by you, and dearest do you really think that I am your "wife"! For a certain anonymous writer in his "theory about wives" says every man is married, has his wife, whether recognized by the law or not; or whether he may have ever seen her or not or ever will see her. Moreover, he thinks very few ever find "their" wives. He has seen four matches which he thinks were made in Heaven and considers that a rare piece of luck—to have seen four. Well, doubtless the man is half right about it, and I will not quarrel with him, if he will only promise ours the *fifth*. Ours *shall* be made by the bright ones above, shall it not, dearest? and it is, if in the love my heart so freely and spontaneously gives, you find that completeness of happiness which your love bestows upon me.

It is again vacation with you, and where may you be this evening? Alone in your room with your thoughts released from labor, turning away to "your heart's home"? If so you are welcomed with my sweetest kiss. Mrs. Earl has furnished the room you occupied when here, and it is now mine, and how I love every inch of it, and how I wish you would come and sit down here by me

tonight and hold me in your arms and talk to me again and let me feel the magic
thrill of a kiss: but you cannot come yet, I suppose. "Old Williams" still claims
you, and I suppose would like to make me believe that you love her better than
me. I do not believe a word of it, however.

You did not give me any of your decisions for the future in your last; and
perhaps you are yet undecided as to the course you will take. I almost hope so
for I want to put in one more plea for the "dear old Eclectic." Have you yet
heard of the Bethany affair? If not you will be somewhat surprised to hear that
almost all our northern students left there.[13] Our friend Burns[14] in a sermon
two weeks ago last Sunday evening alluded to the slavery system, and pronounced the word "emancipation," whereupon many of the Southerners
rushed from the house and forming a mob raised all the disturbance possible
during the remainder of the discourse, and having provided themselves with a
chain were assembled at the door to seize him when he came out and take him
to the river and "rebaptize" him; but his Northern friends surrounded him and
he passed out _____ and unharmed. The boys all determined they would not
enter their classes again until some notice was taken of such proceedings by the
Faculty. They did take notice of it, but to reprimand Mr. Burns and the rest for
leaving their classes, rather than the mob; and one of their *honorable* body—
Pendleton—very *kindly* and *politely* told them in the presence of all the students
that they were not very fine specimens of northern humanity, only *beardless*
boys and *ordered* them back to their classes, but honor to them, they were gentlemen enough to leave such a *rascally place* and everybody here, even "Uncle
Symonds," says that if our northern students cannot graduate at Bethany, why
then there must be a place provided for them in the north; and they begin to
feel that now is the time to do something for the Eclectic. The school is starting
off with prospects very flattering this winter. There has never been a finer
appearing set of students for a winter session before. Miss Booth is feeling in
the best of spirits and so are all the other teachers.[15] Bro Munnell has left them
and Mr. Wilber you know is no advantage, and now they *need you* there. I know
you may do better pecuniarily in some other place now, but if the Eclectic ought
to rise, and there is any chance for it to do so, I feel as though each one who
can, and feels an interest in her prosperity should lend all the aid they can;
unless they are very sure they can do much more good in some other place.

Now James will you not write to me very often and tell me all you are
doing? . . . This is the last day of another Autumn and Old Winter is fast bind-
ing upon us his icy fetters, but nothing like [last year] yet. O my loved James,

fold me to your breast ever more and just one more kiss, and I will leave you for a few days more. Loving you as ever:

Lucretia.

Poestenkill, Rens. Co. N.Y.
Saturday Dec 8th, 1855

My Own Dear Lucretia,

It is now ten minutes past midnight, but I cannot seek my pillow without a few sweet words with you, "my ownest own" one. I received a packet of six letters today, confidently expecting a dear one from you, but it did not come. But if you are not ill, I know it must be somewhere on the way.

Our term closed one week ago last Tuesday, and on Wednesday I came here. Since which time I have divided the days between here, Troy and Millville, at which latter place Bro N. W. Clayton is holding a series of meetings. I have accepted the invitation of Sister Learned and her husband to spend a good share of my vacation with them, for I have nearly worn myself out with the much labor of the past term. They have one of the pleasantest homes here I ever saw and are most excellent and affectionate people. Sister L. sends her love to you.

What adds a special attraction for me is the fact that Mrs. L. has a young lady friend here from Connecticut who resembles you very much and reminds me of you constantly.[16] I have been reading Kingsley's "Alton Locke"[17] and Tennyson's Poems with her and have enjoyed it very much. She is so much like you that *I like her*. Mr. L carries on the lumber business in Troy, and I have been there with him a part of the first week assisting in his business writing, for the sake of aiding him and making myself *generally useful!!* I shall probably remain here a week or two longer, then visit New York and Boston. . . .

I shall write to you often wherever I may be. I am very much to blame in reference to our Bible readings. I forgot to mention about it in my last letter and I made a bumbling business of it when I did mention it last. I have been reading (since the last time I wrote about it) on the principle of *one* chapter if it contained 20 verses or more, and if the first did not contain 20, then read two but never more than two Chapters. In two or three days travelling and no conveniences, I have lost my place and now I want you to tell me where it is and I will go on just as you say hereafter. So here's bungling enough for one job—but hold—this letter itself is a worse bungle still. In my sleepy-headedness, I skipped a page. I would rewrite the whole or rather write a new one but I must leave for Troy early Monday morning and tomorrow I have got to speak. . . .

But darling 'tis late at night and I must sleep. If I could clasp you, my dearest one, to my heart before I say Good night, I should be content. But let me forget there is a legion of cold blast between us and kiss you once before I sleep. With fondest love, I am, my dear Crete, your own

James.

West Troy, N.Y. Dec 31, 1855 11:45

Lucretia, My Own Darling:

Seated in a freezing cold chamber I again lift my pen to talk to you of the dying Year and the expectant one. And I know you too are seated by your table to speak to me through the "silent medium." And is it not a fitting time for our hearts to hold sweet communion once more? The quaint, good-natured Charles Lamb says "Every man has two birthdays; two days at least in every year, which set him upon revolving the lapse of Time. The one is that which in an especial manner he termeth his. The other, the New Year, is that from which all date their Time and count upon what is left. It is the nativity of our Common Adam."

And now Dearest, on this our common birthnight let us sit down lovingly together and listen to the voice of the Old Year before he dies. Already is his breath short and feeble and his life pulse will throb but a few times more. But his words have been registered on our hearts and we can read them when he is gone. But we will call him before us and listen to his dying testimony. To my heart he has spoken words of joy, words of hope, of high and holy comfort. He has unveiled to me the richer treasures of your own dear heart and given me the strongest assurance of your deep and fervent love.

He has matured and intensified the love that my heart cherished towards you. From my soul I thank him for this. He has also given me some few new and dear friends here in this land of strangers. And for that I should enshrine him in my heart had he done nothing more. He has given me, however, many lonely hours and many heart-aches, and though they have sometimes saddened, I hope they have never cankered it. But in return for these privations, he has introduced me to many new and glorious fields of thought in which I hope to roam and gather much fruit in the coming years.

But hark the solemn toll of the midnight bell is sounding through the village, the dirge of the Dead Year. He is gone with all his train of lights and shadows, joys and sorrows left only for the memory to cherish and the heart to love. But the heart bounds and the pulse beats quicken as the path of 1856 begins to open to the view. It's true that the mist that shrouds all futurity hangs over it, but Hope throws in her tints of roseate hue, and weaves bright notions along down the rolling months. It promises (does it not, dearest?) to put you close to my heart before it leaves us. Will it not, shall it not mingle the currents of our lives still more? But I will not dream too much. There are stern questions of duty to be met and settled and acted upon before this year is gone. Over all this hangs the uncertainty of life, and all the unseen Providence that the All-Wise Father has prepared. I enter upon this year with a good measure of faith and hope and courage, and with some strength of heart for the life work that lies before me. My Own Darling. May the hours of our Merciful God preserve you safely during all the changes of the coming year. Should the silent angel claim your loving James ere the year is done, you may know as you read this letter one year from tonight that the heart that indited it, went out toward your own with all the power of its love, and while it throbs and feels, it is all your own. Hoping to hear from you tomorrow when I reach N.Y. City, I am all thine own,

James.

Home. Dec 31, 1855

My own, my fondest Loved:

One by one the last moments of another year are silently dropping off into eternity, and with the thousand starry eyes that keep their watch around his dying couch we too will linger and set upon his cold brow a sweet memory of our spirits union. One year ago I sat where now I sit, beside the same table with my hand engaged as now tracing words for you, while my thoughts wandered away to your bosom, and my spirit held fond communion with yours. Together we saw the old year die, and with one heart bade the new year welcome. It smiled upon us at its birth, and has followed us with smiles through all its course, and dying smiles upon us now. Few have been the shadows "looking over the shoulder of the sunshine" its hour had brought, and with kind and gentle thoughts shall its memory ever be cherished. To me it has brought the opening of a new and bright era in my history—the fading away of many

gloomy shadows and the awaking from a dream of happiness to its glad realization. I know that I have failed in carrying out all those resolutions for the year
that I then made; still without boasting I can say that I have not entirely failed.
For where are you, dearest? Passing upon the billow or seated quietly beside
some glowing hearth? Wherever you may be I know that you are with me in
spirit, and upon my lips I *almost* feel the fond kiss your ardent love there places.
James, you have often asked me when I first began to love you. Memory is a
strange sprite and plays strange pranks with us sometimes. A few days since,
she turned out a little incident which she had kept concealed a long long time;
but as it danced out from its hiding place it approached with an air so familiar
that one might have thought it belonged to yesterday, and I could not but wonder that it could so long have kept out of my sight. Do you recollect the second
exhibition of the Eclectic? Well, I was passing behind the stage when carelessly
stepping into a hollow I came near falling. A pair of strong arms received me
and looking around my eyes met yours as you held me there. Do not start
James—I did not *know* that I loved you then, although a strange wild delight
thrilled my soul as I darted quickly away and forgot it all almost as quickly as
done. I little thought those arms were to receive me for Life; but was it not
almost prophetic? The fire is almost out and I am shivering with the cold, and
must not write any longer. A very happy new year to you, and when it has
grown old and ready to die, may it still find us enjoying all the true happiness
Earth can give. With my kiss upon your lips let the New Year dawn. Good
night, my own dear love.

New Years evening, 1856.

This morning when I awoke the bright sun had arisen and the cold white earth
was flooded with his golden light, and with an unclouded brow all day long he
has smiled a welcome to the new-born year, but to my heart it has been but a
cold and cheerless glare. The very first gleam of the sunshine that met my eye
sent a sickening accusation to my soul which I had no power to struggle
against, nor scarcely any will. I know not why I am at times so foolishly weak. I
seem to lose all self-control and yield to a fit of despondency for which there is
not the least cause.

Do you ever get the "blues"? if so you know how the day has passed with
me. All morning I spent reading "Shady Side" which did not contribute very

much to the removal of the terrible malady. This afternoon I visited the Eclectic hoping to drive away or lose it but all to no effect and came home feeling worse than ever, but it has passed away this evening as noiselessly as it came and I am again as happy as ever. My vacation has all passed very pleasantly and tomorrow bright and early I am away to my school again, hoping to find a dear letter from you there. James dearest will you not write very often this year? write very frankly and fully and trust me as entirely with you in "thought, word and deed." I will try and withhold nothing from you. It is my wish and aim to learn to confide in you as in myself. To feel no more fear in confiding every thought to you than in thinking them. Such is the intimacy my heart asks should exist between us. No more changing, only to love you better every day. I am

Your Lucretia

During the early weeks of 1856 James' relationships with Maria Learned and Rebecca Selleck became very close. He had of course told them both about Lucretia, and he asked the women to begin corresponding with her.

Williams College, March 9, 1856

My Darling *Crete:*

It was a late hour yesterday when the ruthless snows let your dear little message of love pass over the wide wintry waste that lies between us, to reach me, but all the fierceness of the winter storm was unable to chill its warm glow of affection which came outgushing from every line to refresh my heart with its fullness. I still persist in saying that your dear letters are by far your most dangerous rivals; but when we meet I'll very soon decide the question of choice. The difference is like that between a drop and a shower, a rose and a garden of roses, for your letters are only dear little drops of yourself, sweet roses from the full garden of your heart.

And you, too, are weary of the winter. Ah—and am not I also? This is the 74th that the snow has been lying deep on all the mountains and in our valleys. I wrote somewhere a few days ago (was it in a letter to you?) that I longed for the time when with all her "ethereal mildness" gentle Spring should stand upon the mountain tops and breathe upon the drifted snow, till it should repent of its coldness, and weep itself away. If I said so in my last, no matter, for I still feel the same sentiment—strengthened by the weary winter's growing length. And you are soon going to spend a few weeks at your dear old home? I know you will be glad to get back again after the tedious monotony of the schoolroom. How long is your vacation? I shall surely have a few letters from your old room around which cluster so many memories of "auld lang syne." When you write to me from there, I always have a more vivid sense of your presence which links me back to those sweet hours we have passed. Oh, do you remember us sitting by the window of the west room when the peach trees were in bloom and that tall one reached its handfuls of fragrant blossoms in at the window, when the sun was just going behind the meeting house on the hill? What sweetness of spring flowers filled the air, and what calm delight filled our hearts!

I want you to tell me all your feelings as you go over all the old beloved spots where so many times our joy has been full.

Our dear Sister Rebecca lives in Lewisboro, Westchester Co., New York on the Connecticut line. Most of her friends and neighbors live on the Connecticut side and so they call her a Yankee girl. I very much want you to know her. I have received two letters from her since the term began. In the last she says "I shall hope to hear in your next that Lucretia will come to see me, and you must always tell me about her and your mother and Miss Booth."

Really, I wish you and she would correspond with each other, for I am sure you would both enjoy it very much. . . .

Hoping to hear from you very soon, I am as ever your affectionate,

James.

On March 8, Lucretia had written to James from Ravenna an analysis of his character, which he had asked her to do. She speaks especially of his "boundless ambition" which "sometimes makes me tremble for you." "Were you less great, did you possess less strength and energy of character, I should have less to fear. . . . I cannot but feel how great is the need that you examine well the main spring of every action." She spoke of his extraordinary gifts, of his nobility of heart, his expansive mind, and of his future greatness, all in relation to his persistent questions of what vocation he should take up after graduation from Williams: teaching, the ministry, or the law.

Williams College, Mar 16, 1856

My Own Dearest:

"Tell you all"? Well then, I never was prouder of you than at this blessed moment, nor half so proud. Your letters have all been precious, but you never wrote me such a jewel as your last which comes overflowing with strong clear thought, and deep, earnest affection.

But, my dear little woman, you are altogether mistaken about your "little" Jimmy's being such a tremendous fellow. Surely those "giant powers" are merely the beautiful creations which your fancy has thrown around him, and he feels himself just as much the little rollicking rogue of a boy, tonight, as he ever was. Indeed I feel a strong inclination to sit right down on the floor by your chair and lay my head in your lap and tell you of my struggles and successes, and look up for the approving smile and word which I know you would not deny me. Many thanks for your remarks on the dangers of ambition. They are just and truthful, and be assured they shall be cherished by me, both for their own intrinsic worth, and for the sake of her who penned them. I do not deny that the fires have burned within me and still do, but I hope they have not "consumed the brain to ashes," as Willis says, nor seared the nobler impulses of the soul. It is truly a great work to shun the Scylla of inactivity and irresolution, and, at the same time, avoid the Charybdis of lust for power *for its own sake*. I care not how much power, how much influence an individual obtains in a lawful way, *if he use it for the highest good*, when he has obtained it.

In reference to my future course, I hope I am willing to follow the path of duty wherever it may lead. I believe the first great duty of a Christian is to seek his own highest good by the highest and most harmonious activity of all the faculties of his body, mind and heart. This work will include all his duties, to God and his fellow men, which grow out of his relations to them. As a prerequisite to this work, one must find his proper sphere in life, and fill that station to which he is best adapted. Now the serious and practical question with me is, "what is my place and my duty?" O I so much want to talk with you a few hours now! As you have said, I cannot do myself justice by writing. I have a plan or two floating rather dimly on my horizon which I would gladly whisper in your ear were their proportions distinct enough to be sketched. Right at this point I find myself blessed in a strange way. I shall be obliged to teach or do something to clear myself of the debt which will have accumulated by the time I finish my course here, and while thus "laboring and waiting" I shall trust that the same kind Hand which has so often, on my life-path, pointed out the straightway, will again lead me to the post w[h]ere I ought to stand. Before we can hope for such assistance, however, we must use all the means in our power to find the right place. Darling one, I am thrice glad that you have written to me so freely and I want you to do so still more than ever. Why should we not so write? "Our hopes, our fears, our aims are one"; I am already in spirit, your husband, and you my darling wife. How many, many sweet hours have I spent in anticipating the joys of just such a scene as you described! May the time hasten when it shall all be a blessed reality. . . . One kiss from your dear lips.

Your James.

Williams College, April 6, 1856

My Own Dear Crete:

Though the main current of our Senior Studies has led me to the consideration and admiration of Truth, Beauty and Goodness, in the abstract, yet I must here confess that I admire these qualities much more when viewed in the conCrete and hence I find my weekly exercise of filling a sheet for the Ravenna mail the most interesting one in my College course! How well I shall stand examination in this department rests with my Ravenna Preceptress to decide. But metaphor aside, my Darling girl, I am very happy in the knowledge of answering your last precious letter which was just a sweet bit of your own darling self done up in paper.

Our last examinations for the term closed last Friday and so the burden of the term's labor is done, and, to confess the truth, I am about "used up" by late nights and busy days. On the evening of the day that our examinations closed, the whole Senior Class were invited to a party at the President's. He presented each of us in turn to his wife and daughters and to a company of about 20 ladies who reside in the village. After a promiscuous chat of two hours we were regaled with ice cream, lemonade, cakes, nuts and the whole category of sweetmeats. Music by the ladies and class songs from the students concluded the sociability of the evening at about half past ten o'clock. Our President, good noble soul that he is, was all around among us with a kind and familiar word for every body, and so he adds, to our admiration of his greatness, a strong deep love for his good, kind heart. Such a man I love that can be great and move among the sublime grandeurs of the world of thought like a giant, and can at the same time make the social circle bright and cheerful with his genial heart. He is a *Lilliputian* here, who must always stand perched upon his dignity.

I have just received a very dear letter from our much beloved Sister Maria Learned of Poestenkill. She is one of the choicest spirits I have been permitted to meet in this land of the east. You remember that her house is my own home while I am in the Orient. In this letter she says "How I wish you were both in the 'Prophets Chamber' (my room when I'm there) now where I could call to you and our dear sister Lucretia with you. Do you know how I have learned to love her not for your sake alone. I know she is good herself. Remember me with much affection to her and your dear Mother. I expect to see them both some-time." I could not ask for truer friends than she and her husband are to me. Next Thursday I leave for Lewisboro[18] on my way to N.Y. City whither I am sent by the Philologian Society to make a purchase of books for its library. That accomplished I shall return to Lewisboro and spend the vacation with Sister Rebecca. I hope to get your next letter before I start. The answer to this you will please direct to Lewisboro.

I have read the "Song of Hiawatha"[19] and am delighted with it. It will live long years after many of its ungenerous and envious critics are "dead and damned," as Chatterton says.[20] We'll have it as one of the books for our library, won't we? . . . Give one sweet kiss to your own loving James.

Ravenna, May 11, 1856

My Own Loved One:

There is nothing that brings me near to you or makes me feel more entire oneness with you than to know that there are hours-although so many long miles stretch away between us—when our thoughts flow in the same channel; as your dear letter tells me they did one week ago, each longing for the other's presence that more perfect might be our spirits' communion and more entire our hearts' deep joy. But far more intensely does my whole heart long for your presence here today, that we might talk of all those things of which you have written while the fond kiss and the loved caress should be our hearts' sweet lan-guage. Darling, I am lonely and I cannot help it. This morning I awoke with the first singing of the birds, and almost my first thought was of your last letter and what you had written in reference to your future course. Should you devote your life to the ministry? Although what I wrote the last time regarding it is no less true now, still when I thought of the minister's home such as it is among our brethern with his wife alone almost ever, it seemed to me I could never never endure it.[21] I did not know before that my heart was so supremely selfish and crushing back the tears I arose, knelt before my open window and upon the morn's first breath, sent home to Heaven a petition for strength to bear this my cross if mine it must be. My spirit was calmed but all day it has been sad, and more than once I have surprised the telltale tear ready to start from my eyes, and how much do I want you here to talk to me and make me stronger; for if it is your duty to devote your life to such a calling, if it is there you can accomplish the greatest good, I must not, will not be the one to deter you from it, great as may be the sacrifice it will cost me. Although our home will be no home without you, still if duty call you from it, I will try and be happy in sending you from my arms with a cheerful smile and encouraging word, and treasure up all my love to lavish upon you at your return. Yes, darling, I will try and do all this, and aid you all that lies within my power and Heaven helping me I believe I can; for I am proving stronger and happier now that I have told you this resolve; and in a few weeks more I shall be taken to your arms again. Then we will talk of all these things, and whatever may seem to be the right course for you I hope I shall be ready to yield my willing assent to it. Dearest, I hope you are not visionary in your hopes for the future; for I am sure it is my desire to make your life even brighter than you expect. I may fail, but of one thing I am sure: if I do, it will be through inability alone. Friday, I received from Sister Rebecca a darling letter containing that sweet little flower you plucked for me, also two from her garden walk. She is a noble girl truly with a heart so full of love and gentleness. I long to see her and clasp her dear form to my heart, and soon I hope to. You know that you are to be with us when I visit her; consequently, I shall leave it partly with you to decide when it shall be, whether before or after Commencement. . . . If I can I almost hope you will say before, so that our separation may be shortened a few days. I am sure there will be very happy hours that we spend with her in her sweet home, and I look away to them with a great deal of pleasure. Will she not return home with us? She said nothing about it in her letter, although I sent a very urgent request that she should in the note I put in a letter to you. Give my best love to Sister Learned when you next see or write to her. I long to see and know her also. . . . Heaven's choicest blessings be thine. Fondly thine. Lucretia.

Ravenna, May 23, 1856

My Own:

Your precious letter came today to gladden my heart, and though I will not answer entirely until Sunday evening still I feel that I must write a little this evening it is so sweet to talk to you ever, and especially so when I feel just like it. I started away from my drawing lesson this afternoon feeling so weary and spiritless that it seemed to me I could never make another exertion in any way, and the half mile walk through Main Street seemed beyond endurance, so to avoid it I took a back street which I had never traversed before and soon found myself in the coziest little nest of houses you can imagine. Sweet little cottages with green shades and latticed porticoes greeted me on either hand while stretching away before me was the gravel walk shaded with the bright, rich foliage of the beautiful maples; I soon forgot that I was tired and walked on wishing only that you were beside me to enjoy it too, and was almost sorry when I found myself at home. With what a soul-reviving, care-lightening, spirit-charming noise does Nature ever speak to us. Whenever we are gay, joy rests upon her brow; if we are sad she does not upbraid us, does not even bid us drive away our grief, but with her soft and gentle charms woos us away from it when weary and dispirited. Her magic breath restores vitality, gives to the step its wanted elasticity, to the eye its kindling brightness, and to the spirit its joyful glow. So did her kind ministrations restore me this evening to life and vigor again. Yes, it was only Nature that spoke to me in all those beautiful things I saw. There was nothing artificial in these sweet homes however decorated and embellished they may have been; for they were but the natural retreats which love the most natural of all things has adorned and beautified. But I hear nothing, I see nothing beautiful or good which does not remind me of my loneliness without you and intensify my longing for that sweet companionship which I hope may sometime be ours.

Sunday evening. There are a thousand flower-embued paths leading away from my heart to yours, all so beautiful that sometimes I am almost at loss which to choose to guide my spirit away to you, but this lovely evening I make choice of the one which has become dearer than all others. It winds beneath the rich foliage of the Orange, and beside it the myrtle blooms. So quiet and secluded it is that the eye of the world never penetrated into its hidden charms, nor the restless footstep of the intruder darent venture upon its sacredness. How changed has all my life become since I have learned this way to your heart. I breathe the air of Heaven as I traverse it and my whole being is purified and made holier; for while it leads me to that secret door of your heart of hearts, which I alone have found and to which no others may approach, it also opens out upon dearer views of all things good and beautiful, ". . . the Heavens above and the earth beneath," and the nearer I approach to this sacred oneness with you, the more am I brought into communion with the spirit of all love, and all things loveable hold a dearer place to my heart. When I think of the ice cold world in which I once lived, I do not wonder that I was thought so cold and unloving. And it is a mystery which not yet have I been able to solve how you could then have been attracted towards me. Why was it? Did your eye penetrate beyond what others saw and discover that there were really depths of affection concealed in my heart which though chilled by adversity might be revived into life again? Yes into a new and true life which they had never felt before. Did you see this and for this draw me to your heart? I have but one sorrow now; that is a fear that I may never be able to pay the deep debt of gratitude I owe you. You are thinking of me now, yes. I feel your presence here. Your arms encircle me; your lips are pressed to mine. I will keep silence while you speak. No higher earthly bliss is mine than to be held upon your heart and listen to your voice of love. In spirit this happiness now is mine, a few weeks more and it shall be mine indeed. Can I wait for it? I shall go to you and Rebecca before Commencement if possible. Which will be the better route if I go to Lewisboro first? I know that I shall receive another dear letter soon and an answer to this in two weeks. How could I live without these precious messages of affection?

Fondly thine, Lucretia.

Williams, June 1, 1856

Darling One:

"It is the breath of June. . . ."

Such, truly, is today and you could hardly believe that it snowed yesterday, but it did, and we have been obliged to keep up fires for the past four days, and now with the first gentle footfall of June comes all the loveliness and beauty of air and sunshine. Indeed, "here is a great calm" on all the external world, but not on it alone, for it has likewise fallen on my spirit and is giving me a world of sunshine within. But it is a sunshine in which my heart would fain sleep and dream, for a kind of glorious mist, sad though golden, is diffused through it all. Sad, I said, yes, but such a sadness as that of Henry Kirk White[22] when he said

> "A tear-drop stands in either eye,
> And yet I cannot tell thee why
> I'm pleased and yet I'm sad."

For many years, almost as long as I can remember, on Sunday afternoon of the summer season, while the sun is sinking and the evening twilight is coming on, I have felt this very same sensation. I have sometimes believed it came from seeing my dear widowed mother look upon me with those tearful eyes of affectionate sadness at that hour, when cessation from the constant toil of the week gave her time for meditation, and the thought of her lonely condition came fresh upon her. At this season of the year I see her face more frequently than in any other, looking upon me as she used to do, and I long to be beside her again, and I long still more to do something for her declining years that shall testify to a small share of debt of love and gratitude I owe to her. But I suspect that the principal cause of my sadness may be traced to the want I feel of that golden half of my heart which resides just now in Ravenna. Ah, don't you think the hemispheres would fit exactly so that even the places of joining could not be seen. All these _____ to be brought nearer together, which thank Heaven, they will be soon, I hope.

How thankful I am every day that the deep, rich sentiments of your being have come out from the recesses in which they were hidden and have blessed me with their wealth of affection. And if, as you say, my love has given you a new life and new joys, I am twice blessed. I fully believe that we have not done this ourselves but God has done it and to Him belongs the praise. I received a letter from Bro Hayden a few days ago in which he urges me very strongly to go back to Hiram to teach.[23] He did not mention what salary I would have. I wrote to him that if the salary was at all adequate to the occasion, I would go there and teach one year. But as I view the matter now, I could not stay much longer than that under the present Administration.

There are two routes to Lewisboro: one via Erie Rail Road and the other N.Y. Central R.R. and Hudson River. I do not yet know which is best, but I will find out next Sunday when I go to Poestenkill to Yearly Meeting. Did you know that Bro Hayden intends to be here at Commencement? Now I know I shall hear from you again soon. Till then I am forever thine own James.

In the two letters following Lucretia expresses her concern about their approaching encounter at Lewisboro, and James replies confidently, assuring Lucretia that their relationship is "not to be swerved by any trifling accident of life."

❧§§❧

My Own:

I will try and write you a letter although every energy is so completely prostrated by the excessive heat that it seems like a Herculean task to sit here and
hold a pen long enough to cover this sheet with marks. If you would only come
and sit by me it would certainly be very gratifying to my indolence if nothing
more, for I could look at you and perhaps listen to you without much exertion.
I would not promise to talk. That would require an effort greater than I should
be willing to make. It seems to me I never knew a warmer day. The thermometer must stand near the boiling point I am sure. I think it would be very pleasant on the top of some of your Massachusetts mountains just now and if I can
only live through the next two weeks teaching I shall hope to be there before
long. Perhaps five weeks from to day I may be with you. I cannot yet tell, however. James, dearest, how looks to you the prospect of another meeting! Is it all
bright with joy and gladness, or are there dark shades flitting across it which
almost make your heart tremble with sad forebodings? Allow me to quote a passage from the last letter you wrote me before your return last summer. "It
seems to me as if I should not be allowed to enjoy such unalloyed happiness as
I anticipate having. But I hope that the Providence of God may smile upon my
visit and give me a foretaste of what my dreaming visions have painted in the
future." You know how that doubt was realized—how disappointed that hope.
And are the same feelings now yours? I trust not; for if they are I have but little
hope for the future. True, I know that you are all kindness and noble affection,
also that my own heart is most fondly and entirely yours; still if there are
doubts in your mind of my success in making you happy, I fear that I shall
indeed fail. One circumstance gives me a little confidence that our next meeting
will not be like the former. Then I was all hope, never dreaming that there
could be aught in store for us but perfect bliss. I supposed we must be entirely
happy if only in each other's presence. Now I trust I love you in person and am
not so sanguine in my expectations. I have learned that love is a delicate sensi-
tive flower which a cold breath may chill and will droop and die if it receive not
its native climate—smiles and kisses and fond embraces, and I hope that hereafter I shall better cherish this beautiful treasure which you have committed to
me. Then I shall have some reason for hoping to see you happy.

What would you say to hear that Barbara was married, and that when she
found that she could conceal it from Harry no longer sent him a letter requesting

that he return her letters and that their correspondence cease?[24] So H. told me when I was at home last Thursday. The reports came from all directions that she is married and he says that if they are true she was married some time before she wrote him that letter. Of course it causes H. some unpleasant feelings now, but I must confess I am glad that she is not his wife. Her course this winter has been anything but commendable in attending dancing school, dancing parties etc. etc. and I do not believe she is half good enough for him. Harry is a noble fellow and deserving the best of wives, and I hope it may be his good fortune to find such a one.

The commencement exercises at Hiram were fine. The tent was spread just north of the Seminary under which were seated some 3000 people in the finest order you can imagine. There was no confusion, no hurry but all passed if charmingly so quietly and in such good taste. Considering the whole performance I think it was superior to anything we have ever had before. Miss Booth thinks the salary offered you will be $600. Can you come for that? . . . She is talking a little of attending your commencement if the convention at Albany came near the same time. Bro Hayden will be there I suppose. . . . Well I have really filled my sheet and am still alive, not suffering any great fatigue either. That is not strange though for nothing that I can do for you wearies me. Please direct the answer to this to Hiram. I shall be there before it would reach here. One loving kiss and then goodbye From one who loves you.

Crete

Williams, June 29, 1856

My Own Lucretia:

I defy Ohio to produce a more unbearably hot day than this has been and I know I can fully sympathize with your calorific experience of one week ago this evening. At noon the thermometer stood 97 degrees in the shade and last night at midnight it was at 74. Last night I slept on the roof under the open sky. I shall do so tonight unless it rains. It is very fine to watch the myriads of stars and the bright moonlit clouds till your eyes droop in sleep—and then to lie and see the first streak of rosy dawn that dapples the East and heralds the sun. Could I clasp you in my arms and gaze with you upon the beautiful heavens, truly "the night would be filled with music."

You ask me what my heart says in view of our meeting now close at hand—and whether any doubts and fears are before me—any clouds hovering

the bright horizon of the future. I refer to one year ago and its strange experience. My Own Darling One, *I have no such doubts or fears.* I look back upon that
terrible experience of last year as perfectly natural under the circumstances and
from the nature of the case it cannot occur again. It was the rending of the veil
which had not yet been taken away from between our hearts. Hence the
anguish, the terrible agony, and hence the bright glad heavenly joy and sunshine that followed and which has been growing brighter every hour since. One
sentence in your dear letter before me gives me sadness. You say if another
cloud appears "I have but little hope for the future." Now my own loved one,
we cannot expect cloudless sunshine and a shadowless life, but what need have
we of fear; we each know that we possess the wealth of the other's love. You will
find in me many imperfections and many things that you could wish were otherwise, no doubt, but you know that my heart is yours and such as I have, I
have long ago given thee. For this past year, more than ever before, we have
communed "with naked hearts together" and that communion has brought me
only peace and joy. The love that fills my soul is not a wild delirious passion, a
momentary effervescence of feeling, but a calm strong deep and resistless current that bears my whole being on toward its object. Such a love is not to be
swerved by any trifling accident of life—and I feel that your love for me is of the
same kind.—You write of Hiram and the School. I have not yet heard from Bro
Hayden or the Trustees though I ought to have had a letter some days ago.
Have you heard anything in reference to the doings of the Trustees at their
meeting? I regret to hear that Harry is wavering in reference to coming here.[25] I
shall still hope he will come. I am anxious to hear from him. I could hardly
think of going back to Hiram to teach unless Almeda stays and gives her
strength to the school. I don't think she'll go away. You must not let her. I am
sorry to hear such news from Barbara but I have learned not to judge of such
cases till I know more. Love to your folks and let me hear soon.

Your own James.

Hiram, July 6, 1856

My Own James:
    If there is any poetry in the idea of sitting on a protruding rail of the back-
yard fence under an apple tree, surely I am in a fair way of finding it out, and
doubtless I shall too since my occupation is the quintessence of all that bears

the name of poesy: the darling delight in which my heart and hand so unitedly engage. Mrs. Collier and Mattie Lane are spending a few days with us and to be entirely alone with you I have stolen out here where the song of the birds and the soft rustling of the long grass as the summer breeze plays over it and the low sweet music of swaying boughs are the only sounds to greet my pen, and so entirely do all these sounds harmonize with my own feelings—so deep quiet and happy—that I surrender myself to the sweet fancy that you are near inviting me to your bosom in those low love-tones which come stealing to my ear. O that you were indeed here that I might with a thousand kisses tell you how much I love you every hour, and with ten thousand more thank you for all you have written in that last most precious of all letters. It has brought such a wealth of joy and peace to my sadgrowing heart. You will not censure me too severely, my own, will you for not overcoming that strange dread of another meeting which its near approach brought? The memory of those few dreadful hours of last summer arose before me so vividly that my very heart sank, and for a few days it has seemed that all the sunshine of that perfect happiness which our last interview brought was departing forever; but thank Heaven, your words so full of fond assurance, have brought it all out again ten fold more glorious than before. I know James that the awful abyss which seemed opening between us then has closed. I do not believe it can ever open again; still the recollection of its fearful darkness makes me tremble and I almost fear sometimes. It will not be so when I am with you, I am sure it will not; for I know that you love me strongly deeply devotedly, and that my love makes you very happy; and when I am with you the increased confidence of each hour will banish forever the terrors of that hour which knew those fearful heart-struggles. You little know James the entire control your spirit holds over mine. It may be too great. Indeed I sometimes fear it is, but I cannot help it, nor have I the slightest inclination to if I could. It is too sweet a delight to be guided, controlled, yes, ruled by the love of a strong spirit, to wish the golden fetters loosened, and I love to yield my whole spirit to them as I yield myself into your loving arms for protection, and then to know that it is as sweet a joy for you thus to receive me, to know that that control and protection are heart given, renders them doubly dear. The evening here grows chill and I am now sitting in my own room where 47 weeks ago last evening we sat together. Three weeks from to night perhaps I may sit with you again. I hope so, indeed I do. The hours cannot number too few that must yet separate us. I did not return home until Thursday evening and have been so busy since that I have not seen Lizzie but I shall in a few days.

Then I hope to be able to tell you when you may expect me. Just one month from today is your commencement. You know there is one heart which will beat proudly for you then but will feel that it is honored by the love of one so good and noble, and will thus, dearest, be my recompense for the toil which that honor has or may cost you! Will your honors be any dearer to you for the proud joy they will bring to your loving "Crete's" heart? I would not be serious, but it is a pleasing fancy which I love to indulge that my love and interest sweeten all your toil, and give an increased rigor to every effort.

I wrote in my last all that I know of Trustee's doings. I presume you have received a letter from Bro Hayden before this. Almeda is not going away, so Mother says. I guess she did not intend to very much when she was talking about it. She is going into our little southwest room that looks out over the peach tree. I feel a little as though I should like that room again myself, but this is much larger and pleasanter, and convenience is sometimes preferable to poetry!

I cannot tell how much I enjoy being at home again, feeling that I have not got to start away to Ravenna again tomorrow morning. I never knew how to prize the blessing of freedom before. Then it makes my home seem so pleasant to think that you are coming back here again, and so soon we shall all be so near each other. Last week the frame of the new church was raised. A sad accident happened to cast a shade over the people here. Owing to a mistake in the framing, one of the large rafters fell as they were raising it and killed a man— Mr. George Bartoo—instantly. He was the first man in town killed at a raising. I hope it is not ominous of any evil to the Church. . . .

Two or three letters yet I must have from you before I start for your arms. One darling kiss and then goodnight. Most fondly,

Lucretia.

Garfield graduated with top honors from Williams College in August 1856. Lucretia, Almeda Booth, Brother Hayden, Rebecca Selleck, and Maria Learned were all there to hear his oration in the Congregational Church, where the ceremonies were held. James then returned to Hiram to teach and later become head of the Institution. But the "awful abyss" referred to by Lucretia did open. Thus, there are no letters exchanged between him and Lucretia until November of 1856. Beginning then, it is clear a rift in their relationship had occurred. But that is the story for the next chapter.

❧ NOTES ❧

1. Margaret Leech and Harry J. Brown, *The Garfield Orbit: The Life of President James A. Garfield* (New York: Harper and Row, 1978), 70.

2. Harriet Beecher Stowe's *Sunny Memories of Foreign Lands* tells of her triumphant foreign travels after the publication of *Uncle Tom's Cabin*.

3. "Kissath" probably refers to the celebrated visit, upon the invitation of the Congress, of Lajos Kossuth in 1851. He received a hero's welcome in New York, Washington, D.C., St. Louis and New Orleans. "Swedish Nightingale" refers to the Swedish soprano Jenny Lind, whose visit to the United States was sponsored by P. T. Barnum in 1850. She gave ninety-three concerts to tremendous ovations.

4. Joseph Butler was an English theologian and philosopher, whose closely argued *Analogy of Religion* (1736) related "natural and revealed" religion to nature.

5. Almeda Booth spent the academic year 1855–56 at Oberlin, attending Oberlin College and earning her degree there.

6. Paul Flemming is the hero of Longfellow's romantic novel, *Hyperion*.

7. Barbara Berg, *The Remembered Gate: Origins of American Feminism* (New York: Oxford Press, 1978) 112–13.

8. James' Diary entries also tell of these meetings. Under Monday September 10 he writes:

> I am about going to Ravenna to see Lucretia before I leave for the East again. These few weeks of my stay in Ohio have been intensely unhappy and miserable. . . . When I returned to Ohio, four weeks ago and hurried away all full of the brightest hope and the most joyous anticipations, to see her, there came over me, I cannot tell why, the most dark and gloomy cloud, and it has deepened and thickened till the present moment. It seems as though all my former fears were well founded and that she and I are not like each other in enough respects to make us happy together. . . . Tuesday, September 11: Last evening I reached Ravenna and found Lucretia in, if possible, a darker cloud than I was. The agony of spirit I suffered when I left Almeda at Hiram with all the terrible load upon my heart, was not only equalled, but surpassed, when I found her heart so oppressed. She had entirely given up all hope of my calling to see her again before I went away. . . . Never before did I see such depths of suffering and such entire devotion of heart as was displayed in her private journal which she allowed me to read. For months, when I was away in the midst of my toils, her heart was constantly pouring out its tribute of love. When my letters did not reach her her heart was tortured with fear lest I might be suffering with sickness and pain. From that journal I read depths of affection that I had never before known that she possessed. A new light had burst in upon my soul, and I felt as if the vail which had hung between our hearts was [lifted]"

(Harry J. Brown and Frederick D. Williams, eds., *The Diary of James A. Garfield* (East Lansing: Michigan State University Press, 1967), 1: 271–72.

9. The *Queen of the West* was a relatively new lake steamer, having been built in 1851.

10. James and Lucretia had agreed to read a Bible passage each night, the idea being that they would read the same passage at the same hour. But confusion over how many lines one Psalm should have before they would move to another and other problems made this little exercise difficult to work out.

11. Here is the first reference to Poestenkill, a village west of Williamstown, where James began visiting the Learned family and the mysterious Rebecca Selleck during holidays.

12. Streator was a Cleveland businessman and Disciple, who later became a trustee of the college.

13. The "northern students" had crossed the Ohio to attend the Disciples' Bethany College in order to receive degrees, which at that time "the dear old Eclectic" could not grant.

14. "Our friend Burns" is probably Philip Burns, a fellow student in the Eclectic class of 1854.

15. Miss Booth had returned with a degree from Oberlin to teach at Hiram.

16. The "young lady friend" James mentions is Rebecca Selleck, a woman James became enamored of, who was to cause Lucretia many unhappy hours of worry in the years to follow.

17. *Alton Locke* by Charles Kingsley (1819–1875) was a novel written in 1849–50 which dealt with the Chartist movement in England.

18. James' visit to Lewisboro was the first of many sojourns to visit Rebecca at her home.

19. "Song of Hiawatha" is Longfellow's poem, published in 1855.

20. Thomas Chatterton (1752–1770) was an English poet who fabricated a number of poems presumed to have been written in the fifteenth century.

21. Lucretia's concern that a minister's life would mean his frequent absence from home and her resistance to such a possibility are highly ironic in that James' future career in politics kept him away from his family for weeks, even months on end.

22. Henry Kirke White (1785–1806) was an English poet, praised by Southey and Byron, now only known for several hymns.

23. In regard to Brother Hayden's letter, Almeda Booth wrote to James in June of 1856: "Brother Hayden thinks you are morally bound to come back here, but I think the moral obligation resting on him is quite as strong to give up management to you if you do come. I know you can never endure to work under him, for it is ten times as irksome to me as it was before I went away [to Oberlin]. James, would you risk to come here and see what you can do with the school? It certainly is a good location, and I know you would succeed, if you were not embarrassed by dictation or management."

24. Barbara was probably Barbara Fiske, who received her diploma from the Eclectic Institute the same year as Harry Rhodes.

25. Harry Rhodes did finish his degree at Williams College.

CHAPTER 3

Marriage and the Ohio Senate, 1856–1861

UPON HIS RETURN TO HIRAM AS TEACHER IN THE INSTITUTE, *James fell into a deep depression. He apparently was disappointed with the work at Hiram, and his relationship with Lucretia Rudolph had dulled. He felt, in fact, at odds with himself. Lucretia, in order to avoid the humiliation of the failure of the love affair, accepted a job teaching in the Cleveland public schools beginning in the winter of 1857. She moved to a rooming house near the Lake, about thirty miles northwest of Hiram, and their correspondence began once again in a fitful way that spring.*

During the academic year of 1856–57, James was made head of the Hiram Eclectic Institute after a distasteful struggle against former friends and teachers. In the spring of 1858, a year later, James saw no way out of his unhappiness other than by marrying Lucretia: the world about him expected him to do so. Accordingly, in November of that year the two were married in Lucretia's home.

There are few letters written, then, in 1859, their first year together, but beginning in 1860 James spent the winter term at Columbus as a senator in the Ohio Legislature. He continued to administer affairs at the school in Hiram, but with the coming of the Civil War he decided to join the Union Army, which he did in August 1861.

The letters of this chapter follow the years from the Williams graduation in 1856 until James joined the Army. Of the one-hundred or so letters exchanged during the period, thirty-one have been selected to tell this story.

For several months after James' graduation from Williams and return to Hiram, no letters are exchanged. Lucretia was evidently living at home in Hiram during the fall. Certainly, no small part of James' troubled spirit these days was his perplexity over his relationships with Lucretia and Rebecca: did he love Rebecca? could he marry her

instead of Lucretia? James apparently visited Lucretia one night at her home in Hiram,
just before leaving for his late fall holiday. In her letter after this visit, Lucretia mentions
"a great wrong." She seems to have come to the conclusion that James had had an inti-
mate relationship with Rebbeca Selleck while he was in Williamstown. After the new
year in January 1857, when Lucretia had taken a teaching position in the Cleveland
schools, the problem is mentioned more explicitly in her letters from Cleveland.

Hiram, November 9, 1856

Dearest James:

After you left me yesterday morning it seemed that all the shadows of the
last few months were gathering down around me in overlapping each other and
deepening into a terrible darkness. I locked myself in my room and wept. But
wherefore weep? I asked. Could clouds like those be dissolved into tears? And
with the sternness of despair I bade them to their hiding place. This morning
with the first consciousness came the same impression that I was still
enveloped in that dreadful gloom, and if opening my eyes I beheld gliding
around me the pale ghosts of departed hopes mocking me with their unearthly
laugh, I should have felt no surprise. But were such dire sights to greet me? The
room was full of light and quietly lovingly resting upon the floor was the soft,
beautiful November sunlight. Had I awakened? awakened from that long fearful
night of months which had wrapped my spirit in its deathly slumbers? And was
all this glad light of the day, or was it but a meteor flash sent to deceive me, and
leave me there in a deeper darkness? I looked out over the barren earth, and it
was the same beautiful earth it had been to me in other days. I thought of all my
friends and loved them as of old. You no longer turned coldly away and chilled
my heart to ice. Then I recollected it was Sunday, and the thought of meeting
again with the worshippers of God thrilled my soul with delight. Was all this a
delusion? Nothing ever seemed more real and all day long I have been so
unspeakably happy, and as the twilight deepened and the pale "evening star"
looked down upon me I could think of you only as the loving and true being
who in other days blessed me with the devotion of a fond heart. The darkest
hour of the past made no more impressions than would the recollection of a
dark vision in dreams, and it has seemed that you too were again happy, that the
darkness had passed from off your soul. Perhaps it was only because I wished it
might be so.

Monday eve. It was a strangely happy day I spent yesterday, and a strange letter this I commenced to you. Strange that I should tell to James every thought and feeling? Yes. So it has become. But I will not speak of that now. I could not resist the inclination to write as I did last night, let the result be what it might. Whether that awaking, however, was real or imaginary I am very sure that there is a true and higher life to which we should both awake. I do not believe that your course for the last few months is the truest and noblest that you can pursue, and I know that mine has been only downward. O how dreadful that those very hours which were promising only deep, true joys of an earnest happy life should have brought such recklessness, such bitterness and anguish of spirit. James, I am more and more convinced that there has been somewhere a great wrong—where I cannot tell, nor would I say it was intended, but I am sure that this separation of spirits which were once so entirely one is no *natural* result. Perhaps this wrong may never be known, or if known never be made right, but what is more terrible I sometimes fear it will yet prove the ruin and final destruction of us both. Surely it will, unless we work out a course different from that which for the last few months has been ours.

I hope you can pardon me for writing such a letter as this, and I could wish that it might be a pleasure for you sometimes during the long dismal evenings of the coming winter to come and sit by me and read. I would promise to do all within my power to make those pleasant happy hours. But the Future alone can tell of all this. . . . Do not be frightened by this letter from ever approaching me again. I will not call up the terrors of the Past, but be as cheerful and glad as though all were right.

Crete

Orange, Ohio, Nov 13, 1856

Lucretia Dearest:

Half dead with visiting, even with my nearest earthly relations, I have taken the stillest corner of Uncle Boynton's table around which half a dozen are now determinedly chatting upon all topics from [President] Buchannan down to the last batch of neighborhood gossip. From what you know of ranges of feeling about now, you know how much spirit echoes [in] the voices around me. There is no thread of discourse or line of conversation that does not bring me out to Hamlet's conclusion: "How stale and flat and profitless are all the uses of this unfriendly world." And still the fault is probably in myself and not in the world. I came home determined to be as brave and good as I could be and spent most of the time in visiting with mother and the rest of my folks—but really I seem to have lost all that I possessed in common with my kind—is it so or not? I don't know. Tuesday I went to Cleveland intending to go to Cincinnati to take a course of vocal training for my throat's sake, or else spend a week at the Water Cure. I telegraphed to Cincinnati and found that the man could not attend to me now. I then went to the Water Cure and found they could do my throat no good unless I should stay one or two months. So both my projects failing, after I had strolled around Cleveland till I found no more reason for strolling than for standing still and no inducement to do either, I came back last evening to Solon, and today came down here. Oh how the hours drag! Dearest, do you know what these year-days are? Hour after hour full of the insipid commonplace talk of life! I find myself much worn down in strength and flesh, too; yet I long to be plunged again into a whirlwind of work, that I may make life tolerable.—And still my folks persist in supposing me a fortunate and favored one in my life's course! Lucretia, can you tell me what I am and in what a condition? I will not refer to the bright, joyful, hopeful past and the terrible contrast my memory brings back to my heart with such terrible power. I turn away from that past with a tearful eye and I dread to look forward to the great unknown and I stand writhing under the direct piercing rays of the terrible *now*. But I did not intend to pain you more by telling these my bonds of sorrow, for I know something of your own heart-throbs but forgive me—these emotions would ooze out at my finger ends and distil a part of its bitterness upon this sheet. I don't know how I can live through the week. I may go to Hiram on Saturday but I do not know. It has been a long time since I have addressed a letter to you. This is done sorrowfully and tearfully and yet I desire to write on to you till the morning dawns but the household is called to retire. I must lie down. With a heart that is throbbing for you, I am still your miserable

James.

By the spring of 1857 James was a frequent visitor to Lucretia's residence in Cleveland, where she was teaching at the Brownell Street school. When Andrew Freese was appointed Cleveland's first superintendent of schools in 1853, he found that "teachers in the Primary departments were laboring over classes in the second reader,

when [the children] could neither pronounce nor spell half the words they met with; and scholars were advanced to the third reader before they could read with any tolerable degree of accuracy, the simplest pieces in the second." As a result, Freese advocated that pupils go back to the beginning of their readers and spend much more time, advancing with thoroughness.

Cleveland, May 8, 1857

James Dearest:

Indeed you were a very naughty boy to make me promise to write you a letter; for I had fully determined that no letter you should get until I had received one from you; still I don't care much just now for I have wanted you here so much this evening to enjoy with me one of the most enrapturing sights I have ever witnessed. Smith's Panorama of the Tour of Europe.[1] From Rouen France we have followed the artist through France Belgium, Germany, Prussia, Switzerland and Italy, stopping at many of the principal cities, lingering beside beautiful fountains, gazing at the most exquisite specimens of art—then away among the terrible sublimities of the Switzers pride, the snow clad Alps, first viewing them in the clear full sunlight, then at the twilight hour when every peak and crag was tinged with rosy hue—now standing upon the verge of Vesuvius' crater looking down down into its yawning depths—then with the Neapolitan watching it when wrapt in lurid flames and pouring into the sea rivers of fire.

But don't think I am crazy, running on at such a rate as this. I have only been lost in most delightful raptures, and can scarcely restrain tongue or pen from pouring forth the most ludicrous extravagancies. It is all in vain however. I can give you only the faintest idea of the beauty and perfection of those paintings. I only wish you could see them. I do not believe I could have felt any more powerfully the overwhelming grandeur and magnificence of Alpine scenery had I looked upon the original. If you were only to be here tomorrow night, then you too could see and feel it all yourself.—But when do you come again? There is so much here to enjoy that I long for some *old* friend to share it with me. I am at my new boarding place now and have a very pleasant roommate—one of the teachers, a graduate from Mount Holyoke—but I cannot love her yet as one of my old friends and whenever we go out upon the lake-shore or visit any place or thing interesting, somehow I cannot help wishing it were an old *heart friend* near. I cannot learn to love the changes which life seems to bring, and I often find my heart asking for the sweet hallucinations of my early dreams.—I love my little school very much—never felt better satisfied with my efforts than now. I am continually becoming more and more pleased with the method of teaching and drilling in these Union Schools. It may be faulty in some respects, but I am sure is far ahead of anything I have known anything about before. I am getting every day slower and more thorough—I try to teach the children only a very few things, but try to make those few thoroughly understood and leave them firmly impressed. A dissertation on school teaching now!! Well good night; perhaps my brain will be cooler when the morning breezes blow.

Another beautiful morning. How refreshing the sunlight after so many dark, rainy days. Such a nice time I had getting home the morning you left me. Noon. The breakfast bell called me, and I have been busy ever since. I can never tell how much I love you all at Hiram. It seems as though I had no heart left for anyone else. And then to be away from you all and every hour miss you so much. Harry is going to call here soon, and a fine visit I am promising myself. I am so glad Mr. Hayden sent him out here—I wish he would send some of you every day. Harry writes me such a good letter—speaks of Barbara's marriage, but does not regret it—says he is happier in his new love. I am glad if he can be. Dare I hope for an answer to such a thing as this! I believe I might if you could only know how happy it would make me. Tell Almeda I am waiting very patiently for a letter from her.

[Hastily] Loving Crete.

Cleveland, May 19, 1857

Dearest James:

As I cannot be at Hiram this evening enjoying with you the rich intellectual feast there provided by the youth and beauty of the Eclectic's halls, I am glad to be alone. One of our gentlemen invited the ladies here out to a ball given by the "Forest City Lyceum" this evening but as I rarely dance, I declined of course accepting it, and they have left me with my own thoughts, and I have the egotism not to feel in the least sorry. Our "good lady" has voluntarily given me permission to burn the gas . . . in the dining room as long as I chose, and most gladly do I avail myself of this precious privilege, and improve this quiet hour addressing you.—Responding a few words to your kind letter yesterday received. I need not tell you that it was a sweet pleasure to receive again words traced by your hand and were I to follow the impulses of my whole being, the fire would be given to my heart once more. But no I dare not trust it lest I forget the terrible truth which I have been forced to believe, that I cannot make the one for whom I would have lived and died entirely happy. Heaven alone knows the struggle it has cost to yield up that fond delusion. I dare do nothing to call it back. I strive to forget the past, and to have no thought for the future. To meet you, to be with you is a present pleasure of which I have no strength to deprive myself, and when I see you seemingly not miserable in my presence I count every moment that I can be with you a treasure. Sometimes a thought comes over me that perchance our course is only leading on to deeper sorrow in the future, but I have no strength to turn aside into another path, and can only yield the guidance alone to God. With my hands clasped upon my heart daily I repeat the present prayer, "Father thy will be done."

Pardon me James if I have said aught that may awaken a sad thought. I have expressed far more than I designed when I commenced.—You write of the prospects at Hiram, also of the treatment you are receiving from some "good friends." I suppose the decision of the Trustees is already known. I hope they have acted wisely; it is not possible that they are men of so little discrimination as to be influenced by any such baseless reports as those to which you refer. I do not wonder nor blame you in the least that you feel like giving over the Eclectic, and turning your course in some other direction. But James you will not turn all your attention to "Law" before the most careful and candid consideration of Life and all its interests and aims, will you? I presume I have received an unjust bias against that profession but I must confess I cannot see a justification of what its demands are without the feeling that in other fields there is a height and depth of thought and feeling which the law can never reach. My ignorance of it of course allows me no just appreciation of its real nobility, and if I am wrong I hope to be corrected.— . . . I ask nothing which is not your delight to grant. Should it be your pleasure to write again before coming you know that it will be my pleasure to receive it. The Presbyterian General Assembly is in session now, and the streets are filled with ministers. I presume we shall be entertained with some fine specimens of theological talent. . . . Your loving Crete

With her usual insight, in her next letter Lucretia analyzes one of the problems inherent in her relationship with James: the discrepancy between what she is in her letters

and how she is in her person. This discrepancy, she realizes, has been responsible for some of the disappointments James has found each time he returned from a long absence, during which the exchange of letters had led him to expect a different woman from the one he found.

Cleveland, June 16, 1857

James Dearest:

Once it was my sweetest pleasure when away from you to give all my thoughts to the pen and send them away on their little mission of love to you: but the experiences of the last year have inspired almost a dread of this silent messenger. For I cannot but fear that it is not faithful to its trust, or at least that it conveys to you impressions and awakens expectations which my pres‑ ence fails to make you realize, and I have sometimes felt that I would never through it transmit to you another thought. Is it not true that heretofore almost all you have known of me was gained not from my life or my actions but from my pen? And I have determined that it should be so no longer—that whatever you should know of my inner life should be learned from *myself*. Then only such thoughts of me as my presence with you would justify would be awakened. And by this decision I still abide. Consequently, I shall write now not of myself but of you. I sometimes feel that I know you far better than you know yourself, not that one so dispassionate as doubtless I am can under‑ stand all the intensity of such a nature as yours, but so far as deep earnest feel‑ ing may be able to comprehend it, I feel that I know and can sympathize with yours. Youth is ardent and glowing with the brilliant hopes of its own creating. Love is its strongest principle, and around it all those golden expectations clus‑ ter. To common minds the dimming of these glorious visions by the realities of this life cursed by sin is but a quiet change to which they soon become accus‑ tomed, and perhaps even forget that their expected happiness is not all gained. But to a few like you the fading of this promised future into the common reali‑ ties of life is like the going out of the sun. The gloom and terror of the tempest sweep over the soul, and when it has passed by how often nothing is seen but the wreck. And, James, I have sometimes doubted whether one like you could pass through unwrecked; but even if you did, could I who had been so inti‑ mately associated with that darkness hope to appear again in your vision of hap‑ piness? could I from whom every feeling of your heart had turned away, hope to be received home to that heart again? No, no, I could not hope: still a hand, I trust of wisdom, has stayed me from separating myself entirely from you. At times all the pride of my woman's nature has risen in rebellion against my passive course, and bade me sever the last tie that bound me in any way to you, but my woman's heart was too weak for the struggle it must have cost, and I have lived on *waiting waiting* until the riven cloud should reveal all. I felt too that the world had no sympathy with you, that it knew nothing of your suffering and would only blame when rather it should pity, and I dared, indeed I had no wish to do anything which might add only bitterness to your cup already overflowing with sorrow. And however great the anguish at times your treatment may have occasioned me, never have I doubted your sincerity. And I could only exclaim as I contrasted the happiness of the joyous past with that terrible moment. O the bliss and yet the bitter anguish of being loved by such a nature! The vivid imagination of your vain impulsive nature had led you to expect far too much. Away from the idol of your dreams you clothed her with every grace and charm your exuberant fancy could create. Her imperfections were all forgotten, and when the time came which brought her to your arms, how they glared upon you! Had you never been parted from her this terrible revulsion of feeling might have appeared in a milder form and left you more calmly to judge of your true feelings. But, James Dearest, with you I can now say that I regret it not, for if your heart ever turns back to me for happiness, I believe it will be in a purer truer union of deep abiding thought and sentiment our hearts will meet and our lives be made more entirely one than in our brightest dreams we ever before imagined them, and if this is not to be, I can no more than die and every agonizing heart throb will but hasten the hour of my release from a life bereft of every joy. . . .

Your loving Crete.

Bethany, W.Vir., July 4, 1857

Dearest Crete:

At 7 o'clock last Monday morning I found myself seated in the cars and starting away for Wellsville [Ohio]. At Alliance I found Harry [Rhodes] and at 11 we reached Wellsville. In an hour we went on to Steubenville. We spent three or four hours there visiting a Female Seminary in that place and then went on through a wild country toward Columbus. Stopped at Miller's Station and went on foot (2 1/2 miles) to Hopedale. Attended the Commencement of the M'Neely Normal School on the next day and spent another night there.

While we were at Bro Cyrus M'Neely's[2] a fugitive came there in the night from Wheeling Va. She was a very intelligent lady of 22 years and while I conversed with her I could not but feel the enormity of a system which should enslave such as she. Wednesday morning we started and reached Bethany in the evening. That evening there was an exhibition of the American Literary Society and the next evening the Neotrophian. Last evening I listened to a sermon from Bro T. M. Allen of Missouri.[3] I have been very kindly received here by all the brethren. I have been to Bro Campbell's, Pendleton's, Richardson's and several other places by special invitation.[4] There are many interesting old men here— Bro Scott, Bently[5] etc. . . .

I have not received a letter from you yet though I expect one this evening. . . . I would love to read Pickwick with you as we did a week ago today. Can you forgive such a scrawl as this. Hoping to be in your arms ere many weeks, I am ever your Loving James.

P.S. Direct your next letter to N.Y. City.

Cleveland, September 1, 1857

My Dear James:

Yes, mine forever, though a destiny cruel [may] separate us as far as the east is from the west. Whatever our earthly relations may be, we are one and belong to each other, and in view of this truth I no longer fear to reveal to you every thought. I know that my motives will be understood however freely I may speak. The fear which has so long sealed my lips that James might construe any expression of my real thoughts and feelings into a design on my part to gain my own selfish ends no longer haunts me. I believe that you trust me now, and I know that in my own heart has been awakened that confidence which brought such sweet peace to my spirit two years ago. James, do you know that it was the withdrawal of that confidence in me which pressed home to this grieving heart the keenest dagger! How many many times I felt that if you would only love me just enough to come and tell me all, I could endure to know the worst; but to see you shrink away from me as though you could not endure my presence, and hide from me the truth, was almost more than I could bear. May Heaven spare me from ever living again such hours of bitter anguish. Pardon me for alluding to them. It is the last time. They have told upon my heart the lesson I trust they were sent to teach. Their mission has been fulfilled; let them pass unnoticed longer. I would much rather rest with you beside Erie's moonlit waters and feel my heart throbbing against your own, while I talk to you tonight. But I will not wait until I may be so blessed before saying some things so long unsaid.

James, the bright ideal of life and of love which are here held up before us was indeed very beautiful; but was it the true one? Can the human heart bear the tests to which it may be submitted by it? I had hoped it might. Indeed, I had almost, yes, entirely trusted that a love as pure and deep as I believe ours to have been could never never meet with anything that could possibly turn it from its course or prove ever the slightest interruption. I was telling Mother this and remarked that it might be an error. Her reply was if there was no dan-ger of any such thing happening, if two loving hearts could find only in each other all that would satisfy, there would have been no necessity for the mar-riage vow.

May be it is so. If there could be no temptation, no danger of turning to another, why register in Heaven the vow of constancy? I blame you for nothing, for whatever you may have done I believe your heart's faithfulness; and allowed the generous and gushing affection of your warm impulsive nature to go out in all its fullness towards another than the one to whom you had pledged your all. All innocently as this was done, I can not blame you, and could the effect which all the past of our intimacy might have over you be blotted out, I would say to you this hour, go and marry Rebecca; and hereafter trust not your heart so far. Rebecca is a good and noble girl, in many aspects far my superior but she loves you no better than Crete. If, however, you love her better, if she can satisfy the wants of your nature better, and more than all, if you can with her become a good and noble man in spite of all the Past, Crete can give you up, and pro-nounce upon your Love a sister's blessing. You told me that judgment promp-ted you to another course, that to feel yourself an honorable, generous man you must take me alone to your heart. Let feeling dictate whatever it might. I have thought I could never allow that, that I could never be your wife unless every feeling of your heart seconded the decisions of reason. Perhaps I asked too much, but, James, to be an unloved wife, O Heavens, I could not endure it. I am not exacting. It would excite no spirit of jealousy in my heart to know that my husband admired and even loved a thousand others, and know that they pos-sessed traits superior to mine: but I do feel it to be my right to claim this sole assurance, that I am his choice; and that however much he may find to be more admired in others he will not turn away from me to them, but rather seek to correct my faults, and make me like them. I want to find in my husband that strength of love which can steel itself against every attraction that might come between us, which will hold me nearest his heart in spite of every impulse which an ardent nature might feel. Now, James, I freely pardon any error your ignorance of the human heart may have led you to commit, but I do hope whatever course you may take, that hereafter you will be more guarded for your own happiness if nothing more. It pains me to see you so miserable as you are at times, and sometimes I feel that I could dare almost anything, even for the hope of making you happy again. But could I—could I become your wife and see that best hope fail! Oh no, no, no. If it would not fail, may God help me to know it. Then I will make the trial. James, write to me very soon. Keep nothing back that is in your heart. Yours most lovingly, Crete.[6]

The "waking up day" came the following spring. James must have finally settled the matter in his mind, whether he loved Rebecca enough to marry her or whether he should take Lucretia for his wife, for a few months later, in April 1858, as they drove from the village of Garrettsville to Hiram in a buggy, James and Lucretia agreed "to try life in union before many months." It is clear Lucretia realizes James is doing the "honorable, generous" thing. Knowing that he was marrying her from a sense of duty, Lucretia acquiesced to marriage with a sick heart. She finished up her teaching in Cleveland, where she had also been studying drawing, returned to Hiram briefly, and then went to Bryan, Ohio, near Toledo, to teach a course of drawing while living with her childhood friend, Lizzie Atwood Pratt. That summer James and Crete wrote of their household plans, and of their forthcoming wedding.

Cleveland, April 25, 1858

James Dearest:

I did very much wish to receive a letter from you last night but did not very much expect it; for I know how full of busy care are all your hours. I do not need the inducement of an unanswered letter before me however today to make me write, for I am alone and my thoughts will not stay with me, but go away to those I love better. Care has at least one virtue—that of giving swift wing to the moments—and to be so free from it as I am now makes some of these hours that I am alone seem very long.

I am succeeding with my work quite to my satisfaction. Yesterday morning, I carried back a piece to my teacher entirely finished which she expected I would only have sketched. I fancied she was a little astonished and I am sure I was when she asked me which was hers. I shall be ready to go to Lizzie three weeks from yesterday, I think. Can you not come here before I go? I want very much to see you and talk of our plans for the future. I want too that you should sit down beside me and tell me how you feel now—whether or not our decision for the future makes you any *more* unhappy. You will talk to me freely of all these things will you not? I expect James you will see sad dark hours yet. Indeed perhaps it would not be possible that you should not. But do not fear to tell me of them; at least do not hide them from me through a fear that they might awaken in my bosom some dark suspicion. Why James I would not love a man so tame that he had never a wrong feeling to subdue. We cannot hope for a future all unclouded but with the *right* ever before us as it has been in this our final decision, and with our trust in God to guide us I believe we shall find more of joy than sorrow awaiting us. I will use every power God has given me to become the true wife, and if I see you happy in your home and the deep love your wife will give you, I shall have all of happiness my heart could ask.

You will come if you can and see me, but if it is not possible write to me very fully will you not of all your designs.

Mr. Freese has finally resigned.[7] Some fuss was made about his salary, and he resigned thinking—so every one says *very quietly*—that he would frighten them out of the idea of lowering his salary; and that they would of course re-elect him. But there is quite a probability that this opportunity will be improved for changing Superintendants. Should this be the case he will doubtless feel somewhat chagrined. . . .

How soon will you know positively whether you remain in Hiram or not? Love to Almeda and Harry. Your Crete.

P.S. If you can get no other time to come here, cannot you spend next Saturday afternoon with me? There is a train coming in on the Pittsburg road at 2:45 P.M. and another going out—10:20.

Crete

Lizzie's Home, Bryan, Ohio
May 18, 1858
My Dear James:

In Lizzie's cozy little sitting room on the lounge by the south window. I reached Bryan about 9 o'clock last night—found Mr. Pratt waiting for me, and in another half hour was sitting down right here in my Lizzie's home. Today I have been very busy getting my things regulated—looking around to see what kind of place I had found, and seeing some of the people. It looks very new here. Still I think it is pleasant, at least it seems pleasant. I enjoy so much being with Lizzie. I shall not meet my class before Thursday, as it takes a little time for them to find out that I am really here. The prospect is that I shall have quite a large class and possibly I shall decide to remain only for this class. I know I ought not if we commence housekeeping this fall for there is so much to be done before that would be possible; and if I do not go home Mother will do it for me. Then again I do not think it will be very pleasant to go home after the term commences, and have all the fixing and fussing and getting married to do with so many around in the way. I have almost a mind to propose to you that you do not come here until I am ready to go home, and that we be married— "marry" I mean—before going. I dislike so much the parade of a large wedding party, and we could not possibly at home invite in only a few friends. Tell me what you think of this plan. If it does not please you, I am not very particular about the course we will take. The greatest objection I would have to it would be that I should not see you so soon. Mother thought perhaps it would be better for you not to build this summer; but I do not know of any house that we would like to rent. I suppose there would be none except the Institution buildings that could be rented, and it would cost more than they are worth to prepare one for a respectable home, and then it would not be convenient. If you could build I think it would be far more pleasant. Then we could make our little home just what we would like to have it. As soon as you can, you ought to decide what you will do, for if you should build, you will need to commence very soon. . . .

Write to me very soon. I shall get impatient if I wait long. Those boys and girls at Hiram have no right to claim all your attention, and I shall complain if you allow them to do so. Love to Harry and tell him I hope to see him again sometime. Tell him to write to me and Almeda the same. Your Crete.

Hiram, May 30, 1858
Midnight

Dearest Crete:

Today I returned from the State Convention of Churches at Massillon, and I have been at work till this moment arranging our Commencement Programme for tomorrow's mail.

Your letter was duly received. I was glad to hear of your safe arrival. Your folks here are all well and I will only try to write a few items of news etc.

We have issued a call for a convention here to see if any thing can be done for the Eclectic. I fear much and hope little. See enclosed circular. I have been to Massillon to urge it up. . . .

I am in trouble about a home for us. I am hardly able to build as I would like to—and I don't know as I can rent here on the hill. It will not do to go off the hill. Your father suggests that I travel west and locate some land in vacation. I have not yet found room for a thought beyond the work of the school.

I shall come round to it soon. . . . I don't want much parade about our marriage. Arrange that as you think best. I will try to write more fully by and by. . . .

Give my love to Mr. and Mrs. Pratt and write to me soon, and better.
Your own, James.

Bryan, June 8, 1858

Dear James:

The more I think about it the more I am convinced that you will not be able to find a house that we will want to rent; and if you will be satisfied I will consent to board for a while. I do not think it would be as pleasant as to have a home of our own if we could get such a house as we would like, but since we cannot I believe we [will] enjoy boarding better. If you could rent Mrs. Northrop's chambers or their equivalent with some other family, we could furnish them and have room for ourselves and a room to entertain company. I thought of her rooms because there would be just about room enough. There are three rooms in the chamber, I believe. Under present circumstances it seems to me perhaps better to do so as it will save you a great deal of trouble in finding a house, and both of us the vexation of having one that did not suit us. I hope this may reach you before you make any definite arrangement, though I am afraid it will not, I am so late in this conclusion.

Your Commencement will have passed before this reaches you, I presume, but I am hoping a fine time for you. I shall expect you early next week. In haste,
Your Crete.

Bryan, June 27, 1858

My Dear Jimmie:

I fear it will be my painful necessity to persecute you with a real oldfash-ioned love letter; for since you left me, I have done nothing but think of you and wish you back again not because I care everything for you of course but simply that this terribly warm weather has bereft me of all powers to break away from the train of thought your premature departure left me in. I can't quite grow rec-onciled to your running off just as I was ready to sit down and enjoy a quiet lit-tle visit. Why I had a dozen nice little morceaus reserved for it and left here to enjoy them alone they are not worth a fig. Really I am beginning to think *Man too slippery a fish to build many hopes on*, and if the one I claim did not belong to the genus Whale I should expect he would slip out of sight entirely; as it is I have a hope that his dimensions will keep him in view, even when proximity is not to be spoken of.

So after all I don't know but I am really one of the fortunate few who can be congratulated, and I will try and imagine my complainings all unreasonable. But honestly now don't you love to come and stay with me? I hope you do; for if you do not, terrible will be the life marriage will bring to us both. You may think it very unreasonable that such a trifling occurrence as your going away a few hours before I was expecting it should lead to such a query! and I know it is, but do not blame me too much. There are some wounds which the cruel thrusts of Destiny bury so deep in our hearts that the slightest irritation causes them to bleed afresh; but so long as your gentle noble assurances of love are given as a healing balm, I shall secretly harbor no thought which might be unjust. Bravely will I humble my pride to a full confession of each and every one however unreasonable it may appear when the cause for it is understood. I know that God has led us to our present position and I know that if we trust him, doing meanwhile as nearly right as we can, that he will give us light to guide us on to true and lasting peace. I do not look forward to our wedded life with half the doubtings that I feared I might, and I have no desire to put it far-ther away than necessary. Oh my dear Jamie will you not write me as frank a letter as this? Tell me when you are coming back. Lizzie is hoping it will be before I go to Defiance for Mr. Pratt's sake. She says she has not seen him enjoy the society of any gentleman so much for months.

There are no gentlemen here that he associates with except in business and she says it did him so much good to have such a genial body come along to call him from his office and business out into the world of social thought and feeling. Your loving Crete.

Monday morning. Last evening I thought out a design for our house when we are ready to build. I haven't it fully perfected yet or I would send it to you; but I will have it drawn out before you return. I scarcely know what your idea of a house would be, but as far as I do know I think I have introduced into my design all the features of beauty so essential to your eye, also all the conveniencies which I should not know how to dispense with. When you have nothing to do some day will you not draw a plan, too? Then we will compare them, and perhaps out of the two we will get one to suit us both. Do you not love to try little plans and build up prospects for our future? I do. Your Crete.

Indianapolis, June 29, 1858

Crete Dearest:

Your expected letter has just reached me. Of all the hot days and hours I have seen the hottest is this very hour. In the shade the thermometer stands at 94 to 100 degrees. During the last three days 15 men have died in the streets of the sun stroke. I had to lay over Sunday in LaFayette and so did not reach here till yesterday afternoon. I see I am recording my travels wrong end first but no matter the record is about as regular as the travels. I reached Unity before 10AM on Wed. & soon started out on a trip my cousin had laid out for me and was gone till evening. Several letters were then answered. Early the next morning we four (Cousin and wife and Mother and I) started for Stratten Co. Ind. where we arrived at noon. I went ahead as a traveller and stranger and my old aunt who had not seen me for 20 years knew me by my father's looks. I had this Aunt and three cousins to visit and I had intended to stay there with Mother over Sunday but when I had been there about an hour I felt as though I wanted to go on. So on Friday evening I went with Cousin to Bryan where we arrived at 11 o'clock; I passed in sight of your window but I saw no light. I wondered if you were not dreaming of me just then. A little past 12 and I was on the cars for Toledo. Arrived at 3:30. I got two hours sleep and at noon started west as I have already told you. I have travelled nearly 400 miles since I left Bryan and you.

You ask me if I love to stay with you, and if so why I left so soon. The reason I left so soon was that I had agreed with my cousin to be there that morning—

though Mother did not know it. But the first part of the question is of far more consequence, and I will be frank. I do love to be with you, but there is a restless and unsatisfied feeling about a good deal of the time, and I can't tell what its cause is. When I got among my friends in Indiana, I wanted to go on. When I stopped at LaFayette I was anxious for the whistle to call me on to the Capitol. Now, though I expected to spend several days here yet I [am] hurrying my business through so as to start early tomorrow. And I know it will be just so of my next stopping place. When I am sitting I long to be walking, and when I am walking I long to be sitting. I either stagnate and rust with inactivity or am consumed with excess of action. No spot or position on Earth seems to offer contentment unless it be our home. My hope is in that, and yet I will not conceal the fact that I sometimes fear and tremble even for that. Such a state of feeling is strangely miserable, and I think will not continue when we have a home and our interest and love centered there. But yet I feel as though I should need to make an effort to feel more equable, and all who love me can aid me by support and forbearance. I thank God that others—most others—have not such a nature as mine. But probably this is the price of what little power I have. I want to know just what time you will be at Defiance. I will come to Bryan if possible before you leave. But I cannot yet tell. Write immediately to Chicago & tell me as near as possible the day when you must leave. I would be glad to see Pratt again. I have one or two points to embody in that Ideal House. One, a projecting door. I shall hope to see your draft when I come. I can't draw anything. I am making several discoveries for our school. I'll tell you. As ever, your loving James.

Bryan, July 4, 1858

James Dearest:

I did not receive your letter until yesterday and perhaps this will not reach Chicago in time for you as I presume you will be in haste to get on to the arms of your beloved Charles [Wilber]. It is cool and pleasant this morning and after the excessive heat of the past two weeks we can fully appreciate what Willis[8] says of a summer morning: "Life seems a luxury such a morn as this." Bryan is such a shadeless place that it has seemed some of these hot days that it would surely ignite. It answered entirely Dickens description of some city of France, I have forgotten which, where everything was *glaring* and when I have had life enough to express a wish for anything it has been only for a tree. I have not heard a word from Father since he left Princeton and I begin to feel anxious about him. It has been so warm—I am afraid he is sick or that something has happened to him. A letter from Mother last week tells me that Mrs. Van is dead. She was very much tired out with company at Commencement and was attacked with a violent headache. She supposed it was only a nervous headache and that rest was all she needed. But Friday morning of the next week she was taken with spasms which continued through the day and Saturday she died. It seems as though it were almost more than her mother and husband can bear. The burthen of mother's letter is that I must come home and I want to go very much but there are reasons why I think I must stay till September. I shall be ready to go to Defiance about the middle of next week—a week from next Wednesday. July 14 is the day I am decided upon now. If you are ready to return before that I shall be very glad to see you in Bryan again, but if not I shall be just as glad to meet you at Defiance. I hope now to have Lizzie and Mr. Pratt with me one week at Defiance. Mr. Pratt will be there a week on business anyhow and Lizzie thinks now that she will go with him and so get an extra week's work with me. Yesterday we had a tremendous celebration here. Mr. Gunckel from Toledo was present to address the assembled multitudes from the county round about,[9] but just as his speech was fairly commenced, a heavy cloud appeared in the west and he soon found himself declaiming to the brave old woods alone, the most appreciative part of his audience I presume, but he did not seem to think so as he followed the crowd to the courthouse and there finished his speech. In the afternoon, a fantastic regiment of hideous men and women and children appeared in the streets raising an uproar which reminded me of the "Carnival of Venice. "This was followed in the evening by a splendid display of fireworks consisting of rockets, fire balls, fire crackers etc. A fair specimen of a western celebration, I judge. If you receive this in time write me again. I cannot tell the pleasure I felt to open again another letter from you with a few closely written lines. I am glad you wrote so frankly of yourself. Doubtless we shall both need to exercise some forbearance for in many respects we are entirely opposites, but if we center our hopes, joys and love in our home, I believe we shall find the truest happiness earth can give us, and I hope, James, it will bring to your spirit peace and contentment. Loving you as ever.

Crete.

Bryan, Ohio. Aug 19, 1858

Dear James:

By mistake I presume you sent your last to Defiance; consequently I did not receive it until last evening. I have little of surface-life to write about now—nothing save that I am making all possible haste to go home. If I do not meet Miss Booth at Oberlin I think you may certainly expect me the Saturday evening following. Lizzie is very anxious that I remain until the next Monday morning; but I feel very sure that I shall not do so. I am glad to learn of the prosperity of your school, but fear you are taking on yourselves an amount of work altogether too large.

The return of these last days of summer brings to me many sad hours. My heart is not yet schooled to an entire submission to that destiny which will make me the wife of one who marries me because an inexorable fate demands it. And firmly as I have determined to make the best possible of what life has left for me, and govern every action by the Right, yet there are hours when my heart almost breaks with the cruel thought that our marriage is based upon the cold stern word *duty*. Forgive me for speaking of it: I hope time may teach me to be satisfied with the love you will teach your heart to give, and with passing years may pass away all repinings for the lost visions of earlier days. Hoping to see you soon, I am still your Crete.

On *11 November 1858, James and Lucretia were married at the Rudolph home in Hiram. So worried were the Rudolphs that James might not show up for his own wedding that Lucretia half humorously, on her brother's advice, sent James an invitation. But he had bravely accepted the inevitable: the wedding took place. A student at Hiram wrote the following about the occasion: "Near the close of my first term at Hiram and two days after my 18th birthday, occurred the marriage of Miss Lucretia Rudolph to Mr. James A. Garfield. As my brother and I were guests, to us of course it was a grand occasion. Having been her pupil I loved her very much, and Mr. Garfield was my ideal then, as he has ever been, of all that is manly, brilliant, and good—a Sir Galahad, our knight without stain and without reproach. Several young girls were asked to attend upon her and we were expected to help serve refreshments and make ourselves generally useful. We were dressed in white, with low necks and short sleeves, and I remember Harry Rhodes' remark that the bride and her maids were a galaxy of beauty. President Hitchcock of Hudson College [later Western Reserve University] performed the ceremony, which to us young people seemed very impressive."[10]*

While marriage only deepened Lucretia's love for James, James continued on in his restless way, traveling frequently, and later, running for the Ohio State Senate. One hardly has to read between the lines to detect the unpleasant times and harsh feelings during the first years: James' indifference and neglect and Lucretia's bitter criticisms of his behavior.

Crete's first letter to James after their marriage was a note calling his attention to the "anniversary" of their first "interview" in the Hiram Institute's Lower Chapel, five years before.

Hiram, February 25, 1859

My Own:

Do you know this is the fifth anniversary of our engagement? I first thought of it as we were in the chapel this afternoon and Memory has been upon swift wings ever since, and I would not let it pass without sharing with you the sweets it brings. Not that it reveals only pictures of beauty; for there are among them scenes wild and fierce darkened with gathered clouds and terrible with the heaving billows of our tempest tossed life. But we need not stop with those now. There are fairer scenes—fair as this beautiful evening—inviting us to a retreat among their sunny glades, and with these now we would choose to linger. My thoughts go back to the first hour that we drew near each other and when Heaven drew nearer to us both. God, I thank thee for that hour!

And has not each year since brought us into a nearer and truer relation? I believe it has, and were you with me tonight to clasp me to your heart and breathe out words of love, I believe that deeper than ever before would our spirits go down into the mysteries of each other's beings. Since our marriage life has been a deep untold joy—over which the shadows flit sometimes but they stay not—and each day I feel all the tendrils of my heart twining more closely around you. Long ago when talking to me of your nature you compared it to the sturdy oak whose very roughness would hold more closely the clinging vine. I loved the comparison and I have never ceased to love it, and each hour that binds me closer to you makes me love it better.[11] My own husband, draw me still closer to you: bind me to your heart with ties that can know no severing.— The midnight hour draws on and I must away to sleep to dream I hope that a pair of strong arms encircle me. May God bless you, is the prayer of your own little wife. Crete.

James began his career as a Senator in Columbus on 1 January 1860.

Hiram, January 1, 1860

My Darling Husband:

It is a cold glittering morning and every little starry snowflake and pearly ice drop is flashing back the glory of this New Year's morning sun.

Everything sparkles so that I cannot be sad even though you are so far away and my thoughts go out in joyous bounding love to you, my own, my best beloved. I did not write to you last night; . . . I did not know as you were really expecting that I would write—you did not ask me to—besides I did not dare to call up any little reminiscences of the last six years which might lead me away unawares into any of those side passages whose darkness I wish to enter *never again*. So I indulged in pleasant thoughts and conjectures of your whereabouts and doings last evening; until dreams brought you back again to my arms. You do not know how constantly present you are to all my waking thoughts and sleeping visions, not that I am pining over your absence and wishing you back again. To be sure, I had a good child's cry as soon as you were away to lighten my heart of the tears I had been crushing back all day, but as soon as that was over my thoughts of you were *most*—I have to stop and miss you sometimes— all made up of bright hopes and aspirations for you and wishes full of love for your success and happiness and an earnest ever abiding desire that you may be guided by the greatest wisdom. I feel so much anxiety for you that your public career be never marked by the blight of a misdirected step. I want you to be *so great* and *good*. So worthy of the highest respect and love of all. So unimpeachable in every relation that your bitterest enemy can find no just cause for accusation, and I want to be the little wife worthy of such a noble husband. Yesterday I had some serious reflections upon my past life which resulted in some new visions of myself and some new and better resolutions to help guide me in my future course. I believe my nature has been too much of the receptive order. Instead of diving into the honey-cups I have rather lain down among the flowers and waited for them to shake down their sweetness upon my lips, and when for honey they have scattered over me only withered leaves, I have said in my heart this is all life has left for me and have yielded almost to despair. It seems to me I see my error now as I have never seen it before, and I can see a clearer way to carry out the determination I have so often made to make the most of what is yet left to me in life. And my dear husband will you not help me? I know you will—why do I ask. I know you will give me the encouragement of your sympathy and dependence upon me for happiness if I seek it in a joyous loving trusting spirit. I can scarcely be patient to hear from you. I want a letter *now*—this very minute. You will write to me often, very often—twice every week certainly? Tell me all about yourself, your success, your impressions of all that interests you, and sometimes let your heart turn to your little loving wife with some expression of tenderness. I want you to love me better than all else in the world besides. I know you cannot give yourself all up to me but I do want and feel that I must have the dearest places in your heart all for mine. . . . Your little wife, Crete.

By this time Crete knew herself to be pregnant with their first child.

Hiram, February 10, 1860

My Darling Husband:

Last night I had a long letter finished for you; but I shall not let you have it. Its beginning was draped in a radiant web of sunshine, but night came before it was finished, and the shadows gathered around it, and I have resolved to have no more shadows. I have laid in background enough of them to give relief to a long life time. Now for the lights. I have turned my back upon the mists and poisoned vapors of the low valley of life through which we have so long laid our pathway and am hastening to the sun-gilded hill tops: and you will come with me, too. The past shall be a sealed book and we will live in the glorious Now. Living and loving better and truer through each new hour that God shall give us. Will we not, dear Jamie? Can we not? Yes, we can and we *must*. If not for our own sakes, we must for that little one which we are hoping soon to come and bless us. We must ignore all that has been wrong in our Past, and live as though it had never been unless we would embitter that little life with all the desolation that gathers around the homes of those whose parents fail to know that perfect union which marriage should always find. Jamie, we must know the perfection of love for each other, before we can hope for perfect peace. I wish you would talk and write to me of these things sometimes. It seems to me sometimes that you do not care very much whether we are ever any nearer and dearer to each other; but I do not believe this. I know that you desire to become the true husband and to see me the wife who can fill up the whole measure of your happiness and in the clear light of truth we will try to become all this to each other, and let us ever talk freely and kindly of everything. Let us have no reserve.

I am feeling a great deal better than when I wrote you last, though not quite as well as before; my head aches almost all the time now. I am anxious to hear from you again. I am afraid you are not gaining as rapidly as we want you to. One week more finishes up our term, and how glad I am. . . .

Your loving wife, Crete.

Columbus, March 14, 1860

Dear Crete:

I have been expecting a letter from Hiram, but I have not heard a word since I left. Last Saturday I went to Cincinnati and did not return till yesterday. Sunday morning I spoke in Bro Bennett's Church and while I was in the city, with Bro Bishop, the Mayor of the City. He is a fine man, and has a very pleasant family.

Since my return from home we have torn up one former decision in regard to adjournment, and now it is fully settled I think. We shall adjourn on Monday the 26th of March, to meet again in January 1861. So I shall expect to be in Hiram one week from next Tuesday, and resume my work in the school.

I have been and am still very anxious to know how the school is doing and how many students there are.

As the session draws to a close our business becomes more laborious. Events crowd upon each other rapidly and it requires all of one's energies to keep the run of business and act intelligently. I shall be glad when the work is ended. Much of the time since I left home I have felt sad and unhappy but yet a press of duties goes far to keep my thoughts comparatively cheerful. I shall try to make life for you and myself as pleasant as possible. But I have not been feeling as though I could write before. I hope we may be able to get along as pleasantly and happily as is possible [given] the chances and changes of life. I am now in the Senate chamber and a bill has just come up which requires my attention. I hope to hear from you . . . soon. Ever, James.

Hiram, March 18, 1860

My Dear Dear James:

Please don't be "sad," don't be "unhappy" anymore. Please don't think me just an unreasonable little body who will not be gratified only by making you as miserable as possible. I acknowledge my liability to be unreasonable and selfish, but not my intention to be so. I confess too that there is a strong probability that I am too tenacious of my own opinions of right and wrong but it does not seem to be that I am so extreme in this as to make quite justifiable the way you receive everything which I speak of which seems to me not quite right in your treatment of me and of others. Would you not think me unjust if, Jamie, whenever you reprove me for my abrupt and harsh way of speaking sometimes, I should lay it to heart as a wilful desire and determination on your part to deprive me of one of my privileges? You asked from me the promise before we were married that if those things of which I spoke ever became a source of unhappiness to me that I should unhesitatingly tell you of them, for that our own happiness was to be considered prior to all else earthly, and it seemed a little hard to have you tell me in return for so doing that you had for several months felt that it was probably a great mistake that we had ever tried a married life. But, Jamie, I will not treasure it up against you, for I presume I have provoked you to think and feel and say a great many things of which you would have been entirely innocent, had I taken a different course, and I am going to try harder than ever before to be the best little wife possible. You need not be a bit afraid of my introducing one of those long talks—such a terror to you—ever again. I am glad you are coming home so soon, but you must come with a light face, or the shadow of those hours of terrible suffering, which are so surely and steadily coming upon me, will steal over me with its chill of death. . . .

Ever yours. Crete.

In the summer of 1860, just after Lucretia had given birth to their first child, James took a trip from Detroit to Sault Ste. Marie, Michigan. Crete, with their Eliza, nicknamed "little Trot" (after a character in Dickens' David Copperfield) still nursing, could not accompany him.

Sault St. Marie, July 25,
1860. 6 o'clock P.M.

My Dear Crete:

We are now in sight of Sault St. Marie, and I learn that we are not to stop, only time to pass through the locks. So I will take a moment before we reach the locks[12] to pencil a few words as well as my bad arm will let me. We left Detroit about noon yesterday and have come nearly due north 400 miles. It is so cold that I am comfortable with my overcoat on. Our point of destination is about 6 and a half degrees north of Cleveland. We have had a fine passage. About an hour ago I shot a duck from the bow (I, not the duck). Dashing around on every side are huge white seagulls, and a little while ago I saw a large bald eagle. I felt some like William Tell. I could not shoot at him. The band are now playing "Annie Laurie" as we pass along the shores lined with beautiful cedars and skirted with Indian huts. Now we have touched shore and are all going off to walk around by the Post Office and get on at the upper lock.

My love to "Trot" and all.

Ever, James.

Hiram, July 29, 1860

My Dear "Ever" James:

I received your first letter Thursday night and your next last night, but I have not been able to commence a letter before nor am I now. My breast has been getting worse ever since you left. It is swollen very much and at times it is exceedingly painful, and I have grown so weak that for three or four days I have not been able to sit up more than an hour or two. Yesterday and last night it did not pain me nearly as much and the doctor said there was a bare possibility that it might not gather, still he thinks it almost certain that it will. I cough a good deal too which discourages me more than anything else. I want you here so much and sometimes when I am feeling so bad it seems so hard to have you away that I have to cry like a baby. I will write you again so that it will meet you in Cleveland, and if I am not better, you will come right home, won't you, and not stop to spend Sunday at Solon. . . . "Little" Trot is well and good as ever (I guess she is "Ever" Trot). She is lying on the lounge now engaged in her solemn ceremony of extracting the secrets from a mysterious rag. She is very much attached to her bottle—thinks it a great institution and sends a kiss and

a great deal of love to her father. She will look upon the serious side of life however and utterly refuses to smile upon the world she has been introduced into.
She opens her eyes very wide, though, and looks very wise. We presume her
sobriety is due to your absence as she has always manifested such an ardent
attachment to you. I am very sorry that I fail to appreciate the grasp of affection
contained in your signature . . . desirous to see you, Crete.

*Back in Columbus again at his second term as State senator, James and Jacob Cox, a
fellow senator with whom Garfield shared a room, find themselves in the thick of the
debate over secession. Cox later became a brigadier general in the Union Army, and
remained one of the Garfields' close friends for life.*

Columbus, January 13, 1861

My Dear Crete:
    Your letter was duly received and read with a great deal of pleasure. How
much the fact of our little Trot's existence has added to the horizon of our lives.
The laws of perspective have placed her in a point where all other things have
assumed new and peculiar relations to each other. This morning I have been
looking over a volume of fine English engravings. Many among them were of
children of various ages and in various attitudes. Whenever there was not too
manifest a dissimilarity I was seeing the little plump face of Trot peering out
from the picture. Bless her little soul. I hope she will live to know how dear a little creature she is. This has been a very busy and eventful week. I have sent you
the Journal (daily) which I presume you are getting regularly. Its reports are
very meagre. A speech that would really cover two columns being condensed to
ten lines or less. But still you see the current of events. Yesterday, we had a very
exciting day. We had managed to keep on Union Saving resolutions till on
Thursday evening the Republicans of both houses held a general caucus, and
after a whole evening spent in debate a committee was appointed to present resolutions. We drafted them and had Harrison present them. The debate which
sprang up was a very exciting one, but resulted in great unanimity. I think we
shall soon pass a law to arm the State. There is a strong warlike sentiment here.
The members are forming a company of 40 for military drill, so I expect in a few
days Cox and I will be seen on the east portico of the State learning the use of

the light infantry musket. Of course, this is for the sake of exercise as well as to encourage a citizen soldiery.

I have got a new suit of clothes entire costing $33.00 which please put down on our account book. I have a frock coat which cost $16.00 and is very thick and comfortable. The pants are of the same material. I wish you would look in the cupboard below and tell me which volume of the Debates in the Ohio Constitutional Convention I have. I have two there but I believe they are both the same, and I want to get the other one.

I want you to write to me often, for I very much love to read your letters and hear how you are doing. . . . I want to know all about the school. . . .

And now take my love and divide it between yourself and Trot and tell her not to suck her finger.

Ever Your James.

Columbus, February 17, 1861

My Dear Crete:

Your valentine was received and read with a great deal of pleasure. I very much love to read so jolly and sprightly a letter, and I am quite inclined to adopt a suggestion I have lately seen that letters between intimate friends should be far more reflective of outer life than they are. Now I have rec'd a letter from Harry, one from Burke,[13] and one from you, and from these, all my Hiram news for a week. . . .

I have received and accepted an invitation to deliver an address on Washington's birthday at Delaware College.

Having now given you matters of greatest moment, I will subjoin a few words concerning the President Elect. Of course we had seas of people here, a flood of almost boundless extent. In some respects I was disappointed in Lincoln, but in most he surpasses expectation. He has raised a pair of whiskers, but notwithstanding all their beautifying effects he is distressedly homely. But through all his awkward homeliness there is a look of transparent, genuine goodness, which at once reaches your heart and makes you trust and love him. His visits are having a fine effect on the country.

He has the tone and bearing of a fearless, firm man, and I have a great hope for the government. His wife is a stocky, sallow, pugnosed plain lady, and I think has much of the primitiveness of western life. He stands higher on the whole in my estimation than ever. She considerably lower.

Miss Vaughn postponed her reading in consequence of the general excitement till tomorrow evening. She is a lady of rare accomplishments but is quite
affected in her manners.[14] No, I cannot allow Trot to give public readings at
present. Please communicate this injunction to the young miss. By the way, I
think you had better take her to Bro Robbins[15] when you are in Warren and
get her portrait taken, and I will add, send it to me. I have written to Bro Austin
that you would write him and tell him what day you would go. If you go there
first he will meet you at Leavittsburgh. Please do so. I mean write. You will have
a good time. Now for a little more "Laus Jacobe." I spoke three discourses in
the Presbyterian Church at Wellington. Since my return I have received a letter
offering me $400 for speaking to them once in two weeks for a year, to which I
declined of course. How and where is Almeda now-a-days? I happen to have a V
in my pocket which please accept.[16] I suppose Trot has not picked up the flowers yet, has she? With a blessing for you both, I am Truly Your James.

                                                        Hiram, February 21, 1861
My Dear Jimmie:
      Every Monday night since you went away, except the one after your visit
home, has brought me a letter from you; so if you continue steadfast in your
course of writing to me, however guilty you may feel at other times lest I may be
thinking of some of your evil deeds, you may always let your conscience remain
untroubled Tuesday nights, for then I am thinking there never was such a
matchless piece of perfection as you. . . .
      I am not real sorry you could not ferret out all the details of that affair at
the close of the term without any further aid. Why couldn't you? It is so disagreeable writing such things. But I suppose I must try and show due charita-
bleness to your stupidity, so with a patience almost heroic I will guide you over
the ground. The Monday night before the close John Streator was coming past
the Udall house and noticing a disorderly appearance of things, called at Mr.
Gisher's room. He found there in different stages of intoxication, Grace,
Baldwin, Sheldon Beardsley and some others whose names I do not remember.[17] Of course, they were all summoned before the teachers the next morning. They testified that they got their liquor of Mr. Udall, 3 pints. Mr. Udall
acknowledged that he let Baldwin have half a pint of brandy for sickness.
Baldwin said he did not ask for it for sickness at all. I cannot tell all that was said
about it; but the result of all was the dismissal of the students from school and

Mr. Udall from longer keeping boarders. Mr. Udall was inquiring today if you had been written to concerning it. I guess he rather thinks that you will reverse the decision of the other teachers concerning him. But I presume that he mistakes—and that it will be the better part of wisdom for him to leave with as little fuss as possible. The loss of his daughter from classes will be a great affliction to the teachers!

I had intended to go to Warren tomorrow but little Trot is so nearly sick with a cold that I do not dare to take her out. Yesterday she had some pretty severe symptoms of croup. We attended to her right faithfully and today they are nearly all gone. Still she has a bad cold, coughs and is hoarse. I shall be very very careful of her and I think that in a few days she will be entirely well. If so I will go to Warren next week, not before Wednesday, though, so you may direct your next letter to Hiram. Are you coming home at the commencement of next term? I want to see you ever so much. If you should come, what would you think of coming on to Warren Saturday and staying until Monday morning? Please tell me all about it in your next. Your "V" came very opportunely. I was afraid I had not quite as much as I needed before going away. Thank you. Don't you think you were rather severe on poor Mrs. Lincoln? You were not called on to admire her beauty if she possess none, of course, but must you place her lower in your estimation because she lacks it?

Trot and I keep the warmest places in our hearts all for you.

Your loving Crete.

Columbus, February 24, 1861

My Dear Crete:

I supposed I should receive the last letter of yours from Warren, and now it makes me shiver to think that you are detained by the illness of Trot. I cannot endure the thought that that terrible croup should be so near her little life. You will, I am sure, be very careful of her. Still I hope you will not be obliged to stay away from Warren. It would be bad not to go now. Mr. Cox is quite sick and his cold has given him such a fever that I think he will not be able to be in his place in the Senate tomorrow. But it is nothing very serious for he has attended church, and we have been reading nearly all day. I must tell you of a killing time that occurred this afternoon. Miss Vaughan is still here. She read Monday evening, but she has so much affectation in her manner that her performances must always be a dead failure. We have read together several evenings, and she finally told us she had a manuscript novel and a volume of poems she was about to publish and requested us read them and give her an opinion and criticism. So yesterday evening we read a few chapters of the novel and today we finished it. Her advantages in Italy, living two years in the same house with Browning, and a companion of Harriet Hasmer, the celebrated American sculptress, have been very fine, and she has a good deal of native talent, but that affectation, which appears not only in her manners but tones, seems to have filled and vitiated all her modes of thought. Her novel was finely written so far as its literary merit is concerned, but her peculiar affectation of attempting the exquisite makes her plot strained, unnatural and ridiculous. So Cox and I read and laughed immoderately at some of the scenes and characters. We made comments freely as we read and laughed uproariously at the whole thing. Just as we had finished the book, a tap at the door leading into Mr. Wright's room was followed by the entrance of the enraged authoress herself. We supposed the room empty as Mr. Wright and his chum were gone. She had heard all our talk and fun. She sailed into the room, demanded her manuscript and was about to throw it into the fire when we interposed and saved the precious document from the flames. The scene that followed I will sometime describe to you. After it was over Cox and I went on a walk, and when fully out of hearing, we broke the Sabbath by unseemly levity. But we placated the lady, and she seems this evening to be in a good flow of spirits.

Please put down to my credit $18 received for my Delaware Lecture, and a charge of 75 cents for mending my overcoat from a tear received on the trip.

Do you think I ought to be at Hiram at the opening of the term? I don't know whether I can conveniently or not. . . . Remember me to Trot in what way you can best do so, and let me hear from you often.

Ever your James.

On March 10 James wrote "I have staid home from church today in consequence of having been this morning seized with a violent diarrhea, which has rendered me unfit for divine, but assiduous in an exceedingly human service." Garfield's roommate's wife, Mrs. Cox, who lived in nearby Warren, Ohio, had just given birth to a second boy, and James wants Lucretia to visit her, which she does.

My Dear Jimmie:

For once the mails disappointed us, and your letters were not received until last night. I am sorry to hear that your *trouble* of last winter has returned. I was hoping you would escape this winter, and to think too that you should put off on so serious affair one of your long eared puns!!

I received a line from Mrs. Cox Tuesday telling me that her family are well again and inviting me there this week, so I am going tomorrow. I can remain only till Monday and I think now that I shall not probably visit at Bro Austin's—consequently have not written to them. Little Trot—precious little darling—grows prettier and smarter every day. She does not creep but manages somehow to get most any place she wants to, and get hold of whatever best suits her little fancy. A few mornings ago I left her in the middle of the floor and went down stairs. Father went up a few minutes after and found her by the woodbox with the tongs pulled out into her lap, and she was going through the process of making a little darky of herself. Father said she dropped the tongs and looked up as kind of scared when he went in, as though she knew she had been in mischief. She has two little teeth now, and from the bad humor she has been in for two or three days past, I think there may be more cutting. I am glad that you talk as you do about the little creature. It seem to me there is no earthly relation so beautiful as that which exists between father and daughter. The tender delicate loving protection on the part of the one, and the entire trust and affection of the other seems the perfection of all that is most noble in man and most loving and confiding in woman.

Warren. Friday evening. Trot cried so last night that I could not finish your letter, so I brought it with me, and now in Mrs. Cox rooms with little Trot kicking up her heels on the bed. Tell Mr. Cox he has one of the brightest keenest looking little babies here that I ever saw. Kenny was very unfortunate to day. He went out to play with clean apron and all and came in with a good deal of the native soil attached to his garments. His mother said he must go so until night and when we went out to supper he was sitting up at the table with the tears running down his cheeks. His Mother asked him what in the world was the matter. "Why," he said, "I have got to go looking so all day." Little Charlie is a manly looking little fellow. Not a bit behind Kenny. Mrs. Cox says I must stay next week and I wish I could; but I must go back Monday, I suppose. I have two classes in French, a beginning class of seven. I do hope you will soon be through with your Legislature. There is need of you at home in another department of business. The school is starting up more encouragingly than we expected. It numbers now 160. I wish I could tell you your duty in regard to staying longer at Hiram. It does not seem to me best, however, unless you can devote yourself and your time more to it than you have done the past year. I think the feeling that you are not much interested in the school is doing it more harm now than almost anything else. I do not mean this unkindly, James. I know how much you have on hand, but I cannot bear to have people think that you are in anything slack or neglectful, and I have been almost afraid that some did think that of you in regard to the school. I am very much of the opinion that you will not be very entirely satisfied with Law. . . .

I have not been very good to you since you went away last, but perhaps you had not thought of it and I need not have put any such idea in your head.

Hoping to hear again very soon, I am ever all your own

Crete.

James accompanied his old school friend, Corydon Fuller, on a trip to Kentucky and Indiana to see if he could help Corydon acquire a newspaper business. In the meantime, Lucretia's father, who was a Trustee of the Eclectic Institute and one of the founders of the school, asked James about his intentions. Here, too, is the first reference to a possible place in Congress.

Columbus, April 14, 1861

My Dear Crete:

After a long delay I received yours of the 11th. Indeed, Crete, I have not omitted writing to you for a week and a half at any time since I came here. My trip with Corydon did however break into my custom to some extent. But surely, you were joking on the first page of your letter. My memory is quite excellent. I remember that I haven't heard from you for nearly two weeks till last night. Ain't we even now? My whole effort to get a place for Corydon has proved a failure. We found numerous obstacles in the way when we reached McArthur and he remained several days after I returned, but accomplished nothing. He went from here to Mishawaka, Indiana, hoping to get a place in an office there. Put down as a memorandum $35, which I lent him.

I have been quite well for the last week, but the work and exciting news have made me exceedingly tired today. I can see nothing now before us but a long and sanguinary war. The wanton attack on Sumter and the surrender of Maj. Anderson can result in nothing else than general war. When I see the outrageous meanness of the democrats, and the timid and cowardly course of many of the republicans, it makes me long to be in the strife and help fight it out. It seems to me that even in the revolution there was no greater need of men to stand by the country and sustain its authority.

A resolution has been adopted by both branches of the Legislature to adjourn on the 23rd. I very much desire to get away by that time, but I fear we shall not. The war news is causing great excitement, and I presume we shall be kept a week longer. Then the little dear Trot is creeping about the floor! Is it a new trick? You have said nothing about it before. I will get her a willow cart when I come home. Does she attempt to talk any yet? It will seem so very strange to hear her. Do you think she will remember me when she sees me? I guess not. I had a letter from your father a few days ago in regard to the Theological Department and my staying another year. I have answered the letter. . . .

If I should go to Congress, we would move there for the winter (isn't this a fine specimen of unhatched chicken?). Cox and I are spending all our leisure time in reading Military Science and the campaigns of Napoleon and Wellington. I will try to write a letter to Trot as soon as I can. The little grump. She don't care anything about me. Kiss her, though, and write in her journal for me. Please don't fail to write—to

Your James.

Columbus, April 28, 1861

My Dear Crete:

I have been too busy during the whole of the past week, and even now, though it is Sunday evening, I have but a short time which I can snatch away from work. I left Ravenna on the evening train Monday, and finding I could not make the connection at Cleveland, I stopped off at Newburgh, saw mother for an hour, made a speech in the village to a large audience, and staid over night at John Clapps.[18] I reached here Tuesday forenoon, and on Thursday went to Cleveland to help organize two regiments. Returned Saturday morning. Cox has been appointed one of the Brigadier Generals and leaves tomorrow morning at five o'clock to organize a camp at Loveland [Ohio]. He takes about 1200 men with him. It now appears probable that I shall be elected Colonel of the 7th Regiment now at Cleveland. If so, I shall probably be ordered into camp before the week is ended. If not, my military history will not begin just [yet]. The more I reflect on the whole subject, the more I feel that I cannot stand aloof from this conflict. My heart and hope for the country are in it, and I could do no justice to the every day duties of life. I found in the camp in Cleveland a company of Oberlin boys, more than half of them students. Charley Bowler and W. D. Ringland were among them.[19] Their Capt. was a Theological student. I am every day impressed with the character of the men who are going into this war. A few days ago there came a company from Ironton on the Ohio River. They were mostly members of a Methodist Church in that place. When they reached here, there were no quarters for them in the Camp, and the Senate, House and Supreme Court room were already full. They were obliged to sleep on the marble floor of the rotunda. Before lying down for the night they gathered into a corner and held a prayer meeting. Their officers led in prayer, and they sang finely. One song was "I'm glad I'm in this Army." Ungodly men who looked on were moved to tears, and one old fellow said to another who made some slighting remark, "I'll whip the first *damned* man that makes sport of them." Such men will fight.

I shall know in a few days my own course. It seems a month since I was at home. Do write me soon and fully of all that is in your heart and also of what is passing on around you. The state of the times makes me think of my private affairs. Has Dr. Manly paid up that note? How much money will you need for the next three months? Please give me an estimate in your next. How has the war affected the school this week? . . . Kiss Trot—dear soul—and receive my love.

Your James.

After much negotiating with the Ohio Governor Dennison as to what rank he might have should he enlist, James finally accepted a Colonelcy. He saw no reason for entering at a lower rank, as some had been doing.

Cleveland, August 14, 1861

My Dear Crete:

I have concluded to go. Shortly after I arrived, I went to the telegraph office and sent a dispatch to the Governor saying I was ready to go, and asked him if I should leave on the next train. It is now past eleven and I have not heard from him. Probably from the lateness of the hour, he failed to get my dispatch. The reason for my asking him the question was from the tardiness of my response, he may have concluded I was not going and have filled the place. If I get an answer tonight, I shall know, certainly, all about it. If not, I shall go to Columbus in the morning and stay if I am still wanted. I presume there is but little doubt but that I shall stay. So far as I am concerned, it is settled.

But I have arranged to send you a dispatch from Columbus, which is to be sent out in the bundle of papers on tomorrow evening's train. See that the boy gets it. In that I will let you know the final result. Until that time, I want my absence left entirely within the circle of yourself and the teachers. Let there be no hint of its purpose.

Concerning my decision, you know how much of a question was before me. The only new view since I left home was the bad news from Missouri, and the slowness with which recruits come in. In case I am not needed I shall come back on the first train and be home Friday morning. In any other case you will soon hear from me. With kisses for yourself and Trot *for more than a day*, I am

Ever Yours. James.

Hiram, August 15, 1861

Dear Dear Jamie:

I cannot write much to you tonight. Thoughts and feeling to which I can give no expression torture and bewilder me until I grow faint and powerless, and my heart with anxious doubts and fears seems to bursting full. But I will not talk of them. I am glad these terrible hours of torturing suspense to you have passed and you can lift up your soul again to energetic action. I will hope and pray that the course you have taken may be the right one and that you may so guide yourself in it that you may find in the loss "a gain to match." Concerning all the directions you have sent, I have tried and will still try to give them good heed. I send your trunk to Garrettsville tomorrow morning. Your undershirts are getting thin, but you will want flannel when you go out into camp which shall be made as soon as I receive orders from you. Also, some new sleeping shirts. I think people are not generally surprised at your course and quite probably will soon come to approve, but how desolate it seems here; how forsaken everything looks as the thought comes home that your guiding hand is withdrawn. Dear little Trot has been calling "Papa, papa" all day. Every time she has heard a step in the hall she would call out "Papa" and go jumping away to meet you, and when she saw it was not you, she would turn away with such a disappointed look that it made my heart ache. Dearest Jamie, write soon, often, and long and believe me ever loving you better than all else. Crete.

❧ NOTES ❧

1. Smith's Panorama refers to a popular form of art in the mid-nineteenth century. Huge canvases of landscapes and buildings would be hung around four walls of a room to create the impression of an unbroken view. This particular panorama must have been that of Russell Smith (1812–1890), a celebrated theatrical scene painter from Philadelphia, who, after a trip to Europe, developed some panoramic paintings of well-known scenes which he took on tour to various cities.

2. Cyrus McNeely was a convert to the Disciples religious sect. He had been inspired by Alexander Campbell, then president of Bethany College.

3. T. M. Allen was a well-known Disciple preacher.

4. W. Pendleton and Robert Richardson were both professors at Bethany; the former later became president, the latter a trustee of the institution.

5. Walter Scott was a close associate of Campbell, as was Adamson Bentley. All of these men were in the first generation of distinguished followers of Alexander Campbell and his Disciples of Christ sect.

6. This sad, perceptive letter was written in September. In October James made the following entry in his diary: "spent the evening with Lucretia. . . . I wish to God I knew what the path of duty was in this troublesome and soul harrassing labyrinth into which I have been thrown by all the past of my life. But I will not harrow that up at this time. Let it sleep while it can, for there must come a waking up day" (Harry J. Brown and Frederick D. Williams, eds., *The Diary of James Garfield* [East Lansing: Michigan State University Press, 1967], 1: 296).

7. Andrew Freeze had been appointed to both the principalship and the position of superintendent of the Cleveland Schools, but the School

Board terminated the former position and in doing so reduced his salary by $300. When he then threatened to resign, the School Board reinstated his earlier salary, and he did not resign. Crete, who left Cleveland before any decision had been made, evidently assumed the Board would not reinstate his salary (W. J. Akers, *Cleveland Schools in the Nineteenth Century* [Cleveland: W. M. Boyne, 1901], 67).

8. N. P. Willis, a contemporary writer of essays and plays, was one of Lucretia and James' favorite authors.

9. The speaker from Toledo, Mr. Gunckel, was publisher of the *German-town Gazette*.

10. Frederick Henry, *Captain Henry of Geauga County* (Cleveland: The Gates Press, 1942).

11. The well-worn cliché of the oak and vine which Lucretia "never ceased to love" had become an irritant to some women. In Augusta Evans' *Beulah*, for instance, "the heroine . . . repudiated angrily the 'clinging-vine' ideal as an affront to her sex" (Herbert Ross Brown, *The Sentimental Novel in America, 1789–1860* [Durham: Duke University Press, 1940], 295).

12. The Soo locks on the St. Mary's River were opened in 1855, and the boat excursion from Chicago or Detroit up through Lake Huron and into Lake Superior was a popular one.

13. Burke Hinsdale, a graduate of the Eclectic, became a close friend of the Garfields'. He later became the principal of Hiram College and finally a professor at the University of Michigan.

14. Earlier in February, James had written of Miss Vaughan, a recitationist from Cincinnati who was performing in Columbus. She is, he wrote, "a Shakespearean reader" who has "travelled in Europe and is an artist and musician. She is finely accomplished," he added. Later, however, he was not so sure about her.

15. Josiah Robbins of Niles, Ohio, served a term in the Ohio House of Representatives.

16. The "V" James refers to is a five dollar bill.

17. While "Grace" and John Streater and Mr. Gisher cannot be found in the roles of Hiram students, Sheldon Beardsley and Baldwin Bentley can be. Baldwin, expelled from Hiram that winter, joined James' regiment in the fall of 1861; he did not survive the Piketon, Kentucky, campaign, dying just a year from the date of this letter.

18. John Clapp graduated from the Eclectic in 1854.

19. Charles Bowler and W. D. Ringland graduated from the Eclectic in 1859.

CHAPTER 4

The Civil War, 1861–September 1862

ONCE HE HAD REACHED CAMP CHASE IN COLUMBUS, *James' chief objective was to fill up his 42nd Regiment with recruits. He succeeded in this task by December 1861, and was soon on his way to his first battle experience. He fought a brilliantly successful skirmish in the Sandy Valley, Kentucky, in early 1862, was promoted to the rank of brigadier general, and was ordered to Tennessee to join General Buell. He was present at the great battle of Shiloh. During the summer of 1862, after weeks of inactivity on the western front in Tennessee and Alabama, James fell seriously ill with his "old complaint" of diarrhea and piles. He was in a dilemma, however, for just at that time friends in Warren—Harmon Austin, Wallace Ford, Harry Rhodes— were pushing him into the Congressional race for his district. If he came home to recuperate, it might look as if he were actively campaigning or it might seem as if he were attempting to escape the dangers of the battlefield. James clearly hoped to be a candidate (already we have seen him mention that possibility to Lucretia), but he did not wish to be seen as eager for the post or cowardly about the War. In the end, he became so ill with dysentery, fever and vomiting that in early August he had to return to Ohio to recover his health.*

The visit home proved an important first step in the development of the Garfield marital relationship. Crete had moved from the rooming house where they had first set up housekeeping in 1858 and, with Trot, was living at home—the Rudolph house down the hill east of the campus. For James' leave, then, the Garfields went off to Howland Springs, a retreat near Warren, where James could escape publicity. This brief, intimate reunion of James with Lucretia and Trot brought the husband and wife into a fresh relationship. Lucretia, evidently, was able to respond emotionally in an altogether new manner, and James felt a deeper love for her than he had experienced since the marriage. Lucretia's analysis of her feelings in her letter about Howland Springs (the last in this chapter) reveals something of the doubts she has had about James' love for her. She now feels greater confidence in this love. She thinks she has come up out of the darkness of the past, and that their love is "perfect." But bad times are still ahead for her.

Of the ninety or so letters exchanged during this period, twenty-three are here included.

We begin, then, with James' first letter home after his arrival at Camp Chase in Columbus, where he begins his army career.

Camp Chase, August 22, 1861

My Dear Crete:

Your good letter was received Saturday night, and the trunk came at the same time. I am not very well, being still hard pressed with my usual malady. But I have commenced to take medicine, and I think it will relieve me soon. Before I write further I wish to apologize for the looks of this letter. I was suddenly called on to act again as officer of the day for today and came away here leaving my pen at my quarters, and so must write, if I get in time for the mail, on foolscap and with this old steel pen. I was very thankful for the many little comforts you had enclosed in the trunk. I find them all coming in play. I will not say much more about my feelings in leaving you and all the dear associations at Hiram, not the least among which is our darling little Trot, but I will say that while I shall at all hazards keep up my heart and work with my might in the duty before me, I shall nevertheless feel very greatly the need of such full and frequent letters from you all as shall make me constantly feel the full knowledge and sympathy of you all. And our darling! tell me all about her, her changes, developments, and try not to let her memory of "papa" "papa" fade away. Have her say it, so that when I come she may know to call me. I think I have no unmanly feelings in regard to the future and my own place in it, but I have more sadness at the thought that should anything befall me she would not remember me. I know how a child feels under such circumstances, and that by experience. Please copy these last few sentences in her Journal. And now with these lugubrious thoughts we will dismiss all that style of talk and look at the bright side which is always the right side. I am entering on the work of the camp with success and shall hope to be able before I leave to be intelligent and efficient.

It is a little odd for me to become a pupil again, but I came into it easily and have no fear of very disastrous failure in learning duty. I think I must have a lot of flannel shirts, but you may wait until I learn more about what style will be needed.

I want you to have the piano seen to and as good care taken of it as possible. I must receive at least $15 per term from the use of it, over and above the expense of tuning. I cannot now tell how soon I will be at home, but probably in two or three weeks. . . .

Since I began this letter I have probably given a hundred orders—among other things held a trial and sentenced a sentinel to a 3 day imprisonment on bread and water for sleeping on his post. Kiss Trot for me and get her finger marks on your letter in some way if you can. Ever Yours and Hers. James.

Hiram, August 25, 1861

My Dear Jamie:

Not until last night did I receive the letter from you, looked for and desired so much through the whole week. It makes me very anxious about you to learn that you are still unwell, and I fear very much that the exposures and necessary irregularities of camp life will prove exceedingly disastrous to your health. You must try and be just as careful as it is possible for you to be, and I think you ought to be more particular about the kind of medicine you take than you are inclined to be.

Cowles[1] says that the physician of their Reg. gave them a great deal of Calomel when they were sick. Some of them were sent out on guard directly after in the rain, consequently had very sore mouths. Don't let any thing of the kind be done to you. Has not Homeopathic treatment generally done well for you?

Little Trot has been almost as much troubled as you for the past week; but is better now. She doesn't forget "papa" yet but every little while her little bird voice pipes out "papa." I believe she thinks about you a great deal. She called your photograph "papa" the other day without being told, and she begins to call you whenever she sees anyone looking at it. She has just waked now and is sitting on my lap eating a piece of gingerbread. I guess I will have her put in her mark here.

"PAPA" I put the pen in her hand and guided it for her and she looked very much pleased. I cannot tell all the cute little things she does which would please you to know. I can scarcely feel reconciled to have you away from her. I want so much that you shall know all her little cunning ways and love her for them, and that she should learn to love and trust you more than all else. Dark and desolate as all my life would seem were you taken away from me, I don't know but I should feel it more for her than myself. But I must not talk or think that you may never come home to us again. It floods my eyes with tears, and fills my heart with breaking. You will come safe to us and bless us with your love and presence, and our darling will know all the sweet joy of having such a father as you may become to her. I will try and look on the "bright side" and be brave for your sake, too, for firm and dauntless as is your spirit I know you will have the strength which the hopeful hearts of friends can give. If any reliance can be placed in our papers, the prospects of the South are darkening, and it may be the war will end sooner than we had dared to hope. . . .

With a loving heart I am yours as ever, Crete

Hiram, October 27, 1861

Dear Dear Jamie:

I do not willingly think you wicked or neglectful, but how can the heart trust all in silence? I know that you are very very busy, but not so busy that you *cannot* write. And it almost breaks my heart that you do not desire the communion with your home which would prompt you to send if but a word to it as often as you can. I have tried to give you up to the wild chances of war with a brave, cheerful spirit, but when day after day passes and you either do not recognize in me the capability to suffer, or recognizing it feel for it the utmost indifference, I cannot keep back the tears. I know you do not wilfully mean to be cruel but you don't know how your neglect crushes my spirit. I will not talk more of it; but ask yourself, Jamie, if you always do by your little wife as you like to be done by. Then ask yourself if you do not suppose she feels somewhat as you would under similar circumstances.

The coming week is to be a sad one to me. There was nothing said about any arrangements for the winter when I was at Columbus, but I suppose you expect me to go to Father's, and this week the term closes and I shall prepare to vacate our rooms. Every article, every piece of furniture as it is taken away, will be a reminder of the hours we have lived together here, and to see them removed will seem like severing heart-strings. Still it is best that I go. I was thinking to box up all your books that cannot be left in your bookcase and on the What-not. Let me know if that be your wish. The probability is that the Music Class next term will not warrant the teachers to rent the piano; and I very much want it with me. I can take very much better care of it than it gets now, and if any want to practice on it, they can do so. I want to practice a great deal this winter, and I cannot unless it is with me. . . . How nearly full is your Regiment now? There is a company of thirty men in Nelson and Windham[2] which was to start for you tomorrow, but this afternoon Elia Ford[3] passed through here bearing a dispatch to them that they were to go into the 41st. They will some of them be very disappointed. . . .

Little Trot is getting as plump and rosy-cheeked as she was last winter. A week ago she walked with me half way down to Miss Mortan's, and a few days after I left her asleep on our bed, and the first Mrs. Northrup knew she had got off the bed and gone down stairs and was at her door trying to get in. Jamie, dear, you will not forget to remember me with a little word on the 11th of November—the anniversary of our marriage—will you? From the Gazette we see that you went to Cincinnati. We would have liked to have gone with you, but you invited us there so soon that Miss Booth could not stay. I dare not think how much I want to see you.

Love to all. Your Crete.

Ashland, Ohio. Nov. 4, 1861

My Dear Crete:

I did not expect to be out making speeches again but here I am at it at the rate of two or three a day. I found if the regiment was ever to be filled up, we must do it ourselves. We selected Ashland County because it had not sent its full quota to the army.[4] I should have gone home, but I really felt that I could not go through the ordeal of separation again. This is a hard place to work in, but we have got the ice fully broken. There is here a set of men who have not given up their partisan prejudices and are still more than half in sympathy with the South. Added to that, there is a style of over-pious men and churches here, who are too godly to be human. Commencing Wednesday evening, I have made eight speeches and have raised 36 volunteers. They all refused me their churches for last evening, except the heretic J. H. Carman, who has been ostracized by the Disciples of this place. He went on to the platform of the town hall with me and I address[ed] a very crowded house. I felt particularly free and I believe I never succeeded better for an hour than I did in characterizing the Christianity of Ashland and all people who were afraid to "do good on the Sabbath Day." I then called for volunteers and six of the best young men in town and the teacher of the Union Schools and a Methodist preacher came forward.

So I think we shall succeed. Indeed I told the Adjt General that I should never return to the regiment till I brought a company. . . .

Give my love to all our folks and write me at this place. I shall not leave before next Friday. Tell Almeda and Harry to write. Love to Trot and Yourself.

Ever your
James.

Louisville, Ky. Dec 16, 1861

My Dear Crete:

I was unable to answer your last good letter, in consequence of receiving marching orders which admitted of no delay. All along we supposed we should be ordered to this place, but a little before midnight of Saturday, a telegraphic order came from Gen Buell ordering the 42nd to proceed with all possible dispatch to Prestonburg, in Floyd County, Eastern Kentucky. We left camp at 9 o'clock Sunday morning, had the banner presentation at the Depot, and at 2:30 P.M. were in motion toward Cincinnati, where we arrived about 9 o'clock. I had sent Col Sheldon on the night before, as soon as the order came, to provide transportation and determine our route. When we landed from the cars a dispatch was in waiting for me from Gen. Buell telling me to send the Regt on toward its destination, and report myself at his Head Quarters for orders. I worked till 2 o'clock this morning in getting on board our men, and baggage and our supplies and transportation teams, which consisted [of] 150 mules, 25 army wagons, and six ambulances for the sick. The boys were very much crowded and I fear they will not be comfortable. Our route is up the Ohio to Catlettsburg, and up the Big Sandy, as far as the steamers can take us, thence overland to Prestonburg. . . . There is great alarm among the inhabitants of the

"Blue Grass" region and eastward. They say there are 6,000 foot and a pack of artillery pressing on toward Lexington and Paris. It is rumored I am to have command of three or four regiments and conduct the expedition. Humphrey Marshall is in command of the rebel force. I called at Gen Buell's Head Quarters soon after my arrival, but he was not in. I am to meet him at his room tonight at 9 o'clock, after which I will write you the results of the interview. I am stopping at the same house where I stopped two years ago when I met the Legislature. The Union was the object [of] that visit, and is of this. I presume I shall leave by [the] first train to join the regiment. I hope so, for I cannot endure the idea of having the boys meet danger, and I not be with them. My first order as I remember it (for it is not with me) ran thus: "The 42nd will proceed with all dispatch by rail and water to Prestonburg, where its Col. J. Swain will report for duty. J. Swain will take command of our forces there and drive back or cut off the rebel now advancing in that place." So you see, if I have no different orders, I shall try my hand in this new kind of argument.

The flag presentation was a fine affair. The Governor told me that the 42nd was the best regiment that had yet been raised in the State. My health is very good, and though I have hardly slept at all for the last three nights, I am feeling finely. It is now nearly time for meeting the General, and I will leave room to write more when I return. (11:45 o'clock P.M.) For two hours I have either been sitting or pacing the room alone. I have had Collin's large Atlas before me and have been trying to get some knowledge of the territory which is to be the scene of my work for, it may be, many months to come. I returned from visiting the General a little before ten o'clock. I found him a very plain, straight forward, frank, decisive appearing man, and he proceeded to business at once. He said he knew about me, and had resolved, for the present, to put me in command of a brigade. Look on the map of Ky. and you will see the RR from Cin. to Paris. That is the western base of my operations. The 40th Ohio Regt is to be sent there tomorrow, and commence the eastward advance as soon as I am ready to move it. The 16th Ohio is to be at Lexington as a Reserve. Six Companies of Cavalry are on the way overland to join my company. These troops are to meet the rebels who are pushing through the mountains, and making towards West Liberty and Paris. The 42nd accompanied by a Ky. Regt, now at Louisa, are to strike down toward Prestonburg and endeavor to cut off the retreat of the enemy. The General leaves the execution of this general plan in my hands. He says he knows but little about the country, or the real extent of the danger. This I must examine and then lay my plans and act accordingly.

When I reflect that this movement covers an area of 6000 sq miles and has no railroad or telegraphic lines, and think how soon the winter will be upon us in all its severity among those mountains, I feel that my hands are very full indeed. But after all, I must confess that I am pleased with the prospect of work. I will write some of you again soon. I can not now tell you where to direct to me, but you may venture to send the next letter to Paris, Ky. Give my love to all the folks. Thank Father for me for his letter. Kiss Trot. Believe me as ever loving and hoping, Your James.

P.S. I send you $60 by Harry [Jones].

Headquarters 18th Brigade
George's Creek, Dec 25, '61

My Dear Crete:

An express rider is just about to leave for the mouth of the river. I have been writing dispatches for the last two hours. We are now within 18 miles of 2500 rebels who have four guns. Our scouts have been very near the enemy's pickets. We are waiting for our Ky regts to come up and have Gen Buell to send us artillery. As soon as these arrive we shall attack the rebels at Paint[s]ville, who are now fortifying the place. We may be attacked where we are, but I do not expect it.

Conceive of my great hurry and pardon this brief note. God grant you may now be enjoying a merry Christmas. I am exceedingly anxious to hear from you. I have had no word, letter or paper since I left Camp Chase.

Love to all. Ever and forever. Your
James.

James' battle of Sandy Valley was fought with conspicuous success against General Marshall, a West Point graduate. Whether it was luck or strategy is another question. At any rate, the story of that skirmish is told in a letter to the Hiram group of friends, dated January 13 and printed in full in Williams, The Wild Life of the Army: Civil War Letters of James A. Garfield. After the battle, James continued to face problems of his own health, a disastrous flood, and then disease.

Piketon, Ky. Feb 23, 1862

My Dear Crete:

It seems to be my fortune to have a constant round of strange adventures. While I was sick, I kept moving the brigade company by company forward to this place, and when four days ago I got well enough to make it prudent for me to leave, I had the 22nd Ky, the 40th Ohio, one company of cavalry, and six companies of the 42nd already up here. The river had been greatly swollen by rains, and a large steamer came up easily over the shallowest places. Still the river was falling. We were detained by breaks in the machinery so that we did not get here until yesterday at 10 o'clock A.M. It had commenced to rain at 4 o'clock in the morning and continued to rain in fearful torrents till near midnight last night. I have never seen the fearfulness of water before. I detailed 200 men to take our stores further up the bank and secure them. We commenced early in the evening and worked till after midnight. I was conquered for the first time. In one hour the water rose twelve feet. It surrounded the camp of the 40th and they barely had time to get their guns and ammunition and save themselves. This morning discloses a fearful scene. The house where I am staying, which is sixty feet above the usual level of the river, is now surrounded. A wild river roars around it on all sides. It is forty rods to the shore. Two large steam boats are up in the principal street of the village. Houses, stacks of wheat and hay, gigantic trees, saw-logs, fences, and all things that float are careening by with fearful velocity. The terrified people of the village have fled to the hills when they could, or have carried their goods to the upper rooms of their dwellings and are waiting, terror-stricken, the mercy of the flood. At day break, I got a horse and rode through a current which came very near sweeping me away to look after the safety of my dear 42nd. I found them safe but Capt Williams' tent was out of sight under water. The noble fellows had given up most of their tents, which were on tolerably high ground, to the women and children, who had fled from their houses. Co A and two others of the 42nd are surrounded—on an island adjoining the one on which I am. Most of the tents of the 40th are gone. All are under water. Many horse[s] are drowned. I hope no men are lost. It is a strange place to be in, where one is utterly powerless to do anything. I hope the flood has reached its height. Three inches more and it will swash through the room where I am sitting. I tremble for the sickness and suffering which must follow. Four battles would not be so disastrous to us. I am very much worn down, but my anxiety for the boys, and the immense amount of work to be done in consequence of the flood, will, I think, keep me from being sick. I have sent for the steamers' yawls to get up a line of communication with the different parts of the brigade. They will be at the door soon. I am stopping with [a] disciple family, the finest in the place, but they are all secessionists. It is one of the painful facts of the rebellion that nearly all the most cultivated and enlightened people in this country, at least, are on the side of the rebellion. This probably grows out of the fact that the leaders of the rebellion were the aristocrats of the South, and they have led off that element with them. The men are as well as could be expected in such a country. Poor Baldwin Bently is gone. He was a noble, brave boy. I cannot tell you how that regiment grows into my affections. Every hardship they suffer makes them dearer to me. The latest news we have gives me hope that the end of the war is not far off. It would be so great a good, if the grand army of the valley could take Nashville and sweep up the great rebel road, let us join it at Abingdon, and make an attack from the rear on Richmond and the Potomac. But let us have patience. I expect never to see you till the war closes, so let us hope that the blood that must be shed may flow fast and finish this terrible work. But I would rather it should flow for seven years in redding torrents than that the great national question should not be gloriously, fully and finally settled.

The water has begun to fall. The sun is breaking out and is gilding the devastation. I must take the yawl which is now coming and gather up the fragments which the anger of the River God has left us. Try to tell Trot how much I love her and how I long to take her in my arms again. I have not heard from you in a long time. The communication will be very slow now. It is 100 miles in a direct line to the Ohio, 190 by river. Do write me often. You have no idea how much I long for letters. Give my love to all our family and friends and remember now as ever your affectionate and flooded, James.

Hiram, March 9, 1862.

My Dear Jamie:

I am just out of bed waiting for the room and water to warm for a bath—do you enjoy any such luxury now?—and will commence a letter to you with the rising of the bright March Sun and the first robins song of the season. The old Winter has seemed angry that he allowed us to pass so quietly and comfortably through his domain and has been sending on after us his storm legions

with snow and tempest; but he is growing weary of his wrath and is leaving us
to enjoy again the songs of birds and the bright suns of early Spring. How I
wish you were at home again! The hours of your absence begin to grow long
and my resolution to grow not weary in waiting begins to waver. Instead of
looking *over* the time to your coming, I find myself looking *through* it and counting wearily the weeks and months that may intervene. Dear Jimmie, will it not
be the gladest day of our lives, the one most full of deep tranquil joy, when with
this wicked rebellion crushed and peace reigning within our borders, you can
come home to be ours again. But I will try and be patient. Nashville is ours,
Columbus is ours and surely the end comes nearer, but I find people are everywhere trembling for the Potomac. They feel that notwithstanding the concen-
tration of those places where they supposed the enemy would surely make a
stand, they will not give up themselves without a fight _____. It is believed
now that they are concentrating the majority of their force there with a desperate determination to make that the Waterloo of the Rebellion. True, it will not
be that to us, for the cause of humanity must triumph eventually, still a defeat
there would place the termination of the war very much farther in the future
and call for new and larger sacrifices both of life and property than have yet
been made.

Will Clapp[5] reached home last night. I have not seen him yet but hear that
he did not leave you floating down the Big Sandy as we might have feared from
your last letter. I scarcely know what can keep you from suffering with the great
losses you have sustained and the slow means you have for obtaining supplies.
How do you feel staying with a secessionist family! Not only must there be an
entire want of sympathy between you, but a feeling on their part at least well
might be bitter animosity toward you holding the command of a hostile army
quartered upon them.

I received a letter from Mrs. Cox a few days since who wants to be remembered to you and her thanks presented for the kind things you wrote of her to
her husband. Gen. Cox was at home awhile this winter but has now returned to
his command. . . .

Little Trot tries to show that she loves you whether she can understand
that you love her or not. Friday night I received a letter from you and she looked
at and kissed it ever so many times without being told it yours. She would look
at it and say "papa papa" then press a kiss from her sweet little lips upon it. It is
a great pleasure to watch her mental growth now. I noticed a few days ago that
her retentive organs were beginning to develop, and it makes her forehead look

still more like yours. Do write to me as often as you can, Dear Jamie. It seems to me I cannot wait more than a week for a letter. Ever your loving Crete.

Piketon, Ky. March 10, 1862

My Dear Crete:

Yours of Feb 24th is just received. There has been no mail except a few stray letters for nearly three weeks. The terrible state of the river and the weather have made it nearly impossible for me to get or send news. Till yesterday our latest papers were Feb 25th. I cannot comprehend why you had not received my letters. There has been no gap between them as long as the time you stated though there was a space of nearly two weeks in which we got no regular mail sent to the Ohio.

So far as our stores are concerned, we are rapidly recovering from the effects of the flood, but we are suffering terribly in health in consequence of the exposure incident to the high waters. There has never been so fearful a condition as our sick list now exhibits. It is really alarming. There are over 400 sick in the hospital at Ashland, and I am this morning sending nearly sixty more. I hope you will not mention this outside the family. I am doing everything in my power to aid those who are sick and to prevent the well from falling sick. But this country is stripped of every comfort. We need relishes, like pickles, sauerkraut, and other antiscorbutics, but not a thing of the kind can be got here. Fifty have died within the last four weeks. Twenty-two of them from the 42nd Regt. I declare to you there are fathers and mothers in Ohio that I hardly know how I can ever endure to meet. A noble young man from Medina County died a few days ago. I enlisted him, but not till I had spent two hours in answering the objection of his father, who urged that he was too young to stand the exposure. He was the only child. I cannot feel myself to blame in the matter, but I assure you I would rather fight a battle than to meet his father. Two Hiram boys came to me last night, in tears, and besought me to send them home. They said they had been taking the Doctor's medicine for several days and were getting no better. They all have a terrible dread of the hospital. Capt Williams came with them. He broke down and cried, too. I told the boys I had been wrestling with sickness myself as with a giant enemy and they must do the same. I talked to them till they felt brave, and then sent them to Capt Williams' tent to have him bathe them, soak their feet, and give them Hygiene pills. I am glad to say they are better this morning. They are Cyrus Mead and Chapman.

A large number of officers are sick. I dare not tell you how small a number of that noble regiment can be mustered for duty. This fighting with disease is infinitely more horrible than battle. We have had but little snow till since March came in. For two weeks we have had mingled snow and rain and horrible mud. I am alarmed but not discouraged. I dare not be that. I hope, and with grounds for it, that April, at least, will bring us settled weather, and restored health. I suppose we are not worse off, perhaps not as bad, as those in the Great Valley. This is the price of saving the Union. My God, what a costly sacrifice! When I read how considerately, and with what distinguished attention, the Government is treating the Rebel officers, who are now prisoners of war, I am fired with the deepest indignation. The 1200 Nabob officers who were allowed to wear their sidearms, and be attended, in Camp Chase by their slaves—and then find fault with that "Gentlemen were put into such a muddy and uncomfortable camp"—and when I remember that that camp was good enough for me and my noble boys to drill in for three months and nobody complained that we were ill used—If the severest vengeance of outraged and insulted law is not visited upon those cursed villians who have instigated and led this rebellion, it will be the most wicked crime that can be committed. The blood of hundreds of the 18th Brigade will before summer be crying from the ground to God for vengeance. I don't want you to feel alarmed to the extent that our present condition would indicate, for I have great faith in the power of will to resist disease. Particularly I desire that you shall not feel alarmed for me. The effort I am making and must make to strengthen others will, I believe, keep me well. I have now accomplished all in this valley I was ordered to. I have written to Gen. Buell for further instructions. On my approach to this place, the remnant of Marshall's force fled through the Pound Gap and is now scattered all the way from Grantsville [West Virginia] to Abingdon [Virginia]. I have not yet received official notification of my promotion, but presume the accounts of the matter are correct. I am very sad at the thought of being more widely separated from the 42nd. Indeed it has been a serious question with me whether I would accept or not, though I presume I shall. I have been doing the duties of the position ever since I came here. . . . I hope you and Trot are well. How are [you] treating her health? There is much danger of being over-cautious of her. The half-naked, half-starved children of this valley are rarely sick. Don't make her a house plant. Tell me all about it. Give my love to the family and all who inquire. Ever and forever,

Your James.

Louisville, Ky. April 2, 1862

My Dear Crete:

I have never so fully realized the fickleness of Fortune and the chances and changes of war as this morning. I arrived here in the night last night with three regiments, all promising ourselves great pleasure in a new and broader field of operations. Ten minutes after my arrival dispatches were placed in my hand ordering my regiments turned over to the Command of Gen Morgan, and myself to report to Gen Buell at Nashville, or wherever he may be in the field. No hint is given of my destination, but it is supposed I am to be assigned a command in the forces that are now gathering to attack Corinth. No matter—in fifteen minutes I leave. I have wakened Col Sheldon and Maj Pardee to bid them goodbye. I dare not let the 42nd Regiment know that I am going. It might make a scene. I know it would nearly break me down. Whether I shall ever see them again in the war, I cannot tell. One thing is sure: I am their General no longer.

The omnibus is at the door. Farewell. You will hear from me soon.

As ever Yours and Trots. J. A. Garfield.

Hiram, April 5, 1862

My Dear Jamie:

I received your dear _____ letter last night and have done nothing but think of you since, except to give a few hours to troubled sleep. In your whole military career so far nothing has happened to which I have been so unreconciled as to this last change. It seems so cruel both for you and the 42nd that you should be torn from them and sent to the command of men who know nothing of you, and the dear boys who so love and reverence you and so look to you for sympathy and kindness be turned over to the command of one who has only a stranger's feeling for them. Surely nothing is nearer slavery than the tyranny of military rule.

But I try to gather some good out of it on which to build hope for you yet. I say to myself perhaps you need all these lessons, but then I would answer, What for! I am more puzzled to tell. The last week has been one of inexpressable sadness to us. Almost every day has brought us tidings from the 42nd of someone dead or dying, and the fearful desolation of war so brought home to us makes hope for anything earthly seem but a fiction. I sometimes find myself

standing still upon the moment with my eyes closed to the past and daring not
to open them to the future. I have never before so realized the strength and
beauty resting in the motto with which Longfellow introduces his Hyperion:
"Look not mournfully into the Past. It comes not back to thee; wisely improve
the Present. That alone is thine; go forth to meet the shadowy Future without
a fear and with a manly heart."[6] And when I have the power to think or act at
all, it is with these beautiful expressive words rising from my heart and resting
on my lips.

I will not write more now. We must trust not our thoughts to go back-
wards, and the future I know nothing of. May the God of armies guide your
head and your hand to do well and quickly the work you have to do in this wild
conflict and give to your heart some solace in its fierce struggles.

Precious little Trot is well. All our love to you now and forever.

Crete.

James upon joining General Buell's Army was made commander of the 20th Brigade,
in General Thomas J. Wood's Sixth Division. The great battle of Shiloh, which James
describes, had taken place on April 6, when Grant's forces were overrun by a powerful
attack from the armies of A. S. Johnston and Beauregard; and then on April 7, when
the Union armies, with the help of the reinforcements of Buell, retrieved the land lost
the day before. James did not participate in this, the bloodiest battle yet fought on
American soil.

Battlefield, 12 miles from
Corinth, Miss. April 9, 1862

My Dear Crete:

I sent a letter to you from Savannah, just [as] I was embarking my Brigade
to go to the battle. We landed from steamers at a place called Pittsburg, nine
miles above Savannah, about half past one o'clock. The battle had been raging
since early dawn, and the enemy were just beginning to fall back slowly. Gen
Wood sent orders for us to proceed to the front with all possible dispatch.
I hurried my Brigade on and reached the front before three o'clock. I was there
halted to await further orders. For an hour we stood amid the roar of the battle,
the shells bursting around us occasionally, and the grape shot falling on all sides
of me and my staff. We had ridden forward to watch the indications and await

orders, but the tide [of] battle swept over, and as the sun went down our division was ordered to the extreme front where we bivouaced during the worst night of mud and rain I ever saw. Yesterday we pursued the enemy in an armed reconnaisance between three and four miles, where we were attacked by 800 Texan Rangers, and as many more Alabama cavalry. They made a most desperate attack driving back our advance (a Regt of cavalry and one of infantry) killing 19 and wounding 40 with nearly an equal loss on their side. They were, however, soon driven back, and their camp destroyed. On the whole this is no doubt the bloodiest battle ever fought on this Continent, in which has been mingled on our side the worst and the best of generalship, the most noble bravery and the most contemptible cowardice. Gen Grant was encamped on the west side of the river with a very large army, and on Sunday morning, very early, he seems to have been surprised by an overwhelming force of the enemy who came down with a front line of battle three miles in length and a long column supporting it in the center. Gen Johnson was in Supreme Command, Beauregard in the Center, Bragg and Hardee on the wings. By some criminal neglect, not yet explained, their approach was not discovered till fifteen minutes before the attack. Their vast column moved on sweeping Grant's advanced Brigades before it like leaves before a whirlwind. Here and there, some brave officer formed his line and withstood the shock till the long line of dead and wounded was greater than the living. In this way the enemy drove on for four miles, till our force was driven to the steamboat landing, where it must have been annihilated or captured, but for the two gunboats, which sent shells with terrible effect into the columns of the enemy and forced him back from the river. This night closed in over a most disastrous day for our arms and our honor. It was the enemy's evident intention to cut off Grant before Gen Buell should arrive via Nashville and Columbia. In the night, however, our column reached the river and began to cross. Early next morning the battle was resumed, both parties having been strongly reinforced. Inch by inch the enemy were driven back over the ground they had captured, and as night closed in our line of battle, five miles in length, had swept the enemy back over a space of six miles. Such a scene as this 30 square miles presents beggars all attempt at description. If I live to meet you again, I will attempt to tell something of its horrors. God has been good to me, and I am yet spared. After returning from our reconnaisance last evening, we slept again on this ground without blankets. It rained heavily for three hours the latter part of the night. Today we are beginning to bury the dead. I presume we shall soon move on Corinth.

My health has never been better, though I am entirely without camp equipage. My horses and servants, trunks, mess-chest are all back. Indeed, I have nothing of my own, save the clothes on my back. When they will be here I do not know. I shall telegraph for them today.

I have almost been glad that my dear 42nd is not with me—there has been such terrible exposure of the soldiers here. But, Oh how I grieve at our separation.

Kiss our precious little Trot for me a hundred times. God bless you and her with the richest of his infinite love. Remember me to Father and Mother and all the family. Tell Harry and Almeda I wrote to them a short time before I reached Savannah.

My letters must be address[ed] to me "Care of 20th Brig, 6th Division Army of the Ohio—via Nashville—to follow the Brigade." This voluminous direction will cause letters to reach me, and I hope a great number will come.

Ever and forever, Your James.

Hiram, April 19, 1862

My Dear Jamie:

After two weeks of torturing anxiety we begin again to hear from you. Tonight I have just received your letter from Savannah written fifteen days ago. Two nights ago the one came from the battlefield. . . .

These last letters fill my eyes with tears and my heart is near to you with all its sympathy and love, and I live close beside you through all those battle scenes but with my eyes closed to all but you. I cannot think of the horrors this terrible war is planting around our brave boys. I could neither eat nor sleep nor live should I give myself up to the contemplation of the sufferings and miseries of those who are fighting for us. I only make the hours endurable by filling them so full of some employment that I cannot think.

Today is my birth day again, and the anniversary of two days of sorrow to our nation. How full of unspeakable joy would my heart be were you here tonight to read to me this chapter you selected two years ago, and to give to me your blessing to go away with into this new year. May its close find you rescued from all the perils of this war and safe beside me.

Sunday eve. The weeks come and go and each takes you farther and farther away, more and more into the uncertainties which are hidden in the obscurity of the battle smoke until it seems sometimes that I have lost sight of you entirely and my heart stands still with waiting to know if, when that dark sulphurous cloud shall lift, you will again appear. Dear Jamie, our Heavenly Father alone can protect and save you. In Him is all my trust. To Him can I confide all my hopes and anxieties and desires concerning you, as I dare not even to you speak them.

The papers now predict another fierce fight at Corinth. Our Generals have in Beauregard a mighty spirit with which to cope, an adversary they need not despise, and had they known this better, the fields of Shiloh might never have been drenched with the blood of that dreadful slaughter. I am glad you have found some friends in your new Brigade. Remember me very kindly to Ellis. But I hope you will never love another Reg. as you have loved your dear 42nd. I met Harry Jones at Solon, heard his lecture but could get only a moment to talk with him. He was sure that you would get them with you again. . . . I found your Mother not very well. She thinks and worries too much about you. She was mourning that you did not write to her oftener. *Jamie, Jamie!. . . .* Little Trot says papa is "way gone Kucky."

No more now. With all our love, Crete and Trot

Field of Shiloh, April 21, 1862.

My Dear Crete:

After the longest space that ever intervened between your letters [to] me when away, yours of the 5th inst was received. But it was on the way during the confusion and almost entire suspension of the carrying trade consequent upon the great battle, and so only reached me a few days ago. It is the only word from northern Ohio I have had since I left the Big Sandy. I assure you, my Dear Crete, I have never been in so much need of letters from home as since my arrival here. Still, I am getting along as well [as] is possible for me to without the 42nd. I am, by slow degrees, recovering from a violent attack of bloody dysentery, which was accompanied by an incipient attack [of] piles. I never suffered such acute and crushing pain in my life as I did for 40 hours during that attack. I should probably be entirely well, but for the severe and continued rains. There has not been four hours cessation of heavy cold rain for the last three days and nights. From Saturday morning to Sunday evening I was on outpost duty with my whole Brigade, and it rained continually. I was wet through and through, and the effect has been rather bad on my malady, but I am so much better today that I believe I have seen the end of this attack. My pickets and videttes were so far out that they could occasionally see the pickets of the enemy. I found a group of twelve tents in the woods beyond our pickets, where there were 30 wounded rebels, attended by a surgeon and a few soldiers. We sent them food and what comforts we could, but dead men were lying in among the living, and sight and smell were terrible. We buried the dead and were in hearing of the command of the officers of the rebel outposts. The horrible sights we have witnessed on this field I can never describe. No blaze of glory that flashes around the magnificent triumphs of war can ever atone for the unwritten and unutterable horrors of the scene of carnage. I hope you will find a sketch of the battle of Sunday and Monday, written by "Agate" of the *Cincinnati Gazette*. It is in the main very correct and is one of the best battle sketches I have seen. I am still in a rather unpleasant condition in regard to my personal arrangements. I left Louisville with nothing by [but] my trunk overcoat and belt pistol. The trunk I was obliged to leave at Columbia to be brought forward on a government wagon, but I have heard nothing of it since and fear I never shall. It contained all my clothing, letters, commissions etc. so that I have not even a change. When the Aid Society was down with a steamer for the wounded come down from Cincinnati, I found Dr. Beckwith[7] and a Mrs. Noble of Cleveland and also Mrs. Wilcox of Painesville, who came as representatives of the Aid Society, and they gave me a pair of drawers and an undershirt. But for that I should have been wearing the same underclothes more than three weeks. I do not hear from my horse or from Green.[8] I hear incidentally that my boy Jim, who came over to me at the Battle of Middle Creek, was kidnapped at Louisville, but was rescued by a writ of Habeas Corpus. This circumstance caused a panic among the colored men connected with the 42nd and Prof[9] went home partly because he was sick. The Major wrote me he believed it was because I was gone. At last accounts Green was feeling blue about coming down here, and I am inclined to think he thought prudence the better part of valor and has gone home. Still I hope to see him and my horse "Bill". I have telegraphed Capts Plum and Heaton, now in Cincinnati, to send for my horse Harry, now in Elyria, where I sent him when I found what a country we had to operate in, in the Sandy Valley. I have chosen Ben Lake (Lt. in a Cavalry Co in Piketon) as one of my aids. He will be here in a week or two. You remember him when he was a student in Hiram. A few days since I met his father (Bro Constance Lake of Wooster [Ohio]) here in search for his son Joseph. He was nearly distracted. His son belonged to an artillery company, and was very sick with the typhoid fever. When the battle was raging, and while his companions were gone for a team to take him out of danger, he arose from his bed and in his wild fever delirium, ran down to the landing. He was seen on the shore amid the hurrying crowds, and that is the last trace we can discover. His father has searched for days and has now gone down the river to search the hospitals through, to see if he may not in his wild-ness have got on a boat among the wounded and been taken below.[10] Faint hope! but it is a father's. Dear little Trot! how is she tonight? Did you know that I am farther away from you now than ever before? There are a thousand miles between us tonight. I need not tell you how great a joy it would be to me could that space drop out and bring me to you. Do write me long and frequent letters. Tell me what you hear about the 42nd as well as the friends at home. . . . I send you in this $50: a $30 Treasury note, and two ten dollar bills. I should have sent you some before, but I could not get the proper exchange. I have lent some money to Dr. Robison to invest for me. Tell me when you want money and how much. Give my kind regards to all the family and friends. Ever Thine and Trots,

James.

In camp, nine miles from Corinth. May 4, 1862.
My Dear Crete:
    Immediately after leaving Capt Plumb on the boat at Pittsburg Landing, I returned to camp, and at 5 o'clock yesterday morning we broke up our encampment and moved forward to this place, or rather this deserted field. I pitched my tent in a little sassafras grove and here we received orders to pre-pare for battle early next day (that is today). About 4:30 in the afternoon a fierce cannonading a few miles to the left [began]. We turned out and stood under arms, but in about an hour the cannonading ceased. We passed the night very pleasantly, drank sassafras tea for breakfast, and are now waiting orders to move forward. The fight last evening may have changed the aspect of affairs to such an extent that we may not move forward today. I hope not, for there is a sentiment widespread in the army, even among those who are hard men and blasphemers, that battles begun of the Lord's Day are not a blessing to the attacking party. I presume, however, there will not be more than a reconnai-sance and mutual maneuvering to feel of the enemy and learn where he is

located. In this calm Sunday morning of anxious waiting I sit by the rough desk in my tent to write again in the hope that this will reach you before May is gone. The past night and the morning thus far have been strangely quiet for the camp of a great army. There is the peculiar quiet and subdued manner which characterizes men who are on the eve of great events, in which their own lives are at stake. I rode alone in the woods this morning, and saw little groups here and there seated in the leaves in low earnest conversations, sometimes a little group with a bible in their midst, sometimes a man by himself reading a pocket-worn letter. Men who are usually rough address each other with more than usual gentleness of manner. All this tells me that these men will fight with great desperation. It is understood that Gen Mitchell is moving up to form a junction with us and every thing indicates a very great battle. There has been no battle where the preparations were on so gigantic a scale as this. Since the battle of Shiloh, we have been reinforced by Pope's Command 20,000 strong, and the remaining Brigades of Grant and Buell, and all our arrangements of forage and provision betoken vast operations. God grant that this may be the last great bloody sacrifice of the war in the Mississippi Valley. I would not write you on the eve of battle if my letter would reach you before you could hear from me in any other way, for I would not give you the anxiety consequent upon such a letter. But I know that long before this letter reaches you, you will have heard the results of matters here. I have written you so frequently and so fully of late that you will have a full knowledge of all my doings hitherto. I am still in great anxiety to hear from you, not having had a word since April 6th. Yesterday I received a letter from Dr. Robison, dated April 23rd, so you see there is no obstacle in the way of letters reaching me. I trust you will not fail to write to me very frequently, so that letters will keep reaching by and by, even though they may bear an old date when they come. I am very glad to know that Capt Plumb will visit you soon, and carry the hand grasp I gave him directly to you. You will not forget, I hope, to send me your picture and Trot's. Is she growing in size and beauty? Does she learn to talk rapidly? Tell me about her. Harry wrote to me asking me to allow my name to go down in the catalogue as President of the Eclectic. Do you know anything about it? Why does he want it? . . .

My trunk has come but not . . . my horse. I am riding a little yellow Texan horse which we captured from the Texas Rangers in our reconnaisance the day before the battle of Shiloh.

Give my love to all our dear friends and brethern. I hope you and they are enjoying a sweet and peaceful Lord's day in the church. I have never longed so much as now for a quiet day in Church and a good religious sermon from some good man.

Ever and forever, I am Yours and Trot's,

James.

Captain Ralph Plumb of Oberlin, who was James' friend in the Quartermaster Corp, visited Lucretia in Hiram with letters from James and news about his health. Crete has something to say about the cigars Plumb is carrying in the following letter, in which she also speaks of the Hinsdale wedding. Burke Hinsdale, who had been a student of James', became president of Hiram College before going on to become a distinguished professor of education at the University of Michigan. He and James developed an important intellectual relationship over the years.

Hiram, May 25, 1862.

My Dear Jamie:

Every week of this bright moon of blossoms has brought me one or more letters from you, and, dear Jamie, do you know how much lighter is my heart and brighter my life when these sweet tokens of remembrance and affection are scattered thickly through the months?

Yesterday we were all up at Cleveland to attend Burke's and Mary's wedding—all but Harry. He was called to speak the funeral discourse of Ann Calender of Newton Falls, Mr. Calender's oldest daughter. The wedding was a very quiet, pleasant affair. The day was extremely beautiful. A little company of twenty or thirty select friends were gathered, and the ceremony took place at two o'clock P.M., Harvey officiating.[11] Burke and Mary both looked well, Mary the best I ever saw her. She is in fine health now, was dressed very neatly in light silk with no ornament but a simple wreath of bridal flowers around her hair put up in plain style and a few prettily arranged in the fastening of a neat little collar, and we all said that we felt when we saw her standing beside Burke so womanly and dignified that she was indeed very good looking. Mary is intelligent and interesting company, and I hope that her love and respect for Burke will make her more careful to attend to all those little comforts which make a home inviting. I believe she has the ability to do so, and I hope that her desire to please Burke will be sufficient enticement to make her come up to the full measure of her ability. We all missed you, and Burke said that it had been one of the brightest anticipations of his boyhood that you should be present on this occasion. Your absence and his mother's illness were the only drawbacks of the most entire happiness of us all. Mrs. Hinsdale is suffering with an attack of some nervous affliction which has completely prostrated her, so that she is unable to be about at all. Mr. Hinsdale, nor Louise, could leave her, so that none of Burke's family were present except Boldan. So much for Burke's marriage.

Perhaps the next [marriage] will be Harry's, but I have far less hope for his and Libbie's happiness than for Burke's and Mary's.[12] I have written so much at length because I know that you are interested in all the minutiae of your friends' doings, even more than if you were one of those little souled men who never get beyond little things. What would you say to know that little Trot had started out in life for herself? A few days ago Mr. Brown found her in the street down by his house crying "Mama, mama"! The little thing had opened the gate and gone through and not being able to open it from the outside started off. We had not missed her at all and when I thought of how far she might have gone and what might have happened to her, I can not tell you how I felt. It seemed to me that I should never dare let her get out of my sight again. And to think of the terrible feeling of loneliness that must have come over the little creature as she traveled along calling for Mama. It almost makes me cry to think of it. She says she loves papa, and I think she begins to understand what she means when she says so. The 42nd have been seeing some hard times from lack of provisions. The roads have been so bad that it was almost impossible to get anything to them. The boys say that nothing on the Big Sandy can compare with their marches to Cumberland Ford. Joe[13] says Napoleon did not encounter more difficulties crossing the Alps.

Jamie, I cannot help thinking about that box of cigars I saw in Capt Plumb's valise, and I cannot but feel kind of sorry that they were ordered. It does not make me love you less, but it makes me feel sad that you do not show your strength to desist the temptation of such gross pleasures of appetite. I am glad that you were so entirely well again. Try now to keep so. The warm season, as it approaches, will try you _____ unless you use great care. My letter of April 19th you had not yet received, it seems. I presume you have received most of the others before this.

Forever thine. Crete.

Near Corinth, June 10, 1862

My Dear Crete:

By some oversight Capt Farrar went away without the letter, and it lies here yet. I have now received yours of June 2nd. It is a great comfort to me to hear from you regularly and to know that you and the dear little one are well. Of course, everything in her growth and happiness are full of interest to me. I am, however, made anxious by the confession made in your last letter, where you say: "She is such a little mischief that she nearly gets the upper hands of me sometimes." Her young intellect knows almost instinctively where the vulnerable point in parental authority is, and just when is the opportune moment to storm it. When you ask her what you shall do for such mischief, and she recommends "pak" as a remedy, I fear it indicates that your authority has followed the track of your medical faith to become Homoeopathic to some degree. Of course, I am at so safe a distance from her witcheries that I can give advice of so staid and proper a kind as this without committing myself for inconsistencies. I will say concerning your passage about "spanking" as another has said of smoking: "It does not make me love you less, but it makes me sad that you should not show more strength in resisting the temptation to such weakness." Seriously, is there no danger that you are letting her will remain undisciplined? You see I changed the word from "get" to "remain," for the will of a child is in the beginning wholly untamed and undisciplined. I have no doubt that gentleness of spirit is to a great extent an acquired possession and that only by control. Please write me a letter about it.

I am taking some purgative medicines and so am not so well today though my general health is improving. . . .

Poor Augustus[14] has had a terrible time. It will be doubtful whether he gets back into the army this season. His recovery must be very slow. I want you and Almeda and Harry to go and see him.

Since I have been sick here, I have been indulging in novels. I have read Bulwer's "Strange Story"[15] and Dickens' "Great Expectations." Almeda sent me a book just before I left the Sandy Valley, which was locked up unread in my desk and is now in Cincinnati. Tell her about [it]. I have never acknowledged the receipt of it, though I have intended to, but forgot it when I have been writing to her. I hope to read it sometime. With much love to you and Trot and all, I am

Ever your James.

After weeks of inactivity on the western front near Corinth, Garfield was ordered into Alabama.

Tuscumbia, Alabama, June 14, 1862.

My Dear Crete:

We reached this place early this morning, having marched since daylight. We spend the day here taking in a supply of forage and provisions. We shall move on tomorrow morning. Our immediate destination is Decatur. It is very severe on our poor boys to march in such hot weather in this sultry climate. For two days we have passed through a splendid country. Great plantations with magnificent residences fill this rich Valley of Tuscumbia. No one who sees the splendor and luxury of these wealthy planters' homes can fail to see that the "Peculiar Institution" has great claims for the rich and yet no one can fail to see that it is the poor man's bane. We pass these fine plantations and see the slaves toiling for masters and masters sons who are in the rebel army fighting us, and we let them stay at their toil. A regiment preceded us a few days ago, and as it passed a cotton field, the whole drove of slaves came to the road and shouted for joy, saying, "Now we are free!!" One who acted as foreman for the rest said, "Take us with you, we will work, we will do anything for you." The Union Colonel answered with terrible blasphemy which I will not repeat, "Go back to your plough, you black villain, or I will put a bullet through you." The poor slaves went back to suffer not only their terrible bitter disappointment, but all that is in store for them in consequence of this expression of their wishes.

I could chill your blood with the recital of horrors that have resulted to slaves from their expectation of deliverance and their being abandoned to death at the hands of their overseers. But I have not time nor heart to write these things. The full day's march nearly exhausted me. Yesterday I stood it better, and today I am quite strong. I shall be busy drawing my supplies and preparing for the march.

Direct your letters as before and they will follow me. I presume the address will be changed when we reach Decatur, but I don't know what it will be.

Love to Trot and all
Ever your James.

In Camp near Decatur, Ala July 5, 1862.

Dear Crete:

By some unaccountable delay your letter of June 9th did not reach me till last night, though I had ten days ago received one from Harry mailed at Solon June 16th. One also came last night from Harry mailed at Newton Falls June 28th. There would seem to be some fault at the Hiram office. Till last night I have had no mail since we left Tuscumbia ten days ago, but we are now in R.R. communication with the North, and I hope our mails will be more regular and rapid. I am sorry to have to tell you that my health is not only not improving but getting worse. I have kept hoping that each attack of my besetting disease would be the last, but it has lately returned with a vigor and stubbornness which I am quite unable to control. I had begun to regain strength and weight, was weighing 177 pounds, but the last week has run me down to 168, and I am suffering a good deal of pain as well as weakness. If I do not get better soon, I shall get a sick leave to go as far as Cincinnati if not all the way home. Still I am hoping to be able to work on till I can set myself right, though I have not been so much discouraged about my health since I came into the army. We have rebuilt over a hundred miles of railroad, and are now lying still with no apparent aim or future purpose. It has been supposed we were going into East Tennessee, [and] it may still be our destination, but there seem to be no vigorous symptoms of any movement. Gen Mitchell has accomplished a good deal, but his men have committed the most shameful outrages on the country here that the history of this war has seen. He, Gen M., is reported to have resigned. At any rate, he has gone to Washington to see about his future in some way.

A number of people have written me about running for Congress this fall. I have not determined what to say about it until I can learn more of the [state] of feeling throughout the district. I would, of course, rather be in Congress than in the Army, if there is to be no more active service, for I have no taste for the dull monotony of Camp Life, and then too I can dispose of my life to more advantage than to confine it to the inglorious quiet of a Brigade Camp. Still, I am very unwilling to do anything that would look like a desire to leave my place in the army, nor will I, as long as my health will hold out. It is that which made me say I might go as far as Cincinnati if I did not go clear through home— should I continue unwell very much longer. To go home just now would, I fear, be misconstrued into a purpose to make political capital for myself. I have been

[so] thoroughly dead militarily since I came to the Tennessee that I hardly see how I can be sufficiently remembered to make my return a matter of much comment. Still it might be, and I don't [see] why it is, but I have a more than usual horror at being hauled over the coals of political persecution again. What do you hear said about the Congressional matter?

I wish you would send me a catalogue of the Eclectic, and also tell me about the Commencement. Have you recd a letter from [me] enclosing $50? I sent it about the 12th of June. I thought of our little darling a thousand times on the 3rd and wondered how many of her birthdays I should be permitted to enjoy with her. Dear little creature, I cannot tell you how anxious I am for her growth in beauty, health and intelligence.

Yesterday we had a celebration of the 4th. I was hardly able to sit up but the officers of the Division insisted that I should speak and I went out and spoke about 20 or 30 minutes. I did not know but I had lost the trick of speech, but I found the old feeling coming back to me with all its memories of other days. We had a very pleasant time, though a strange one. Several Disciples of the vicinity had been here to visit me. There is a church in the village of Mooresville near by and they have sent up inviting me to speak to them on Sunday next. If I am not too unwell I have a notion to speak to them.

I hope to hear from you again in regard to what you think about the mat-ters referred to above.

Love to all
Ever your James.

Reference to Colonel Turchin in the following letter is to a Russian émigré who allowed considerable pillage by his troops in northern Alabama. James sat on the court martial, which concluded with a decision against Turchin. Before the punishment could be meted out, however, Turchin was promoted to brigadier general without prejudice.

Athens, Ala. July 17, 1862
My Dear Crete:

Your two favors, one of June 27, by the hand of Col Hazen, and the other by post, dated July 6th, were received within a few days of each other, and since I have been in this place. This is the 13th day of the Court Martial, and we have only just closed the evidence for the prosecution. The case is a very important one, but exceedingly tedious in the almost endless extent of its details. The horrible character of the outrages which have been committed here are in striking contrast with the character of the officer (Col Turchin) who is charged with the responsibility of allowing their perpetration. From the accounts we had heard of him and his doings we had expected to meet as fierce and brutal a Muscovite as the dominions of the Czar could produce. But though he is a Russian by birth and education, yet when he came into Court, we met a fine manly figure, with broad expansive forehead, mild blue eye, with an unusual depth of piercing intelligence which at once won respect. Though he was suffering from the effects of fever which gave him a most severe headache, he was not excused by the Court, and for ten days he has sat patiently while citizen after citizen (rebels all) have rehearsed and we have recorded the outrages of the men under his command. Though by a fiction of military law, the prosecution has been striving to fix upon him the responsibility for robbery of citizens, rapes of female slaves, yet during all that time he has borne himself so much like a noble souled man that he has quite won my heart. In conversation with me today I gathered his history as follows. He was educated in the artillery school at St. Petersburg, and after serving some time in the Army entered the Imperial Military Academy, and there graduated, winning a place on the Imperial Staff. During the Crimean War he was Col on the Czar's staff and had the control of 30,000 men. There are few places in the American Army that afford more honor or emoluments than that, but saith he to me: "The dream of Freedom was before my eye and in my heart, and I could not rest. I abandoned my post in the Army, gave up my serfs (for I owned a number) and came to America. I had studied engineering in my native land, and having settled in Chicago, I became an engineer on the Ill. Central RR. When the war broke out I was called to command a regiment and have lately become nominated by the President as Brig Gen, but I do not want a military position. I left the art of war in the old world to reap the peacable fruits of freedom in the new, but since I have been in this army I have tried to act for the best interests of this noble country. I have tried to teach rebels that treachery to the Union was a terrible crime. My superior officers do not agree with my plans. They want the rebellion treated tenderly and gently. They may cashier me, but I shall appeal to the American people and implore them to wage this war in such a manner as will make humanity better for it."

I have tried to give you the substance of the thoughts of a man who will probably be dishonorably dismissed from the Army in a few days, but who, nevertheless, has won my heart and whom I will always be glad to call a friend. My duties are exceedingly unpleasant. Col Stanley, a brother senator in 1860–61, and Capt (prof) Edgaston of Cleveland, are both to be tried before us.[16] I am glad to tell you that I am considerably better; indeed I am here got almost entirely well since my last letter. I am stopping [at] a Dr Maclin's, a wealthy planter, where I have a fine room and the best of accommodations. I take a shower bath every morning. Doesn't that astonish you! Tomorrow, during a recess of the Court, I go out with him nine miles [to] visit his plantation and 95 slaves.

As I have long expected, the enemy has run through our extended lines, and cut off several important lines of communication. We have been cut off from Nashville several days and our whole army is on half rations.

Again I repeat the sad truth that we have no Generals. In this respect, the South has far outstripped us. How long I shall be on this Court I cannot tell— I fear, a long time. Write me at this place and it will reach me whether here or not. Give my love to all the folks. . . .

Kiss our dear little Trot for me. I thought of her on her birthday, but was too ill to write.

Ever yours, James.

One cannot help noting the irony of Lucretia's remark in the following letter: "I don't know but politics *is to be the death of you yet." Just nineteen years from this July James will lie dying of "politics."*

Warren, July 20, 1862.

My Dear Jamie:

The past week finally brought me another letter: the first for almost four long weeks. I need not tell you how glad I was to hold in my hand and let my eye follow the lines of another letter from you; but I am made exceedingly anxious by what it contains concerning your health. I don't know but *politics* is to be the death of you yet. If life and health are to be made secondary to political interests, I shall certainly regret that your friends have made any move regarding them. Since the move has been made, however, I fear you cannot come home on any plea without subjecting yourself to much severe and unkind criticism.

It is too bad, but if you can do no better you must come as far as Cincinnati. And I hope you will do so immediately, unless you are getting better.

Miss Booth and I came down here (to Bro Austin's) last Friday morning. Harmon is feeling great anxiety about the best course to pursue in regard to you and is working in his quiet cautious way to accomplish what he has undertaken. Yesterday morning he went with Almeda to attend a Methodist Conference now sitting at Youngstown with the secret purpose of sounding as many as he might be able of those he would meet there from southern Trumbull and Mahoning Counties. I met Maj. Hall on the street yesterday.[17] After chatting a moment he remarked that he noticed in one of the Ashtabula papers that your name was proposed as candidate for the coming nomination. I did not know whether to count him as friend or foe, so made only an indifferent response. He then went on to say that he was afraid from the style of the article that it was not authorized and would not make much impression. From some remarks that followed I thought I might count him friend, so drew him on to tell what he thought your prospects were. He said he thought there was no doubt but that Ashtabula Co. would go for you if it were generally known that you would accept it. He said the impression was quite general that you did not want it and some of the other candidates were trying to strengthen that impression for their own advantage. I did not think best to say very much but told him you did not want any great effort made to gain the nomination, still if the people gave it to you voluntarily, I presumed you would accept it. He seemed to think there was not enough being done in Portage [County]. I shall tell Mr. Austin what he said when he returns, and he can take it for what it is worth. I sent you in Miss Booth's letter of a week ago a letter to you from Mr. Spencer[18] regarding the matter, and asking you if you would allow your name to go before the people as a candidate. We sent the letter via Nashville and perhaps you may never get it. Are you not growing discouraged at our present prospects? It seems to me the night grows darker.

I should have had a very pleasant visit at Aurora had it not been for my face. One of my teeth ulcerated and my face was so swollen as to shut one eye. But it soon gathered and discharged a good deal, so that it is now almost entirely well. Trot has behaved herself like a little lady. She and Charlie Harmon had some grand plays. She is so pleasant and happy and behaves so well most of the time that it seems to be a pleasure to every one to have her around. Yesterday she went down town with us and I took her to a barber's and had her hair shingled. She was a little afraid but I held her on my lap and with a little coaxing and telling her that she must sit still, we got along very well with her. This is the first time her hair has been cut, and I send you a little curl to put in with her picture. You cannot think how much she looks like you with her hair cut. Do you remember the image of Wellington Hanna [Austin] has standing among her house plants? Trot persisted in calling it papa, and one day I found her sitting on the stone hearth holding it close in her arms. When she saw me coming she hugged it up close to her little heart and says "O I dot papa." I do want you to see her so much.

I don't know why my letters do not reach you. I write every week and wait two three and sometimes four weeks for a word from you. I sometimes feel as though I must cry. . . .

Wednesday morning. I had no idea of keeping this unfinished until this time. But it is just as well for Mr. Austin and Miss Booth have returned and Miss Booth will write, too. Mr. Austin tells me that Hall is blowing around about you, saying that you ought not to have the nomination. That you have done nothing yet militarily to deserve it. Of course, he has a right to his opinion but I cannot tell how indignant I am that he should have shown to me such a false face, and in the guise of friendship urged the necessity of your friends making more strenuous efforts for your nomination. He need not have said anything about it if he did not favor you. Thanks to my *reserve* for once I said nothing out of which he could make any capital. Darling Jamie, I feel as though I wanted to take you ill home to my heart and hide you away in some corner of it where the bitterness and calumny of political foes and the envy of little souls could never reach you. But you are too big and brave, and I can only stand by you and let my presence shield a little spot.

Yours most lovingly, Crete.

Augustus Williams, the captain in James' 42nd had contracted typhoid fever when in Kentucky. For many months he had been near death, and in July he finally died at his home in Ravenna, near Hiram.

Solon, Ohio. July 27, 1862

My Dear Jamie:

I scarcely know how to tell you of the sad news which now fills all our hearts with pain. Augustus is dead. We had all supposed him well and he thought himself so until he suddenly grew worse and died. I have not heard the particulars yet, did not hear of his death till yesterday, the day of his burial. Had I heard in season I should have tried to attend the funeral service. I cannot tell how shocked and overwhelmed with grief is my heart. It seems to me I cannot be reconciled to it. All through his long illness we waited and watched so anxiously for its every word of hope, even when it seemed there was no hope, and when he began to recover we felt so sure of him again, and now he is snatched from us so suddenly. When he was up at commencement his face was so bright and hopeful, and life seemed coming back to him so gently and in such a healthy current that our hearts were filled with thankful gladness. In all that large circle of his old friends gathered then, every eye turned to him with such delighted surprise and gave him such glad welcome that life seemed almost assured to him. It seems to me as I think of it now that I never felt surer of life for any one than I felt for him then, and to think now that he has fallen back even into the grave, down, down into that cold sleep from which the last faint clinging hope of agonzied hearts has lifted, I can scarce endure the thought. Augustus was very dear to me. I love him little less than my own brothers, and not often has death reached nearer to my heart. I know, too, how you will grieve, but I cannot think of the suffering of those from whom life's all has been taken. I can only weep and pray for them.

More than a week has passed since I received your last, a week of anxiety and torture concerning your health. The weather has been very warm, and I cannot but fear that your disease instead of abating is getting a stronger hold of you, and, Jamie, there is danger more than you are perhaps aware that it may lead on to quick consumption. I do greatly desire that if you are no better you will come immediately as far as Cincinnati, at least. It will be better for you there than where you are, and after the convention you can come home I suppose with safety to your political life. I wrote you a long letter last week telling you all I know of your prospects, and Mr. Austin and Almeda will write you soon if they have not already. With that letter Miss Booth sent you a remedy for your disease which I hope you will try if possible. It seemed a very reasonable one. Harry Jones is at home now and he and Dr. Robison speak here this evening. I will leave the remainder of this to fill after this evening.

Monday morning. The meeting last night was held in the public square in front of Lockwood's store. The Doctor, Harry Jones, and Mr. Riddle were the speakers. I took Trot with me so did not dare to venture into the crowd; consequently, lost much of the speaking. [The] Dr.[19] bellowed as usual. I discovered, however, Harry reveled in "the merry music of mirth," and Riddle[20] tortured himself and everybody else with his agonized gestures. Harry Rhodes was there and told me he received a letter from you last Friday saying that you were growing worse and that you would come home as soon as the Court Martial was through. I hope you will indeed.

Trot behaved herself better than any little child I saw there last night; but she grew very tired and when the crowd began to disperse, she was determined to rush right into the street among the horses. She seemed not to have the least fear. I waited until the people were nearly all away, and she grew so angry that she threw off her bonnet and screamed with rage. I made her pick up her bonnet and put it on her head quite to the distress of Aunt Anna, who said the poor child shouldn't be made to pick it up when she did not know what she was about. She was not subdued even then but marched on alone clear to the swamp allowing no one to lead her, or touch her, and I thought it was as well to let her walk off her spunk. The friends here are all pretty well and all extremely anxious to see you again. Harry Jones[21] is very sure that you will get up to the Gap with the 42nd again, and he said last night, "Will he not be greeted with such cheering and shouting, such throwing of caps and firing of guns!" He is out on a recruiting expedition to raise 140 men to fill the Regiment again. With the hope of seeing you in a few weeks at most, and with love without measure, I am your own Crete.

p.s. I hope you will find Col Turchin guilty of nothing unpardonable, for the sympathies of the North are far more with him than with the proslavery tendencies of Gen Buell, and as someone has expressed it, we feel that the General's severity and sternness should be turned to the punishment of rebels for the barbarities committed on our boys rather than to the punishment of our own for their own severe and prompt action. It seems very strange that as soon as a man begins to accomplish something in the way of putting down the rebellion, he is at once recalled, or superceded, or disgraced in some way. I am afraid there is a world of iniquity in our own army to be crushed out yet—before we can do anything effectively. But we must labor and wait; perhaps time will show all to be right.

Again, your own Crete.

TO: MRS. J. GARFIELD
CLEVELAND, AUGUST 6, 1862.

I AM HERE UNWELL. WILL WAIT AT WEDDELL HOUSE [HOTEL].
ANSWER.

SIGNED. J.A. GARFIELD, BRIG. GENERAL.

James' sick leave lasted two weeks into September. Lucretia, Trot and he isolated them-selves in a farmhouse on a hill at Howland Springs outside of Warren, where there was a medicinal spring. He was nominated to run for Congress from his district on September 2, but his state of health did not allow him to participate in political activ-ities. Instead, he and Crete, and their beloved Trot, lived quietly through the September days until James' health had improved enough for him to return to duty. He was ordered to Washington to await further assignment and left Ohio on September 17. The following last two letters of this chapter refer to this idyllic sojourn.

Pittsburgh, Sept.17, 1862.

My Dear Good Crete:

You did not expect a letter so soon. The fact that my trunk was left led me to think it most safe for me to wait here for its arrival, as it might be lost if I should go on without it. Then I found myself somewhat sleepy and tired, and I took the leaving of the trunk as one of the "providential interferences" to give me more rest. I am sorry that Green did not go with me, and yet my future is so indefinite that I can't tell what is best. It may be just right that he didn't come. He forgot to bring my revolver along. I hope it will come with the trunk, for I shall need it. The trunk will be along at 3 o'clock tomorrow morning, at which time I take the train for Harrisburg. I shall go to bed in a few minutes, and try to rest before starting. When I got here I was quite weary, but I took a good bath and have just taken a frugal supper. I caught myself eating warm bread and remembering your wishes, it was a great pleasure to lay the tempting hot roll away, while I thought of you and wished you were with me. I cannot tell how glad my heart is at the remembrance of my visit with you. It has been so much more than I have dared to hope for the last two years and more, that my soul is full of thanksgiving. If this still, lone room could now be filled with your presence, I would not even be tired nor sick. I do not me[an] to say I am sick, but I think I am coming right out of the valley, but it would make my heart so light and happy if you could be with me now, and shed around me the brightness of the new light that I might breathe the fragrance of the "alabaster box," which, so long sealed, has been broken at last. Everything conspired to make the visit dear to me, and its close was worthy of its whole course and character. Our little darling never put her arms around my neck and hugged and kissed me so lovingly as in the fare-well embrace. You walked and talked with me till the train whistled, and you tossed a sweet kiss after the flying train. It was all as my fondest wishes could ask, and it all augurs good for the future. I shall hope soon after my arrival to receive a dear letter with a heart full of love from you.

I send you a slip from the Portage Democrat which I found as I came along the road. Mother may be pleased to read it. The news today looks still more encouraging. God grant we may soon see the end of the war, though I dare not hope that the end is very nigh. As I draw nearer Washington, my own future looks more and more uncertain. It seems as though the individual would be lost in the magnitude of the whole great movement.

I must close and rest. I will read a chapter in the little Testament for you and me, and ask God to be with you before I sleep. And now, my precious darling, with my heart very warm and full of love to you and with my best "God bless you" and warm kisses for you and Trot, I give you Good night. Ever and Forever,

Your own James.

Ravenna, Sept 18, 1862

My Dear Jamie:

My own darling husband! I did not as I promised write you yesterday. When you left me yesterday and the long weary months of another separation loomed up before me, I must either have yielded to wild passionate grief, or let all be forgotten in physical weariness. The latter triumphed, and after dragging home through the burning sunshine, I threw myself on the lounge and slept. When I awoke it was only to a stupor which could neither think nor feel, and a little past seven in the evening I shut myself in our room and was soon dreaming of you. But now, dearest, I am wide awake to all the precious sweetness of the last few weeks and to all the unutterable loneliness your absence gives.

My heart was so full of happiness to see you so happy; and so full of that old love was my own heart. James, I do love you with such fondness and nearness as

I have never known before. I have dreamed of it, have thought about it and hoped for it, but never have known it before. From the pierced side gushes the healing stream. Through the crucifixion of our own desires in yielding up ourselves to that silence of death we have passed through the grave to the resurrection morn. Like the poor disciples at the tomb, we waited hoping yet fearing and doubting; but forth from the darkness has passed our risen love and a day of eternal glory and brightness has beamed upon us. In my heart there is not one doubt, not one fear. What I have never known before I *know* now: that our love is perfect, and all is peace. I trust in you most entirely. Though I can scarcely comprehend all that has passed, all that you said to me only a few hours ago, yet I believe in you and have not one doubt that you are now and ever have been a *true man*. From our baptism of sorrow I have risen to a new life into which no doubts or questionings enter, a life of faith and love and holy joy. O how good is God for all his mercy toward us; and with all my gratitude to Him is mingled the petition that not many shall be the days of our separation. I have never so missed you before, never so desired that you might remain always with us.

Evening. I have just returned from the fair, where I went more to please others than myself. Still I have had a pleasant time. Saw several old friends who inquired about you and expressed their regard and anxiety for you. Aunt Fanny Gage said how much she wanted to grasp your good old hand again. I hope you are nearly through your journey by this time and are none the worse from the fatigue. I cannot but be extremely anxious about you, there is so great a liability that you may be thrown back into a condition worse even than you have ever been. Still I am at the same time hopeful for you. I have so much faith in your native vigor. Try and use as much caution as you can. Tell me about yourself, and write often and long.

Little Trot asks if papa is coming every time she hears the cars. I think she too misses you.

Your own loving Crete.

NOTES

1. Frank Cowles, an Eclectic graduate of 1860, died in March 1862 after the Big Sandy battle.
2. Nelson and Windham were nearby villages.

3. Elia Ford graduated from the Eclectic in 1861.

4. The Ashland *Union* called these volunteers "hired Hessians going to the sunny Southern soil to butcher by wholesale, not foreigners, but good men, as exemplary Christians as any of our men who believe they are fighting for God-given rights. This is a damned abolition war, and we believe Abe Lincoln is as much of a traitor as Jeff Davis."

5. Will Clapp, a student at the Eclectic, was a second lieutenant in Garfield's 42nd Ohio.

6. Longfellow's *Hyperion* was a favorite of both Lucretia and James. This quotation is from book 4, chapter 8. The passage begins as follows: "He bowed his stubborn knees, and wept. And, oh, how many disappointed hopes, how many bitter recollections, how much of wounded pride and unrequited love, were in those tears through which he read, on a marble tablet in the chapel wall opposite, this singular inscription:—Look not. . . ."

7. Dr. S. R. Beckwith was first president of the Cuyahoga County Homeopathic Society, the first privately owned hospital in Cleveland and a surgeon for the railroad.

8. Green was a hostler for Garfield.

9. "The Professor" was Garfield's cook.

10. Joseph Lake had boarded a steamer and was put into a hospital in St. Louis. He died there before he could be traced by his father.

11. Harvey Everest, who officiated at the wedding of Burke Hinsdale and Mary Turner, had been at the Geauga Seminary in Chester, Ohio, with James and Lucretia, as well as a student and teacher at the Eclectic.

12. Harry Rhodes did indeed marry Libbie Woodward of Lordstown, Ohio.

13. Joe is Lucretia's brother.

14. Augustus Williams was a classmate of James'.

15. This is Bulwer-Lytton's, *A Strange Story* (1862).

16. Timothy Stanley of the 18th Ohio and Warren Edgarton of the 1st Ohio Light Artillery—both under Colonel Turchin's orders—were acquitted.

17. The Major Hall mentioned may be Halsey or Lyman Hall, co-editors of the *Portage County Democrat*. James, in a letter written on July 24, said he thought the Halls might favor the opposition candidate, O. P. Brown. Through the years, however, the Ravenna paper generally backed James.

18. Platt Rogers Spencer, a well known penmanship teacher, had taught at the Hiram Eclectic.

19. This is Dr. Robison.

20. A. G. Riddle, a Cleveland lawyer and later congressman, wrote one of Garfield's campaign biographies in 1880.

21. Harry Jones was the chaplain for the 42nd Regiment. He distinguished himself for bravery at the battle of the Big Sandy with James. He was the principal speaker in Cleveland at Garfield's funeral in 1881.

CHAPTER 5

The Civil War, Washington, Chickamaugua, and Congress, 1862–1863

THE SIXTEEN MONTHS, *from September 1862, through December 1863, were momentous for James and Lucretia. Despite the new relationship they seemed to have achieved at Howland Springs in early September 1862 the same coldness which had so disturbed Lucretia before returned to their marriage. A serious misunderstanding took place in December when Crete accused James of neglect and indifference. James wrote back angrily. With Lucretia's abject apologies this was cleared up before the first of the New Year.*

James' lot in Washington was not easy. His illness had interfered with his hopes of receiving an assignment to rejoin his 42nd Regiment at Cumberland Gap, and once in Washington he was kept on tenterhooks for week after week while Secretary of the Treasury Salmon Chase (former governor of Ohio)—with whom James was living— and Secretary of War Stanton attempted to secure a suitable command for him. The city was resounding with rumors and suspicion about the competence, even loyalty, of the Union generals—men like McClellan and Halleck. At first, James thought he would be assigned to a Florida campaign; then an expedition to Charleston, South Carolina, seemed in the offing, but that, too, failed to materialize. The forced inactivity brought low James' morale, and he was subject to fits of depression, despite his rather pleasant life of social rounds, led by Secretary Chase's charming daughter Kate. At last, however, James was assigned to General Rosecrans' command with the Army of the Cumberland in Tennessee. He passed through Hiram on his way there in January 1863.

But again there were long delays, and that great army tarried ingloriously through the spring and summer months, as James became more and more critical of Rosecrans for his reluctance to go into action. Finally in September, the Battle of Chickamauga was fought near Chattanooga. Once again James distinguished himself under fire, but it was clear now that he would serve in Congress, for he had won his election the preceding October. He traveled to Washington, via Hiram, to carry official reports for General Rosecrans to President Lincoln. Then a great calamity for James and Crete occurred. Trot fell ill with diphtheria. James returned from Washington to sit by her bedside. She died on the 2nd of December. James and Lucretia suffered this grievous blow together, and the emotional bond between them was strengthened accordingly. James then returned to Washington to take his seat in the next session of Congress.

If this had been a momentous period in James' life, as he moved from battlefield to Congress and suffered the death of his beloved child, it was still more a profoundly difficult time for Lucretia. Beginning with renewed hopes for a secure and lasting love with her husband, she had experienced within a few months a harsh reprimand from him that must have stung like a lash; she then had to endure the weeks of separation and fear, while he rejoined the army in Tennessee, during which time she was pregnant with their second child. A son, Harry, was born in October; eight weeks later her precious Trot was taken from her. James speaks of suffering, and so does Lucretia, but one can only surmise how much more profound was Crete's.

Of the more than one-hundred letters exchanged during this period twenty-nine are included here, beginning with a letter from James shortly after his return to Washington at the end of his September sick leave in 1862.

Washington, Sept.27, 1862

My Precious Crete:

Your two dear letters of the 19th and 21st were received last evening. I had inquired every day at the Post Office, but by some means they had either been delayed on the way or covered up in the mass of matter, not having been directed to my hotel here. I had become very lonely without a letter from you, but do not, my darling, think for one moment that I doubted you or supposed you had not written. I have no words to tell you how precious these two letters are to me. It is indeed a "baptism into a new life" which our souls have received and which, after so many years of hoping and despairing has at last appeared in the fullness of its glory. I bless our Good All Father who has brought us through it all, and I trust our love will be all the more perfect being made so through suffering. You write as you never wrote to me before and my pen is in the hand of my heart, as it has not been for years. It is a joy to me to sit down and let my heart write itself out to you, and yet I tremble in the very fullness of my joy. It is not, I trust, the trembling of doubt or fear but of joy, the trembling that one feels when the danger is past and the light of hope, peace and safety beams gladly in upon him. Bless your dear true heart for the sweet words you have written to me. My heart followed you back to Uncle's and shared the loneliness with you. But you, my dear, have our blessed little one to be with you, and I have only the great world. You can fondle and kiss your companion and be kissed in return. Mine is a great unlovely unloving, unkissing comrade, to be frowned and whipped into respect even.

For the last three days I have been busy in the study of Florida—its geography and topography—and in planning a campaign there. It is still unsettled where I am to go. I think [it] will be Florida or South Carolina. If they determine to retake Charleston, I shall choose the latter. If not, the former. I somewhat dislike to be under Gen Mitchell, but I am resolved not to be faultfinding. The Pres. and War Dep. has trouble enough without my adding to it, and they are kind to me. I should have written to you oftener, but I have been hoping every day to hear from you, and waiting so as to have the pleasure of acknowledging your letter. I sent you $500 on the 20th, which I hope has been received before now. I see by the papers that Spaulding[1] is nominated. I am sorry, though I suppose he is a good man. Give my love to all our folks. I am getting better and stronger every day. I have scarcely had a symptom of Diarrhea since I left home. I am sorry I did not bring the Diarrhea medicine. Kiss Trot a score of times and receive my love. Ever anew and forever, Your Own James.

Evening, September 27th

Dearest Wife:

I add an appendix to acknowledge the receipt of your dear letter of the 25th. It makes me very glad to read such true good words from you. I beg of you, give me as much of your time as you can. It is a great blessing to be so near that your letters can reach me the second day after they are mailed. Mr. Chase and his daughter Kate have insisted that I shall stay with them while I remain in Washington and so I came here this evening with all my luggage. I have a delightful room and am much better pleased than at the Willard's [hotel]. You may still direct my letters there, however, and I will get them more certainly and speedily than I should if they went to the General Post Office.

I am rejoiced that Gen Cox has been doing so well. It is now due to him to be made a Major General, and I have been doing what I can with the Heads of the Department to effect it. If they respect seniority of Commission, they cannot resist his claims, for his Commision dates May 1862 and many who were made Brigadiers since then have been promoted. I have received two letters from him. He is well, and has grown very much in the esteem of his men since the late battles. The President's Proclamation gives great satisfaction among all strong vigorous men. It can only have an adverse effect in Ky and Tenn. and that, whatever it may be, is a thousand times overbalanced by the great moral force and significance which the measure will add to the war. The President's head is right, God grant he may have the strength to stand up to his convictions and carry them out to the full. I wrote a gossiping letter to Harry last night which I presume you will see before this reaches you. I am getting very anxious about my good Capt Swaim[2] and the rest of my staff, and particularly about my horses. They have all arrived safe in Louisville, and I hope soon to be able to order them forward here. I have met Root, a college classmate, and hear that Gilfillan another classmate is a Clerk in the Treasury Dept.[3] If so, I shall find him. I am glad you are pleased with the prospect of keeping house. Would that I could be with you to help you enjoy the reality. You had better close an arrangement with Brown soon, lest he may see that you are preparing for the work, and will keep up his price.[4] Do write me often and long. Love again to Trot and yourself.

Ever, ever Your James.

Hiram, September 28, 1862.

My Darling Jamie:

It seems to me I was never so sad and anxious about you as today. Your letter of last Monday to Harry was so desponding that I cannot but think about you and feel sorry for you all the while. I think of you as wandering around with weak and weary steps, finding nothing to interest you, and scarcely desiring anything, so enveloped in gloom has everything become; then when you go to your room there is nothing to greet you but the cold uninviting silence. Dear Jamie, I wish I were there to make one little spot brighter, to keep away from

your heart the desolateness which reigns supreme over everything else. I wish
you were here. You would be happier, wouldn't you, since it is for so little purpose you are there. What can be the outcome when selfishness and corruption
bear rule? It seems to me we are almost on the banks of the Red Sea where we
can do nothing but stand still and see what God will do for us.

As for you, I think you must feel somewhat McCawberized,[5] waiting for
something to turn up, and I think too that you will feel none the less that unfortunate gentleman's condition when that something turns up to you only a position subordinate to another Gen Wood.[6] I don't wish to say anything unkind,
but I feel a little as though your call to Washington was but playing out one of
Doc Robison's big farces.

It seems as though the command at Cumberland Gap would have been
more desirable than anything, but since sickness prevented your going to it I
call it a "Providential interference" for reasons we cannot now see and perhaps
never may, still I believe it was best that you could not go. Some of our friends
here think western Virginia the place for you now; but the paper last night
stated that Gen Milroy was to take the command there so you will be prevented
from that, will you not? It states also that Sigel is in Washington without any
command again. I wish you were at home with me. You will be obliged to take
some place where you can do nothing but expose your life to the most immi-
nent danger. I am afraid now that your health is not improving very rapidly and
that you will be induced to take the field too soon. Don't, my darling, I beg of
you, do not, for I cannot but fear that it would prove fatal. I request you to live,
not for the country's sake alone, but for my own; and, Jamie dear, I want to live
with you now, to be near you, to bless you with my love and be blessed, Oh so
blessed with your love so grand and good. I have written a dolorous letter and
will not continue it much farther, but when I look out over our country's
prospects, all looks so dark. It is not dark within tonight. Never have I lived
such days of heart-joy. The new light is so perfect and the peace it brings so
sweet, and with such passionate desire do I long for the warm sweet pressure of
your lips upon my own. I want another letter from you, full of your own heart's
love. Write to me, my own, very, very often and tell me all about yourself. The
little one is well and talks a great deal about her big papa way off in
Washington. Try and be as cheerful as you can, and when you get to looking
right well, have a card photograph taken. . . . With my whole heart. Your Crete.

Washington, October 3, 1862

Dearest Crete:

Your dear letter of the 29th was received yesterday. I cannot tell you how full of gratitude is my heart, that your soul goes out so strongly toward me. It is so new and so delicious a joy to know that at last I have found the fountain in what I had supposed to be desert. Indeed it has sprung up joyously in the desert of my life. But, dearest, you must not be so desponding in reference to myself. I have felt, it is true, and still feel great impatience at being kept here in suspense, like Coleridge's Ancient Mariner:

> *"Day after day, day after day*
> *We stuck, nor life nor motion*
> *As idle as a painted ship*
> *Upon a painted ocean."*

While it annoys me very much to be kept waiting so, and particularly to keep my staff waiting so impatiently at Louisville for orders from me, I am still assured that it is meant as no lack of confidence in me but rather the contrary, for they are endeavoring to get me an independent command. Again I have not been till lately able to take the field. It is two weeks this morning since I arrived here, and it has dragged very heavily by, I assure you. But the personal discomfort of being kept here, and the positive loss of reputation I shall suffer if I do not do something soon, are overborne by my painful and anxious interest in the welfare of the country. Men do not usually grieve for national calamities as for smaller, specific sorrows, but when I see what is unfolding here every day, of the weak, timid government, on the one hand, and the deep plottings of the old Breckenridge wing of the Democratic Party in connection with Gen McClellan, when I see the criminal vacillation that has marked the course of the Government in its desire to remove him from Command and its cowardly drawing back at the very important moment when hesitation was surrender: I am filled with most anxious forebodings. Only think of it. McClellan lay still in the field of Antietam one day and two nights and let the rebels cross the Potomac in perfect safety, when he could have destroyed them. He has been reinforced until he must now have near 140,000 men. He now refuses to cross the Potomac into Va. till the river is permanently swelled by rains so that the rebels can't get around behind him into Maryland—at which time of course the roads will be bad and the winter near. To complete the disgracefulness of this sad picture, he has sent to Washington for an immense supply of intrenching tools and for all the Topographical engineers that can be spared from the various Departments of the Government. You have probably seen the account of the dismissal of Maj Key from the Army by the President. He was a brother of Key, our Ohio sena- tor and on Halleck's staff. His crime was that on being asked why McClellan did not follow the rebels after Antietam, he answered: It is not the plan to whip the rebels. They are to be kept from invading the north, and the two armies are to be kept in the field till both sections of the country are exhausted, and the[n] the armies and the Democracy will compromise the matter. From all I can see, I am almost convinced that McC is not misrepresented in that statement. The President has gone out to see McC. and there [is] great commotion in the official circles here. No progress can be made in any other enterprise till that is settled. Four days ago Buell was suspended from command the papers all made out. But Crittenden and a few more, half and half patriots from Ky. protested and the Government backed down at once and restored him.

I shall spend the day with Gen McDowell, who will show me the history of the Va. campaign. I believe he has been greatly wronged.[7] The Pres and Cabinet know he is a true man but dare not come out before the people and vindicate him. Do write to me. I may be here weeks, but rather than stay much longer I will take command of a Brigade, Regiment, or Company, or do guard duty. I am sick and tired of such terrible weakness. I am quite well, except a little Diarrhea yesterday. I found the vial of Diarrhea medicine in the box in my trunk. Kiss the dear little one for me. She is twenty-seven months old today. Ever your own

James.

Hiram, October 4, 1862.

My Dear Jamie:

I saw Mr. Brown last evening. He still thinks his house ought to rent for $100. He says he has had an opportunity to rent the two front rooms and bedrooms adjoining for $50 a year, and he thinks the whole place ought to bring him $100. He says he will make all the repairs we want, and when done he will let it go for a little less if he can. Miss Booth and I looked over the house, and considering the size of the lot and the amount of fruit there is on it, and the probability that he could rent it to students for even considerable more, we think he ought perhaps to have $100. Still I did not think best to take it without hearing from you again. I presume you will think best to take it, for I presume we cannot do better here and perhaps not in any other place we would want to live.

Please write as soon as this is received as Mr. Brown wants to know certainly about it as soon as possible. I will not finish this out for a letter, but write again soon. Peaches are just in a nice condition for canning today, and I must make a busy day of it. I think about you and love you more and more every day. Hope I shall get another letter tonight.

Yours forever with kisses and love, Trot and Crete.

Washington, October 8, 1862

Dearest Crete:

Your note of Oct 4th stating Mr. Brown's proposition and asking my opinion is just received. I have only time to write a word in answer, as I am about going by appointment to meet Mr. Giddings,[8] who is now in the city and has sent for me. Accept his proposition without hesitation. If he will let you have the house after it is repaired according to your wishes for $100, it will probably be as well as you can expect to do. Let it be understood in the bargain if you can so do, that you are to have the house the next year also at the same rate, if he rents it. I think he ought to put it in a good state of repair for $100.

I have no news to write in regard to my own future. The Florida scheme is maturing but the troops are not at hand for the expedition. Gen Halleck has got to be consulted. My heart burns with indignation, when I see these beautiful autumn days pass and McClellan's army idle. In a few weeks more the rain will be upon us and the campaign will be ended. The rebels are unmolestedly moving back toward Richmond. Shame! if not treason.

Write me soon. Don't call this a letter. Love and kisses to you and Trot from your loving

James.

Hiram, October 19, 1862

My Own Jamie:

A whole week has passed since I wrote to you but I know you will forgive when you hear how busy I have been. The week of getting ready to keep house is altogether more of an affair than I had supposed, and in order to be ready as soon as the house is ready I am working every moment that I am not sleeping or eating. I wanted to write you a letter during the week but there was no time till bedtime; then I was too weary to write anything but a weary letter, and I have now three of your unanswered letters all of them dearer and more precious than words can tell. To begin with the first. I have seen Mr. Brown, and he promises to have the house all ready by the second week of vacation so that I hope to be fairly established before the 11th November. How I wish you could spend the anniversary day with me. It will be the first we have spent apart; and yet the one more than all others when our hearts will be nearest. Jamie, darling, you will remember me that day with a letter from your heart, will you? In the next place, you made me very glad and thankful by the letter and long article giving us an insight to many things before mysterious. I had become thoroughly impatient and disheartened trying to know any thing about the motives influencing our Administration or our Generals. And I was almost ready to adopt the opinion becoming very general that they were all either a set of cowardly fools, or wicked plotting knaves. It is very hard from the outside views we get to discover who are acting with wisdom and loyalty or otherwise; and it was very satisfactory to follow you in your penetration to the center, and know your judgment and opinion of men and measures. From all you have written I can gather a little faith yet to look ahead with some hope for the dawn of a brighter day. Indeed I begin to feel that there is a faint streak of daylight in the promotion of Gen. Cox and his being allowed two such Generals with him as Morgan and Milroy. But is it not a great shame, and very discouraging too, that the Ohio elections have turned the way they have? . . .

I suppose you are with Rebecca today. I have not heard either from her or Maria since you left. Jamie, I have been passing through a great struggle since I received your letter last night, and whether I should write anything to you of it has been a serious question. Before you came home last summer, I had settled down on this conviction that the threads of our lives had become so entangled with others that it was only useless to try and unravel them, and the best we could do was to gather them up as they came and finish out the rest of life as best we could. But during your visit you know how unintentionally and almost unconsciously we turned back together and looked through the tangled past, and with what surprise and great joy we found the links we called broken only hidden. Then from mutual explanations and confessions we found more that was unfortunate than wrong in what had once seemed all wrong, and I saw as I never had before that a large part of our great sorrow was due to the mask my own heart had worn; and in the new light and life and love which sprang up around and before us, I then resolved that—cost what it might—no conceal-ment of anything in my heart should ever again be allowed. You should know all the love and tenderness it felt, and if the darkness of doubt or distrust fell upon it you should know that too. Now, darling, don't begin to tremble lest something terrible is to come. When I read your purpose to visit Rebecca, the old pain came back to my heart, and I seemed to be going all back into that cold darkness, and in all that you had said to me I began to fear there was only inconsistency which showed nothing but a desire to deceive me. Now, Jamie, I have confessed all. Most solemnly and earnestly did I pray to the All Giving Father for a just and generous heart, and He who hears the young ravens when they cry heard and answered my prayer. And there is in my heart today only love and trust, and I have asked myself why I should tell you of it at all, and it is not so much that you should know it as to school my own heart to a perfect freedom with you.

Your letters are priceless treasures to me. I will try and write again during the week, but if I do not you will not think that I do not want to. I think of you every hour, and desire to see you more than ever before. Your own loving Crete.

Hiram, October 26, 1862.

My Own Dearest One:

Your letter from Lewisboro I did not receive until last night; tho' delayed so long it was loved just as much; and I searched through every line for each word or expression of the new tenderness and love, and to each and every one my own heart gave such full and ready responses.

Dear Jamie, I cannot tell how great is my joy in this living love which has sprung up in my heart. The little germ so carefully hidden away in my heart, which I knew was there, and wondered sometimes that you could not see it, is so full of perfection and beauty now that it has burst into life, into living breath-ing life, that I can scarcely understand my life heretofore and I no longer won-der that you thought it so cold and dead. It seems to me something new has been infused into my whole nature, a warm glowing passion, which is trans-forming all my thoughts and feelings, and giving me such new desires. I loved you way down in my heart before. I love you now with my whole being. Before when you were away my heart missed you, now my whole self mourns with it and longs and pines for your presence, my lips for your kisses, my cheek for the warm pressure of yours. In short, I understand what you meant when you used to say, "I want to be touched!" and were it not that I have got enough pride left to want to keep my reputation for being *so sensible* about your absence, I am not sure but I should be as silly as the silliest that you must be so much away from me. With all sincerity I can now say I thank Thee Our Father for the suffering and great sorrow through which I have been led, since it has brought me to such a life of rich enjoyment. And I hope, dear Jamie, that enough of new joy has been given to your heart so that you may feel that it has not been all in vain that you have suffered.

I have concluded the bargain with Mr. Brown for his house, and shall soon be in our *first* home. I go to Cleveland next Thursday with Miss Booth to make purchases. I have not succeeded in finding a girl yet such as I want, and we have decided that Nellie shall live with me this winter, and we will do our own work. I think it will not keep me [so] very busy that I cannot entertain company and do a good many other things I want to. Miss Wilson is going to board with us, but there will be only six of us when Mother comes. I could have started with quite a family. Harry and Miss Martan both wanted to come and get their meals with me, and if I could have found a good girl I would have taken them, but I thought that with a poor girl I should be obliged to do more than I will now. I shall keep a look out, though, for a good girl so that we can have one when we need. (Will you be very sorry for what I am now to write? We shall have no *special need* of more help at present). *Do you understand?*

I hope you know something of your winter's work before this. The paper last night states that Buell has been again removed; but perhaps only to be reinstated tomorrow. It is rumored too that Gen Hooker is to supercede McClellan. We hope so. This week the Fall term closes up. . . .

We awoke this morning with two inches of snow. It looks very strange indeed; for the grass and many of the trees are yet green and scarcely any leaves have fallen yet. The bright autumn tints of the forest, and the fruit in the orchards peeping out from their heavy covering of snow gave to me, who love snow so little, a very unpleasant impression. I called Trot up to see the snow. She looked very wonderingly at it but finally decided it was pretty. Mother sends love to you, and Nell is talking of writing to you. All love you and love to hear from you. That you may be kept safe from every harm, and guided and blessed in all you do is the prayer each night of your little wife.

Crete.

And so Lucretia set up housekeeping in her own home. With her were Trot, Almeda Booth, Nellie (Lucretia's sister), Miss Wilson, a teacher from the Institute, and James' mother, sometimes referred to as "Grandma." Professor Mary Ryan has pointed out how frequently nineteenth century housewives would contribute to the family income by taking in boarders, as Lucretia did[9]. Here domestic skills are converted to a source of income. It is evident, too, from this letter, that Lucretia has had a miscarriage and that no plans now need be made for a second child.

Washington, Oct 25, 1862

My Dearest Crete,

I left New York night before last, but the train missed connections at Philadelphia, and I was left there till yesterday noon, and so I did not reach here till last night. I had a conference with Thayer just before leaving N.Y. and found that the Florida plan is winning friends and supporters every day. The only thing now needed is the action of the government and we seem as far from that as ever.[10] I have not learned what the War Dept has been doing in my absence, but from all I can gather they have done nothing. It is exceedingly discouraging to see how weak and dilatory they are. I am growing into a feeling of personal shame at being kept here in idleness. I am really ashamed to be seen on the streets with the U. S. uniform on. In New York—here—everywhere—there is a settled gloom on nearly every face. A great nation groaning in an agony of sus-pense and anxiety to have something done. A people that have poured out with a lavish hand their life and treasure to save their government. A people that have trusted their Executive head with a constancy and faith which in these des-perate days is really sublime—are now beginning to feel that their confidence has been betrayed, their treasure squandered and the lives of their children sac-rificed in unavailing slaughter. The failure of the late elections is the natural and inevitable result of the management of the war. But I will not distress you with any further views of the dark and gloomy picture of our times.

I am glad to hear that you are perfecting your arrangements for a home of our own. I only wish I were well through this war and could enjoy it with you. I am glad to have you write me frankly and fully as you do in the last letter of the 20th now before me. I was however sorry to know that you had been sad and had passed through a struggle on account of my visit to Rebecca. I hope you will not harbor any thought that I have practiced any deception toward you in my late communication. I hope you will see me as I am conscious of being, indeed a true man, and that I am true to my *whole* history. I had a very pleasant and yet sad visit with Rebecca, pleasant because I was glad to revisit the scenes of six years ago and was enabled to do so without having my horizon clouded or having the thorns again pierce me, pleasant because I am more than ever assured that he that is true to his own nature is happier and better in being so, and I can say in truth that I love you none the less for having seen Rebecca again and she is no less dear to me from the fact that the sunshine has sweetly dawned upon your life and mine—pleasant because I took pleasure in telling her that I had passed a very happy month with you and that henceforth my life with you was full of promise of sweet peace and sunlight. I was sad in this that I found her just arisen from a bed of pain and suffering, that I feared the insidi- ous approach of consumption, that I found her surrounded by those who do not contribute much to make her life agreeable, nor do they seem to be worthy to be companions of so noble a woman. She has been sorely disappointed in Maria's not going to visit her before her return to the West. Eben Ayers[11] has got home from the Army sick with a fever, and worst of all has a fever sore on his knee, which threatens to make him a cripple for life. . . .

Kiss our darling for me. I regret that I cannot be with you on the 11th Nov, but I am preparing something for you which will answer nearly as well.

Loving you and hoping to hear from you very often, I am forever

Your own James.

Hiram, October 28, 1862.

My Own Jamie:

Your letter of three days ago is just received, and I will make a little leisure for a word or two. It is a great pleasure to have you so near; but Jamie I do feel real indignant that you are so long delayed, and I wish you would resign and come home.

If the country doesn't need you or doesn't want you for fear you may have the audacity to do something, we need you, and are not at all afraid here to let you have *full swing*. I will give you a job at wood sawing, and board you for noth- ing, or at least for a little of your aid in getting settled and provided for the win- ter. I was thinking today how much easier it would be if I could make an occasional draft on your executive talent. I am not sure that my providence may not prove inadequate to the demands made upon it. But in good faith, Jamie, why do you stay longer? I very much fear that your reputation for earnestness and zeal in serving your country now in her trial is suffering not a little. I do not wish to aggravate the mortification I know you already feel at your long detention, nor do I doubt your ability to judge of the motives of those with whom you deal, but I feel that in some way you are becoming a victim to their dastardly slowness, and I wish you were away.

Do you know that Harvey has resigned his position in the school? I think he has been dissatisfied ever since the last meeting of the Trustees, and all through the Fall he has been sulkily opposed to everything Miss Booth has desired for the school, and finally in a very *unmanly and ungenerous* way (I think the Trustees who know of it will endorse those expressions) declared his determination to resign. I have ever felt friendly to Harvey and desired in every way to sustain him. But I do feel that he is unreasonable and wrong in the course he is taking. I do not see what is to be done. No one who knows Harry [Rhodes] feels [ready] to rely on him to stand at the head. Father says he would like to know what you would propose in case Harvey does leave,[12] but I presume your inclinations are not to think very much about the school now. I am truly sorry to learn of Rebecca's ill health, but I trust your fears in regard to it are unfounded. It would be a great pleasure to me to visit her. I have loved her as I never did any other woman, and I trust we understand each other in a measure, though we never may entirely until beyond the veil. Perhaps I can never be as just and generous to her as I ought before. I don't know but the remembrance of life's great trial[13] must follow me even down to the Jordan of death. May the dark river wash it away. Do not judge me too severely, my dear Jamie, though I love you too selfishly. You would not, I know you wouldn't, if you could know how much I try to be generous. Help me by kind forbearance and love. My eyes are full of tears as [I] write to night; but it is not often now that any thought of you brings ought but the sweetest happiness. . . .

Loving you forever, Crete and Trot

Washington, Nov 11, 1862

Dearest Crete:

I take my pen on this quadrennial anniversary with mingled feelings of sadness and happiness. Sad, as I review the past, that it should have been so strangely, painfully trying to us, who groped about in the darkness and grief trying to find the path of duty and peace, and being so often pierced with thorns. Sad that so much of life which can never be recalled should have been, by a kind of fatal necessity, devoted to a sadness almost bordering on despair, and that possibly those dark years may have left a residuum of bitterness, which the whirling eddies of after years may stir up and mingle with the sweet waters of life. But I am also happy in the reflection that we were both seeking the path of duty and honor and that we each bore in silence many griefs, and each drank bravely and uncomplainingly many a bitter cup. Happy that in those days we were each borne up by the trust that the other was of true noble soul, and however great the errors might be, there was still integrity of heart. Happy above all that this patient waiting and mutual forbearance has at last begun to bear the fruits of peace and love, and that the buds of this hope give promise of and harvest of calm, joyful peace, as we go down the lengthening shadows of life. I have watched the new hope with great anxiety to see if it were a transient flower, or a perennial growth. I have rejoiced with trembling, and I will not, even yet, speak with that full assurance that can lay all the future under contribution, yet as the days wear on, I rejoice more and tremble less. I hope strongly and happily that we have passed through the valley and shadow of that death, which for so long a time we "died daily." But I here pray you to be still ready to bear with me if at any future moment my heart should for a time go down again into the deeps. I do not say this because of any such experience since I left you. I have had none. Were I with you today, I would let you see in my eyes and heart that the cloud has not returned. It would be a great joy could I go with you today and occupy our first home, and tonight kneel with you and Almeda around the new altar. I hope you have gone into the house today. I cannot tell you how I long to see our little darling Trot again. Precious little soul. I have ordered a present sent you by Express in commemoration [of] this anniversary. It is now in New York City and may not reach you for a week. I tried to have it reach you by today but could not. It will explain itself. I have directed it to be sent to Garrettsville and you may have to send for it there. It's only a little token, but I thought you would be pleased with it.

I was to have sailed yesterday, but news came that the Yellow Fever was raging there, and we were ordered to wait. It will not be safe to go till the black frost sets in. Of course, I don't want to take troops in where an epidemic is raging, but I was greatly disappointed at being again disappointed in getting into the field. I think, however, we shall not be very long delayed. The cold weather and snow we have had here during the last week has I hope frozen the fever out, so that it will soon be safe. My staff has not yet arrived, but will be here tonight. On the whole I am very much pleased with the proposed expedition and the place I was, and probably still am, to have in it. It will give the government a great moral power to have retaken Charleston and Sumter, and I shall be glad to bear a part in that work. One year ago today I was just leaving the northern part of Ohio not to return again for three quarters of a year. Now I am near the time of leaving the northern Capitol to go where and how long I know not. I try to look to our good Heavenly Father and trust that what the next year brings forth may be to His honor and our joy. Pray for me that I may not forget His mercies, but may be true to Him and to my own manhood in every place. Give my love to Mother, Father and Nell. . . .

Write me often, here, as usual. It may be weeks before we leave.

Ever and forever, Your James.

Hiram, November 16, 1862.

My Own Dearest Jamie:

In our own first home I sit down for the first time to write to you. I am not entirely settled yet but have the lower rooms looking cozy and comfortable. I have had a hard week's work, I assure you, and yet there is a great deal to be done before everything will be in order. Almeda comes over tomorrow and I hope by the close of another week to have made great improvements here. We shall be fixed very comfortable. Still the house would be very undesirable for a permanent home. The rooms are so very small and Mr. Brown is very much *smaller* than his rooms. When you come home I shall tell you of several things I do not choose to trouble you with now. It was very amusing to watch the astonishment with which little Trot looked around in her new home when I first brought her here. But the next morning she very complacently claimed all as her own, saying "This is me's house." It is a great joy to me that she remembers you with so much love. She asks about you so often and says, "Will papa come home to see me sometime?" Just now she is turning over the leaves of a book and reading to herself, and only this moment whispering "papa come home." O Jamie, my darling, I do so wish you could come. I feel that I have risen up to such a high and perfect trust in you, and my heart so full of loving love that you would be happy, happier, than you ever were before with me, were you here now. As your letter of the 11th was an expression of both joy and sadness, so does it make me both sad and joyful, sad that you will almost distrust yourself, but very glad that you have so little reason for that distrust. Jamie, should again I be called to that fierce trial for which you can ask me yet to hold myself in readiness, I hope God may give me the strength I need. Of you I only ask, try not to conceal it from me, for you cannot, and to see you try to do so only adds another pang. Your eye never deceives me. I always know the moment it is turned upon me, if the veil is before your spirit. My heart is full of breaking at the very thought of it. Let us put our trust in God with our souls' greatest strength and pray to Him that this "rest and peace" may remain with us forever more. Whatever the present may be you have sent me, my heart will thank you for it with all its fullness of love. I scarcely know whether to joy or sorrow that you are still left in Washington. It is a great trial to have you go so far away, still I desire for you the pleasure and satisfaction which the service will give you. . . . I hope you will write just as often as you can, both freely and fully of all your heart feels. It seems to me I never so needed you, never so desired you, and your letters are the only compensation your absence can give. Pray for me, dear Jamie, that I may be hopeful, trusting and loving, and that [you] may be good and noble, and that you may be kept through all harm to return to me shall be the constant prayer of Your loving Crete.

James' comment in his letter of November 11 that he prays Lucretia "be still ready to bear with me if at any future moment my heart should for a time go down again into the deeps," suggests he may not yet be confident he is immune to the temptation of female charm; and in concluding the letter he prays he "may be true . . . to my own manhood in every place." Lucretia's response, that she is sad "that you will almost distrust yourself," confirms this weakness in James. In fact, at this time James may have met the woman who is to figure a year and a half later in this epistolary history.

November 19 had been James 31st birthday. He took the occasion to write a gloomy letter to his good friend Harry Rhodes, in which he complained of the poverty which had been his lot in life to endure. "I, an over-grown, uncombed, unwashed boy . . . was at that age compelled to begin the work of exhuming my manhood from the drift and rubbish which every chance had thrown upon me," he wrote. "Hardly a day passes in which I do not find sad traces of the 17 years' chaos; hardly a day when some fortunate young son of early opportunity does not make me feel my inferiority to him in things whereof I lament." Harry Rhodes let Lucretia read this letter.

Hiram, December 4, 1862.

My Dearest Jamie:

The first day of winter brought to me your picture from New York. I thank you very very much for it, and my reasons for prizing it are more than words can tell. The face is so grandly serene, so unlike any picture of yourself for the last years. There is not in it a trace of those lines which have shown so plainly the restless chafing spirit within. In the quiet eye I see an assurance of your happiness which gives me more hope and gladness than all the assurances your lips could give. I look at it with a new pleasure each time and feel that you are drawing me home closer to your heart. Jamie, you cannot know the sweet pleasure it gives me to feel that you desire and prize my love, and that you feel a quiet joy in the hope of our future love. I felt a little sorry to read such a desponding, almost complaining letter as your birthday letter to Harry. It is with me a positive certainty that whatever be the circumstances beyond our control which surround us, they are the very best—just what we need—to make us what God designed us to be, if we use them as we have the power given us to. And I believe, Jamie, if you will question yourself as to the time when you have developed most rapidly, not only strength but refinement and purity of sentiment and feeling, you will find it was not when you were helped in any way but when you stood all alone, and, from some tendencies of your nature, I do not believe you would have been as good or noble and not half as great had not your career been one of struggle. Jamie, how it would break your little mother's heart to read that letter, and I beg of you do not indulge in any more such *wicked*—yes, I do feel they were wicked—reprovings. You can be all that any man ought to be if you will continue to strengthen and cultivate the powers God has given you. You will pardon me for speaking as freely with you, dearest, though perhaps I have been unjust, for I do presume you were in a very morbid condition of feeling due to your bilious state of health.

I am glad to hear that you are so much better, and since the weather is getting so cool I presume you will soon be away to Carolina. I dread so much to have you go; still I quiet my fears with the hope that He who has so far preserved you will still protect. Little Trot says, "I want me papa to come home and stay all longer." She has learned her first tune, "We are marching down to Dixie." She sings, Good news, good news from Dixiesland, from Dixiesland, from Dixiesland, rebel cause is at stand . . . and she gets the tune perfectly. . . .

Write as often as you can, and remember that I am loving you and desiring you more than ever. Your own Crete.

My Dearest Crete:

Yours of the 4th was received last night. I am very glad you are pleased with the picture. It was made by Mr. Ulke, my German friend here.[14] He took a photograph and then I gave him two sittings of half an hour each. His brush did more for the picture than the camera. When I was in New York an engraver, I. C. Buttre, wanted to make a steel engraving of me for a volume he is publishing, and I sent him the picture. It was three or four weeks before he had completed the engraving. I think the engraving is very good, though of course I cannot tell. I will have some copies sent you. I would not have you think I would be so foolish as to incur the expense of my face in steel, for it would have cost $80 or $100. Mr. Buttre got the engraving up on his own account. The picture I sent you was made as a present to you and cost $30. Does little Trot know it? I hope so. . . .

I have lately drawn my pay for the last two months, and I enclose you in this letter $100 which I hope will meet the necessities of your household till I have a little more pay. I will try to get a draft. In case I do not, I will enclose a $100 Treasury note. I know it is not a good way to do business, but the mails are very regular and safe, and there is but little risk. I am writing in the Court, which [is] now progressing finely. We have a phonographer here who takes down the testimony as fast as the witnesses can talk. Gen Pope and Capt DeKay have been examined, and Gen Roberts is now giving his testimony. I this morning received a letter from Dr. Robison saying that he and his wife are now in New York and are coming here to see me before they return home. I am sorry you all seem to think that my letter to Harry in regard to the advantages and wealth and opportunity in early life and the disadvantages of being poor and having no strong cultivated means to direct the growth and development of character [was unjust]. It was the farthest possible from my thought to find any fault with my good mother. I have no doubt, as you say, that much good has resulted to me from having been obliged to fight the battle of life alone, but it is none the less true that I lack much which I would not otherwise. The chief thought which led me into this train of reflection was in my heart longings over our dear little Trot. I was thinking what her future womanhood would be if she had neither your counsel or mine to guide her, and were obliged to struggle along as [a] hired girl in some kitchen at one dollar a week, as compared with what it might be, aided by us and such a competency as would enable us to give her the best culture that our educational institutions can afford. Do you think I was very *"wicked"* in thinking that to be poor and alone in early life is not so fine a thing as poetic views of the gallant fight in life's battle would sometimes lead us to think it? I am always glad to have you speak whatever you think of all my doings and I thank you for your suggestions on that subject.

Try to tell Trot how much I love her and how anxious I am to go home and live with her and you. Write me often and often.

Ever and forever Your James.

James, fully occupied as a judge in the Court Martial of Fitz John Porter, had decided not to return to Hiram—to his first true home—for Christmas. This combined with the fact that several of his letters somehow were delayed caused Lucretia to chastise him for his neglect. She wrote a letter she later wished she had not written.

Hiram, December 21st 1862

My Dearest Jamie:

Little Trot is sitting beside me with one of your quill pens I have given her for hers, an empty inkstand, and a piece of paper writing a letter to papa. I just asked her what she was writing to you. "Bout tissing me" was her reply. She is a perfect little chatterbox talking all sorts of funny things. Every little while she gets off some droll thing which I think I will write to you, but I can't think of one now. She remembers a great many things about you, and talks about you a great deal. She has taken a great fancy lately to talk to your picture and the other day got up and put her little fingers to your mouth and said she was "feedin papa candy." She grew quite disgusted however because the mouth wouldn't open and said, "When me big papa comes home he'll open his mouf." She has got to understand that you are the one she is to depend on for the supply of her wants and every little while she comes to me with something she wants you to get. You know she has always had a great admiration of jewelry; and the other day she came to me saying she wished papa "to dit her ring" and this morning when I was dressing she said, I want me papa to dit me great big chemise (Don't think I call this article a jewel!) like yours, mama. She says the bed in our room is hers and papa's and she says she "wish papa would come home and sleep with her." She is growing very fast and was never more rosy cheeked and healthy.

The weather is very cold again and I am thinking of the poor boys again shivering over scanty camp fires with not half the hope to cheer them that they had one year ago. What do you think of Burnside's last movement?[15] Can it be anything more than a disastrous defeat? Were it not easier to hope than to despair, I am sure we would cease to hope against all hope. This year, which we hoped would accomplish so much, is almost to its close, and the Rebellion stands up with a more formidable and threatening front than ever before, and it does seem as though it was due almost entirely to the aid given them by our traitor generals in doing nothing themselves and letting nothing be done by those who would do.

I hope you may get this on Christmas, and let it be to you the bearer of many wishes for your happiness. We would love your presence here, but if it must be withheld we will think of you with kindness and love. If it is possible I wish you might come to Harry's wedding. You who have been so faithful in sending him such *frequent eight-paged Congress sheet* letters ought to show him sufficient regard to honor his nuptials with your presence. More than another week has passed and yet no letter comes to me.[16] If woman's name be *frailty* where in the whole catalogue of human failings can be found one comprehensive enough to be man's name? Jamie, I should not blame my heart if it lost all faith in you, but I hope it may not. Indeed, I am not going to let it; but I shall not be forever *telling* you how much I love you when there is evidently no more desire on your part for it than present manifestations indicate.

Yours as ever, Crete.

Washington, Dec. 26, 1862

My Dear Crete:

Yours of the 22nd came to hand this morning as I returned from a Christmas trip across the Potomac. The Ohio people here in the city gave a Christmas dinner to the Ohio soldiers (about 800) who are located in a convalescent camp at Fort Gaines about four miles out of the city, and a large party went out to cheer the boys. There was a fine dinner given them and after it speeches made by Judge Spaulding, John Sherman, Gov Chase, Mr. Hutchins, myself and others. After the dinner was over I went to the Chain Bridge and over to the Va shore to visit Capt Allen of the 169th New York. He is Bro Allen of Millville, N.Y., whose wife visited us in Hiram in 1860. He has lately raised a company and come into the service. I was pleasantly surprised to find his wife there, and also to find some half dozen old College acquaintances. The Colonel was at Williams a few years before me. The Surgeon graduated the year before me, and the Major (Alden) was a class mate of Harry's. I knew several others. They had a fine Christmas supper concluding with speeches and songs. I staid over night and came into town this morning. The Court has done a good day's work, and I hope we are moving with accelerated velocity toward the end of the business. I am delighted to hear all those dear little pranks and traits of our precious little Trot. I constantly feel that I am losing very much of the most interesting part of her babyhood by being away from her so much. It is very hard for me to let all that period pass without leaving my finger marks upon her childhood's history and development, but the outlook for the future, as the war is now developing itself, is by no means flattering to my hopes of enjoying much for a long time to come.

The next sentence after this must not be mentioned. Mr. Chase told me a day or two ago that the Secretary of War said he was going to make me a Major General and give me Gen Wright's Department with authority to go into East Tennessee and hold that Country. I am now inclined to think I shall refuse the other star if it is offered. I would rather earn it in the field than to take it on trust of what I might do in the future. It may be necessary in order to settle some question of rank. But I have no expectation that the War Dept will hold one mind for a whole week. If it should I may see the Cumberland Mts again instead of the Carolinas. The war must be long, and the more I reflect on it the more I am doubtful about taking my seat in Congress. But we shall see when the time comes, that is if we have eyes.

Private and Confidential

I have taken this new sheet to say a few words in regard to ourselves. I know you want me to be frank in everything, and I want to assure and reassure you that I write what follows with the tenderest regards for our mutual happiness. In your letter which now lies before me there is the following passage: "Jamie, I should not blame my own heart if it lost all faith in you. I hope it may not, indeed I am not going to let it, but I shall not be forever telling you I love you *when there is evidently no more desire for it on your part than present manifestations indicate.*" I had to read that sentence over several times before I could become fully convinced that you had written the passages which I have underscored. Waiving the consideration out of which this sentence arose (my letters to you, their relative brevity and infrequency), for I have spoken of that in my last letter which you have received before this, I presume—waiving that, I say, I want you to look at your words again and ask yourself whether you ought to have written them to me. A husband should not only be a faithful husband but should also be a noble manly friend and a wife should be a noble womanly friend. Now Crete, if a mere friend should write such a sentence to me, I should consider it an imputation upon my honesty, a direct slight to my manhood which if unexplained would compel me to drop that correspondence. I am clearly of the opinion that [it] is very wrong for you to write to me in that way, and I beg you with all the earnestness of my heart that you will not do it again. We came so much near[er] to each other and have been, Oh, how much happier than before in consequence of my late visit home. It is a perpetual source of thanksgiving to me that we were so blessed. I am all the more rejoiced to know that that new joy was not an ephemeral existence but a fixed and permanent part of our lives henceforth, and I believe that nothing, unless it be such things as that above written, can fling me back into the old darkness and shadow of death in which my soul dwelt so long. Understand me: I don't want you to write what you do not feel, nor indeed do I want you to conceal your real feelings from me, but it seems to me that you wrote that in a temporary feeling of dissatisfaction which was not at all an exponent of your fixed belief. If you really felt what was there suggested, I should consider it wrong for us to continue any other than a business correspondence. But I hope and most fully believe we love each other in a nobler and truer way than that. Be assured that I say all this (an hour and a half after midnight) from a heart that longs to clasp you to it and answer all your doubts by the warmth of its presence and love. Write to me and forgive me if I have wronged you. Ever and forever, Your James

Hiram, January 2, 1863.

My Dearest Jamie:

I received your last Wednesday morning, just as we were starting for Harry's wedding, and I have felt like chiding the merry nuptial hours that have so long kept me from responding. I need not tell that I was pained by what you had written me there; you meant, I suppose, I should be, but I was pained not that you wrote me as you did, but that I had been so unfortunate as to give you the occasion. I had felt hurt, not a little, at the indifference your letters were growing to manifest. When you first went away, you wrote me frequently and with a warmth of feeling which made me very happy and hopeful. After a while, your letters became more infrequent and business like, in fact containing no expressions of feeling on your part, save that you were glad *I love you*, and finally when a long letter I wrote you when you were sick was not even noticed and ten or twelve days passed without any letter at all, I felt that I might as well go back onto the old plain, where nothing was hoped for, nothing expected. And I should have done so without a word had not the recollection of your last visit made me feel that I could not give up all again. I then thought I would not find fault, but in a half laughing way as I sometimes talk to you I wrote what I did. I saw after I had written it that the words looked forbidding, but the impression that followed was that Jamie will know that I was only laughing with tears in my eyes, so I let it remain. Your last letter before had explained the delay of your letters and I was sorry for having written any thing at all, still I hoped you would not think I was in serious earnest. Since you did, however, I thank you for writing what you did. I will keep it as another lesson to teach my lips more gentleness. Jamie, I do desire to be the good and loving wife your heart desires, and I do desire to be with you more that our spirits may grow into more perfect harmony.

I have been very anxious about what you wrote me concerning the probability of your not taking your seat in Congress. I thought there would be no harm in speaking to Harmon Austin about it, and did so. (I did not tell him what Sec Chase had told you). He was a good deal troubled, and said he thought that only circumstances the most pressing could make it allowable for you to resign your seat. He wished me to ask you to write to him fully before you decided to do so. Almeda and Harry have felt for some time that you could not do so without seeming to trifle with the confidence the people of the District have placed in you, unless it was very manifest that your presence in the field was very much needed. Perhaps it is all useless to have said anything about it since we know nothing [of] what a day may bring forth; but although we do not distrust your judgement, we feel that all the influences about you are tending war-ward, and they may in a measure influence you to think less of your political duties than you otherwise would.

We had a very delightful time at the wedding, although not so pleasant getting there. The snow and mud were so deep that we were three hours getting
from Warren to Lordstown, but the sunshine was very bright and we suffered
only for the poor horses. Harry went down the night before, and we found him
in one of his most radiant moods, and Libbie[17] looking very sweet, quiet and
happy. Harry is proud of Libbie's personal attractions at least, and the more I
see her the more I think she is capable of exerting a stronger influence over him
than we have feared. She is pretty, self-possessed and gentle with a very nice
taste, and I felt as I looked at her that in her personal appearance and qualities
she was the most perfect counterpart of Rebecca I had ever known. I looked at
her and thought of Rebecca, while my own faults and imperfections trooped
before me until legion was their name, and my heart filled with great sobs of
anguish, and I felt as I never had before that had it not been for me, you too
might have been blessed with a wife to whom it would not have been necessary
to say as Harmon Austin said to me, "You ought to be in Washington with
James. You need the [friction] of the kind of society you would meet there." O,
for your sake I would be more, but I am what I am, and I thank you for bearing
with my faults as kindly as you do. I cannot write any more—my heart is too
full. May Heaven keep you through all the new year and guide you to all that is
good and noble.

Your own Crete.

Washington, January 6, 1863

My Dearest Crete:
Your good letter of the 2nd came to me a few minutes ago. I have just read
it, and will answer it at once. In regard to the letter which [was] as painful to me
to write as anything in the world could be, I will only say I wrote it because I
thought we ought to become to each other in all the better and nobler senses of
the word "true," and I am thankful to you with all my heart for the noble manner in which you have responded to it. Only good can come from faithful statements to each other of our convictions and mutual admonitions. I would not for
a moment have it seem that I assumed [myself] to be so free from faults as to
give me the right to criticise you, for I know fully and sadly how many faults I
have that need to be forgiven. In this letter you speak of a letter written to me
when I was sick that I did not answer. On that I say as I said before that I have
answered every letter I have rec'd from you, and if mine have been infrequent,

yours have been equally so. But you have spoken so nobly and earnestly upon the whole matter that I hope and believe that you will not think I have meant to be in any way unkind or unjust in the premises. I most fully believe that we can live happily and joyfully together, and never so much as now. So I long to be with you, and with those dear assurances of the living presence, to make plain the obscure, render light the dark and joyful the sad, as this poor pen is wholly unable to do. I pray you do not be sad but hopeful about our life and love. There is more reason to be hopeful and joyful than ever before since we took up the journey of life together, and I feel sure that we cannot only "clamber up the hill of life" but "totter down the farther slope" hand in hand with more light and genial warmth of heart than if we had never felt the snows about us, and the cold wind blowing. And now, dearest, a truce to sadness and an all hail to happy thoughts of love and each other and our blessed little Trot.

The evidence is all now before the Court. Tomorrow we begin to review the evidence. Saturday, the defence of the accused will be read, and that day or Monday we shall give sentence, and close our work. It has been a tremendous job, full of difficulties requiring a great deal of labor and patience. I have no doubt but I shall get away into the field somewhere south or west as soon as we are through. I was told a few days ago by Mr. Chase, that the Stanton plan of sending me to East Tennessee was probably vetoed by Halleck and that South Carolina stood fairest to be my destination. In regard to the Congress matter, you have solved the question correctly in your remark that we "know not what a day may bring forth." I should not need to resign till late next fall, and before that time the question has a great many chances of settling itself. Of course, I shall take no action without full consultation with you all and many of my leading Constituents at home. Meantime, let nothing be said that the thing is thought of at all. Indeed I doubt if I shall resign the Seat. I shall not, unless, when the time comes, it clearly appears as a matter of higher duty.

I hope Harry and Libby may be happy, and that all the fears we have had for Harry may be groundless. As I once said to Burke [Hinsdale] there is a certain unknown quantity in Harry's nature which can be represented by "XY" and whose value it is quite impossible to determine with accuracy. Whether there will ever be equations enough to enable us to eliminate and deduce the value of X and Y, I don't know. But such strange things happen in human nature, that we can form no judgment as to how Harry will come out at last. He and Libbie may be just fitted for each other; their mutual influence upon each other may be every way salutary. Let us hope so. . . .

Kiss our dear little one for me over and over again, and write to me soon on the arrival of this or it will not find me in Washington. Loving and hopeful, I am your James.

P.S. I attended the Italian Opera a few evenings ago and heard the celebrated Angiolina Cordier sing.[18] The opera was La Traviata which I find is the same as Camille. I send you a copy of it.

In mid-January James traveled to Tennessee to join General Rosecrans. He stopped by Hiram on his way. From his Hiram visit until the following October, no letters from Lucretia are extant. Whether they were lost, or Lucretia in later years destroyed them (which is most unlikely) cannot be known. Nothing is mentioned of them; they simply are not to be found.

Murfreesboro, Tennessee.
January 25, 1863.

My Dear Crete:

I reached here at 5 o'clock this evening after a ride of seven hours in an ambulance. I had a cavalry escort of 20 men and narrowly escaped a fight with a large body of rebel cavalry, which came down the Nashville pike from Franklin and destroyed a few cars and captured 25 of our men, only two or three miles from us as we were on the route here. But we are here safely now and will soon be in shape to return any little affectionate compliment of that kind they may see fit to give us. I have never seen more disagreeable weather than we have endured for the last four days. It has been one continued drizzle of dreary cold rain, soon converting the earth into the rarest mud for the last two days. Today, however, there are symptoms of turning sunshine, and it promises that for a while "the rain is over and gone." It is exceeding strange that even the thought of camp life should bring back my old malady. For two months I have been almost perfectly well. But last night I was wakened in the small hours by a most frightful diarrhea which has been running riot with me all day. I presume it is the result of a sudden change of water and diet. I have one thing in my favor, and that is a very slim appetite. I shall try fasting, or at least abstemiousness for a time and hope soon to have adjusted myself to the new conditions, and be all right again. Don't feel troubled about it, for I feel a great power of health in me, which I think will show itself soon. I have had an interview with Gen

Rosecrans, who is now quite sick, indeed has been confined to his bed for several days with an attack of lung fever. He was very friendly and received me with the familiarity and kindness of an old acquaintance. I did not introduce business but as I came out he asked me to come in again in the morning, saying he was glad to have me with him and that there were two or three Divisions "fishing" for me. I will not write more tonight but will write more in the morning when I have taken a night's quiet. In these dreary days it is sweet to have a loving center to let my heart wander back to and to think of you as loving me and to feel the warmth and glow about my heart which is full of hope and joy. And our happy home and dear little Trot: God bless you all and many sweet dreams and loving thoughts of me visit you. Good night, Dearest. Your ownest James.

Monday morning, January 26.

Dearest Crete:

I am feeling quite well this morning after a good night's rest and though I have not yet surmounted my attack of diarrhea, yet I am [feeling] better than I did yesterday. I have met quite a large number of my old friends of this army. I have not, of course, been here long enough to form a very comprehensive judgment of the state of affairs here, nor of the prospects of our cause here. I am however greatly pleased with some features of Gen. Rosecrans' character. He has that fine quality of having his mind made up on all the great questions which concern his work. In a military man this is a cardinal virtue. The whole texture of Generalship is made up of theories which his mind must form of the position, force and intentions of his enemy, and he must shape his course, take his resolutions, and act upon them in accordance with his theory. Hence a man who does not think decisively and place full and implicit reliance upon his own judgments cannot act with confidence. Gen. R. thinks rapidly and strikes forward into action with the utmost confidence in his own judgment. In this he is perfectly unlike McClellan, who rarely has a clear-cut decisive opinion, and dare not trust it when he has. The officers whom I have met since I came here seem to have the most unbounded confidence in Rosy, and are enthusiastic in his praise. He is the most Spanish looking man I know of, a kind of Don Menendez face, and though he swears fiercely, yet he is a Jesuit of the highest style of Roman piety. He carries a cross attached to his watch dial, and as he drew his watch out of his side pants pocket, his rosary, a dirty looking string of friars beads, came out with it.

There is much in his appearance that is striking and singular. He remembers me very well, commenced at once to talk of my Sandy Valley Campaign, and our correspondence while I was there. Nearly midnight last night he came out after I had gone to bed, and though he was sick he staid and talked for an hour, till his darkey came and took [him] by the shoulder, and led him back away to bed.

I shall look for a letter from you in a short time. The mail comes here daily. Until you hear from me again, direct to Care of Gen. Rosecrans, Murfreesboro, Tenn. Ever and forever,

Your James.

Murfreesboro, Feb. 26, 1863

My Dearest Crete:

Harry arrived yesterday afternoon bring[ing] your letter. It had been a long time since I had heard from you, or any of the family. I am sorry that my letters have, some of them, failed to reach you. From what Harry tells me I am sure that several of my letters have been strangely delayed or entirely lost. I full[y] sympathize with all you say in regard to gloomy feelings, for though I have long made it a point to use philosophy and not give way to sad and gloomy feelings, I do so now, but the complications of questions congressional and military and especially my long stay here in comparative idleness, and official inactivity conspire to make me dissatisfied and sad. The continual dreary rain, the broken and devasted country with its impassable roads and the dreary battalions that go dripping and soiled to their daily monotony of mingled labor and idleness— all act with depressing force on one's spirits. I am most happy to assure you that no part of my sadness is referable [to] any of the old causes of darkness which once haunted my heart. On the contrary, I turn from all this sadness here to our happy home and long with an ache and an earnestness stronger than ever to enjoy it with you and our blessed little Trot. The question of what I shall be assigned to has not been a mere formal matter. If I was to have been put in command of a Division, the decision would have been easy, but the place of Chief of Staff was one of more gravity and more important results. In the first place, Gen R. wanted to know me so thoroughly as [to] be sure that I was the man he wanted. It was, in the next place, necessary that he should find out what the opinions and feelings of such officers as his leading Corps Commanders were in reference to the matter. These consultations have been held, and long and searching conversations between the General and myself have been held in reference to it. I have almost wholly abstained from writing to my friends till I should know what my work was to be. I have not been unaware of the fact that I should lose credit and my personal and military reputation to some extent injured by the long delay. My experience in delay, in Washington and here, has been one of the most trying of my life. It has tried my powers of endurance and my natural restlessness more than it was ever tried before. I have gone through all the cycles of restlessness and chafing impatience until I think I have learned to endure with a considerable degree of patience if not with meekness what is laid upon me. Since I began to write this letter at the General's table, he has written an order, and has just now shown it to me, assigning me to duty as Chief of his Staff. It will [be] printed tomorrow and I shall proceed to duty at once. So that the long agony is over and true [to] perverseness of human nature I shall no doubt often regret that I am not in command of a Division, but I shall nevertheless go to work throughly and vigorously to make as much out of this army as I can. I presume that the first impression of my assignment to duty will be unfavorable in the minds of my friends abroad, but I am willing to bear that from the knowledge that I am chosen here because it is regarded as a great necessity and though I may not make as much reputation as I could in another place, yet I can exercise more influence on the army and more fully impress my views and policy on its administration.

I am very glad to see Harry.[19] I have had a delightful visit with him, and shall hope soon to be set up in an independent mess where I can make him feel more at home. I had a telegram on the 24th from Professor[20] saying he was on his way here. I am glad to have him come here with me.

In regard to the little addition of which you speak to our house, I leave it wholly with your own judgment. If you conclude to build it, try to get along with using as little of our invested money as possible. You had better have [your] Father superintend it, and then settle with him, if he has the time. Will it disfigure the house any to have such an addition put on? Tell Almeda I will answer her letter soon, probably tomorrow. One of my letters to her seems to be lost. Give my love to all the household. Kiss little Trot and tell her it is from me. It is now 1 o'clock at night. Ever your own James.

By mid-March Lucretia knew she was again pregnant, and that the danger of another
miscarriage was past. From the remarks James makes in the letter following, it would
seem she had written him the news.

Murfreesboro, April 1, 1863

My Precious Little Crete:

Yours of the 26th March came to hand yesterday, but the letter of the 22nd
did not reach me till today. From the Office marks on it, it appears to have had
a trip to Cairo and left that place on the 26th of March. I am glad always to
receive a letter from you, but this last that should have been first of the two is
most welcome. From my heart, Dearest, I thank [you] for writing it, and the
beautiful and tender way in which you wrote it is only surpassed in my regard
by the message itself. I thank you for the fact, even more than for the record.
You know how I have felt on that subject for a long time. The heading for this
letter was written late last night, and just as I was ready to commence the first
line, a pile of dispatches was brought in which occupied me till past one o'clock.
I then went to my cot and for nearly an hour my thoughts of you and your letter were very sweet, solemn and joyful. There is such a mystery about life in
any form that the comtemplation of it always fills me with awe. But of incipient
life, of life that is to be, with all the grand and fearful possibilities which may
attend it, I have no words to tell you what my thoughts were. And then the
thought that it is my life, a life which I may never see, that there may be a period
of oblivion between the sunset of my own, and the morning of that new life.
Should this be true, that little life will be so strange and singular a one in its history. It is impossible for me to tell you how overwhelming and deep an interest
I feel in the future of that precious hope. I beg you to be happy and cheerful during all the awfully mysterious days through which you will live till the consum-
mation. It is matter of great regret to me that I cannot be with you and share
with you the hopes and thoughts that shall be yours during those sacred days,
but you must write to me frequently and fully. I agree to your last views in
regard to the house. Can't you make the "Library and Parlor" a little larger by
reducing the width of the hall or by letting the hall run out a few feet into
Mother's room? Do so if you can. I fully agree with father's views that the house
can never be made to suit us by additions. It is like the prayer that old Bro John
Smith of Ky was asked to finish. He declined, saying he had rather make a new
one than to try to patch up that one. Get some thorough man to build it, and

bind him to finish the work by a given time, and not far distant. A horse barn must be built under the same contract, as it will cost less. Also a Lew. Toodles should furnish the plan for the latter and send me a drawing. I want the horse barn large enough so that a carriage may stand in between the stalls on the opposite side and still have full room to lead horses out and in. I want some good plan made out and sent to me. If I had time I would get one up, but it is not possible for me to do it. I want the barn finished with upright boarding, battened over and painted some light color, say slate, trimmed with white.

Economy is the word in all this work. I sent you a draft on New York of $183 in my last. I forgot to enclose the stanza. I send it now together with a song which Gen McCook sings. His wife copied it for me. The Gen. (McC) sings it finely. It is very beautiful. Kisses and love to Trot, and always to you.

Ever and forever, Your James.

Murfreesboro, June 24, 1863

Dearest Crete:

The whole army is in motion. Head Quarters moves at 1 P.M. I have only time to tell you this, for we are very busy. I have just issued an order interdicting all telegraphic dispatches to the press until further orders. You may not hear from us for several days. We shall test the strength of Bragg's Army before this reaches you. I send you love and a thousand kisses to Trot. Love to Mother. I shall send you a line when I can.

Ever your own, James.

TO: MRS. J A GARFIELD

HIRAM, PORTAGE COUNTY, VIA CLEVELAND

FROM: NASHVILLE. JULY 23, 1863

IF YOU CAN COME, DO SO AT ONCE. THERE WILL BE TIME FOR YOU TO ARRIVE BEFORE WE LEAVE HERE. MRS. ROSECRANS IS HERE. ANSWER WHEN YOU WILL LEAVE CLEVELAND. THIS DISPATCH WILL BE A PASS.

SIGNED: J A GARFIELD, BRIG GEN. CHIEF OF STAFF.

But Lucretia did not visit James.

Winchester, Tennessee.

August 1, 1863

Dearest Crete:

Yours of June 27th came to hand last evening. I had been waiting anxiously to hear from you not knowing whether to look to the mail, the telegraph, or the cars for the first intelligence. I knew it would be a question of some doubt in your own mind what you ought to do, and I did not feel sure myself, but yet I hoped it might be consistent for you to come and visit me. While thus waiting I did not write, and in addition to this reason I was so overcrowded with business that I did not write to anybody. I have never passed so long a time before for years without writing a letter. But from the date of my last letter to you (in which I enclosed $500) I have not written a private letter till today. We staid in Nashville much longer than we at first intended to. We didn't come back here till the 29th July. In addition to my work I had a very severe return of the piles which made me a great deal of trouble all the time I was there, and I have not yet entirely recovered. I hope, however, the worst is over. We are busy again preparing for another advance and I earnestly hope it will be begun soon. I don't feel at all satisfied with the slow progress we are making and I expect to hear complaints and just ones soon. There are the strongest possible reasons for using every moment now before the rebels can recover from their late disasters. I have been paid for the month of July and I enclose you a government check for $200. I hope you are using the funds as economically as is consistent with our wants and decent appearance. I don't say this to intimate that I have any doubts on the question but only to show my anxiety on that point. I am running myself rather shabby in the way of clothing, thinking to keep but a small amount of military clothing on hand this fall, in case I should quit the service, but I presume I shall be compelled to get one more suit at any rate. I am living as frugally as I consistently can. I hope the aspect of the war may be such that I can go to Congress this fall, but I will defer a decision for the present. Tell mother I will write her in answer to her letter soon. Dear Little Trot—How much I long to see the little codger. Kiss her for me, and tell her the "webbles haven't hurt papa yet."

Ever your own James.

P.S. If you don't need to use this $200, you had better put it in bank or purchase US 6—20's. JAG.

On September 19, 20, and 21 the great Battle of Chickamauga took place near the border between Tennessee and Georgia, just south of Chattanooga. Rosecrans' forces gave way at the center and the right when the General ordered a withdrawal there just at the moment and the place where Longstreet's Confederates had massed for an attack. The Rebels overran Rosecrans' headquarters, while the General along with his lieutenants and chief of staff, James, rode in panic to the rear. But the battle had not been lost. General Thomas—"the Rock of Chickamauga"—held his line against great odds. James suggested to Rosecrans that Thomas was still fighting and they ought to return to the line of battle, but General Rosecrans had somehow lost all will to fight. As General Rosecrans withdrew to Chattanooga, dazed and listless, James rode back to General Thomas to encourage him to continue the fight. His horse Billy was wounded and his orderly killed, but James arrived at Thomas' front unscathed. Thomas, however, had received orders to withdraw and did so, missing an opportunity to smash the tired and battered rebel forces. Thus, the Union army retired to Chattanooga awaiting a further attack from Bragg and his Confederates. But that never came. James felt that the great battle might have been won more decisively, that the rebel forces once and for all might have been destroyed, had Rosecrans, or even Thomas, risen to the occasion.

Chattanooga. Sept. 23, 1863

Dearest Crete:

I know you will pardon me for not writing sooner and even now I have only time to write a few words. I would not now, had I time, recount the events of Saturday, Sunday and Monday. The recollection of them fills me with pride and grief commingled. We are now in the peninsula which this place fills, and the masses of the rebel army are closed in around us. There is no doubt that they have double or triple our numbers. Burnside will not reach us for six days. We must therefore save ourselves if saved at all. I expect the battle will be renewed this morning and with fury. If calamity befalls us you may be sure we shall sell ourselves as dearly as possible. It is now the early morning and all is still. I would not if I could tell you all that is in my heart. I will only say that a picture of unutterable dearness is in my soul as I think of you and Trot and our dear circle of precious ones at Hiram. Give this word to them for me. Yours of the 14th came to me yesterday and made me glad. Keep up a brave cheerful heart. The country will triumph if we do not. Kiss little Trot for me a hundred times.

Write me frequently as usual, whatever betide. I hope you will never have cause to blush on my account. Love to mother when she returns to you. I hope she is well.

Ever your own James.

Chattanooga, Sept 25. 1863.

Dearest Crete:

I have been so perfectly overwhelmed with work and weariness for the last three days that I have not been able to write to you or any of our friends at home, and I will only now write to assure you that you need have no apprehension for the safety of the army. I will not attempt now—perhaps not till I see you—to give you a history of the battle which was much the fiercest we have had in the west, perhaps anywhere during the war. I will only say it was won and then abandoned, giving the enemy an opportunity to follow and injure us, but he was too much crippled to do so till we had strengthened ourselves in this place and were able to repulse all his attempts. The campaign is successful, and Chattanooga will be held. Thus the great end of our movement has been accomplished, even if the battle be considered lost. I am very much worn down with fatigue and diarrhea. I kept up finely till the trouble was over, and now the reaction has come on, it will take me some days to gather up again. I hope I shall be able to spend some weeks with you before Congress convenes. Let me hear from you soon. . . .

Love to all our friends. Kisses to dear little Trot.

Ever your own James.

Hiram, October 4, 1863.

My Dear *dear* Jamie:

I cannot tell how inexpressibly glad we are for the loving words you have sent us from the battlefield, and you do not know how tenderly and lovingly my thoughts turn back in clinging fondness to you during those hours when after the night's weary work, the little rest, the early morning glare brought only to you a keener sense of your loneliness and that longing for friends and love which only such a heart as yours can know. O dearest, with a proud love I think of you standing up in all the strength of brave noble manliness, and my heart leans upon you and trusts to your protection, but when such hours come upon you I feel the stronger one, and long to draw your head close down to my heart and fondle and caress you as I would the trusting love-needing child. Yours of the 23rd ult. did not reach us till last night; Mother was growing almost sick with anxiety lest you were from the exhaustion and fatigue of the battle ill again and unable to write. I did not feel that you were, still was very glad to have added your testimony. The papers give no account of fighting since the date of your last so that I am feeling very comfortable about you. It seems to be understood now that there is little danger of the rebels renewing the attack. I hope Rosecrans may soon be so strongly reinforced as to be able to assume the offensive again. . . .

Harvey [Everest] is sick with what seems now to be typhoid fever, so that the school is thrown almost entirely upon Miss Booth's hands. It is well the term is so nearly through. There are only five weeks more, I believe. I have finally got down my last carpet and have the whole house in living order. I should have been perfectly discouraged had I known at the beginning of the term that eight weeks would pass before I should be as far along with the work as I now am. The barn is nearly ready to raise and I begin to hope it may be finished before you come home, unless you take us by surprise much sooner than we dare expect. The report was very current a week ago that you were to be at home last week, and speak at a Union Meeting at Mantua Station yesterday. Mr. Leach came up here to inquire about it. He said if you were to be there he must go; if not he could not spend the time. Trot is very well now, and getting to look like herself again. She went to church today with Grandmama, the first time without me. It rained when they were coming home, and Mother put her handkerchief over her hat. She had seen the horses go past yesterday with flags on their heads, so Mother says she said when she put the handkerchief on her, "The horses had flags on their heads, but I have a 'haffin on mine.'" She has taken a fancy again to have a ring, and wants me to write you to bring her one. We are all well and hoping and praying that you may be kept to come home to us again. Your own as ever,

Crete.

On October 15 James was relieved of his duty by a grateful General Rosecrans. He returned to Hiram, via Louisville, where he was questioned by Secretary of War Stanton regarding Rosecrans' behavior at the Battle of Chickamauga. He stayed a few days in Hiram and then went on to Washington to deliver the official report for Rosecrans to General Halleck and President Lincoln. He again returned to Hiram to be with "little Trot" in her final illness. She died on December 1. James then went back to Washington in time for the opening of his first session in Congress, which took place on December 5. Though Trot was now gone, Crete and James had a son, Harry, born on October 11.

Washington, Dec. 6, 1863.

My Darling Crete:

I arrived here at six o'clock last evening, having been detained at Harrisburg six hours by our train failing to connect with the one for Baltimore. Mrs Parmlee and her friend did not get the morning train at Bedford, but came on in the afternoon and overtook me at Harrisburg next morning.

I cannot tell you what a lonely dreary ride it was to me. On reaching Pittsburg I fell in company with Capt Pearce of Cincinnati, whom I knew in the days of my Senatorship. He was accompanied by his wife and her sister and all were accompanying the remains of a third lovely sister of 19 to their former home in Washington. I joined the party and seemed far more at home with stricken mourners than with any others. I told them the story of our precious little Trot, and they told me of their grief. The way seemed very long and very dark. I reached here just in time to attend the caucus at 7 in the evening, when we elected Mr Colfax of Indiana as our candidate for Speaker.

Today I have resigned my commission in the army and am now for the first time since Aug 12, 1861, a citizen. I have come away this evening to my rooms at the corner of N.Y. Avenue and 13th Street, and am now here alone. The rooms are very large, and I more alone than ever before in my life. It does seem to me that I cannot stay here alone this whole winter and spring, and Heaven knows how much of the summer besides. How constantly the image of our precious lost one leaps into my memory and heart! I took dinner with Sec Stanton today, and his little ones were there to haunt me with contrasts between them and Trot. Her brightness so far outshone theirs that I almost wondered any one could love them and not worship her. I find myself sitting alone calling her by her pet names and asking her if she loves me and almost hoping to hear an answer. Precious little Darling, I wonder if she can know how her papa loves her and longs for her? I find here awaiting me your letter of Nov 6th in which you tell me of her crying that I came away without kissing her. In my leaving for Washington this last time I could say that the little darling had left without kissing me. I grieve more than she did. I find a ponderous pile of letters awaiting me, and I sit down drearily to the task of answering and Sec Stanton assures me that he will hold my place in the army open for me at any time I choose to return, and if this terrible weary work and desolateness of heart continues, it seems as though I must go back into the wild life of the army.

There is some prospect of a difficulty in organizing the House, and the members have been advised to go there assured _____ tomorrow. I don't think there is any real danger, though some think there is. I was appointed as one of a committee of five to manage the matter, and the other members of the caucus promised to sustain us in any measure we deemed necessary to take. The other members of the committee were Thaddeus Stevens of Pa., H. Winter Davis of Md., and Blaine of Me. We have planned a small campaign which has a fight as one of its remote contingencies, but I trust very remote.

Do write to me Dearest, often and long. How much I want you with me. Give my love to Mother and Almeda, and kiss the little boy. (How sadly this sounds to leave out Trot!) for I am as ever your own James.

Hiram, December 6, 1863.

My Dear Precious Husband:

I have just come from kneeling beside the bed where our little one breathed out her life. I have asked of Our Father a more perfect resignation of spirit to this great sorrow which has fallen upon our lives so heavily, and I hope that He has given it to me—to us both. I hope, dear Jamie, that you are trying to look up, through tears though it be, to our Savior's face and from His words of comfort gathering peace to your soul, and a larger strength to do well the work of life. These words have been much in my heart today: "The Father chasteneth whom He loveth," and the thought has come to me that not only has He honored us in giving us to keep a while a little nature so pure and noble but that he also loves us so well that He will make surer our clinging to Him by taking our cherished one to Himself, that where our treasure is, there may our hearts be also. These have been, Oh, such sad strange days that I fear there have been in my heart questionings and doubts which were almost wrong; but I hope God is lifting my spirit out from the shadow and that I am gaining a hold on a larger truer life, and I trust it is so with you, my dear one. Surely we can be thankful for this at least that we have come to be so much nearer and dearer to each other, that our love has been made so perfect through this great suffering. I feel that we need each other now as we have never before, and that we can the most truly live when near each other. Still I submit to whatever seems best and will try patiently and faithfully "to labor and to wait." My dear Jamie, you do not know the large place you won in my heart by your gentle care and attention when at home. It surprised me and made me love you so tenderly to see you taking care of our little girl, and watching beside her so gently; and so much dearer is our home now for the notice and care you took of it. I have almost feared that your heart was so saddened by the loss of our darling that you would dread to return here, and that our home would have little attaction for you now: but I hope it is not so. To me it is now a holy place, and I want it to be so to you. I do not feel like writing more now; but we will write to each other very often and live very near each other. I did not write yesterday as I promised since a letter would not go until tomorrow. . . .

That you may be blessed and kept good and noble and true is the prayer of your loving trusting little wife, Crete.

P.S. Commencing with the 13th verse of 1st Thessalonians, 4th Chapt, read through to the close of the Epistle. I find there much to comfort and strengthen my heart. Crete.

Hiram, December 11, 1863.

My Dearest Jamie:

It is a week this morning since you left us, and we have no letter from you yet. I am perfectly sure you have written and that the mails alone are at fault that we do not receive the kind words I know you have sent, and which I so much need. The perfect trust with which my heart leans upon you now makes me feel more than ever before my loneliness without you and it seems to me the days instead of diminishing the sorrow over the little lost face which was ever turning to me in its brightness and love are only adding a new edge to the sharpness of my grief. The want in my heart for that little presence grows larger and larger and when I look into the days and years which may remain of life, there is a spot in every place so blank which nothing can fill, nothing hide. Our little boy is very dear to me, but he seems to me so incomplete without his little sister to lead and guide him.

Dear Jamie, do not let me murmur. I am afraid my heart is growing more rather than less unreconciled. Pray earnestly for me, my darling husband that I may gain that resignation of spirit which can look calmly through life to that perfect life beyond where our darling has gone to wait for us.

We were gratified to see how successful our Union party were in electing their Speaker in the House, and your name once occurring in the report of Monday's sitting assured us that you were safely at Washington and well enough to be about.

Our affairs here are progressing slowly. Mr. Pinney had some trouble to find lumber for the ice house but has succeeded, and will build it as soon as the weather will permit. He says he would like a hundred dollars now as soon as you can get it for him. He has some notes due which he would like to take up.

Baby is two months old today. He is growing nicely and can finally *laugh*. Write as often as you can and come home Christmas. Yours most lovingly, Crete.

P.S. I sent you a letter last Monday.

Washington, Dec. 13, 1863

My Precious Crete:

Your dear noble letter of the 8th inst. came to me yesterday. It was balm to my heart, and it made me feel more than ever before how noble and true you are. Pray for me, dearest, that my heart may, like yours, become more resigned and see the hand of our good Father in this great sorrow. It is a lovely day, after a cold and cheerless morning of storm. I ought to be cheerful and happy as are the sun and the sky, and though your brave words have made me calmer and stronger, I still struggle with my grief and think [of] our precious darling with such a yearning agony of heartbreak that at times it seems as though I could not endure it. I have read twice over this morning the passage you told me of from Thessalonians. It is touchingly tender and hopeful. I would that my heart could rest upon it as I when a child rested in my mother's words. I pray that my faith may grow stronger. I try to be hopeful but Tennyson speaks for me when he says:

> "Yet in these ears till hearing dies,
>   One set slow bell will ever toll
> The passing of the sweetest soul
>   That ever looked with human eyes."[21]

How her image and little nature has grown upon me since she is gone. "Death has made His darkness beautiful with her." You must read "In Memoriam." It really seems as if it were written for us. Only a change of gender is needed to make it seem direct and real. I hope you have gotten my letters by this time. They have all been very hurried, but I know you will appreciate something of the amount of my work and will forgive my meagerness in what I write. Really, Dearest, I wish you would think whether you cannot manage to come back with me after the Holidays, if I return home then as I now hope to. It really does not seem as though I could stay here all this lonely winter. We will talk of it when I come. Do not fear that I will not love our home. It is more sacred to me than ever. I did for a little while think I could not live in it any more, but I think differently now. Tell me about the little boy. Is he well? How is your own health now? I hope you are being very careful and getting strong again. I sent you a draft the other day: did it reach you? Give my love to Mother and all the family. I am still stopping at the corner of N.Y. Avenue and 13th St. and logging away at the letters.

With all my heart, I am ever, Your own James.

Years later Lucretia wrote to a close friend who had lost a child as follows: "I read a little while ago a few sentences from a Swedenborgian, which have in them so much beauty that I will give them to you. 'Those who pass into the other life in infancy and childhood, will be the embodiment of loveliness. They will be like the privacy and sweet peace of home.' And the thought came to me that perhaps your baby who seems so unaccountably taken away from you here, was taken to help people your home in the spirit world. Our children who grow to mature life, go out from us to be centers of new homes, and, were all to grow to man's estate, perhaps we would be childless in the spirit life. And maybe this little one was taken for your new home after death."[22]

⚜ NOTES ⚜

1. Judge Spalding was a Cleveland lawyer, a member of the Ohio House of Representatives, and a Democrat. He later became a member of the U.S. House of Representatives.

2. David G. Swaim, a close friend, later managed Garfield's presidential campaign.

3. James Gilfillan, a fellow graduate of Williams, became Treasurer of the U.S. in 1877.

4. Orin Brown was prepared to rent his house to the Garfields. The house, still extant, stands at the northwest corner of the campus of the Eclectic (now Hiram College). Early in 1863, the Garfields bought the house, making some additions to it that year; it was their first home.

5. Mr. Micawber was a character from Dickens' *David Copperfield*, well-known for his expectations of something turning up.

6. General Wood commanded the 6th Division, which included Garfield's 20th Brigade during the Kentucky campaign. At this point Wood was in command of a division in the Army of the Cumberland.

7. Major General Irvin McDowell, maligned after the Second Battle of Bull Run, had been relieved of command. He told Garfield his story, and Garfield obviously took his side. For a while James had been assigned McDowell's enquiry case, but in the end did not sit on that board.

8. Joshua R. Giddings, an Ohio member of the U.S. House of Representatives (1838–1859), became Consul General to Canada in 1861. James and Lucretia had heard his abolitionist point of view in 1850, when they were at the school in Chester, Ohio.

9. Mary P. Ryan, *The Cradle of the Middle Class* (Cambridge, 1981), 201.

10. Eli Thayer, a Massachusetts congressman, advocated the Florida scheme which James was hoping to lead. The scheme never came about.

11. Eben Ayers was a friend of Maria Learned, whom James visited while at Williams College. Ayers had attended the Hiram Eclectic when James was Principal there.

12. Harvey Everest, who had taken the principalship of the Hiram Eclectic when James entered the army, did not in fact resign until 1864, when he accepted the presidency of Eureka College in Illinois.

13. When Lucretia mentions "life's great trial," she must be referring to the revelation that James had fallen in love with Rebecca and had perhaps consummated that relationship.

14. Henry Ulke was a Russian-born artist working in Washington. He painted portraits of many prominent men.

15. Burnside publicly accepted the blame for the massacre of union soldiers at Fredericksburg, December 13.

16. James had written Harry Rhodes letters December 5, 7, 14, but he only wrote to Lucretia once during that time, a letter she had not received.

17. Libbie died a few years later, and in 1868 Harry remarried.

18. Angiolina Cordier made her New York debut on November 24, singing the title role in Meyerbeer's opera *Dinorah*.

19. Harry Rhodes visited James in February. As well as a letter from Lucretia, Rhodes also brought two volumes of Carlyle's *French Revolution*, requested by James in a letter to Rhodes written February 7.

20. "The Professor" was James' personal cook.

21. James quotes *In Memoriam A. H. H.*, verse 57, stanza 3.

22. Frederick Henry, *Captain Henry of Geauga County* (Cleveland: The Gates Press, 1942), 275.

CHAPTER 6

"The Shadows Passed," January 1864–December 1865

It was many months before Lucretia and James fully recovered from their grief over the death of "little Trot," but as time passed references to her gradually disappear from their letters. In the meantime, they decide to name their baby Harry Augustus and he begins to replace Trot as a focus of attention in the letters.

James took rooms in Washington with his good friend Major General Robert Schenck, a warrior turned congressman like Garfield. In the early spring James arranged for Crete to visit him in Washington, which she did, often attending the Congressional sessions to watch James from the Diplomats' Gallery.

Back at Hiram, the Garfield household seemed more peaceful in that James' mother and Almeda Booth were adjusting to each other, perhaps both having been sobered by the death of Trot. The bitterest blow for Lucretia then fell. It seems that James had met and fallen in love with a widow sometime during the many months he had been living in Washington alone. Perhaps it was a fear that just such a thing as this might occur that caused him to write to Lucretia on their wedding anniversary in the autumn of 1862: "I here pray you to be still ready to bear with me if at any future moment my heart should for a time go down again into the deeps." The "future moment" evidently arrived in May 1864. Harmon Austin, having heard an ugly rumor that James had become involved in a love affair, wrote asking if it were true. James denied the rumor emphatically. But suddenly in June James appeared at his home in Hiram, saying to the women there that he was depressed and discouraged with his work. He said he might go back to school teaching. But with Lucretia and Almeda that night he made a clean breast of it: he told them he had fallen in love with Lucia Gilbert Calhoun, a widow from New York. Little is known of Calhoun; she was a writer on domestic and social issues for the New York Tribune, and after her affair with Garfield, she married Cornelius Runkle, a New York lawyer. What is clear is that James had fallen very much in love with this young, twenty-year-old widow. Lucretia could do little more than forgive him and ask that he break the affair off, which he promised to do immediately. But James must have had a difficult time following through on this task, for both he and Crete refer repeatedly to the courage necessary to carry out the mission. The summer of 1864 could not have been a pleasant one for either James or Lucretia.

However, daily life went on as usual with James campaigning through Ohio during the fall of 1864, again successful. He then returned to Washington. But this time he found a rental to which Lucretia and little Harry came to be with him. For part of the fall and during the winter, then, the little family was together. Crete and Harry returned to Hiram in March to await the adjournment of Congress.

But that spring James could not return home until he had concluded arrangements for an elaborate business venture in Chicago having to do with the purchase of Pennsylvania oil fields. Once again Lucretia was pregnant and dreading the months ahead; she needed James to spend more time with her. Almeda Booth, in the meantime, decided to resign from the Eclectic Institute, much to James' sorrow. A child, a boy they named James, was born in October. The Garfield marriage, having weathered the grievous blow of Trot's death, endless separations, and James' infidelity, seemed by the end of 1865 to be strengthening. There would be no more long separations, and only Rebecca remained in the background to return occasionally to haunt Lucretia's thoughts.

About one-hundred and twenty-five letters were exchanged during this period, of which twenty-nine are here included.

Like the preceding letters exchanged between the bereaved wife and husband, the following contain sad and sentimental remarks about "little Trot." But, as has been pointed out by Nancy S. Dye and Daniel Blake Smith in "Mother Love and Infant Death," children in the mid-nineteenth century "were gradually slipping out of the hands of God and into their mother's warm, if nervous, embrace. And infant death, like so much else in the increasingly intimate world of family, became a private tragedy."[1] Such domestic tragedies took a powerful emotional toll.

❧

Hiram, January 22, 1864.

Darling Jamie:

You do not know how sweet and dear and treasured are your letters to me. I receive and read them, and hide away in my heart each loving word; then begin to count the days which will probably hold me from the repetition of this great joy—the greatest when you are away from me. I am glad you are getting along so well with your work, and I judge you will not be able to let me come to you before the close of this term, so that I shall have Miss Booth and Harry for company. Do you think you will want me to stay with you through the Spring? I would like to know very soon now, as I will need to arrange affairs at home for whatever time I stay away. You do not know how much I desire to be with you. There are yet four weeks of school. Will Gen Schenck leave you by that time?

We have now the deepest snow we have known for years. The two days it was falling the cars were unable to run, and we received no mail from Monday till Thursday. The weather is just warm enough to make sleighriding delightful, and if you were here I would love a ride through the frosty night, with the tinkling and jangling of the bells. Do you remember almost our only sleigh ride of three years ago, with our darling little five months old Trot? Now this snowy mantle wraps her little grave. Oh, how full of breaking my heart grows at every thought of it, and I feel there is nothing of life worth living for but you and the little boy. I used to feel sad sometimes to see how our lives were hurrying on; but now I want rather [to] hasten the days and hurry the work we have to do that we may go home the sooner to our little girl. Will she be waiting for us, and will she know us, and clasp her little arms around our necks with her sweet little "I'm glad to see you, papa and mama"? Have you any faith, Jamie? I wish you could see the little boy now. It seems to me he has changed so much you won't scarcely know him. He has got his first tooth, and yesterday pulled Grandma's glasses off from her eyes two or three times. Lizzie [Atwood] staid with me nearly a week and I enjoyed her visit very much. Mother is better than she has been for a week or two. She has been so miserable some of the time since you left that I was afraid she was going to have a fever of some kind. I think her worst symptoms have passed off now; still she is feeling very weak yet. . . .

I see from the Paper you sent Mother that you are to be, or perhaps have been before this, one of the speakers before the Lecture Association at Washington this winter. Tell me something about it. I received also the Paper with Charles G. Ames Poems.[2] Is it not very pleasant to take up now and then a thread linking us back to the long ago! Hoping to hear from you soon and often, I am ever yours most lovingly, Crete.

Hiram, February 8, 1864

My Dear Jamie:

I have just tonight received yours of the 3rd Inst. and hasten to respond. The vacation commences the 19th and we shall be ready to start the Monday following, the day I think the Sanitary Fair opens, and we shall be very happy to meet you in Cleveland or rather see you here the Saturday night preceding. I hope to perfect an arrangement by which Mrs. Hart will keep the little boy while I am gone. For several reasons I have decided that it will be very much better to leave him at home on his account more especially than our own. If I were going alone to see you, I would give it up entirely, but since Almeda expects and desires to go, I will not disappoint her. We can stay a couple of weeks and that is about all the time that this monstrous great world will ever feel I suppose that I need ask. I thought Gen. Schenck was to leave your rooms in case I was to go there, and I think it would be about as sensible for him to go to a hotel as for you. I know it is not pretty for me to say this, but full of sadness as is my heart tonight over a great many things, there is a spice of real ugliness flavoring it sufficiently to dry up all tears.[3] I will not torture you with any more of it. I am very glad and thankful for all your love and kindness and wish that circumstances would allow me to do more for your comfort and happiness. I am proud of the work you are making in Congress, but if it is at the expense of so much of your life and health I shall be more grieved than proud. . . . Pardon this letter miserable both in body and spirit, and love a little yet; for my heart is all love for you. Crete.

Washington, Feb. 14, 1864

Dearest Crete:

Let me be your Valentine, and write you a word at the close of this beautiful day. For almost the first time since I have been here, I have broken away from work and enjoyed a part of [the] Sabbath. I went to the hall of the House to hear Rev. Mr. Furniss of Boston,[4] and he preached a strong earnest sermon which did me good and I hope made me better. How I wanted you with me to enjoy it. I came back to my room, and as Gen Schenck's daughter is in town and he went away to stay with her, I was left alone. I have thus had a little rest. It was needed for I was very tired. How I longed while here alone to lie upon your breast and tell you how deep and true is my love for you. The memory of our precious Trot came back to my heart so fresh today as if she had only just left us. Where is the dear one now? Can she not send us one word—sign or token—to tell us she still knows and loves us? How I yearn to know of her new life and its wonders! The time seems long that we must wait to see her, but it may be very short. Blessed little soul. Were not my hours so full of work and weariness they would overflow with sorrow that she is gone forever.

I hope to be with you on Saturday eve next. I sent you a letter I have lately received from Mrs. Cox. She seems to be a very unhappy woman. If I ever "fall into the sere and yellow leaf,"[5] and you feel that I am neglected by others, I pray you never say so to others as she does. I need not caution you for I know you would never do so. Why hasn't Almeda written me? I haven't had a word from her in a long time. The evening bells are ringing and I must go to work on my pile of letters, which seems immortal. Ever and forever your own, James.

Lucretia had been with James in Washington for a few weeks in March and April. She has now returned to Hiram, where the household with Almeda Booth and James' mother has settled to a more peaceful atmosphere than had been the case in the past. James' mother and Miss Booth evidently disliked each other.

Hiram, April 24, 1864.

My Dear Precious Husband:

It is more than a week since I received your last letter, and I cannot but feel really lonely and sad notwithstanding my promise to remember that you do still love me and think of me even when no word comes to assure me of it. I have been waiting several days with a hope of hearing from you before writing again; but I am getting so overcharged with things to say to you that there is no alternative but to write; and the first is that I want you to know how happy we are here together this Spring. There is no unkindness shown or spoken and I think more thought and you will remember, my darling, not with a sword but in the spirit of peace you are to return to us. Oh, how earnestly I desire you to be here. Jamie, you will surely come home and stay with me this summer, will you not?

I do so want you to. I will love to have all the company you desire and be so happy if you will only love *me* better than any other one, and not make me feel that you want company because you are not happy with me alone. That isn't wrong or wicked in me a bit. I do want you to love me so well, and I can't help it. I love you just as well as that; so I ask for nothing I do not give. Now please look at me through your bluest eyes, and let the bright halo, which love exhales, gather around your face again.

I wish you could see our dear little boy. We call him Harry Augustus to please Grandma, and I remembered too that you at one time suggested that. He is larger now than dear little Trot was when a year old; and is so strong and active, and getting so smart, that I cannot but be proud of him. He is getting to understand a good many things we say to him and will peek round into our faces with such a look of mischief and with so much appreciation of fun that we cannot help but feel sometimes that he knows a great deal more than I suppose he does. Grandma says sometimes he is getting altogether too smart, but I quiet her fears by telling her he has a big neck and a big body to match his big head, and I guess he will come on all right. I wish you could see his ear. As Physiognomists would say it has so much character. It is large and stands out well from his head and every line and angle is so nicely defined that it looks like the ear of a matured person. Jamie, I think we have some reason to be proud of our babies, and since you desire more I wish we had them now. I have received the papers you sent and have read them with a great deal of interest. I fancied how you all looked through those exciting debates,[6] and wished I were there again to watch you from the Diplomatic Gallery. I suppose you have no expectation of adjourning before the Baltimore Convention, so I suppose we need not expect you here Commencement. I wish you could be here at the close of term, but I think Commencement is the 9th of June, and the Convention is the 7th. But you will come as soon as you can after, will you not! What is best to do with the deck roof of the porch? It leaks worse than ever this spring. Shall I try canvassing it; or make sure work by covering it with Zinc or Tin?. . . .

I hope you can write to me again. I try to feel that you are not neglectful; but love is so exacting, the desires of the heart will overpower even the dictates of Reason and the trusts of the strongest faith. Your own forever, Crete.

As the Army of the Potomac was preparing for a decisive battle with General Lee's Confederates, James once again toyed with the idea of returning to the army; but it was

only a loose thought, as was his dream of going west to the Pacific Coast to settle down there. More practical about such things, Lucretia, thinking she is once again pregnant, requests that James come home more often, especially during the difficult months she has ahead of her. In fact, she does not prove to be pregnant after all.

Hiram, May 1, 1864.

My Darling Jamie:

I have just laid the little boy down asleep in his crib besides me and I wish you could see him as he lies here with both little fists doubled as if to defy any-body or thing to disturb his slumbers. You don't know what a world of happi-ness you lose in your separation from his baby life. It would bring back to you so much of life's springtime to hold the little rolicking fellow in your arms. I feel sorry for you every time I think of you away alone, knowing so little of your lit-tle boy and so unknown to him.

Jamie, I don't want you to return to the Army. I want your heart to turn to your home, loving the feeling that you owe something to it. If what now seems *more than possible* in regard to myself prove true, it seems to me that under no circumstances can I consent to your staying away from me, and I almost feel that there could be none which would make it justifiable. If I knew that you would come home and stay with me, I would try not to complain; but if you will not, I feel that it would be almost better to lie down in the dust beside the pre-cious lost one. Jamie, I do not feel that I can live through another such trial without you. Perhaps my fears may be groundless. I cannot but hope they may. Do not chide me, darling. You speak of a home on the Pacific coast. I could live with you any place; but judging from the past, you will be almost always away from me. You would probably be sent back to Washington to spend a large part of the year with your old friends all around you, while I should be left a stranger alone in a strange land. Do not think I am feeling bitterly. I hope I do not express myself so. I only feel very sad, and I cannot help it. . . .

I shall do what I can in the way of gardening, but the great scarcity of labor-ers will make it perhaps impossible to do as well with it as you would like. Father thinks it will not pay to take the piece of green sward Mrs. Smith pro-posed; but she will let another piece, already broken up, on shares, and he thinks it best for me to take that.

We are all very well, and Mother sends her love and promises to write to you soon. Your letter of last Sunday reached here on Thursday—sooner than any one before since I came home. Uncle Thomas writes that Charles paid him for you when at home in the winter and that he will make it right with you when he sees you. I love and desire every letter you get time to write. Your own forever, Crete.

P.S. Don't have any more photographs taken, I beg of you. They grow worse and worse every time. You look a great deal better than the best one. Ever, Crete.

The Battle of the Wilderness, May 5–7, had been fought between Grant and Lee, and the wounded—over ten-thousand—were beginning to flow into Washington. It seems not unlikely that James' restlessness, to which Lucretia responded in the letter above, may be an indication of his attachment to Mrs. Calhoun. Recalling those days in 1856 and 1857, when James seemed to be in love with both Rebecca and Lucretia and expressed this conflict by bouts of depression and restlessness, James again is not sure whether he wants to stay in the Congress, rejoin the army, or go out to the Pacific coast. At any rate, a rumor of James' affair with Mrs. Calhoun has surfaced.

Washington, May 8, 1864.

My Precious Crete:

Your dear letter of the 2nd came to hand yesterday. There is not a word you say that I don't appreciate and sympathize with most fully. From the tone of your letter I saw you were sad. I have been sad too for many days past. I wish you were here with me this quiet Sunday evening. I would take you to my heart and talk with you, and be comforted by you. I have been feeling how very hollow and empty is the world and all its pursuits, and how little all this struggle of one head and heart will amount to when the world's great balance sheet is made up. I have been harder worked for the past ten days than ever before this session and I suppose that body, brain and heart all share in the weariness.

Dearest, I hope I am not wrong, and you will not think me lacking in the gentles[t] tenderness for you when I tell you I was rejoiced at the possibility of what was a grief to you. I will not do so, however, but by your own union with me in rejoicing. Should it prove true, I assure you, Darling, that nothing but the most imperative necessity shall keep me away from you again. I do hope, and shall try to realize it, that I may be with you a good deal of the coming summer, and have you with me next winter. But remember, dear, if anything occurs that you cannot come, the session will only be 12 weeks long. You will always be dearer to me since your visit here, which was very perfect in its sweet remembrances to me. I hope it was so to you. I shall not go to California. If I cannot make my way in life where I am best known, I will go down to the unknown in quiet. I think I shall not re-enter the army. Certainly not if the present campaigns are as successful as they promise. But if disaster befalls us and I am really needed, I am sure you will do as you have so nobly done before—cheerfully give me to the country. We are waiting with suspended breath for the issue of the great struggle going on just beyond the reach of our ears. The long train of wounded is beginning to pour into the City. We have steadily gained thus far, and if Grant is completely successful in crushing Lee, the rebellion is substantially ended.

I have been made very unhappy by the letter of Harmon Austin which I sent to Almeda and which I suppose you have seen. The story is wickedly and maliciously false, and I have no doubt it has been manufactured in the interest of some one who wants my place here. . . .

I am delighted at the account you give of our boy. Try to convey to him the idea that he has a father who loves him more than all his precocity can comprehend. Give my love to Mother and tell her I am looking for a letter from her. I send you a proposed catalogue of books. Please mark with a pencil such as we already have, and you and Almeda and Burke [Hinsdale] add 75 or 100 to the list. I shall make a purchase through the Congressional Librarian. Ever and always your own James.

Lucretia must have heard something of James' love affair, or of his philandering in general. For his weakness for women is discussed in the household, perhaps in regard to Mrs. Calhoun. The acid remark of James' mother, typical of her outspoken nature, reflects on her dislike of Almeda Booth, bitterness stemming from James' early days at Hiram when he was much under Almeda's influence. Wallace Ford, the visitor who was so humiliating to Lucretia, remained a close friend and advisor to James. From his crude comments before her, to say nothing of "grandma's" remarks, one can feel the occasional suffering of Lucretia in the early years of the marriage.

Hiram, May 29, 1864.

My Dearest Jamie:

I did not intend to let so many days pass without writing to you, but last week was given up to house cleaning, and I was really too busy or too tired to write a word until the last day or two, and then I had a reason for not writing which I am not going to tell you now. I received yours of the 23rd inst. Friday evening and though I do not desire you to be unhappy and miserable, still I was so glad to know with what longing your heart turns to our home. It is a dear pleasure to me to know that you do love me and love to be with me, even though the world will not believe it. Perhaps I should be too proud of your love were I not reminded occasionally that no one can understand how it is that you can love me, so the kind hearted and judicious Wallace takes to himself the infinite satisfaction of thrusting it before my unwilling eyes, always selecting of course the most propitious time and place. A few evenings since when here and talking about you—as he always is—he took occasion to say before Mother and my hired girl, "James will not be contented with any one thing any more than he will be with one woman," and when by various and sundry remarks nearly as pleasant, he roused Mother to say, "If Miss Booth should tell James the moon was made of green cheese and he had got the first slice, he would believe it," he, Wallace, chuckled over it and said, "Grandma, good for you. I am glad we have had this talk," showing that he was delighted to find anything to confirm his notion of you.

Jamie, I have felt so angry with him and almost indignant at you for keeping such an audacious presuming ignoramus around you that my head and heart have been full of thoughts—real wicked, I suppose—but I could not help them. And then to think, too, that you show to him so much friendship as to give to him that pretty little watch that you gave me when you went into the army. It hurt me clear to the quick, and I could not but feel the world was more than half right in what it thought and said. There I have said all the naughty things that I did not mean to tell you, and which have kept me from writing this two days lest I should say them. But, Jamie, I did want to say this, that I do feel that for your own good you ought to keep Wall away from you. He is to say the least of him a fawning flatterer without much good sense or judgement, and for your own reputation I hope you will at once put a veto on the book he and Gilmore are planning. Miss Booth will tell you what she thinks of it, and her judgement is worth more than that of a whole world of people like Wall. I feel real sorry that the time of adjournment is being so far removed. I did hope that you could spend a few quiet days before the electioneering campaign began. If you go into that or into the school as you propose to Miss Booth, there will be very little time for me. I sometimes think there is no hope of anything but to live through this life at least as far away from you as possible. Little Harry's plump and well as ever. He is getting to know your picture. I say to him, "Harry see papa," and he looks up at it and jumps and laughs. He would soon learn to love you, were you with him. If your jewels cost you what they do me, you would not sigh for more, I am sure. I wish you were here with me tonight. I want to look into your eyes again and see that you do love me. Is there any hope that you will be here Commencement? I do wish you could, and yet it would be more lonely than ever to have you go away again. If you write as often as you can, I will try and have no more reason for not writing to you. . . . Mother is at home for a few days. I hope you will have a letter here for her when she returns. . . .

Your own Crete.

Baltimore, June 6, 1864.

Dearest Crete:

I have delayed writing to you for three days because I intended to present myself instead of a letter. I should have left for home Friday evening last, but Harry came that day and I could not well leave him. I then proposed to leave Sunday evening, but our visit to the Ohio troops around the city made it impossible for me to get away, and Gen Schenck was taken quite sick so as to throw some military committee duties on my shoulders which required me to stay in the House today. This evening I came this far hoping to take the night train to Harrisburg but the delegation from Ohio insisted that I should stay tomorrow. I find they think if I go home now, it will look like an intentional slight to the Convention, and I don't want to make any unnecessary quarrel with our friends in this matter. If you do not see me before this reaches you, you will not see me till Congress adjourns. It is a disappointment to me not to see you at Commencement. I am very weary of the crowds and the politicians and long for the quiet and affection of home. I fully sympathize with all you say in reference to [Wall] Ford. I will explain most of the points you mention when I see you or when I write more at leisure. Love to mother and Almeda and Harry and excuse this scratch written among a noisy crowd.

Ever your J.A. Garfield.

James did arrive home, however, despite the Republican Convention in Baltimore, and he told Lucretia of his illicit love affair with the Widow Calhoun. Of course, there were different expectations for the sexes' moral behavior. Infidelities after marriage for the man were treated as venial sins which the sensible wife would be advised to overlook. Still, we might recall James' own comment in a letter of just four months before: "A husband should not only be a faithful husband but should also be a noble manly friend and a wife should be a noble womanly friend." One finds it difficult to forgive James for allowing himself to be drawn into this affair, considering the crisis he and Lucretia have recently lived through with the death of their daughter, as well as the fact that Lucretia has been in Washington with him the previous month. But Lucretia was able to forgive James and even sympathize with him. This and some of the following letters make clear how difficult it was for James to break off his relationship with Mrs. Calhoun.

New York, June 12, 1864.

Dearest Crete:

I reached here at eleven o'clock this morning, a little too late to hear Beecher as I hoped to do.[7] I found I did not save much pecuniarily by coming this way, for my pass on the Atlantic and Great Western was only good to Salamanca, N.Y., and the balance of the trip cost me $9.30. I got a fair night's sleep however and have done tolerable justice to a breakfast since my arrival. I shall leave at seven this evening for Washington and arrive there at seven tomorrow morning.

I hope when you think over my trip home and balance up the whole of my wayward self, you will still find, after the many proper and heavy deductions are made, a small balance left on which you can base some respect and affection. I still believe that I am worthy to be loved after all the books are balanced. Still, I do not know what I shall be after I have fathomed the deep waters of the gulf through which I shall try as bravely as I can to wade.[8] If I strangle and go down, I want everybody, but you and Almeda, to think it was a case of accidental drowning. I don't intend to whine any more, if I can help it, nor to talk about the matter. I want to thank you again for the brave words of good sense you spoke to me night before last. I believe after all I had rather be respected than loved if I can't be both, and I am quite sure I can't be the latter without the former. I ought to have a great deal more head, or a great deal less heart. Either would be better than my present proportions. The preponderance of the one makes a man a lubber, the other may make him iron, but a storm won't hurt him. So I tender my obeisance to those happy mortals who are not troubled with those elements which Horace embodies in his "puer flebilis."[9]

I called at Austins and visited them about an hour on my way yesterday. I saw Mrs. Cox ten minutes. She went to the Warren station with me, talked most of the time about her "noble and greatly neglected husband" and wanted you to visit her this summer very much. Whatever shall happen to me I beg of you never to whine for me or pity me before folks. I do not fear that you ever will. To be practical a little I meant to say to you yesterday morning that I thought your garden could be improved a little in the way of hoeing. I suppose it is not easy to get any one to do it, but I hope you will find someone to keep it up till I come, and I will try to play husbandman—in double sense. I noticed that the gatepost on the Northrup side could be improved in the way of uprightness and steadfastness. It is now too much like its nomadic master. Tell Almeda if she won't think me quite a fool in my mental inanity, I will get her recitation room carpeted.

And now, Dearest, write to me and try to make Harry love me. I think the little fellow can afford to do that at least till he gets well acquainted with me, and maybe by that time I can get along if he don't. Wouldn't it be glorious to get so one would [not] care about it?

What do you think of the philosophy and good sense of that couplet that says, "And he's an heir of Heaven that finds / His bosom glow with love"? Wasn't it written by some very young girl? At any rate, kiss the little rascal for me. Even his oscular tastes can't stand a mustache. The thorns on the upper lip outweigh the rose in his estimation. I suspect he is more sensible than his lubberly father. I will write to mother before long. Get rested and keep cheerful. Such as I am is Truly Your

James.

Hiram, June 12, 1864.

My Darling Precious Jamie:

It is one of those beautiful summer days when the outer world is so in harmony with a quiet loving spirit, and I cannot but feel cheerful and happy in spite of the sorrow you left in my heart when you went away yesterday morning with that great crushing pain on your own heart. I thought about you all day yesterday, and wished O so much that I could take it all to myself and bear it for you, and yet, Jamie, is this not one of those struggles of the spirit by which a new life is gained? Have you not so often said to me as we have passed from some fierce sorrow into the light of a new and holier peace and joy, "There can be no birth without pain"? and now, Jamie, the question is to you: Will you through dread of the suffering hold back the fearful struggle until the new life shall die before its birth, or will you with all your strength and courage seize the pain _____ and give to that life a living birth? I know what your answer will be, and I wait the issue with a trust and a hope in you which I cannot allow to waver. And I pledge you anew my heart and my hand to aid you in carrying out any arrangement which shall help you most in the work you will try to do. I have felt for a long time that you would not be all that you might and ought until you had gained a more independent life, and I think Almeda has felt the same from a remark she made concerning you not long since. She said she felt almost impatient with you that you would allow yourself to be so influenced by those around you. That she began almost to fear that you would never be the man you might. I told her we must keep trying to hold you right. Yes, she said, that is best, is it? but it seemed that there was a kind of despondency in her tone which bordered fast on to hopelessness. And yesterday morning after you left, she came into my room and finding me crying said, "I feel as though a nightmare had gone away," and going out again she continued, "it is perfect childishness for him to feel so." It seemed to me cruel for her to say so, and I thought at first that I would not repeat it to you for a world, it would hurt you so. But the more I thought of it, I felt that I would tell you, not to hurt your feelings or make you feel unkindly towards her, but with a hope that it would do you good. She might think I had no business to tell you; but I am just as sure that under the same circumstances, she would do the same thing. Now understand me, it is only with a hope that you shall become worthy of the highest esteem of Miss Booth that I tell you this, and now I leave you, my darling, with a heart that would break with tenderness and pity for you should you fail.

Yours most faithfully whatever be the outcome . . . but perfectly sure that for you "there's no such word as fail."

Crete.

Hiram, June 16, 1864.

My Darling Jamie:

I received your letter from New York last evening and can assure you it was very dear to me. I have felt anxious and sad about you ever since you were at home; still I did not despair of you, and your letter gave me new assurance that you need not be trembled over. My letter of last Sunday was perhaps a little cruel, but I think it will do you no harm. "Love you": of that be the surest of any thing in this world, and know that I shall not let you *drown*, and it will be the most perfect folly you were ever guilty of to attempt it—even that of having attached to your destiny such an *insignificance* as your humble correspondent would be nothing compared to it.

Almeda did not start for home until last evening. I communicated your message to her which she thought ought to stand in connection with some promise for the school. I am very grateful for the notice you took of affairs here. I confess to a little keener appreciation of the interest you manifested while here than perhaps you suspected. I came to about this conclusion concerning it that it did not pay very well to sacrifice so much time and labor to make a home pleasant and agreeable to my husband if he would entirely refuse to be pleased or to manifest the least interest because some other woman failed to bestow on him all her regard. However, the garden has been hoed since you left, and the gatepost is waiting for the new fence between Mrs. N. and us to be built. We have engaged Mr. Canan to build it. Now I hope we shall both lay aside all our unkind and unpleasant and desponding thoughts, and be the true and noble man and woman doing the work we have to do with earnestness, and living to make each other and those around us good and happy. Little Harry will love us as we deserve to be loved, and we must feel that in him at least there is something to live for.

In haste and with a heart full of most tender love for you, Your Own Crete.

Washington, June 19, 1864

My Own Dear Crete:

Your two good letters came duly to hand, that of the 16th this morning. More than ever before I am glad to read your good sensible loving words, which put my own silly weaknesses to the blush. My own history since I wrote you from New York is easily told. I came through Sunday night reaching here for early breakfast Monday morning. I found seventy letters unopened awaiting me. I have spent most of the week in reading the testimony for the Treasury Investigation and making the memoranda for my report, which I shall hope to complete the coming week.[10] I have taken up my old habit of pushing away sorrow by filling myself with work, and I have succeeded better than usual. I can't yet tell you how I shall come out in the struggle, but I hope I shall be found not altogether worthless, nor unworthy should I see some promise that the process of getting weaned and concentrated on some plan of work will be at least partially successful. To be a nightmare is no more comfortable to ones self than to his friends, and is at best a poor cavalry service. By a lucky piece of meddling Ford look[ed] at one of your late letters, wherein he saw no very vigorous eulogium upon himself, and came to me in his grief. After censuring him for looking at your letter, I read two passages in another in which you tell me of his talk when at Hiram, and I gave him your view and more in full. I think it brought him to a sense of his own unworthiness and will do him good. The session is rapidly drawing to a close. I think we shall wind it up by the 1st of July. I may have to remain here a week longer to finish up some neglected work, but shall get home as soon as I can.

Mother must excuse me for delaying to write. I have had no time this week. Kiss the boy, and consider yourself kissed in spirit every hour.

Ever your own James.

James was home in Hiram for the latter part of July and most of August, and then, as usual, in September he took to the campaign trail.

Hiram, September 22, 1864

My Darling Jamie:

It is one of the glorious days that our fickle Mother sometimes pets us with when she is very gentle and with many smiles puts to our lips the goblet filled with the wine of life! And I am happy, very happy in the full enjoyment of all she gives, and alive, so alive, in my love for you. I have set aside the bitter cup—

would it might be forever—and can think only of the warmth and light and beauty of our love. I long so much to see you and be with you again. I want you here to perfect the glory of the sunshine with your presence. I want you here to hold me close to your heart and sweeten the wine with kisses. I want you here to draw me so near to yourself that my whole being may be permeated with the glory of your own glorious life. Jamie, I do love you! love you with all that is deepest, truest and best in my nature, and I do want you to feel that the whole wealth of my love is all yours.

I am very anxious to hear from you and know how you stand this campaign. I hope you are not breaking down again, and are having a pleasant time; and I hope too that you are happy. Write me a letter and tell me all that is in your heart. Your books have come and the book case is to be set up today. In haste, your own Crete.

Cincinnati, Sept. 23, 1864.

Dearest Crete:

Your note of Sunday was handed me at Hamilton, just as I was taking the stand to speak. I was very sad and unhappy that we should have parted as we did, and, Dearest One, I do not know of anything I did which had you known fully would have pained you. If I could have had the time to talk with you, I am sure you would have felt differently. I do not willingly give you pain, or do anything to make you unhappy. I hope you will try to judge me as leniently as you can—try to rest your whole weight upon my love—which I assure you is no longer a weak or bruised reed. It is growing stronger every day, and I hope the time is not far distant when you will feel the strong consciousness of knowing my heart and all its depths of love and truth. For notwithstanding all the paradoxes and contradictions of my life, I dare assert that I am a man of true heart, worthy to be trusted and loved.

I reached Solon in time to attend the afternoon meeting and went to Mary's and staid till dark. I found mother quite well and in the best of spirits. She has not said a word to any of our folks about anything unpleasant in Hiram, and Mary said she would not have supposed from mother's manner that an unpleasant thing had occurred. Almeda's name had not been mentioned.[11] Mary told me many things which lead me to believe that what we have seen is only an exhibition of that common infirmity which has grown out of a peculiar nature and the advances of second childhood. I talked of the trip to Muskingum, and if I had the leisure to go with her, it would all be right, but I doubt if she will go alone. I asked her when she would be at home. She said in two or three weeks.

I have stood my outdoor meetings better than I expected to, but I am quite hoarse and each speech costs me a great deal of muscle and nerve. Phil Sheridan[12] has made a speech in the Shenandoah Valley more powerful and valuable to the union cause than all the stumpers in the Republic can make.

Our prospects are everywhere heightening and I am trying to bury my own petty and great griefs in the great cause. I would love my country with the same devotion that Richlieu loved France and try to find my happiness more in the performance of duty than in the particular moods or phases of my wayward heart. Pray for me, my darling, that I may be a man in the larger and nobler meaning of the word.

It makes me happy and glad to have you say that you long for my return. I shall joyfully press you to my heart when we meet. I lay awake till two this morning reading a book which I will tell you of and will get as soon as I can. Kiss our darling boy for me and give my love to Almeda. . . .

I shall hope to find a letter from you at Peru {Ohio}.

Forever your James.

During the fall, James and Lucretia were together in Hiram most of the time; in December James made arrangements in Washington for the family to join him during the winter, so it was not until spring 1865, that they were again separated, when Crete and Harry returned to Ohio. It was at this time that James entered into elaborate business dealings with the Phillips brothers of Pennsylvania, hoping to secure his family financially. Again, the distressing problem of James' absence from home occupies the correspondence.

Hiram, April 10, 1865.

My Darling Jamie:

I have thought about you a great deal since you went away and with a feeling of real pain for the sadness in your eyes as you said you were never more sorry to leave home than then. Were I not sure that you better understand me, I should almost fear that you think my strongest desire to be, that you gather up all the wealth you can, even at the risk of life, to leave me, in case you die first. So far from that am I, my dear Jamie, that could I direct I would not have you put your life in jeopardy one moment for all the treasure of the world. And if I have ever seemed indifferent to your absence from home and to the constant dangers to which you expose yourself, it was due alone to this, that I felt you loved the excitement of such a life better than to stay with me. You do not know how much I hope something may prevent you from starting on that perilous California trip; still I do not want you to stay here and be unhappy.

You started away in such haste or rather I was thinking so much more about you than Washington, that I forgot to send my kind remembrances to our friends there. I hope you improvised them for me. I dreamed of you last night a dream that made me so unhappy that I awoke and could not sleep again for a long time. I will tell you nothing now, except to remind you of a little German poem you spent a Sunday afternoon copying a few weeks ago. To me you said not long since, "be gentle" to you; allow me to say "be prudent." The glorious news of Lee's surrender has reached us. I have no words to tell what my heart feels that the end draws so near. Never before has a people had such reason to lift up their hearts with one voice in praise to God.

Little Harry has whooping cough without much doubt, but I think will not have it very hard. I think he was never so full of mischief as he has been for three days past. He goes bobbing about putting his head and hands into every thing he can reach. Mother looks on and says, "never was a child so like his father. He acts exactly as his father did." Last night he got the kitchen stove door open and tried to crawl in head first. He covered his hands and face with ashes and only gave it up when I took him away.

I hope you can be at home on Saturday. The days and nights are long and lonely without you. I send the letters received Saturday and today, and will send tomorrow's mail. Harry is just starting away and will take this. . . .

With all my heart, Your own Crete.

On April 15, while James was in New York on business, he heard the news of Lincoln's assassination. It was at this time that he was negotiating with the Phillips brothers and, at the same time, planning a trip to the west coast. Lucretia, who was now pregnant, hoped very much this trip west could be canceled, as indeed it was, but not because she opposed it.

Metropolitan Hotel, New York.
April 17, 1865.

Dearest Crete:

My heart is so broken with our great national loss that I can hardly think or write or speak. I reached here Friday night at midnight and in the morning heard the shocking news. Places of business have been closed. Nothing is in the heart of anyone but our great sorrow. Saturday night I went out to Lewisboro and spent Sunday at Rebecca's. Her Mother is just able to sit up part of the day, but I fear will never be well. I came back early this morning, but such is the deep grief and sorrow that no one seems capable of doing any business. The day is nearly gone and I have as yet done nothing. If I could see the men with whom I desire to transact the business in reference to land and other matters, I could leave for home in a day or two. When I can now leave I don't know. I may have to go to Washington tomorrow to attend the funeral. If so, it will very badly break in upon my plans. I am sick at heart and feel it to be almost like sacrilege to talk of money or business now. More than ever before in my life I want to be at home with you. Could I have you and our precious boy in my arms I could almost let the world and its work go without a thought or a care for them. From present appearances I shall not start for Cal. before the 1st of May. I want you to know that there are not the dangers attending the journey that you have supposed. Mr. Stanton tells me that the route is well guarded by troops, and Warren Leland, one of the proprietors of this Hotel, with whom I have talk[ed] an hour or two today, has lately come across the plains and says the route is very safe, and the journey a pleasant one. Your dear good letter was found awaiting me on my arrival here. It came close to my heart with its loving tenderness and found a . . . quick and joyful response. I thank God every day for the tender love with which He has filled our hearts, and I trust we shall grow nearer and dearer to each other as we approach the confines of the silent land. Dearest wife, with all my heart I long to be with you now as the sun is setting and tell you in words and kisses of my love. I shall not fail, I think, to be at home before the week closes. Kiss Darling Harry again and again for his papa. Your dream had no basis in reality. Ever your own James.

After leaving Washington that spring, James went directly to Chicago to conclude business arrangements with the Phillips. He was due home in May but kept postponing his

return, finding that he had to be in Detroit and even Virginia before he could return to Hiram, which he did over the 4th of July.

Hiram, June 4th, 1865

My Darling Jamie:

Another Sunday has come and still you are away. It makes the time seem so long, to wait half expecting you and every week disappointed. I think each time I will not look for you or expect you until you come, but in spite of myself I go on the porch as car-time comes around on certain days when there is the least probability that any combination of circumstances could bring you and find myself looking with expectant eyes for you, and though I do not intend now to look for you one bit before Commencement, still I know I shall and feel real sorry if you do not come. It makes me almost discontented to be here now when I think of the pleasant time I could have with you; but I know that it is better that I stay quietly at home. I think I am very careful, and am feeling pretty well, but find I can endure less than ever before. This will be a hard week, and I scarcely know how it will be possible to take the care I ought of myself; but I will try, and if you can come home it will be easier for me than with you away; and if you can come consistently I hope you will. Mother came home last night. She found Aunt Calista at Newburgh and had a grand visit with her. She is coming out here before she returns to Michigan. I hope you will be at home when she comes as she is very anxious to see you. Aunt Anna is dead. She died the first of May, and Aunt Calista felt as though she could not stay away from her friends here any longer, and came home with Phebe Clapp. Mother says Phebe wishes to buy your piano, and I think you had better let her have it at almost any price. It will soon be entirely ruined if left in the Seminary.

. . . . I am glad of your success in Detroit, and I hope for your sake that you will be successful in your present work. I think your life is worth too much to be given up to a continual struggle against poverty, and I greatly desire—not alone for your comfort, but for the freedom it may give you to fulfil the high destiny God has given you . . . that your summer's work may lift you into a competency which will place you beyond any anxious thought about our manner of merely living.

Darling Jamie, you do not know how fondly and tenderly I love you now, how much I desire to see you lifted into the enjoyment of all that your rich and noble nature entitles you to. I want you to know how much I realize the blessedness of my lot in being loved by you. I thank our God each day that He has placed me beside a husband so good and noble, where life is worth so much more than I could have ever made it alone.

With my heart full of love and gratitude I am all your own: Crete.

Dear little Harry loves papa too and wants to see him.

Chicago, June 6, 1865.

Dearest Crete:

It is very hard indeed for me to stay here with the thermometer at 90 degrees Fahrenheit, and not take this evening train for Cleveland. But both Phillips and I are persuaded that this week is the crisis of our work and will determine whether we succeed or fail. I have therefore abandoned the hope of seeing you at Commencement and must content myself with writing this note. I wish I could tell you that the California question was settled, but I cannot. A new and annoying element has been added by the rumor now afloat in the press that an extra session of Congress is to be called. Of course, if that were so it would settle the question, but I don't yet believe it.

A rascally German Barber clipped my whiskers this morning in such a way as to disfigure them so much that I had them partly cut off, leaving them only on my upper lip and chin. I have not been recognized by acquaintances since till I tell them who I am. I shall have to tarry in some Jericho till my beard is grown, have all the rest cut off, or present myself to you in the character of a Dutch Landlord whose face mine closely resembles at the present moment.

With much love but little beard I am your late husband.

James A.G.

Hiram, June 9, 1865.

Dearest Jamie:

Wednesday night came and brought Harry [Rhodes] and Jennie and John Hawley[13] together with several others, but to me it brought not the one most desired. I could not help but expect you, and when you did not come my heart was so sorry that the tears came almost up into my eyes. But now that the time has passed over that you would probably have staid with me, I console myself that I am not suffering the utter loneliness which comes over me whenever you go away. Dear Jamie, when are you coming to stay with me *all* the while? I desire your society so much that it seems to me I must have you with me for the next few months. I think the crisis of danger is passed, and from present indica tions I am quite sure the time is much nearer than we supposed, and I do beseech you with all the earnestness of my heart that you do abandon entirely your trip to the Pacific Coast this summer. I do entreat you to leave me not alone through another of those dreadful hours. So terrible not alone, nor chiefly for the bodily suffering; but for the shocking accompaniments which make me feel that I cannot pass through them again without your protection. I am trying for your sake to be very careful. I have attended none of the Commencement exercises, but used every moment I was not obliged to work for rest, and have come through without any injury, I think.

Commencement has passed off very pleasantly, I judge from the satisfac tion expressed by all parties. John enjoyed his visit, but whether it was *satisfac tory* I do not know. He attended Nell to the Lyceum last evening and called there again today. I have not seen Nell in the meantime and know nothing how they were either of them impressed.

From your own account I think I shall choose to see you entirely beardless. I think I should like to see your face again as I first loved it. With a heart con tinually loving you and desiring to see you, I am your own as ever, Crete.

Chicago, June 10, 1865.

My Darling:

I am exceedingly anxious to hear from you and to know how you have got through with the work of Commencement. It has given me very great anxiety to think that you were having such a crowd and so much to day. We have had a very serious occurrence in our enterprise, which for a time threatened to destroy it altogether, but I think we are nearly recovered from it, though it will delay us still longer. I want so much to sit down beside you and tell you the whole story of the work, that is, if it succeeds.

So completely have I been absorbed in the work that I have not been to the fair till today.[14] I went to see Zenobia and General Grant. I wish you could have been with me to see that exquisite work of art. You must see it sometime. The marble is most perfect in its purity and the whole figure is filled with an unde finable grace and sadness. I can almost read the sad story of Palmyra in her face. I send you a photograph which though fine does not do justice to the marble.

I saw General Hazen here at the Opera last evening. He came in town yesterday and went away on an early train this morning. I have received a telegram from Ravenna asking me to deliver the 4th of July oration, and I hardly know what to say. I would be very glad for many reasons to speak there on that occasion, especially from the fact that I spoke there in 1860. But I am yet in a miserable state of doubt as to what I ought to do. Of course, if I continue in the same state of uncertainty, the question will settle itself in the negative.

Darling, you must be patient with me and sympathize with my long delay in coming to you. If I fail I want to fail decently after a fair trial. Do write me often and bless me with all the fullness of your love, for which I daily and hourly thank God.

. . . Sweet kisses to little *Snubby Ann* and to Mother and all. Ever Your James.

James came home briefly before July 4 in order to speak at Ravenna, which he did on the 4th, going directly back to Chicago from his speech. Crete, not at all well, did not accompany him to Ravenna. Much of James' time at home was spent with Almeda, who had resigned from the school at Hiram and would be leaving permanently.

Hiram, July 4th, 1865

My Darling Jamie:

In most utter desolateness I sit down to sympathize with you if I can, but fear I can only give expression to the loneliness which is preying on my heart. Your visit home has been so unsatisfactory, so short and so crowded with work, that I scarcely know how to endure the disappointment. I feel that you cannot stay just a few days before another long wearisome absence. The pain is so cruel when I think that you will not come back tonight and, Jamie, I feel so hurt, too, I cannot keep back the tears, that the little time you were at home almost the only leisure you took from your work was given to mourning over the infidelity of Miss Booth, and sighing over that past which gave to me only anguish unutterable. I cannot feel that my love at all satisfies you when you do so, and it makes me feel real sad—*not unkind* as you sometimes seem to think. Your love is so entirely my happiness that I cannot understand how you can be so sad over the past when I love you so well, if my love is worth anything to you.

I suppose you have finished speaking before this and notwithstanding my own selfish griefs I am feeling very anxious to know of your success. I have so much faith in your ability to succeed that I cannot but feel that you have now, in spite of your fears. I hope you will tell me all about it; I want to know how you feel about it yourself. You don't know how much I wanted to go with you today; but I knew it was not best. I could scarcely get through with the work this morning, the pain in my side was so severe, but I have been lying down and feel much better now. I want you to love me and think of me and write to me all you can, assured that thus you make me as happy as I can be away from you.

These are Harry's little mischievous marks. I went out to get him a piece of bread and butter, and when he heard me coming back, he began to jump and laugh and I found him jabbing my gold pen into the letter at a great rate and almost to its—the pen's—ruin.

Poor little soul: how badly he did feel when you left this morning. I sat down and had a good cry with him that he could not have his "papie" to ride with him ever.

Well, my darling, I have verified the truth of your Methodist Hymn. Speaking has relieved me, and I am on the rising wave to a *moderately* happy and contented spirit again. But not yet reconciled to your speedy departure, and I do believe I would be willing to give most all of my fortune if you were only coming home tonight.

Ever your own little wife, Crete.

James' intense loyalty and high regard for Almeda Booth are fully expressed in his next letter, defending his devotion of time to her, rather than to Lucretia.

Chicago, July 9, 1865

Dearest Crete:

I arrived here Friday afternoon and found the meeting of the stockholders and the report of the committee had been delayed and came off Friday evening. It was very fortunate that I was present for there were several perils which promised to give us trouble; but it all went off well. The Committee reported in favor of the lands and the stockholders accepted them. It now only remains to secure enough subscriptions to pay a few thousand dollars more to the Phillips Bros. and the work will be done, so far as I am concerned. I hope we may be able to get through here the coming week. I am still quite weak and my head has not lost the echoes of the 4th, but I think I shall soon be sound again. I think I am quite bilious and I will get some cathartic and rinse myself out.

Yours of the 4th came to hand the day I arrived. I was very sorry you were dissatisfied with me and unhappy in consequence of my talk about Almeda. You greatly misunderstood me. Had I been in grief over a lost friendship and unsatisfied with yours, it would have been the last topic I should have discussed. Indeed it is surprising to me how completely I have learned to live without that intimate friendship which has been so large a part of my intellectual and social life for so many years. I will not deny that it was a very great struggle for me to lose it, much greater than I have ever told; but I am equally clear that it is better for me that it should be as it now is, and it is only at times that the sadness of the old struggle comes back upon me. It was forcibly called to my mind during the preparation of my oration, because she helped me in that of 1860, and wrote the first three or four sentences herself. I could not fail to be struck with the great contrast of then and now in her feelings. To me, it is no small matter to see a human soul cast loose its moorings from another and have no more care for vessel or cargo—whatever may befall them on the voyage of life—and I wonder at myself that I have learned to expect no inquiry or anxiety for me or my fortunes from her, and that she is now so small a part of my thoughts. If this had happened by my fault or neglect, I should never cease to upbraid myself both for want of heart and friendship. But as it [is] not my work, as it is the part she has chosen, I congratulate myself on having so soon and so nearly perfectly adapted myself to the new conditions. I have no doubt it is better for me and for you and for our love, and I hope we shall be able [to] look back at it all as sea voyagers escaped from a peril look back from the shore upon the wreck of the vessel that once bore them over the waves.

I cannot bear the thought that our happiness shall now be marred by these memories of the past, or that the consideration of them should do aught else but strengthen us in our perfect confidence and love. . . .

Write soon and let me know that your sky is not dark. Ever Your James.

James spent most of the summer in Chicago but returned, as usual, for the fall campaign, when he was in and out of Hiram as he traveled to various Ohio towns to

speak. *A second boy was born in October, to be named James. Of course, the reference to "your sickness" is to Crete's giving birth to the baby.*

Petroleum Center, Pa.
November 11, 1865.

My Darling Crete:

I greatly regret that I cannot be with you this anniversary of our wedding and with you review the seven years that have led us through such various paths in which doubt and hope, joy and sorrow are so strangely blended. We should be sad in that review, were there not so happy a conclusion to it all, had not our paths which so long led us apart through deep shadows, yes, a gloom that shut out the sun and stars, united at last and wound peacefully along the happy valley where love dwells and doubt does no more enter. My Darling Wife, more than ever before, I bless the good Father of all Mercies that he has permitted us to see the end of our long sorrow and has given us the promise of a future that shall be joyous to our hearts, whatever outer ills may betide.

It is sweet to be able to say, as I can tonight, with all my heart, that I rejoice that we met and became each the life and love and hope of the other, and were I this night free from any tie, I would choose you for my wife as against the world of noble women.

My stay at home, during my lameness and your sickness, has given me new and deeper views of your nature, and I feel that I know you as I never have before. Life and sorrow have done very much to develop your nature, and bring out its rich tints and fix them in fadeless hues. If you have found that I meet the wants of your nature to any considerable degree of satisfaction, as you do mine, you must be very happy. I know at this hour (8 P.M.) you are thinking of me and of our past and present and looking at the two precious pledges and fruits of our love. Were I with you I should know that my joy would be full. I shall rest tonight in the sweet assurance that our spirits are not asunder as are the bodies. I hope you will think to write some word for me. I shall hope to be with you by Wednesday evening next, possibly not till Thursday morning. I regret the necessity of this trip and doubt its utility. I fear for my Ashtabula lecture. Dearest Darling, kiss our two little ones and know that you are love[d] with the whole heart of your own James.

Hiram, November 22, 1865

My Darling Precious Husband:

I have been awake a long time thinking of our conversation your birthday night. I cannot tell how full of new thankfulness is my heart to you, and to God who gave you to me, for the light you let in upon my hitherto blinded soul. I scarcely dare try to frame in words the glorious beautiful truth concerning Christ and his Religion as it begins to dawn upon me lest I fail to choose those which can reveal what I feel to be true—lest like an unskilled artist I use the wrong color or otherwise distort the beautiful form I would represent; nor would I yet attempt to tell anyone but you lest I be thought toppling over with heresy. To you, however, let me talk, for you can understand and help me. The light you gave me reveals this to me. That Christ is our Redeemer, our Savior, our Atonement in the *example* he has given us, our Redeemer and Savior in the example of a perfect life by which we are to guide and model our own so far as we can, and our atonement in that he took upon himself the suffering of death thus showing us that not until we had passed through the shadow of death could we be entirely purified from sin. Never having sinned, he could not have suffered the penalty only as he yielded himself up to be put to death that he might be to us a perfect example. I know this is but vaguely expressed, but I must learn to tell this truth which has begun to be revealed to me. My heart is so full of gratitude to you that you have so opened my eyes. I have always felt afraid to talk with you lest you were in the same troubled state with myself. All that I could see was mysterious and arbitrary and my nature would rebel however much I tried to bring myself into subjection and I thought, if you felt the same, to talk of these things would but unsettle the little faith we had. But from the moment you said in that night's talk which was ventured on so tremblingly, "The Bible is chiefly valuable to me for the example it gives me of a perfect life in the life of Christ," a new light sprang in upon my soul, and I felt for the first time that I had "experienced" the saving power of Christ. My Dear husband, let us talk of these things a great deal that we may ourselves understand the truth more clearly and learn to enlighten others also, and let us pray often for each other that we may not only know but practise what we know. My Jamie, I cannot tell how much the last few months have heightened and strengthened and deepened my love for you and my perfect trust in you. You have come home to me and taken me so near to yourself, and made me feel so strongly the wondrous power of your love that I am lifted up into the heaven of life. I miss you so much now that you are away and the house is so desolate without you, and yet even now every hour is bright and happy compared with the hours which have gone before. I hope you will write as often as you can, and feel what I believe to be true, that there is no place in the wide world where centers so much love for you as in your little home, nor any one heart which clings to you so fondly or loves you so well as that of your little wife. Did you get your satchel? I shall hope to hear a full account of your Poughkeepsie visit, especially of your success. With my heart full of love and hope,

your own Crete.

❧ NOTES ❧

1. Nancy Schrom Dye and David Blake Smith, "Mother Love and Infant Death," *Journal of American History* 73 (September 1986): 346.
2. Charles Gordon Ames (1828–1912), clergyman and writer, was at the Geauga school at the same time as Lucretia and James.
3. This strongly suggests Lucretia has heard a rumor of a love affair.
4. William Henry Furness (1802–1896) was a Unitarian clergyman and abolitionist.
5. This is from *Macbeth*.
6. This probably refers to the furor over Frank Blair's attack on Secretary Chase, whom he accused of treason and corruption. The climax was reached on April 23 when Blair delivered a long and vitriolic speech to the House.
7. Henry Ward Beecher, Harriet Beecher Stowe's brother and one of America's best known preachers, spoke at the Plymouth Church in Brooklyn. James later attended Henry Beecher's trial in 1874, when he was accused by a woman identified as "Mrs. Tilton" of adultery with her.
8. This is surely a metaphor for the unpleasant prospect of speaking to Mrs. Calhoun, an ordeal which was yet ahead of James. He saw that it would not be easy to face his lover and bring the affair to an end. He may have had his first interview with Calhoun in New York before taking the train to Washington that Sunday.
9. The reference to Horace's 5th ode, book 1, is interesting. There is no reference to a "puer flebilis" (crying boy) in the odes of Horace. But the 5th ode is about the "gracilis puer," and it has to do with faithlessness of Pyrrha, who now has him in her arms. The relevant line is "Alas, how

many times will he weep [flebit] for faith and changed gods." James could still find an appropriate classical reference, and Lucretia could still understand it.

10. James was chairman of a committee to investigate the charges made by Blair against Secretary of the Treasury Chase.

11. From this letter it seems clear that James' mother had left the Garfield home in Hiram, having had some kind of a bitter conflict with Almeda Booth.

12. Major General Philip Sheridan commanded the 3rd Division, 20th Corps.

13. John Hawley was courting Nell, Lucretia's sister.

14. The Northwestern Soldiers Fair was held in Chicago in June 1865. The Fair emphasized public health and was called a Sanitary Fair.

CHAPTER 7

Washington and Hiram, 1866–1869

Beginning with his winter term in congress, November 1865, James rented a house in Washington so that his family could be with him "all the while." Though Lucretia had made several brief visits to Washington in the past, this was the first time a home had been established for her and her two boys. Accordingly, the number of letters exchanged between Crete and James decreases, for their separations now were only for the fall campaign, or for the those occasions when James was called upon to speak away from home. When Congress was not in session, the family would be back in Ohio. Letters then exchanged would characteristically be when James was away campaigning.

One important event during these years was a trip to Europe James and Crete made in July 1867. James had intended to sail alone, but, as he wrote his mother on July 12: "I have been away from Crete so many years that I felt it was due to her to enjoy the same advantages of travel that I do as far as is consistent with the safety and proper care of our children." They visited England, Belgium, Germany, Italy and Paris, returning to America in November.

Another important event in this period was the birth of their third child, Mary (called Mollie), their only girl after Trot.

In this chapter the letters begin to take on a tone of convincing affection; James appears for the first time genuinely to need Crete as a companion, and one senses his growing dependence upon her. He must have been aware that his brilliant career in the House was slowing down—for example, he did not receive the appointment to be chairman of the important Ways and Means Committee, as he had expected—and he was only just coming out of the emotional trauma of his love affair with Mrs. Calhoun.

Perhaps most important of all for the stability of the relationship of Crete and James was the decision of James to build a house in Washington. And so in the fall and winter of 1869 we find James happily involved in the progress of their first real home, watching it rise from its foundations at 13th and "I" street. No more brief vis-its, no more rentals. From now on, as James writes his little son, Harry, the family will be together in Washington during the winters and will "roll in the grass" in Hiram during the summers.

Of the more than one-hundred and fifty letters exchanged during this period, twenty-eight are included in this chapter.

Washington, Dec 3, 1865.

My Dearest Crete:

Your two precious letters came duly to hand, but I have delayed answering you until I knew definitely the result of my negotiations for a house. Yesterday I closed the bargain and signed the contract of lease from now to Nov. 15, 1866 at $135 per month for the house I referred to in my letter of last Sunday. I lease it of Mrs. Bache, a relative of Prof Bache of the coast survey,[1] a lady who evi-dently moves in good society here and has been accustomed to live comfortably. The house is a three story brick with dining room and kitchen on the first floor and hydrant in the yard close by the kitchen door.

The second floor consists of two parlors with folding doors and a hall.

The third floor has two large and one small bedroom and the attic has two rooms used for storage and one a bed room for servant. Mrs. Dennison went with me to look at the house as did also Lily Schenck[2] and we carefully exam-ined the furniture. All the fixtures are in good condition and you will only need to bring silver and bed linen. That is, knives, forks and spoons and sheets pil-low cases and towels. I think it will be a pleasant home for you and Nell[3] and me and we will have room for a friend when we want to entertain one. Had I known we could have been so soon settled, I would have asked you to come on with me and if I thought you would be ready and could conveniently come, I would go for you next Wednesday night and get here the Monday following. Mrs. Dennison thinks you could make up your wardrobe here as well as at home and Lizzie volunteers to go with you to Philadelphia to do your shopping where they trade. The Schenck girls do their shopping in Baltimore and say they would go with you there. Please think this over and if I telegraph you next Wednesday be ready to answer me whether you will come or not. I have been staying since Monday with the Dennisons[4] who make me at home but I go into our house tomorrow morning and I shall feel so much alone without you and shall want you very much. In order to state the whole case to you I will say that I shall be compelled to go home to deliver some lectures and also to visit Columbus and Cox between the holy days and should probably be away from you about ten days.

I think I can get a cook here and a little waitress and could I suppose get a nurse, but I presume it would be better for you to get the nurse there.

Our prospects are brightening in the congressional way. At a caucus last night there was developed a robust spirit which gives me great hope that the fruits of victory will not be thrown away. The rebels have no hope of being admitted to seats in the organization of the House. I am glad to tell you that our friends seem glad that we are to be here in a home of our own, and Mrs D sends love while several of your friends send kind regards. It is very gratifying to me to know that my so precious wife has won the honest admiration of so many good people.

Had not my letter already reached so far from its beginning I would write on the grand theme of Christ, so well expressed in yours of the 22nd. When we meet, or when I write another long letter, I will speak further on it. I so much want to see little Harry and watch the development of his stormy nature. Bless the dear boy. Tell him papa has got a nice yard for him to play in and a nice crib for his little brother. Give my love to Mother and tell her she must not hesitate to ask for any thing in the world I can get for her.

With all my heart, ever and always your James.

Lucretia did not go to Washington immediately, but waited until after Christmas to join James. Their rental was on F Street between 18th and 19th. They continued to rent this house the following year, but in 1867 they gave it up knowing they were going to Europe.

By April 1866 Crete was again pregnant. She remained in Washington through the first part of the summer and then returned to Hiram for a visit to her parents in the fall.

Luna Island, Niagara Falls
October 31, 1866

My Darling Crete:

I believe it was on this very spot that I wrote my Niagara note to you thirteen years ago. I have taken a few moments while waiting for the train to take me to Albion to renew the dear memories of that first written word and to pledge my love anew to you, with all the remembered dearness of the intervening years. The eternal roar of the cataract is again in my ears, and the imperishable echoes of our love are ringing through my heart. God bless you and our darlings and make us a joy to each other till the gulf of death divides us, and then in the calm waters beyond, in the peaceful eternity may we love on forever.

With all my heart and soul I am more than when I first wrote and more than ever your ownest own husband, James.

After the 1866–67 session of Congress, Lucretia went back to Hiram for the hot weather, while James had to return for a July session of the House which was to be devoted to the passage of a third Reconstruction Act (against the will of President Johnson).

Washington, July 3, 1867

My Darling Crete:

After a frightful roasting of 27 hours, I came in sight of this metropolitan focus of heat, and jumping off the train at a crossing just before it reached the station came straight to the bath room of the house and dedicated three quarters of an hour to the spirit of cleanliness which is said to be next to Godliness, and whether worthy of such rank or not, I know that I could not better please you than to pour out a libation of Potomac water upon my muddy person. I came upstairs and got my seat in time to answer to the roll call at 12 o'clock, and now while Jim Brooks is "roaring" us less gently than "a sucking dove,"[5] I will write you a word. And first, my Darling, recall to your mind the days and nights of July 1866 when you and I lay awake night after night to fan away the fires of the Dog Star that drove all sleep from our eyes. These days are here again, and have pushed the thermometer up to 98 degrees with a prospect of an indefinite additional upward slide. A thousand fans are busy in the gallery and on the floor, and I have used one a dozen times since I began this letter. In short, after a miserable, weary ride, with a weary homesick heart, I am here in a state of exquisite discomfort, wanting you more than I or my pen can tell you. We have a quorum of both houses, and I have some hope that we may be able to restrict our legislation to the single purpose for which we have met, the correction of the President and Attorney General in their attempt to stop our work of reconstruction. If so, we will not be here more than two or three weeks. I don't yet know anything in reference to my own future, but hope to be able to write you something definite before long. Do write me, darling, very often. Kiss the precious little ones for me, give my love to all the household. Of course, I have no stopping place yet, but will try to get one tonight. In the meantime I am and shall always be more than ever before, Your own James.

James had planned to sail for Europe after the session; it now occurs to him to take Lucretia along, too, if he can only arrange his finances to afford it.

Washington, July 4, 1867.

My Darling Crete:

I have rented a back room of Mrs Schoolcraft (Widow of the famous author of several works on North American Indians)[6] about three doors east of Witmores on F St, and shall board either at the Ebbitt House or at Welcker's Restaurant. The Senate and House adjourned over till Friday and I have come away to my old committee room to answer my letters and do what I can toward keeping cool. I am almost ashamed to tell you that I am so childish (perhaps it is manly) as to be both homesick and desperately lonesome. Really you have spoiled me for being away from you, and I would cheerfully endure the roasting of the next 26 hours if I might be with you again.

I find myself miserably unwell and quite unfit to do any work. A heaviness in the head and a general lethargy through my whole body make me feel as uncomfortable as one need wish his enemy to feel. I think now that I shall never consent to stay long in Washington without you. It is wonderful how you have grown on me and how fully you now fill all the wants of my heart. It is almost painful for me to feel that so much of my life and happiness have come to depend upon another than myself. I want to hear from you so often, and I shall wait and watch with a hungry heart until your dear words reach me. Now Darling, in reference to Europe, I fear that Congress will not adjourn by the 13th, but unless I feel better than I now do I shall not stay, but shall sail as I have arranged to do. I have this morning written to the agent of the Company asking him if the stateroom which he has assigned to me is large enough for you and me. I shall hear from him by Saturday or Monday I presume. Now let me state the case as it appears to me. 1st from my side, 2nd from yours. If the Company will extend their invitation to you and if I can see my way financially to meet the expense of the trip, and can feel assured that Mary[7] will come to help the two girls take care of our children and home, I shall feel that I ought to have you with me both for my sake and your own. On your part, if you feel sat-isfied that you can leave the children in safe hands and can be happy with me so far from them, it seems to me—I say that these ifs concurring, you ought to go. Now it is very cruel to keep you in suspense on so grave a question, but I know of no other way (the time is so short) but to write the matter up now and make provisional arrangements, so that I may not happen to find out, when it is too late, that you could have gone. Indeed I have seriously thought of giving it up myself, if you cannot go with me.

If I find you can go, and are willing to go, and telegraph you by Tuesday, you can take the A&G.W. train and be in N.Y. in 28 hours, or perhaps less. I shall stop at the Metropolitan Hotel and shall probably not leave here till Thursday night or Friday morning, unless some part of the arrangement makes it necessary. If you go, you only need two suits, a street dress, and a travelling dress. I presume you could put all into the leather valise. Now my dear, I don't say what you ought to do. I shall try to be content with your decision, if it is left to you, but if I can arrange my end of the lever, I shall leave the decision to you. In the meantime, write me fully on the whole case. Make an estimate of how much money I would need to leave at home, if you go, also if you don't, and know that staying or going, alone or with you, I am in a constantly increasing strength of affection. Your own James.

In the following exchange of letters, the topic has to do with whether or not Lucretia will accompany James on his trip to Europe. But Lucretia and James have another concern: James' relationship with Mrs. Calhoun and Rebecca. With James in New York once again, Lucretia worries about both women, only hinting in her letter of July 6 that a danger is present; James mentions "the skeleton" of the Calhoun affair in his letter of July 6, and Lucretia avers on July 7 that she is confident that James' relation-ship with Rebecca is no longer a threat to her, but she is not so certain about Mrs. Calhoun, whom she hopes James will not visit.

Metropolitan Hotel, New York.

July 6, 1867.

Darling Crete:

The House adjourned last evening until Monday, and I thought it best to come on here to make preparations for the passage. Ward [a lobbyist] was coming on . . . to help me in reference to raising money and getting gold for the trip. By coming now I can sooner determine whether we can both go, and I can save more time to stay at Washington next week. Now, my precious Darling, do not feel at all disturbed that I am here. The skeleton shall no more appear in our closet. I have not seen the shadow of it and don't know that I shall. If I conclude to, it will be because I wish to better the status of affairs as we have talked. Here where I have come nearest to wronging you,[8] I avow that my heart is more yours than ever, and I long for you with all there is in me of heart and faith. I was in hopes of receiving a dear word from you before I left last night but it did not come. I shall go back tonight or tomorrow to meet your sweet message and shall hope by that time to be able to know definitely what can be done about your going. After dinner I shall visit the "City of Liverpool" and see what her accommodations are. I know that she has already arrived at the pier. I have been miserably unwell ever since I left home. The terrible heat has greatly added to my discomfort, but a shower last night has made the weather tolerable today, and I am better. Among my small annoyances is a little boil over the rim of my ear which keeps one side of [my] head in petty misery. My corns have also raised a rebellion again. I tell you these things only because I want to say that I constantly feel that your presence would make me well. I enclose one pass on the Atlantic and G.W. R.R., for you will need it whether you stay or go with me. If you come on, you had better come by the A&G.W. and the Erie. In that case, the pass will bring you as far as Salamanca at least, and they may know it on this end of the line. They did so once for me. If you are short of money, you can use Harry's bond temporarily and we will replace it, or you can borrow of Streater. Kiss the dear children for me, and give my love to Mother and all the rest.

Ever and Only Your own James.

Hiram, July 6, 1867.

My Dearest Jamie:

I have not received a word from you yet and am getting lonely and almost sad. It seems to me I never missed you so much before nor felt so unreconciled to your absence. I am going to stop right now lest I write a gloomy letter. I saw from the Thursday paper that you were in your seat at the opening. Every time little Hal[9] hears the cars, he jumps and says O papa is coming. He and the other darlings are not yet up or they would all join their mama in love and kisses to you. Write your word to me very often, and don't allow any one or anything to come between us and our love.

Ever your own Crete.

Hiram, July 7th, 1867.

My Good Husband:

After all the conflict of contending emotions through which I have so far passed in regard to Europe, whether to go with you or stay with our babies, or if I stay to know whether I most desire to have you go or stay, I think I have arrived at this stoical conclusion, to be utterly resigned to whatever fate this coming week may bring. My duty to my children and my anxiety for them will make me think it for the best, if I am left; and my love for them will make me happy; while if the word from you comes that I can go, I shall go in the most perfect confidence that I am doing right—such is my love for you and such my relations to you and to your position. Yet I have little expectation that it will be otherwise, that you will go and I will stay. I desire to say to you before you go that which I think will give you happiness as it does me. I want you to know that the last trace of bitterness over the past which was in my heart toward Rebecca is removed, plucked up by the roots and thoroughly cast out. I feel sure of this. I thought I was sure of it weeks ago, but lest it might prove to be but a temporary feeling which came on some moment of exaltation, I did not tell you of it. I have tested it thoroughly, and not once since, even in the darkest, weakest moment I have passed, has there come into my heart aught but love and tenderness for her. I want you to go and see her before you go, and if you can tell her that I love her and would love to see her, and only I dread the utter breaking out into weakness which I know would occur were we to meet again.[10] Write to me before you leave New York, and tell me of all before you sail. I almost wish you would not see Mrs. Calhoun. Somehow I cannot but feel that to her at least you would compromise our love were you to go into her presence. And for her, too, it would be better to let the fire of such lawless passion burn itself out, unfed and unnoticed. If she is a good but misguided woman, you will neither be more harmed than now, and if she is wicked or malicious, she has less occasion to harm you now than she would have after another interview. But whatever you do, I shall ever love you, and I hope you love me too well to ever be untrue to our love or do aught to give anyone occasion to say that you are.

I hope to get a letter from you tomorrow. I want so much a word of love from you again, and to know how you are. Harry says tell papa he has got to be a good boy, and Jim says "oo oo boy" too. Loving you as ever, most tenderly. Crete.

In New York James is able to retrieve the letters he has sent to Mrs. Calhoun. The affair is now officially over, much to the relief of both James and Crete.

Washington, July 8, 1867.

Dearest Darling:

I returned this morning and found your dear words of the 4th awaiting me. I cannot tell you [how] sweet and precious they were to me. Every dear word of tenderness and love is responded to from the depths of my heart.

Shortly after writing to you on Saturday in N.Y. I found the steamer "City of London" had not yet arrived and was not expected till Sunday evening. After doing what I could in reference to my departure I went in the afternoon to Lewisboro and visited Rebecca, and returned to New York on the Sunday morning train. On Sunday I called on the business of which we talked before I left home, and I am glad to be able to say to you that I feel happy in the consciousness of having done both you and myself better justice than I had hoped and in getting possession of all the papers which I was fearful might some day and in some way be troublesome. I cannot write as I would talk with you on this subject, for I do not want any ink mark by any mischance of the mail or otherwise to reach any other than you on this subject. I tried to deal kindly, honorably and firmly in all the premises, and I feel sure my Darling that you will most heartily concur in all the outcome. You cannot be so much relieved in heart and mind as I am, and I now say with a fuller, broader and deeper meaning than ever before that there is between our hearts and lives neither substance nor shadow of sorrow, except that we are separated even for a day. I here and now renew with new fervor and completeness of devotion the covenant of my heart and life to you till there shall be no more on earth or in heaven. And now, my darling, if I go away without you, I shall go happier for the knowledge that I leave behind me on this hemisphere no human being who can say aught against the fulness of our love. I had so much hoped to find on my return an answer to my first letter, or some intimation of what you were thinking in reference to going with me. The agent in N.Y. has tendered a free passage to you, provided Mr. Allison[11] don't go, but that I shall not know till tomorrow, when he (Allison) reaches here. I will hold this letter open till tomorrow in hopes of hearing from him and of hearing further from you. I am greatly distressed by the uncertainty which haunts me in reference to your going or not going. I would go home now [to] talk it over if I could get away. I so much hope you will think you can go. I have a fair prospect of being able to raise sufficient amount of money for us both. Shall know tomorrow or next day. I am trying to sell some of my Ocean oil. For today goodbye and may elect angels guard and keep you, my most precious jewel. James.

Tuesday, July 9th.

My Dearst One:

Your precious note of the 6th came to hand at noon today, but you had not received any word from me. I wrote you on Wednesday the 3rd, on the 4th, and from N.Y. on the 6th. It is very trying that my letters did not reach you. I am still at a loss what to expect. You speak as though you had given up all thoughts of going, but yet you did not know what I had written. I will wait one day more before I give it up in hope that your answer to my Thursday's letter may reach me. It is very strange but it has not yet seemed to me that I am going to Europe and so great is my unfaith that I shall not feel sure of it until the steamer sounds the signal for sailing.

I have been miserably unwell ever since I came here, and I would leave here soon had I no thoughts of going abroad. The little ear trouble of which I spoke has terminated in an angry boil which made my ear look like a boiled lobster. But the boil has at last broken and I am easier on that score. . . .

By the way, I have made a mistake—so they tell me—in not bringing an old suit of thick clothes with me to wear on the passage, and throw away on landing. I write in the midst of such uncertainties that I hardly know what to say. Allison will not go and so far as the passage is concerned the way is open to you.

I will send this off, and wait another day in hopes of hearing from you. Kiss all the dear children and mother for me, and set me down again and again your ownest own James.

James and Crete sailed for Europe the middle of July, traveling extensively in England and on the Continent for four months; it was the longest period of their lives when they were constantly together. They returned to America the first week of November, Lucretia went straight to Hiram where her children had been with James' sister, Mary, and "grandma," and James took up his congressional work. He set about immediately finding a house for them to rent. Crete, who was pregnant when they left, had a miscarriage after returning home.

Hiram, November 20, 1867

My Darling Precious

How many things occur in the lives of the loving to make more sweet their affections. Your letter of July left unread at home has dropped down into my loneliness now—a bright ray from the Eden of our ante European love to link the sweetness of the past to the riper joy of the present. It made my heart very happy to read it; and the desolation of my loneliness even grew brighter. I cannot tell you how the months of our shared times have deepened and perfected the earnestness of my love for you, nor the glory and majesty with which they are beginning to rise up before me in the inestimable privileges they conferred in giving me so much to enjoy with you, my loving guide and princely giver, and I condemn myself that bodily discomfort ever for one moment made me forgetful of my perfect happiness, and your loving patient and tender regard make me know how noble and genuine is your love for your faulty though very devoted little wife. . . . I held baby on my lap a long time this evening while the little boys laughed and played around her, and my thoughts wandered back through the years into the beginnings of our love, and their little lives grew as precious as I gathered them into my heart as the sweet pledges of our life. I hope you are in Washington before this, with a hope of rest before you. I shall watch with great anxiety the development of affairs there. But whatever may be done, don't fail to take your medicine twice a day. You must take care of your health or you will surely break down again. Hoping to hear from you very soon, I am all yours, and yours forever. Crete.

Willard's, Washington, November 24, 1867.

Precious Darling,

It is nearly ten o'clock Sunday night, and I will not lie down to sleep till I have told you again that I love you. Surely "love is the fulfilling of the law," and the law of our love is liberty. We no longer love because we ought to, but because we do. The tyranny of our love is sweet. We waited long for his coming, but he has come to stay. I wish, my dear love, that God would let us die together when we die; that neither of us might be left in the empty world for a single hour. It would be unkind in me to tell you, if I could, how lonely and lost I am without you. Part of the machinery of my life seems to be gone and I wander around unconsciously as if in search of it, that I may set nature at work again.

Your precious words of the 21st came to me this morning and fell down into my heart like benedictions. Did you know how unutterably sweet it is to be praised by you? The words you wrote have lifted me and made [me] proud and happy all day. How sweet the privilege I have had this summer! The alchemist sought to transmute other substances into gold. I have done far better. I have been able to transmute gold into esthetic joys, intellectual growth, heart life, and, better than all, have been permitted to see it transformed into sweet and beautiful decorations of the noblest and truest woman I ever saw, and she as glad to be mine as I to be hers. This surpasses alchemy. It is divine. It is a new proof of the truth that "God is love."

Well, Darling, I have done nothing of worth except to hunt houses and read. I am satisfied that the price of the house I wrote you of is too great and we ought not to pay it.[12] I hope I can do better. I am thinking of buying a house on time and hope to sell it again when we are done with it. If we had done so four years ago, we should have owned it now. I am anxious to receive your answer to my letter of Thursday. It may help me to a decision. Tomorrow morning the committees will be announced. It looks as though I should be Chairman of Ways and Means, but I do not know. I am glad to tell you that I have not spoken to Colfax on the subject and have made no efforts to secure it.[13] So if I don't get it, I shall not fail. If I do, it will be all the better for coming unsolicited. The Impeachment Report is to come tomorrow and great anxiety is felt in regard to it. The path before us is full of difficulties. If I should be at the head of W&M it will be the most arduous and responsible work and the severest trial of my life. Dear Love, do write me very often. Kiss the sweet three and tell them Papa loves them all. Ever your ownest own. James.

Hiram, December 1, 1867

My Dearest One:

The first day of Winter has come with its cold cold but did not bring another letter from you to warm and cheer me. It is very cold and the snow is deep, and the past week has been one of the most dismal I ever saw—scarcely a ray of sunshine through the whole of it. But don't think I am dismal, too. I am only lonely without you. I am very, very busy trying to get some clothes ready to keep the children warm, but almost the only time I get to sew is when they are all in bed at night, but I would not complain of that if I could only be a patient good mother. It tries me more than anything else that I am not, and I am afraid I never can be.

Evening. Just as I had written so far, Matt called with our yesterday's mail, and with it was your most precious letter of last Sunday. I asked George Northrup to inquire at the office for me last night, and supposing he did so concluded there was nothing for me, but sweet and most delightful has been my disappointment! It seemed to me that never before did words of such infinite and sweet worth pass from heart to heart. I have read and reread them with my eyes filling with tears, and have pressed them to my lips and heart with a feeling that I must hide their visible presence and their loving spirit away there forever. Truly, Darling, such happiness and such joys can come alone from the infinite Giver of all good. . . . I cannot tell how gratifying are all your successes to me, and I know how worthy you are of them, but especially am I pleased that they all come to you unsolicited. I am glad you did not speak to Mr Colfax for the Chairmanship you have received, and I cannot help but be proud of you that you are esteemed so worthy of such distinction as to have it bestowed unasked. I hope it will be best that I go and live with you again this Winter, it seems so hard to be away from you. I have not urged it, lest you should feel that I was discontented with what seemed to be a necessity, and feeling also perfectly sure that if it were best that I go, the way would most surely be provided, so perfectly do I trust all that pertains to our love and happiness to the dispensation of the

Infinite Love which has so far guided us. I shall quite approve of your buying a house if you can find one to suit us. A few years more of such rents as you have been paying would pay for a house. And again when you have any spare funds to invest, if they go into a house they will be quite as sure to be safe as they would be if invested in stocks. Little Mollie is getting to be a picture of life and health. She has not had a sick day since you left. Can sit alone and is fast losing the look of feebleness which made her seem so frail. Mother came home yesterday and says she never saw a child that had gained more in the same time. Hal too is growing fat and hearty, and roguish. Jim is as hardy as ever. The marks on the first page are Harry's. He says that he wrote these to you, that a deep snow has come and he wants to know if you do not think Old Santa Claus will come pretty soon. Mother had a pleasant visit with Aunt Alpha and her cousins, and I think is feeling pleased with the idea of going to Washington if you get a house. I hope we can make her feel happy and pleased with us in case it is so. . . . How I would love to cheer you with my presence. Your own Crete.

Washington, Dec. 2, 1867.

Dearest Love:

Your two precious letters were awaiting me this morning on my return to Washington. I went to N.Y. Thursday and reached Lewisboro Friday morning. Came back to N.Y. on Saturday evening with Rebecca and some of her N.Y. relatives who were visiting her. Went with her to hear Beecher yesterday and came through last night, arriving here this morning. I made a short call on Mrs. Calhoun, and am glad to tell you that I am confirmed in the wisdom of the course I adopted. I think she will marry a N.Y. lawyer before very long, who has long befriended her and who is able to support her in her literary life.

And now, Darling, let me say that out of that darkness we have made, and surely shall make, good come. It was a terrible hurt to your love, it was a test and proof of mine. I know more surely than I could have known before how deep and abiding, how pure and never failing is that love that binds you to my heart, me to yours. That night showed us that the star of love was fixed in our heaven forever. With all the past in view, with all its possibilities, with what might [have] been, in any conceivable supposition, I here record the most deliberate conviction of my soul. It is this: Were every tie that binds me to the men and women of the world severed, and I free to choose out of all the world the sharer of my heart and home and life, I would fly to you and ask you to be mine as you are.

During the past week I have been almost ashamed of my weakness in having my heart so full of love lorn longings for you and the dear little ones. Bless you and them, and Preciousest One, do write me very very often. I have not yet settled upon a house to suit me, though I came nearer buying one than anything else. I shall try to find some place for you and have my darlings near me. Life is too short to spend so many of its sweet hours away from you. I do not yet hear from Mother. Do you? Maria was called home some weeks ago by the sickness of Jonas.[14] Rebecca is giving her time to the care of her mother who is very feeble. Ever and All your own, James.

Hiram, December 6, 1667

My Precious Darling,

I have been making such a violent effort to sew this week that I did not realize until this morning that I had allowed so many days to pass without writing to you. I resolved at once that another mail should not go without a message for you, and your precious words of last Monday, just received, have given a new impetus to my resolve and with my open sewing machine for a desk and in the quiet of Jim's and Mollie's nap, I am scribbling as fast as I can to catch the love that is running over from my heart. Again and again my heart thanks you and would pour out its whole wealth of love and gratitude to you for all your dear and loving words. To know that you so love me is the extremist happiness that this life can give, and it seems to me it must be the same through the endless years. Such endearing words of love and tenderness give me strength for all the work of life, and nothing seems very hard with one so good and strong and noble to lean upon. I wish you could look into my heart and see how gushing full it is of love and fondness and sweet desire for you, and know that notwithstanding my many shortcomings how earnestly I strive to be as worthy of your love and pride as you are of mine.

I feel a good deal indignant that Mr. Colfax has turned you over to the Military Committee after your years of hard work on the Ways and Means. Still, out of it I hope will come this good, that you will have more time for rest. I cannot but hope that you can have us with you this winter. I know we need each other more than we need anything else in this world, and it seems almost wrong the thought of so many months of separation. . . .

I hope to hear from you as often as you can spend time to write, and I will try not to be so neglectful again.

With my whole heart of love. Your own forever, Crete.

In the winter of 1868, James again found a large house to rent on Capitol Hill at $125 per month for Crete, his mother, and the three children, Harry, Jim and Mollie. In February James had to go to Bethany, West Virginia, to argue a case in law; on the 22nd of that month, the House voted to impeach President Andrew Johnson.

Washington, Feb. 23, 1868

My Dearest Life:

I put fresh coal on my fire last night at eleven and went to bed with a half hope that the 5 o'clock train this morning would bring you home, for I had received no letter from you since Wednesday. The fire was still alive when the train came, but all the morning brought for me was your letter of Friday, next in priceless worth to you, but not you, and it gave only the sharp pain which lies nearest to keen pleasure, the pain of waiting so many long days yet for your return. I am made so anxious, too, for your health. Why did Judge Black leave you? Was it to come back here to give his aid to the new trial of Presidential folly? So it is whispered. Yesterday was a fierce day in Congress. At eleven they were still in session, but what was done or when they adjourned we have not heard. The morning paper did not report the evening session. Mother was there from noon until 5 o'clock. She says the excitement was intense, and impeachment more threatening than ever before. You will doubtless see all the reports of the whole proceeding before this reaches you. I am reading After the Verdict now.[15] Mr. Spofford[16] gave it to me a few days ago. I am growing very much interested in it since I find you and your Sandy Valley campaign introduced. The story is written by the author of Margaret Howeth, and, like it, reveals the attempt to make words tell those sentiments and passions of the heart which are only *felt*. But I find myself less and less able to criticize anything of this kind. My own heart is so full of quick throbbing life in its love for you that it beats a ready and approving response to every thought or sentiment which struggles for expression, and casts about it a halo from the brightness which so transfigures all my life. My darling precious one, when I stop to think, and I do very often, how priceless is the gift of your great love, the love of one of the very few whom the Great Giver sends to bless mankind, my soul lays hold of strong and holy purposes and my happiness lifts me beyond all the annoyances of life, and I reproach myself that the frailty of my own nature can ever drag me down for one moment, even among the shadows of discontent and repining. When I look into the faces of our darling little ones, and take home to my heart the precious thought that they are *ours*, yours as well as mine, they seem to me so sacred that I wonder how I can ever be impatient with them. They all love you so much and want you to come home. Jimmy says every day "papa home at dinner Mamie" and Hal says "I wish papa would come home" and their mama responds to all with unutterable longings and tenderest desire. My precious, remembering you every hour with fullness of love, I am your little wife.

Back home in Hiram that fall, as the couple approached their tenth wedding anniversary, James once again took to the campaign trail. Lucretia and family resided in the Rudolph homestead since their own home had been rented to the Burke Hinsdale family.

Hiram, September 7, 1868

My Darling:

   The cool days and falling leaves are bringing to me some very sweet reflections. The years tell me that we have passed the period called "bright youth" and that whatever more of life there is for us belongs to the less enviable time, to the maturity which sobers us for the swift-coming future. But with our love so perfected the coming years promise me so much that is sweet and beautiful in the loving, trusting gentleness and peace of our united and uniting lives that I look to them with more joy than to all the past. I hope darling that this is truth to you, too, and that the perfecting harmony of our lives satisfies and sustains you as it does me. I hope you will take care of your health and not let this week count more than seven days in moving you on to the end.

   We all love you most dearly and long for your presence.

   Yours forever, Crete.

Cleveland, Sept. 15, 1868.

My Darling:

Before leaving for the cars I write a word to repeat the same sweet story that I love you with all the sweet yearning tenderness of which my nature is capable. It grieved me to think that any old memory should come up out of the past and smite my sweet one, and I could hardly leave you. Dearest, you must not doubt the depth and tenderness of my love which has been and is growing with every new month of my life. I have written this in the little moment before the early train. Aunt Alpha goes with us.

Ever your own, JAG

Write me at Belfountain [Ohio]. J.

Hiram, September 16, 1868

My Darling One:

I received your letter today and thank you for its kind words. You are mine and I love you with all the tenderness and devotion of my woman's heart. To each of us the past of the other would have been so impossible that we can scarcely understand all that the present now inflicts. I would not be unjust as I know you would not be cruel, and yet there are moments, short ones I hope, when each to the other does thus seem. If the sober years, nor the whitened, bleach not this spot from our lives, then the grave will hide it, and it shall not be known in the life beyond.

Wallace [Ford] and Mary are still with me and I am very grateful for their society. They make the hours of your absence much lighter. I hope you will not get sick. I hope you will live to bless me through all my life, and that we may both be spared to our children and each other for many years.

Remembering you with all my heart's love, Yours forever,

Crete.

P.S. I send you all your letters except some large official looking documents. Crete.

I hope you can be home on Sunday.

Hiram, October 2, 1868

My Darling:

Two of the letters received yesterday asked to be forwarded immediately; consequently, this package to Dayton hoping it may meet you there. There is also a letter from Bryan [New York] in a hand I think I do not mistake. If it contains an invitation to you to meet Rebecca there, I hope you will not go. It would hurt me so to have you meet her there among so many of your friends, who would think if they did not say, James loves her yet better than he does Crete, and add what a pity it could not have been otherwise. My disgrace is all I can bear now; do not make it more. I have just torn off a half sheet on which I had written out the bitterness of my heart. I will burn it, hoping that all that is wrong in thought or deed between us may thus be consumed.

How soon may we hope to see you again? Do write to me and give a little cheer to your absence. We are all well. Mother has just returned, and is looking quite as well as when she went away. Aunt Phebe did not come. Is it of any use to ask you to take care of yourself? I wish you would. I feel anxious about you all the while. I shall look for you at home next Thursday evening.

Yours in loving patience.

Crete.

The winter of 1868–69 James and Crete were again together in Washington. During this period they decided to build a home at 13th and "I" streets in the City. Lucretia returned to Hiram for the summer, while James remained in Washington overseeing the new construction and working on a special committee assignment, overhauling the outdated provisions of the census bill.

Washington, May 30, 1869.

My Darling:

I don't know that you ever experienced the full meaning of homesickness, but you know I have, and I thought it was, like ague and kindred diseases, worn out—but I have come very near having it since I left you. You have spoiled me for being alone in the world, and all the children have conspired to help you. To be here at the old place, with many of the old faces, but with a silent, empty room to come to every day, is almost too much for me, and I am reminded of my old Twinsburg [Ohio] days of crying. Do the *savans* of homeopathy set down "nostalgia" among the diseases? If so send me some pellets to nub _____ the case.

I have been very busy with my committee and other work since I reached here and have thus been able to keep off the very hard stage of the malady. But, my darling, sport aside, there is a spot in my heart that aches more than I can tell you, that you are not with me. All the past week I have been anxious about your dear health, with some apprehension that your illness at Cleveland might return and make you suffer without me. Not until this morning was I blest with the coming of your precious letter, which assured me you were well. You must take the utmost care of yourself. I beg you to feel that you are no[t] all your own, but that the happiness that I hope for in this life resides in your health and loving kindness to your own precious self.

I go every day to the little spot of earth where we are planting a home, and think of what it will be to us if life and prosperity are spared to us. I have spent several hours half dreaming, as I watch the spade fulls of earth going out to make way for us and our little ones. It was found on excavating that the wall of the house north of us did not reach low enough to meet our wants, and so we have had to build a wall three feet in height under it. I watched the bricks as they were laid, and felt how sweet it would be, when all our little darlings should be in happy and safe shelter under its roof, to remember that I had thought of you and them as each brick of its foundations were being laid, and that my love and prayers for their happiness were in the very mortar that held its walls. The work is going on bravely. The underpinning spoken of above is completed and tomorrow the other walls will be begun. In the shop the window and window and door frames are nearly done and the sash are being made. The material used is very good and dry. I think the builders show a determination to make a good and honorable completion of the contract. I have already made some changes and incurred some new expenses:

1. The N. wall was not provided for in the contract and I am to pay $50 for it.
2, On examination I have changed the brown stone from Manassas to Connecticut. The former is too red and makes too little contrast with the brick, and I believe the house will be worth more than the difference in cost, which is $60.
3. I have concluded to adopt your advice in regard to the Library, and have a window in place of one of the book cases. But I am in doubt whether it better be put on the north side of the chimney or the south. The builder

thinks it will be too near the corner if we put it south. What say you? This change from bookcase to window will make no change in cost. I think however that I shall have to get another book case for some other part of the room. What say you?

It is not possible for me to say how long I shall be kept here. The work before the committee is enormous and will take a deal of time, and I may find it necessary to make a martyr of myself by staying much longer than I expected. I see no hope of getting home to Commencement, though I want to very much indeed. Do write to me, Darling, often and often and often. I am a beggar for crumbs; don't turn me away from your table. Love to Mother and all the dear little ones.

Ever and fervently your own James.

Hiram, June 3rd, 1869.

My Own Darling:

Your long precious letter of last Sunday is just received, and I thank you for it more than words can tell. It is so sweet to know that you love me so well as to be anxious for my health even though there is no occasion for it. But remember that to me your health is of far more consequence than mine can be to you. The thought that it is even possible for you to be taken from me makes my heart sink and tremble with fear. Except for being away from you I am almost glad that you can watch the building of the house alone, and have it ready for me before I see it. It has always given me pleasure to know that the home I built up here is so pleasant to you, and I know that I shall love the one you are watching and preparing. The prayers of your loving heart laid in with the foundation stones to send up their incense through the whole superstructure will make it a sanctified, a holy place, and I feel that with such an earnest desire to do and be all that is right, we will be blessed and see many happy days where so much love is centered. I think the changes you propose are wise. As to the Library window, I think there is little choice in the sides of the chimney and if the builder thinks the north side better, I should not object. I think a bookcase to stand on the north side of the hall door opposite the window would look well. But you will decide that as you think best. I am sorry and yet glad that you are homesick—sorry for your loneliness, but glad you love us so well as to be lonely without us. I hope you will not feel compelled to stay very long now. It is growing so warm that I fear you will suffer in health as well as be made very uncomfortable. Will it not be better for your committee to postpone some of the work until cooler weather comes in the Fall? I hope you will think best to do so. I want you here so much at Commencement. I am sorry I did not send your summer vests. I am afraid you are needing them. I think I sent one pair of pants. The other pair I find are nearly worn, so if you need them you had better get some.

We are all very well, and wanting nothing but you. Love to all our friends and remember every hour that we are all loving you and longing for you more than words can tell.

Ever Lovingly Yours, Crete.`

Hiram, June 30th, 1869.

My Precious Darling:

Not a word for you for two days. Most surprising. Nor a word from you. But today's paper reports in the telegraphic column your address last night so I am assured that you reached Washington safe enough at least to speak last night. I did not receive the note you sent from Garrettsville until evening and until after I had mailed the letter to Mr. Austin telling him I had decided not to go, and on the whole I thought it not best to go. Mother and Harry start for Solon tomorrow morning, and I shall be more alone still. Can you not come home early next week? I wish you could, and if you do not go to N.Y. and Boston, you will, won't you? I am so anxious to hear from you. I gather a little comfort concerning your health from the cooler weather and from your staying with the Spencers. It will be so much more like home with friends who will think about you and take care of you.[17] I hope you find our house still progressing satisfactorily. It seems to me almost like a beautiful dream, the home my darling is building up for my kingdom, and I believe I feel more a bride than I did eleven years ago. I am sure if your home should be really finished and you permitted to take me into it, that I shall feel more than ever before that I am your wedded wife taken to your hearth and heart. Precious one, my heart is so full of sweet emotions and tender loving thoughts which the eyes alone can speak or understand. I hope you can stay in our bird's nest a little while when you return and rest. I will stop and rest with you, too, and we will forget that we are not in the sweet dawn of love dreaming the dreams that the perfume of early flowers brings. Darling, we will be Lotus Eaters or anything that the enchantments of love can make us. Come, Darling, Come. Lovingly and longing ever.

Your own Crete.

In the summer of 1869, while doing his committee work in Washington, James was invited, along with Sam Armstrong, a Williams alumnus, President Mark Hopkins of Williams, and Professor Northrop of Yale, to inspect the Hampton Institute, a newly established school for African Americans. After this trip, James then went to New York and Boston with David Wells, commissioner of revenue, to investigate matters relating to the new census bill his committee was working on.

Steamer "Louisiana" on Chesapeake Bay, July 3, 1869. 6 A.M.
Darling Mine:

I have found a scrap of paper in the cabin and will make best use of it known to me, to say "I love you" and to tell you where I am. I left Washington at 12:30 day before yesterday and at 4 P.M. took steamer at Baltimore for Fortress Monroe. Had a delightful passage down the bay with the special and unusual satisfaction of finding no person on board who knew me. I was therefore permitted to revel in the full freedom of privacy, to hear public men and measures discussed without being taken into the account personally. At 5 o'clock yesterday morning we reached Fortress Monroe, or Old Point Comfort, and I thence went by wagon about three miles to Hampton, the seat of the Industrial School, which has been established by the joint effort of the Am[erican] Missionary Soc, and the Freedman's Bureau. I [waited] there for Dr. Hopkins and wife, Prof Northrup of Conn, and two or three other prominent men, with whom I was to serve as a committee of observation and report. We spent a busy and delightful day visiting in the fort and the schools, sailing on the bay. It was a great pleasure to be with Mark Hopkins and receive so many proofs of his approval and kind regards. He and Mrs Hopkins inquired kindly after you and while they were talking I promised myself that you and I would not let another winter pass without visiting their daughter, Mrs Knott. Will you try to remember it? After a busy day which concluded by our agreeing upon the substance of a report which Dr Hopkins is to write, I took the steamer at seven P.M. and now we are within 30 miles of Baltimore steaming up this beautiful bay. I do not wonder that the people of Old Va were so enthusiastic in the love [of] their state. It is certainly one of the noblest, if not the noblest, of all the 37. In its water system, mountains, climate, soil, and indeed all the physical conditions which make a beautiful country, I know of but few places on the Earth which are its equal. How I wanted you with me! The next thing to having you was to promise that I would bring you down there next winter to spend a day and night with my friend Gen Armstrong, the Superintendent of the school. I think you will be glad to go. I shall go back to Washington this morning and finish up some work I left undone and probably shall make another payment on the house. Not later than Sunday night I shall leave for N.Y. where Wells[18] is to meet me and we go thence to Boston. My heart is turned homeward and my head will soon be. The date I cannot yet tell, but not far from the 12th. Ever and forever, Your James.

Hiram, July 3rd, 1869

My Own Darling:

I have felt so near you all the morning. I have found myself dreaming so many times with my work fallen into my lap and my eyes looking away to you. Perhaps it was your dear letter so near, or perhaps it was the memory of nine years ago coming back into my heart. Our mutual lives first lived in the little girl who came to us nine years ago this morning. The little life soon passed away from us, but the beautiful brightness into which it kindled stayed long enough to show to us each the other's heart, to show to us the way into the dawn. The little girl did her work; and O was it not a great work? A work for which we will thank God through all the coming ages. Darling I cannot tell how my heart longs for you.

Sunday evening. I used to write you love letters which I did not dare to send you lest they should meet with no response, and I feel almost like doing with this as I did with them—commit it to the hungry flames, and it is only that I now know that you love me and respond to every heartthrob that I do not so dispose of it. I recollect Mrs Hawley[19] once said something like this: "Truth comes to us infinitesimally." So do all the lessons of life, at least we so receive them. But when once received they are indeed like leaven, and we are so transformed, almost transfigured by some of them, that of our former selves we scarce discover a trace. Since the first faintest glimpse of the truth that you did really love me dawned into my heart, I seem to myself to have died to all that long dark life of untruth and to have been raised up to a new life, and really the things that I did then in that former life I cannot do now. Darling, I sometimes feel that our love has touched the extremes of more experiences than any other human love this Earth has yet known, and is to become the most perfect example, and the exaltation which the love brings, makes me feel that it is not all *human*, but may be divine. I treasure up all these things in my heart.

Monday evening. The quiet of these days makes me think of you so much and wonder if we really would be so happy as it seems to me we would be were you only here. We could be so devoted to each other. Maybe we would be too selfish and so you are kept away. I shall look for you through morning and night until you come with a hope that we shall enjoy one uninterrupted day. The two babies amuse me but they can scarcely break the thread of my thoughts remaining ever loveward.

Even the Great Frederick and his rugged old father Frederick William, about whom I am now reading, I believe interest me more for the thoughts they suggest of you, more regal than themselves, than for the fascinations of their own magnificent lives.

July 8th. The fates have been adverse surely in regard to our letters during this absence. Today yours from New York is received with the one returned to you, and I have just opened a package of Washington letters to find my last to you. I thank you so much for the sweet solemn words of assurance your letter contains. I read them with my eyes filling with tears, the tears which great joy brings. Darling, do you think we have brought up out of that fearful night only a love to last till the high noon appear and then to fail with the passing day? Rather have we not arisen as from the night of death into an eternal day? "And there shall be no night there."

I shall think of you now as with your face homeward turned, and wait for you with infinite longing. May the Father's outstretched arm guard you and preserve you and bring you soon.

I seal this now to keep until you come. Forever thine.

Crete.

New York, July 4, 1869.

Darling Crete:

I reached here this morning and now at half past five in the afternoon, have awaked from a long sleep to find dinner over, and I must wait half an hour till the Dining Room opens for tea. After I ceased my letter to you yesterday morning on board the Steamer, I went to Washington, where I arrived a little after noon and waited very diligently till nine P.M. closing up my work there. I found the brick work of the second story all up and everything ready for the floor joists of the third story. The roof is all done on the wing except the tinning. As I stood on the roof last evening and looked out over the city, I thought and hoped that we would often step out of our chamber, and sit there together in the cool of the evening, and I would tell you what I saw and thought as the work was going up, and I alone with it. By the 15th July, they will have the house enclosed. If they make as rapid progress hereafter as they have done thus far, the house will be ready for us before the end of September. My trip to Fortress Monroe, the hard days work in Washington yesterday, and the sitting up all night in a hot car last night have made me half sick today. I have however slept nearly all day and am feeling better now. I was to have met Mr Wells and the Sec of the Social Science Association here this morning. The latter came and spent several hours with me, but a telegram from Wells tells me to come on to Norwich which I shall do in the morning. Thence we shall go to Boston, and as soon as Monday week, I hope sooner, I shall turn my face homeward. This public drudgery in such terrible weather is a hard and thankless task. But I shall have so far got my Census and Banking work into shape that I can do nearly all the balance of it at home and shall accept your kind offer of help in getting through with it. Swaim got back on Friday morning and will now watch the progress of the house and thus save me the feeling of anxiety I would otherwise have. Do you remember when you and I stopped at this hotel?[20] It was on our way to Boston with the Congressional Committee. My room is nearly straight across the hall from the one we had. It makes me homesick to think of you away from me.

Darling, I want you to know that New York contains no force that can make the least ripple on the waters of my soul. You are the only orb in the firmament that controls the tides which ebb and flow in my heart. The very fact that I am in this place makes me feel the need of you all the more, for it awakens the memory of your noble magnanimity and largeness of soul. Your greatness in my eyes, has never been surpassed among women. Bless you, My Darling, and let me once again thank you that by your grand faith and truth and endurance our love was saved and purified through the fiery ordeal of the years. Ever and forever. Your Own James.

54 Portland Place, Quincy, Mass. July 8, 1869.

My Precious Crete:

I have arisen before the family are stirring to enjoy the scenery, to regale my heart with the associations personal and historical which belong to the interior and exterior of this delightful old house, the ancestral home of the Adamses. The main part of the house was built long before the revolution and each successive generation has made additions to it. It is in the green fields of the country, eight miles southeast from Boston. I have slept in an upper chamber in the third story under the roof with dormer windows and from the east window I look out on the bay and catch a glimpse of the open sea beyond. The room is hung with pictures, four of them German engravings of sketches from Silesia brought by John Adams when he was foreign minister. The rest are engravings from classical subjects. One side of the room is filled with books, Latin, Greek, French, German and English, and most of them bear the name of John Quincy Adams, who purchased them. The furniture is rich but quaint, of the last century pattern, and in keeping with the venerable aspect of the room. The house is an elegant and charming relique of antiquity. Every room is full of history. On the next floor below is the room where John Adams died. It is now used as the library of his grandson, Charles Francis Adams, the paterfamilias of the mansion. Many original portraits are scattered through the house, one very fine one of Abigail Adams (the wife of John), the writer of those charming letters you were reading last winter. One of Washington, taken before he was President, and what is of more consequence to our personal impression of him, before he had his false teeth. It gives you a vivid impression of the humanness of his face with its wrinkles and sunken mouth. Beside him is the jolly Martha with a stunning head gear which does not appear to have come down to our times with her standard pictures. There is also a fine French portrait of Jefferson. What a remarkable history this family has made. Two cousins John and Samuel Adams leading spirits in the revolution, made its first mark. John, the second President of the U.S. and decorated with all the other high offices his country could bestow; then his son John Q. . . . but though he had not the rough sturdy grasp which characterized his father, he was a man of much more culture and learning and really made a more lasting impress upon the policies and opinions of his day. He was in public life longer, I believe, than any other American and held nearly all the highest offices including the presidency. His son Charles Francis Adams did not perhaps shine in Congress as brightly as his father did at the same age, but his very solid abilities displayed during his long residence in London as American minister during the most trying period of our diplomatic history have shown him every way worthy of his father and grandfather. And now his family are showing even more marked ability. His oldest son John Quincy is the leader of the Democratic party in Mass. and I shall not be surprised to see him elected Governor before long. Charles Adams is a very forcible and brilliant writer on the North American Review and is just appointed Commissioner of Rail Roads for Mass. He is not more than 33 years old. Henry Brooks Adams, still younger, writes financial and other articles for the Edinburgh and other foreign reviews, as well as for our own, and is rapidly rising as a clear and powerful thinker and writer. Mary Adams, who is not more than 22, is very bright, very like the picture of her great grandmother Abigail, and Brooks, the youngest boy, is now a senior in Harvard, where every male Adams since and including John in his direct line has graduated. I doubt if any family in England or America can show such a history.

Groton, Noon Thursday.

Dearest, I stopped at the foot of the previous page and went down to breakfast. The family were as wide awake and jolly as when we dined with them in Portland Place. They remember our visit and us very kindly and I keenly regret that you are not with me to enjoy the rare visit I have had and am having here. You see by the heading of the page that I am writing on paper brought from the place where we saw them. After breakfast we talked finance for an hour, as we had talked it till near midnight the night before, and then Henry Adams took us to the old church of Quincy, built many generations ago, and where are buried the remains of John and Abigail and John Q and his wife. We also went through the old burying ground where is the tomb of Henry Adams, the American founder of the family. He was one of the original founders of the town, in 1639.

Near the Adams house, between it and the old church, are the ruined foundations of the House where John Hancock was born. So you see there is a great mass of revolutionary history in Quincy. Before I left the Adams House, I looked through a few of the manuscript journals and letters of John and

John Q. Adams. Charles Francis is now at work preparing a mass of them for publication.

Do you suppose Hal or Jim will ever care to look over your letters to me and mine to you? Bless the dear boys and little Moll. I hope we may be worthy their love and veneration.

This forenoon since I came into town I have visited several people in reference to the Census and other public matters. We are going to take a trip on the Bay this afternoon with a party of Boston gentlemen. I must close this long and, I fear, dull letter by saying for now, I love you and good bye.

Ever your James.

Boston, July 9, 1869

Crete Dearest:

As soon as I closed up my long letter to you yesterday, I went to the Custom House, where a party of eight gentlemen met us and embarked on board the Government tug or revenue cutter, for a trip on the Bay, and a fish dinner. At first, we took a turn up toward Bunker Hill and the Navy Yard, and on the way passed the U.S. Man of War "Sabine," on which my little cadet Harber[21] is shipped for his year's cruise. We hailed him and saw him a moment as we passed, and I made arrangements for him to come ashore to meet me in the evening. We then passed down the harbor and boarded several foreign vessels, which were coming in. I thus had an opportunity of seeing how our Revenue officers discharge their duties in regard to the foreign imports.

At half past four o'clock we landed on one of the islands of the harbor, where there is a celebrated Hotel, kept by a Mr Taft, who is the cuisine celebrity of Boston. His father was a famous tavern keeper in his day and the son, like the sons of whom I wrote you yesterday, has followed the career of his sire. Taft has studied the subject of fish and also of birds with the enthusiasm of an artist and the pride of a caterer, and is the authority of the Hub. I confess I did not expect so much. But it really seemed as though Neptune and Pan had combined to make Taft successful. The first was a course of soup, in which clam chowder and fish chowder played a chief part. Then followed dishes of fish, the delicacy of which I cannot expect to describe. The rock, the bass, the perch, the deep sea flounder and, to my taste best of all, the turbot, each in turn elicited rounds of applause and were then received with inward satisfaction. Over the turbot came a classical discussion touching the comparison between the merits of this American fish and his transatlantic relative the turbot of England, and the story was not neglected of the Roman Emperor Domitian, I believe, to whom, when a live turbot was sent from Briton, he assembled the Senate to discuss the best mode of cooking it. This fact was satirized by Juvenal.[22] After fish came wood-cock and other birds, dishes that vied with the fish, and then the dinner was ended with strawberries and ice cream. After dinner we went down to the offing where lay at the mouth of the harbor, a beautiful ship from Spain, laden with wine. We boarded her and then came home, the bay gleaming with lights, and after a visit of an hour at the Club, where "finance," the theme that puts you to sleep, was discussed for an hour. Then we came to the hotel and found my Harber awaiting me, and I took him to my room and entered into his young hopes and ambitions in a talk that lasted till midnight, and now, while I am waiting for him and Wells to come down to breakfast I have written these notes to you. Don't think I am a gourmand to spend so much ink over dinner, but I thought you might want to know how men talk and feel about that theme. Wells has come down and we must go to breakfast. With all my heart longing for you and hoping soon to be with you, I am all your own James.

James was back with his family in Hiram for the annual reunion of his beloved 42nd Ohio Regiment, as well as for the fall political campaign. He wrote Lucretia faithfully from the various Ohio towns and villages where he was making his speeches.

Hiram, September 26, 1869

My Darling:

It makes my heart ache to think you left me to day looking so sad and hurt. Honestly, My darling, there was no occasion for it. You must and do know how entirely I am yours and how perfectly and with what great happiness I love you, and how unspeakable the joy which your precious love gives to me. Sometimes I find myself turned quickly and sharply around and unconsciously looking straight into the fearful darkness of our night. I do not intend to do so, nor do I want you to know that I do. I always turn away the moment I become con-scious of its shadows, and try to hold myself steadily with my face to the great light of our glorious day. I do not mean that it costs me an effort to do this, for it is a delight from which I would never turn, but as I have written above sometimes an uncontrollable circumstance turns me, and when you surprise me with my face set and rigid, I feel somehow that I cannot tell you, that you must not know what it is, lest you think me willingly and perhaps wilfully going wrong. Darling, do not question my love. I trust you in spite of some very grave reasons why I might not. Reasons stronger, I believe, than any you can bring for doubting me, and if you cannot have perfect confidence in my love for you, I shall be driven into that despair which can neither speak nor move, nor give any sign. Tell me that you know I love you and that you love me, and I will be always happy.

Monday evening. We are all very lonely without you. We are all spoiled for life without your immediate presence. Tomorrow I go to Nellies and think I will stay with her until Saturday. Will hope to meet you at home then. With many hopes and loves for you, I am All Your Own, Crete.

Hiram, October 18, 1869.

My Darling:

I have worked all day and am very very weary, but cannot go to our bed without saying to you in answer to your question of this morning that I am indeed lonely without you. The house is empty and desolate the moment you go out of it and however unresponsive I may appear, or in truth be, there is ever a great longing in my heart which your presence alone can satisfy. I do not think I was born for constant caresses and surely no education of my childhood taught me to need them. Still I do not believe you know how vacant is every place without you. Nor am I sorry that life to you means demonstration. It has made you the great moral and social power that you are. I am only sorry that my own quiet and reserve should mean to you a lack of love. But, darling, we have a whole eternity to perfect the harmonies which our natures are beginning to touch.

I have reflected also over our talk of last evening. I must be brave enough to be happy with the great good given me without asking that it be made perfect through the suffering of another.[23] The truth, whatever it may be, alone can live. Whatever is false will die of itself and by itself. There is not need of violence to destroy it.

I hope you will be happy until I come; then I will try not to lessen it. My love to all our dear friends. I shall be anxious to hear from you.

Ever wholly and entirely your Own Crete.

❧ NOTES ❧

1. Prof Dallas Bache (1806–1867) was the great-grandson of Ben Franklin. He had been a professor at the University of Pennsylvania and superintendent of the United States Coast Survey since 1843.
2. Lily Schenck was wife of the Ohio politician and close friend of Garfield's, Robert Schenck.
3. Nell, Lucretia's sister, was yet unmarried.
4. William Dennison had been governor of Ohio and was then Postmaster General, appointed by Lincoln.
5. James Brooks from New York was democratic leader of the House. The reference to his "roaring" is from Shakespeare's *A Midsummer Night's Dream*, act 1, scene 2: "I will roar you as gently as any sucking dove."
6. Henry Rowe Schoolcraft had died in 1864. His second wife, Mary Howard Schoolcraft, rented James a room. Schoolcraft's great work is *Historical and Statistical Information Respecting the History, Condition, and Prospects of the Indian Tribes of the United States* (1851–1857).
7. Mary is James' sister.
8. When James writes, "where I came nearest to wronging you," he may mean that he not only nearly consummated this relationship but he also almost left his wife for Mrs. Calhoun.
9. The Garfields usually called Harry by his nickname, "Hal."
10. Lucretia may think she has become reconciled to that relationship, too. But her attitude toward Rebecca continues to haunt her for many more months.
11. Mr. Allison, a Republican member of the House from Iowa, later sat in the Senate. James offered him the Treasury after his nomination to the presidency.
12. The house James decided not to take was a three-story home on the corner of 10th Street and New York Avenue, facing south. The rent would be

$175 per month, and the owner would live in two rooms on the second floor.

13. Schuyler Colfax was Speaker of the House. He did not appoint James Chairman of the Ways and Means Committee, though it appeared that he had at first—at least Lucretia thought he had.

14. Maria Learned was the woman James came to know so well in Poestenkill, New York. It was she who introduced him to Rebecca, encouraging that romance. Her son, Jonas, then about thirty years old, had gone to the school at Hiram, but was too frail to finish the course.

15. Lucretia refers to *Waiting for the Verdict*, a novel by Rebecca Harding Davis (1831–1910), published in 1868. Her other novel, *Margret Howth: A Story of Today*, was published in 1861.

16. Mr. Spofford was Librarian of the Library of Congress.

17. The Spencers were old friends. Platt Spencer, the noted originator of Spencerian penmanship, had held classes in penmanship at Hiram. His son, Henry, and wife, Sara, lived in Washington.

18. David Ames Wells (1828–1898), an economist and friend of James' from Williams College, advised James on tariff matters. He was a special commissioner of the revenue.

19. Mrs. Hawley was the wife of Richard Hawley, a manufacturer from Detroit. The Garfields visited the Hawleys at their Lake Huron cottage in the summer of 1872.

20. James likely refers to Astor house.

21. Giles B. Harber was an appointee of James' to the U.S. Naval Academy. He came from Youngstown, and later became a good friend of the Garfield family.

22. The reference to the turbot mentioned in Juvenal's 4th satire has to do with a mammoth turbot caught in the Adriatic and sent to the Emperor Domitian. Too large to fit into any dish, the fish was discussed by Domitian's cabinet, and it was suggested that a potter be ordered to make a jumbo pot big enough to broil the turbot.

23. "Our talk of last evening" must have had as its subject the matter of visits to Rebecca. Lucretia's submission to James' insistence that he continue his friendship with Rebecca is evidenced by her conclusion: "I must be brave enough to be happy with the great good given me without asking that it be made perfect through the suffering of another." James had just left for Washington and New York and (no doubt) Lewisboro and Rebecca.

CHAPTER 8

1870–September 1872

JAMES MOVED LUCRETIA AND HIS FAMILY *into their newly built home in the fall of 1869, and they settled into an ordinary routine. Separated only by James' occasional engagements to speak or plead law cases in faraway cities, the family wintered in Washington and summered in Ohio. In August 1870 a fourth child, Irvin McDowell, was born. The following autumn, in 1871, James took his mother and aunt on a trip through New England so that they could visit their childhood home in New Hampshire, and the following June, James was at Williamstown receiving an honorary degree from Williams College, the last official act of the retiring president, Mark Hopkins.*

Later that summer James and Lucretia, with two younger children—Mollie and Irvin—and Major Swaim and his wife, made an excursion to Fort Leavenworth, Kansas. The women and children remained there while James and the Major traveled to Montana on Congressional business to treat with the Flathead Indians.

Of the one-hundred letters exchanged between 1870 and 1872, twenty-one are included here. The end of December 1869 James was in New York visiting General Irvin McDowell, his old army friend, for whom his fourth child had been named. This chapter begins with the letter James wrote Lucretia on the first day of the New Year.

New York, January 1, 1870

My Darling:

A happy new year to you and to all our dear ones. I so much long to be with you and them and begin the year with you. May we end it happily and all feel that the world is better and each of us happier for the other's having lived in 1870.

We all went to Wallack's Theatre last evening and listened to a very stupid play. Then came home and and {sic} visited till the new year came in and the "wild hello" told it to the "wild sky." No work can be done here today and I shall go this evening to see Rebecca. I shall make a few calls here today and on Monday morning resume my work, and finish it as soon as possible. I can't yet tell what day I will be with you, but it will be as soon as possible, for I am bereaved every hour without you.

I have never felt so constantly and deeply as now the need of you. I hope you will not be worn and discouraged by the many vexations which the household imposes upon you. Loving you with all my heart and soul, I am more and more

Your own James.

Washington, Jan 1, 1870

My Own Darling:

That each year you may be made happier and lifted into a larger life is the truest wish of her whose strongest desire is to be to you all that is sweetest and best, and to aid you in all that is the most noble. We have passed a very pleasant day, but the chief enjoyment I have gained from it, was a kind of consciousness that in all my arrangements for the day, and in the welcome I have given to our friends you would feel that I was not unworthy of you or of the position you have given me. Over fifty persons called and Mother and Mrs. Swaim assisted me very handsomely. I will tell you all about it.

The express package from Stewarts came just as the visitors began to arrive, and I did not get time to open it until just a few minutes ago. The shawls are both very pretty but I think I could scarcely be comfortable in the *red*. And I do not feel sure that it will be best to keep either. I can get along this winter without one, and I find every day so many ways for money to go.

I cannot begin to tell you all the kind things that have been said about you today in this, but I have them stored in memory for you, and please don't stay away until I *forget* them. I shall look for you without fail as early as Wednesday, and if you can come sooner I shall be so glad. Thank you for your sweet letter.

I shall hope to get one every day. Dr. Pinkerton still stays in town, but comes here only occasionally—says he will let me rest while you are away.[1] My love and kindest regards to all the General's family. I am so glad to hear that Mrs. McDowell is better. Come soon and know that I am loving you always.

Ever yours
Crete.

Washington, Jan 2, 1870.

My Precious Darling:

I awoke from one of the most loving dreams of you last night that ever came to glorify my sleep. I cannot tell it to you until I see you, but my faith and trust in your immeasurable love and tenderness for me was so awakened and vivified that I awoke feeling that I had passed into a new life, and I could not sleep any more, but with life and love transfigured I waited for the morning thinking only of you, and with no thought but of sweet solemn holy trust. I have no explanation of it. It came to me and it abides in my heart a living truth, and my soul worships the All Loving Father for this latest richest gift. Darling, come home, to our home which is growing to me so much dearer each day. The children are well and giving me far less trouble than I expected. Thank you for the severe trial through which you made me pass before leaving. I believe it has inspired me with something of your own regnant power which the children recognize as well as the servants.

I have only to add *come home.*

Yours more and forever, Crete.

Garfield had been admitted to the bar in the early sixties, and his first case was argued before the Supreme Court. On that case he had worked with Judge Jeremiah Black, who had often urged James to abandon politics and enter the law profession. In the summer of 1870 Lucretia was once again in Hiram, and James was returning for work in Washington.

York, Pa. July 6, 1870.

My Darling:

When I awoke at half past seven this morning, I found myself alone on the sleeping car on the side track at York, and the train gone for three quarters of an hour. Some slight accident had happened to the car, and it had been left. The conductor had neglected to awaken me, and the porter had carried my sachel into the next car and here I was, with nothing in the way of luggage but the first volume of Ernest Maltravers.[2] I took the occasion to visit the noble old Judge and his family. I take it that I came here to his house on the banks of the Codorus as dirty a traveller as ever entered that hospitable dwelling. I found the family at breakfast and joined them in the same place where we ate a year ago. After breakfast the Judge's colored boy took me in hand and gave me such a washing and shampooing as only a negro can, and then put on me one of the Judge's shirts with a fixed standing collar. So think of me in that ancient and honorable attire. The Judge has again made me a business offer, which makes me almost hope that the Convention which meets at this hour (11 A.M.) in Garrettsville [Ohio] will relieve me from further service in Congress. I am, at this moment, greatly tempted to resign. At any rate, I shall think further of the proposition of Judge Black and may conclude to accept it before you see me again. I shall go on to Washington this evening and the Judge will go with me. I wrote you a word from Cleveland yesterday, and shall try to send you a word every day, and I hope you will not fail to do the same for me. Bless you, Darling, and keep you and our jewels well until I see you again. Ever and forever your own, James. . . .

Lucretia is now within a few weeks of giving birth to her next child, Irvin. The Hiram household is an obvious trial to her at this point in the summer, particularly in that Lucretia felt she had to do an extra amount of cleaning after the house had been rented to Burke and Mary Hinsdale.

Hiram, July 10, 1870

My Darling:

I received your letter from the Judge's standing collar yesterday, and expect the next paper will announce your resignation; for so much dignity will surely

stand appalled before the tempestuous roaring of "the Core." There must have
been a conspiracy between the Judge, the Conductor and the Porter to have
thus entrapped and drawn your legislative head into the legal stocks. Well, from
whatever surroundings I am glad to hear from you again, and know that you
have been alive and well since you left Cleveland up to the 6th of July 1870 at
least. To the 10th we still continue in usual health and strength and hope for
another week of like continuance. Then, my precious, I trust you will be ready
to start for home, if not here. I hear nothing from Miss Ransom yet nor from
any other person in regard to more help. Mary scrubbed in the kitchen yesterday to bring it to its former color, until almost crippled, and was so lame this
morning that she could scarcely get about. I think I was never so impatient for
strength to use as now. There, darling, I will stop and not fill my letters with
complaining longer. There is nothing that you could do that you have not done
and I begin to feel ashamed of my seeming ingratitude. We will come through
all right yet, and bless the providence that set us down in our country home for
the bright autumn days, but darling hereafter we will shut up our house unless we can leave for it something more practical than a *talented* man with a
gifted wife.

The weather is delightful here now, a little too warm for comfort during
parts of some of the days but the nights are luxurious in their coolness, and I
wonder if it can be that you are suffering with the heat as before I left. I find I
have kept two of your sleeping shirts here, and I half fear that I did not leave the
other where you could find it. The boys betake themselves to the edge of the
woods two or three times a day where they have found a big log which they call
a boat, and they—especially Hal—give glowing accounts of its marine capabilities. Their unsatisfied want now is a *big* . . . wheelbarrow, and their mother's
desire to gratify them leads her to think that perhaps something of that kind
which would be recognized as possessing value per se might be treated with
more respect than toy wheel barrows and carts. At least they have played with
Mr. Streater's wheelbarrow ever since they came home without breaking it. If
you should think best to make some such sort of a purchase on your way home
at Garrettsville, for instance, I think you would afford great delight to the *puer*
element of the family. For myself, think about me, love me and come home to
me, and I have nothing more to ask.

Hal has made an attempt to represent papa in standing collar, but never
having seen you so attired he has put it on hind side before. He seemed to recognize the need of the swallow tail to complete the figure.

With my heart full of love and tenderness, I am ever and forever and entirely yours. Crete.

Hiram, July 12th, 1870

My Precious Darling:

I have just received yours of the 8th inst. How slow the letters are in reaching us. Yesterday we got some effective work done. Mr. Hemming came and took up my carpet and blacked the stoves; and Mary set in order the big closet at the head of the stairs. We have had no tidings, however, of the carpet and paper, and I have to send to Garrettsville today to have them telegraph to the freight agt. at Cleveland, and if he knows nothing of them, to send a dispatch to Mr. Beckwith.[3] This morning I felt that my bad luck could take only one step lower, and that I almost began to expect. Mary awoke with her feet so crippled that she could not step nor bear her weight on them. The terrible cold she took getting home has been at work ever since and I now fear has settled into inflamatory Rheumatism. I am doing all I can for her, but if she is not better tomorrow I shall call the Doctor in to see her. I felt so miserable myself, that I about concluded to be sick, too, and so reach the ultimatum of misery. I did not, however, and the mail brought me a letter from Miss Ransom[4] telling me of a girl she had found to be sent on hearing from me. I have telegraphed for her to come tomorrow morning. Eunice has just been in and says "Till" has come home, so she (Eunice) can come and stay until the girl comes, so I am on the rising wave again, and hope to be lifted safely on shore; but, darling, I hope you can arrange to get home on Saturday. I felt for a while this morning that I must telegraph to you to come immediately, but if we get along as I now hope we may, I shall not send for you, knowing that you will come the very earliest moment possible after reading this. Hal is as good as a boy can be, runs errands, brings in wood, and helps every way he can. My respect for him this morning has reached almost to adoration. Jim, poor Jim, would help if he were not so full of mischief, and was not in such constant antagonism with Grandma. She talks to him as though he were the worst boy alive and manages to make him so saucy to her that I am driven to my wits ends to know what to do. I have had to switch him twice, and I try to keep him out of Grandma's sight as much as possible. I did not write to you yesterday and think you must be glad of it, my letters are so full of our distresses. I think we will not need to have Mandie come, for Mary heard of a girl this morning too from one of her Cleveland friends, so that I think among them all we will be provided for. Dan is just starting for her and I send this to reach you sooner.

Ever yours, Crete.

James, in Washington, is attending a session of Congress and seeing through some repairs needed for the new house.

Washington, July 13, 1870

My Darling:

Your letter of the 8th reached me last evening and filled me with great anxiety. Nothing but the overmastering demands of the public business keeps me here another hour. I am so involved in the pending legislation that I can hardly leave with honor. Again, the carpenters and plumbers are now at work, and I want to see them as near through as possible before I leave.

The door is cut through the kitchen wall toward the laundry and cased, and the new door nearly finished. Your wishes in regard to the dining room door and to spring hinges on the basement door will be carried out. I am having the plastering in the basement (north and east walls) taken off for about six feet in height and shall have a coat of hydraulic cement put on them, a coat of slate, and then on the slate a coat of plaster. I am having the edges of the basement floor cut off, so that all the moisture which soaks through the brick may work down under the floor and get off in the drains. It looks as though we were to have a good job, and a dry house at last.

I am pained beyond measure at the difficulties you meet with in getting help. To add to it prospectively I have just recd a letter from Mr. Hitz saying that the girl he spoke of can't be had. I have written him asking him to try again to get such a girl as we need.[5] I still hope to leave here Friday evening and to reach you before Sunday morning. Precious darling, know assuredly that I am loving you with all my heart and soul.

Ever Your own James.

A vivid picture of the Garfields at home in the summer in Hiram has been given us by William Dean Howells, the Ohio novelist who visited Hiram in 1870: "I was then living in Cambridge, in the fullness of my content with my literary circumstance, and as we were sitting with the Garfield family on the verandah that overlooked their lawn I was beginning to speak of the famous poets I knew when Garfield stopped me with 'Just a minute!' He ran down the grassy space, first to one fence and then to the other at the sides, and waved a wild arm of invitation to the neighbors who were also sitting in their back porches. 'He's telling about Holmes, and Longfellow, and Lowell, and Whittier!' and at his bidding dim forms began to mount the fences and follow him up to his verandah. 'Now go on!' he called to me, when we were all seated, and I went on, while the whippoorwills whirred and whistled round, and the hours drew toward midnight. The neighbors must have been professors in the Eclectic Institute of Hiram where Garfield himself had once taught the ancient languages and literature; and I do not see how a sweeter homage could have been paid to the great renowns I was chanting so eagerly, and I still think it a pity my poets could not have somehow eavesdropped that beautiful devotion."[6]

That fall, 1870, James, who decided to continue his political career, was once again campaigning in Ohio.

Hiram, September 19, 1870

My Own Darling:

After the children were all quietly asleep this evening, I sat in our room by the stove, just warmed enough to make one dreamy, a long time musing over the years so long gone and the friends and loved ones who belonged to them. Then the thread of our lines grew tangled in the web, and ran wandering through it disturbed and disturbing until I stopped amazed to find myself sitting by our fireside, the loved and loving wife, and the conviction came anew, strengthened and deepened that the All-loving Father had done all for us. That his arm of strength alone had lifted us up from the confusions and out from the entanglements and had set us down alone with souls to each other transfigured by the light and glory of love. I felt that we are not living on the same plain as heretofore, that we are scarcely the same beings, but like conquering sovereigns we live in high isolation, wedded in heart and soul and life.

I am sitting now at your desk to tell you this although it may not go to you before you come to me, but however it fulfill its mission whether by going to meet you or staying here to greet you, I want it to reveal the abiding joy that reigns in my heart, and the trust which no more forsakes it. With kisses and love my spirit and my pen say to you good night.

Your own forever. Crete.

Chicago, November 1, 1870

My Darling:

I reached here at half past eight this morning and after taking breakfast at the Sherman House have come over here to the office of my friend Major Hubbard[7] to write you a word before I go to look at my lots on Milwaukee Avenue. I shall go to Milwaukee tomorrow morning, speak there tomorrow, thence to Racine where I shall speak Thursday and thence go to Iowa City to look after the land there. I don't think it will be possible for me to get home this week. But I shall get there as soon as possible. The weather here is delightful and this wonderful city is more than ever a surprise to me. It has grown prodigiously since I was here in 1865. If I were free to go into business I have no doubt I could put you and the little Garfields out of reach of the wolf that howls at our door. Still, there are worse things than the howlings of wolves and I would not exchange the happiness that dwells in our little home for a thousand times what we have in property.

The Major is now ready to take me out to see the city and I must close. Kisses and love to all the dear ones and always most of all to you.

Ever your own, JAGarfield.

Hiram, November 3, 1870

My Darling:

I received your first from Chicago today and answer not so much in expectation that it will reach you before you reach home, as in the hope that the silence of your absence will not seem so long if broken. I have been so busy with *velvet bands* and *fringes* and *over skirts* and *sashes*, and all sorts of garments for children and women that I have a feeling that I have been in some way neglectful of you. Every minute I have a feeling that I have been unfaithful to you, and my soul tells the confessional. I am growing very hungry for some long quiet days alone with you. It seems to me the cares of life have grown very impertinent and exacting this summer, crowding themselves in between us in a very uncomfortable way, demanding time which ought to have been devoted to things more precious than cotton or woolen fabrics or even to crying babies. I look into the future though with hopeful eyes, trusting that it will *by and by* give us more of the sweet companionship of wedded love. I believe I do nothing now but work and sleep and even now I find my eyes constantly closing and my thoughts standing still with weariness and I can only add, come home soon, and remember ever that we all love you, and more than all this does your sleepy sleeping Crete. We are all very well. I think baby is much better than when you left. With a heart full of love, I am always yours. Crete.

In the ten months following this letter, James and Crete were together most of the time. Only about a dozen letters pass between them. The summer of 1871 had been difficult because James had been so undecided, wondering whether or not to push for a seat in the Senate or if he might win the chairmanship of the Ways and Means Committee. In the fall of 1871 James once again went on the campaign trail.

Hiram, September 3, 1871.

My Darling Precious Husband:

I was so glad to hear from you again yesterday, and am so glad to think today that possibly you have turned your face homewards again; but I am especially glad to be able to tell you that I hope I have grown more worthy of you and your great love since you went away—in this—that out of all the toil and disappointments of the summer just finished I have risen up to a victory; that the silence of thought since you have been away has won for my spirit a triumph. I read something like this the other day. There is no healthy thought without labor, and thought makes the laborer happy, and perhaps this is the way that I have been able to climb up higher. It came to me one morning while making bread. I said to myself, here I am by an inevitable necessity compelled to make our own bread this summer, and why not consider it a pleasant occupation and make it so by trying to see what perfect bread I can make. It seemed like an inspiration, and the whole of life grew brighter. The very sunshine seemed flowing down through my spirit into the white loaves and, darling, I don't believe my table was ever furnished with any better bread, and this truth, old as creation, seems just now to have become fully mine that I need not be the shirking slave to toil but its regal master making whatever I do yield me its best fruits. You have been king so long, darling, that may be you will laugh at me to have lived so long without the crown, but I am too glad to have found it at all to be entirely disconcerted even by *your* merriment.

Now I wonder if right here does not lie the terrible wrong, or some of it, of which the "women suffragists" complain. The wrongly educated woman thinks her duties a disgrace and either frets under them or shirks them if she can. She sees man triumphantly pursuing his vocations, and thinks it is the kind of work he does which makes him so grand and regnant, whereas it is not the kind of work at all, but the way in which, and the spirit with which he does it. I had received a copy of the Chronicle from Mrs. Spencer[8] before the paper you sent came, and have thought over the article you noticed a great deal. She sent also a printed copy of the rules and resolutions of the "Woman's Franchise Movement." I laid it aside to read and cannot find it again, so I am unable to pass my judgement on it except as it is revealed in the newspaper article. I certainly approve any effort to release women from the terrible bondage of crime and to lift them out of their degradation. But to publish and send broadcast through the country such an article as that looks more like unscrupulous revenge than any desire to benefit the fallen. The cry has been by the women asking suffrage. You men are so influenced by bad women that we virtuous women must have the power to help make laws to put down all these bad influences. They have been defeated in the courts; now with lofty heroism they go to these women and promise them *justice* and protection "legally financially socially & morally" if they will but give them aid in bringing to woman the law making privilege. If this does not *out Tammany Tammany* itself, then what can?

Well, darling, I have written you a long letter, and have not said anything yet. I am hungry for your words, want to see you more'n tongue can tell, and talk to you, too. Come home just as soon as you can. Mr. Howells'[9] letter I have answered but send it so that you can tell him more definitely about Jefferson [Ohio] if you think necessary. All send hearts full of love.

Ever Yours in all love.

Crete.

In October, James began a trip to New England with his mother and aunt.

Spencer House. Niagara Falls.
Oct 17, 1871

My Darling:

We reached Buffalo at six this morning, a little too late for the early train to the Falls, and after breakfast and a delay of three hours we came on here, arriving at ten. It is now three P.M. and we have made the round of the whirlpool, the two suspension bridges, the Clifton House, Horseshoe fall, Goat Island, Luna Island, the Tower, and back to the hotel. Our two young ladies enjoyed themselves exceedingly and do not appear fatigued. Perhaps you do not know that my first letter to you was written on Luna Island. I sat on a log which is still there amid the everlasting rush and roar of water. The course of our love has been not unlike that of the great stream whose waters I saw when I wrote. First the turbulence, then the cataract, the wild swirl of waters, the mad and awful whirlpool, and then the broader, calmer Ontario, and now the Thousand Islands dotting and glorifying the broad, peaceful river as it sweeps onward to the Sea. God grant, my darling, that we may sail it with the joy and peace you deserve. I have no words to tell you how I want you here to go with me to that trysting place where I began our trip alone.

We leave at five forty this P.M. for Keene N.H. via Schenectady, Saratoga, Rutland, Bellows Falls. I choose that route mainly because you travelled over most of it with me a few weeks ago. If you need to telegraph me, send to Tremont House, Boston, until Saturday. We now intend to go to Boston (for it is about as cheap as to Keene) and thence to New York, where I shall leave the party and go to New Jersey. Please send all my letters that reach you up to and including Saturday next to the Metropolitan Hotel, New York. And, my precious one, do write me there, a full long letter, or series of letters as your heart may dictate and your hand permit, with the work that fills it. Tell the dear children that Papa thinks of them every hour and loves them all the while. I must now go with Mother and Aunt Alpha to the shops, where they want to get some views of the falls.

Ever and wholly Your Own,

James.

Hiram, October 20, 1871

My Own Precious:

It is so good of you to have written me so many times since you left. Until today I have had a letter each day since you went away. The best was from Niagara, and the postmark sent through my heart a thrill of that first new joy which came to me one winter night when your first letter to me was placed in my hand. How long *long* ago that hour seems! Since then the fierce rapids, the cataract roar and plunge, the sullen silence of the deep river beyond and the ter-rible whirlpool have been but faint pictures of the terrible beginnings of our love, but, my own darling, fainter still is the picture which the broad peaceful river gives of our own perfect peace and blessedness now.

It makes me so happy to know that you are making Mother so happy, and I think of you with infinite love and tenderness for all your goodness. I should love to be with you so much, but, darling, we are losing nothing in doing our duty. All will be repaid to us a thousand fold in larger richer love in the here-after. I am ashamed to send this hurried scrawl for all your good letters, but I am hurrying so my work this week that I can only think of you and love you. All the children are well and doing very well for such *live* children . . . Come home as soon as you can. It is so lonely without you. Love to Mother, Aunt Alpha and Silas. All join love to you. Ever and Forever Yours,

Crete.

In June 1872, James returned to Williamstown to receive an honorary degree from Williams College. It was the occasion of President Mark Hopkins' retirement, and James spoke on behalf of the alumni. Lucretia and family were back in Hiram for the summer, and this year were again staying with the Rudolph family in the old home-stead, having once more rented their house to the Hinsdales.

Hiram, June 25th, 1872.

My Darling Precious Husband:

If the good Fates have been with you, the cool shades of dear old Williams are now blessed with your presence. Thoughts strange, beautiful and sad, throng through my brain and cluster about my heart. Again I look through the same windows, out from the same room where eighteen years ago I sat and looked into the far East towards you, so unknown to me, wishing and longing to be nearer, to let my eyes rest on the places hallowed by your presence and your dawning love for me. Now [that] my eyes have seen the beautiful spot my heart has been filled from the sacred fount of that undying love, and I have no desire to lead you again through the shifting lights and shadows of intervening memories. My lips touch yours with holy delight, and my heart lives in the sacred confidence of your own heart's love. The Jordan is passed and Heaven is gained, and I rest in the arms of your love tonight though the same miles of hill and valley intervene that then threw their darkening distance between us. Darling, I would love to feel the strong close embrace of your "trusty" arms; I would love to be with you; but I am happy here with all the knowledge of the past and present to give me faith in your abiding love, and with our precious children. They are being very good, and I am happy to be with them.

Wednesday.

Darling, I did not finish my letter last night since nothing can reach you until you reach New York. I have been trying to discover why our little home here is so much dearer to you than to me. I felt almost sad that it should be so and had almost concluded that it was due to some radical fault in my own nature, but think I have found the reason to be one much more consolitary. Nearly all my life in that home has been spent there without you, and I have passed so many lonely days and nights in it that it was only the preciousness of the memories of you when you were there that made it very dear to me. On the contrary, it was to you the place of all others where when you did come to it you found gathered all that was nearest and dearest to you. I don't believe you loved it very much when I was not there, did you darling? I confess that when you are away I am happier here in my old home than I was there, except for the things and places lacking to remind me of you. . . .

I hope you have given up the *Flatheads*. I don't want you to go so far away, and I still think it better to go to Canada first whatever you do. Especially if I go to Leavenworth with you. I hope to hear from you almost every day and I will send letters whenever they can reach you. All the darlings send love to their blessed Papa. Loving you more and more forever and forever. Your Crete.

Williamstown, June 28, 1872

My Own Darling:

I reached here late Tuesday evening, and on driving to Prof Perry's I found that Dr. Hopkins had provided that I should stay with him. Everywhere I was then, and have since been, met with expressions of regret that you were not with me. My Darling, it is so sweet to find that wherever you go, people love and admire you. You can hardly know how much I have needed you. Wherever I enjoy anything like a triumph, I feel bereaved without you. Dr. Hopkins and his family (they are all here except Lawrence) received me most cordially. At 9 o'clock Wednesday morning the Alumni Society met, and I was re-elected President for the ensuing year. The work and exercises of the Society occupied the whole day. I will try to send you a programme of the Exercises. In the evening I took tea with David A. Wells at a friends a little out of town. Yesterday was Commencement day and the forenoon passed in the usual manner. At the dinner no speeches were made, but at 2 P.M. a very solemn service was held at the church. Dr. Hopkins delivered a most touching address, resigning the Presidency and delivering the College Keys to Prof Chadbourne.[10] Then followed Dr. Prime,[11] in an address on behalf of the Trustees to the retiring President. Then an address by Prof Bascom[12] on the part of the faculty to the old and the new Pres.; then a similar address on behalf of the students now in college. Then I spoke on behalf of the Alumni and the exercises closed. My friends here say I have seldom done so well, though I had no time to write it out. When we came to the house, Dr. Hopkins said to me that he was glad to remember that the last official act of his Presidency was to confer on me the degree of LL.D. which he did yesterday, at the close of Commencement proper.

P.S. Troy, 10 A.M. Friday

I had written this far, when I was called to an early breakfast and then bade goodbye to Dr. Hopkins and his family and went to the cars, and I have just reached this place, and in a few moments shall be enroute for New York, where I shall look for your dear word of love. The Commencement has been one of deep and solemn interest and I do so much regret that you were not with me. I hope we shall some day have the joy to witness the graduation of our dear boys at Williams. Tell the little fellows what papa says about it, ask them if they want to go to college. Kiss all the dear ones for me and know how deeply and wholly I am Your Ownest Own James.

New York, June 29, 1872.

My Own Darling:

I reached here last evening but found no letter from you. I was sad and almost alarmed lest some evil had befallen you. But today I have been filled with sweet proud joy at the arrival of your last and best letter. It is almost compensation for being absent from you to have such a treasure as this letter.

Washington. June 30, 1872

Darling:

I was interrupted by callers and was hurried around so that I did not finish this letter, but threw it into my sachel and took the evening train for this place, where I arrived this morning. I went directly to Welcker's and got breakfast, and then came to the house, where I think I am safe in saying I have spent the hottest day indoors I have ever experienced. The thermometer has stood 94 degrees to 98 degrees in the coolest rooms of the house, and now at 9:30 in the evening, I sit in my shirt sleeves, with a towel over my head and face to keep the sweat from dropping on the page as I write. The air is dead calm with no sigh or motion in all its still, furnace heat. A profane man passing by today said he would like to go to hell and try it as a summer resort, for he believed it cooler than Washington. I do so rejoice that you and the children are in a cooler climate. I shall hurry away at the earliest moment I can, Wednesday, I hope.

Lizzie has put the house in excellent order. The turf is down, the old fence away, although the new one is not yet in place. You can hardly imagine how the appearance of the yard and area are improved by the change. I fancy that it gives the house itself a more stately and imposing appearance. Rose and his family are neatly and comfortably provided for and I think will use the house well. Rose[13] is still ill, and I am quite anxious about him. The Spencers buried their baby on Monday last. There is much sickness in town. I have heard from Chittenden[14] and think it is almost certain that the business I undertook for him is successful. I hope to be able to tell you when I reach home that my fee is secured. Ward will be here tomorrow, and I think something will come out of our business. So Darling, the wolf will not howl at our door so loudly as has been his wont. Did you know that I forwarded by express my Sandy Valley records, and the Cedar box with my military letters? They were here when I arrived and I have spent more than six hours of today in looking them over. In the cedar box are great

numbers of my letters to you. I have read them today, beginning first for the
purpose of getting up the dates and facts of my career in the army, in order to
write out the military history called for by the War Dept.

But before I had read far, I was much more absorbed in reading the letters
addressed to you, and noting the spirit that animated them at the different
dates. I read some 20 written to you while I was in the Senate in 1860–61
which everywhere showed signs of the great darkness in which our love was
groping. Still there were rays of light and gleams of hope, for which we both
struggled. Then came the period of war, the Sandy Valley Campaign, and later
the Shiloh and Alabama Campaign of 1862. In that period I can see from the
letters how great a part our sainted child played in bringing our souls together.
Then came the Washington letters of the fall of 1862 and the Army of the
Cumberland letters of 1863 in which the star of hope and the light of joy began
to beam out with a ray doubtful and timid at first, but growing ever steadier and
brighter. But still clearer and brighter were the Congressional letters of 1864
and the Campaign and Chicago letters of 1865. Darling, I sat and read till twilight deepened into dusk on the world without. But the reading brought no twilight to my heart, only the clear full high noon of love. The reading, and the trip
to Williamstown taken together form a curious and sweet review of our whole
course of love. Starting from the house where we sat together, almost children,
looking on the blushing blossoms of the peach tree from your window, I went
to Williamstown which was so full of memory and struggle and then the letters
in the cedar box carried me on past our marriage, through the two winters in
the Senate, the anxious work in the school at Hiram, the questions of law and
the ministry, the great war, with its inspiration and its absence, then the illness
and Howland Spring where the light began to dawn, and so on down through
the years that brought me with swimming eyes to the deep twilight of last
evening, when I folded away the letters, and looked up to the shelter and rest of
our dear home here, built as a monument of our love, built for you and ours
because they and I were all yours. Darling, when has lover had such a review or
such a sweet heart? I hail you here from our temple and I hasten to you, for I am
forever Your James.

*By Executive Order from President Grant, the Flathead Indians had been required to
move from their home in the Bitter Root Valley in Montana to a reservation north of
Missoula. James was appointed commissioner to oversee the removal of the Indians to*

their reservation in June. Accordingly, James and Lucretia in August 1872 went with their two youngest children, along with Major Swaim and his wife, to Kansas City to Fort Leavenworth. From there the Major and James traveled together to Montana.

Fort Leavenworth, August 12, 1872

My Precious Darling:

Yesterday I read about eighty pages of Bonneville[15] and left them in the region of the Snake river not far I imagine from the Flathead country. I suppose you must be on the road from Cheyenne to Ogden this morning. It seems to me you move over the map very slowly and when I think of the wilderness above Ogden which you have not yet reached and which seems illimitable since we have no good map to show us where in the great unknown it may be, it almost seems as though you would never find those Flatheads. I want you to remember that just as soon as you reach a telegraph on your return, you must send us a dispatch. I know you and Major are having a glorious time and when I think how much better it is for you than campaigning would be, I am glad you have gone, if you only will come back in any reasonable time. Mrs. Swaim and I are doing the best we can to pass away the time. Saturday we started out and answered all the visits made us except one. This morning we were going to town, but it is raining, so we are going to have a good time at home sewing and reading, etc. You gentlemen have no conception of the blessing a woman's work is to her. I believe the contentment which flows into the spirit through the delicate operations of the fingers is almost greater than from any other source. All employment is good but it seems to me when a woman's fingers have learned to work successfully with the needle, her spirit grows quiet and free unless there is some great and positive occasion for sorrow or anxiety. In your rich exuberant enjoyment of mountain travel, of scaling heights and dashing through wild ravines, I suppose you will pity the tameness of our home enjoyment; but be glad that we are not at least too miserable without you. We are all in very good condition this morning, the children all pretty well. Mrs. Swaim's finger is better, and my hoarsness [sic] nearly gone. We shall certainly expect to hear from you today. All join in love to you and the Major.

Ever and entirely your, Most lovingly. Crete.

Black Rock, Idaho. 107 miles north of Corinne.
Midnight. August 13, 1872

My Darling:

We have reached the end of the second driver's run, and the supper is being got ready. We have had a beautiful night thus far, clear and cool, but not uncomfortable. Just before sundown, we passed the divide and came down into the Marsh valley which is tributary to the Snake River. At 9 o'clock we entered Port Neuf canyon and have rapidly descended toward the valley of the Snake. We are still in the canyon, but in two or three miles more we shall reach the broad valley. I have caught a few snatches of sleep and so has Swaim, but sleeping is no easy matter with nine in a small box. It may amuse you and Jennie to know the *personel* of our inside company. The back seat is occupied by a very gossipy Englishman and his fidgety, gabby wife and a dunce of an impertinent boy. They are now sitting across the table backbiting all their neighbors, and especially the passengers who are now asleep in the coach. On the front seat sit three people facing the rear. One is a Salt Lake banker and a fine fellow of middle size.

Next to him sits a good looking portly doctor who is returning to Montana after three years' absence, sick of civilization and the dullness of N.Y. City. Next him sits a jolly, burly German woman weighing 200, who left Hamburg July 15 and has since then made 6500 miles of her way back to Montana, which she left last October, not intending to return. In the middle seat, which is six inches wide and 18 inches distant from the front seat, sits a lank Methodist preach[er], with a big basket full of chickens and apples, and who shuts down his window to keep from catching cold and thus suffocates the rest of us. By his side sits Swaim and by him I sit. The six pairs of legs interlock in the closest possible fit. The lean Methodist and slim banker, making one set; Swaim and the plump doctor another, and the fat German woman and I are the third. If you can imagine a more united party than that telegraph the result at my expense.

But supper is nearly ready and this is a region of mountain trout and their savory odor already greets our nostrils from the next room. Wish that you and Jennie were eating them with us. I am as ever and forever, Your James.

Yam Patch Station, Idaho. 143 miles from Corinne.

August 14, 1872.

My Darling:

When we had finished our midnight supper, which was ready when I closed my note, we were packed into the coach in the order I have already described, except that the banker on the front seat courteously offered to let me take his for one station so that I could lean my head back and sleep some. That arrangement, however, brought the three fat people (the German woman, the Dr. and myself) on one seat. As I squeezed into the seat, the German woman said, "This is worster as it was before." We rattled down the canyon, and in a few minutes were in the great plain. When we had gone three miles from the station, an iron that held up one side of the coach body broke, and we had to send back to the station for a chain to butter up the break. Seeing we should be compelled to wait a long time, Swaim and I took a buffalo robe and getting on the prairie where there was at least room for our legs, we spread one end of the robe on a sage bush for a pillow, threw a blanket over us and slept what we could till the stage was toggled up and then, the dawn breaking, we came on, five hours behind time. At ten o'clock we passed an Indian agency and saw a crowd of painted Indians, who are trying to do a little farming. We are now on the banks of the Snake River, and are waiting for breakfast with appetites sharpened by five or six hours delay and the long ride. The mountains are always in sight on each hand, but the wide reach of desolate plain makes this day's ride thus far one of wide and cheerless desert. We have not quite completed one third of our stage journey and I think it will be likely to take us till Saturday morning to reach Helena.

More than my desire for sleep and rest at the end of the ride is the desire to find a dear letter from you that shall bring me its message of love and shall tell me of the dear boys in Hiram. I hope you are resting quietly and sweetly in that paradise of Leavenworth. Remember me kindly to Gen Pope[16] and to any others who shall enquire. We are well and as jolly as the case will permit. Ever and always your loving James.

❧

Fort Leavenworth, August 21, 1872.

My Darling:

Last night I received the inclosed and hoping, or rather thinking another letter might possibly meet you at Corinne, I forward them to you. The weather still continues very warm and this morning is exceedingly sultry. The children are both feeling badly, and I begin to fear that we have made a mistake in bringing them to so warm a climate so late in the summer. August they tell me is the worst month here, and I am surprised that I did not think of it since it is so nearly the latitude of Washington; but they will get through safely, I hope. If you receive no dispatch to the contrary when you reach Corinne you need feel no anxiety. . . . Darling, the days are passing rapidly, still it is so lonely without you, not lonely either in the common acceptation, but I want you. Want you in the morning, want you all day, want you in the quiet night when the whole world gives you all up to me, want to hear the sound of your voice and look into your eyes and through them down into the deep wells of thought and precious love. O, how I want you to come and be near me and stay near me. I begin to feel anxious to have the time come to settle down again in our own home, but it will not be many weeks now and I will try to be patient. Unless I hear something more from you I scarcely think it worth while to write you more to send to Corinne, for I am sure if you have no very bad luck you will be back there by the time this reaches there.

Loving you and longing for you more than words can tell, I am always and forever,

Your own Crete.

Missoula, August 23, 1872

My Darling:

I have returned to this place and will now post up the record from the place where I left it off, at Helena last Monday. A little before noon, the Supt. of Indian Affairs for Montana (Mr Viall) took an ambulance and four horses and loaded in Sanders and his little boy, a driver and Swaim and me, and took us to Deer Lodge City 55 miles distant. At half past 9 P.M. we arrived and at 3:30 next morning we took the stage for Missoula. Gov. Potts and Mr. Claggett joined us and the stage was crowded. At four and a half in the afternoon we reached here, having made 90 miles in 11 hours and nearly 2 hours of that time we spent in changing horses. Most of the way was down the canyon of the Hellgate. Sometimes our road lay along the beautiful plain among forests of yellow pine; sometimes for miles along the treeless valley, beside the river; and sometimes it moved along the precipitous sides of the hills five hundred feet above the river. Along all these places our four horse team dashed at a rattling gallop. But for the fine excitement of the motion I should have felt the peril of such a drive. The proprietors of the stage company had heard of our going on their line and had directed their drivers to make a notably quick trip, and we did [out?] distance all former time.

Missoula is the farthest verge of settlement and civilization until we reach the Oregon settlements. It is a small town in the valley of Clarke's fork of the Columbia, near where the Bitter Root and Hellgate rivers unite.

We remained here over night, but sent a messenger up the Bitter Root valley to inform the Flatheads that I wanted to meet them in council at 9 o'clock Thursday morning. Wednesday morning, getting [into] three wagons and buggies, we made our way up the valley, passing the Lo-Lo fork, which was called by Lewis and Clark Travellers' Rest Creek, it being the place where [they] crossed the last range of mountains which separated them from the main current of the Columbia River. I have so much to tell you about this wonderful country, that I cannot undertake much now. But we went up the valley 35 miles to old Fort Owen, which is the Head Quarters of the Flathead tribe. There we spent the night, and yesterday in a great lodge made by uniting three lodges of buffalo skins, we held a solemn council with the Chief and headmen of the tribe. The Council lasted five hours and closed with an apparently absolute refusal to be removed from their Reservation. I pressed the case as skillfully as I could, and asked them to go with me to see the reservation before deciding. They asked for another council with me this morning and I staid over and met them again. They are now softened and their three chiefs agreed to go with me and visit the Jocko Reservation. When the Council broke up, we returned to this place and tomorrow morning will go with them to the Reservation, which lies north west from here about 30 miles. I greatly regret this detention, but I feel bound to do all in my power to save these noble indians from the mistake they will make if they refuse. Moreover, I greatly dislike to fail in anything I undertake. It has looked as though I could not succeed and I still fear I cannot, but I will make one more good try. I am more anxious than you can know to hear from you. To think that I have now entered upon the third week since I left you, and though you have written many times, yet I do not get one word you write is very hard. I know your letters [are] awaiting me at Helena, and I shall hasten back at the earliest moment to find them. We are in the best of health and this mountain air is almost pure oxygen. We eat and sleep marvellously well. I wish I could tell you when you may expect us, but I cannot.

With all my heart, I am Ever and forever

Your own
James.

Garfield did succeed in persuading the Flatheads to move to the Jocko Reservation.[17]

❧ NOTES ❧

1. Lucretia knew she was pregnant by this time.
2. *Ernest Maltravers* (1840) is a novel by Edward Bulwer Lytton.
3. Sheldon Beckwith was teamster for the city of Cleveland. He had been a Hiram student.
4. Miss Ransom, a close friend, was a portrait painter.
5. Mr. Hitz was Swiss Consul General. He found a Swiss housekeeper for the Garfields, Mary Bauchert.
6. William Dean Howells, *Years of My Youth* (New York: Harper Bros., 1916), 204–5.
7. Gordon Saltonstall Hubbard Jr. was a Chicago real estate and insurance agent. Garfield had bought seven lots in Chicago at Armitage Street near Milwaukee Avenue. He wrote in his Diary, "If I keep them till Jimmie is of age, they may be worth $30,000" (Harry J. Brown and Frederick D. Williams, eds., *The Diary of James A. Garfield* [East Lansing: Michigan State University Press, 1973], 3: 63).
8. Mrs. Spencer, a friend of the Garfields in Washington, became an advocate of the women's rights movement.
9. This is the father of William Dean Howells; he was an important newspaper editor from Jefferson, Ohio, who became a staunch supporter of Garfield.
10. Paul Chadbourne, a former professor of chemistry and botany at Williams, had been president of the University of Wisconsin before accepting the presidency of Williams.

11. Samuel Prime, an editor of the New York *Observer*, a writer, and a pastor, was a trustee of the College.

12. John Bascom, a professor of rhetoric at Williams, went on to replace Chadbourne as president of the University of Wisconsin.

13. George U. Rose was Garfield's clerical assistant. With his family he sometimes "house sat" while the Garfields were summering in Ohio.

14. S. B. Chittendon was a New York businessman.

15. Washington Irving wrote about Benjamin Louis Eulalic de Bonneville (1796–1878) in *The Adventures of Captain Bonneville* (1837).

16. James said he did not admire Major General John Pope "very much," though he thought Pope had been "greatly wronged" by his superiors. After losing the Second Battle of Bull Run, Pope had been relieved of his army command.

17. See H. J. Brown and F. D. Wiliams, eds. *Diary of James Garfield* (East Lansing: Michigan State University Press, 1967), 2: 81–85: "In return for the agreement of the Indians to remove to the reservation, Garfield pledged the government to build houses for them, give them during their first year 600 bushels of wheat . . . enclose and break up land, furnish agricultural implements, pay to the Indians as much of the $5000 appropriated by Congress for removal as was not expended in carrying out these other provisions, and pay in ten installments the $50,000 provided by Congress to compensate the Indians for land and improvements which they were giving up in the Bitter Root Valley" (2: 81.n241).

CHAPTER 9

The Credit Mobilier, the Salary Grab and the California Trip, 1872–1875

JAMES AND CRETE'S MOST DIFFICULT TIME *as public figures came in September 1872, after the notorious Credit Mobilier scandal broke. When the government subsidized the building of the Union Pacific Railroad from Omaha to Utah, some unscrupulous businessmen organized a company called the Credit Mobilier, which was to build the railroad, using, of course, public funds; they then paid themselves three times the cost of building the railroad. When the matter had been brought to the attention of Congress and it looked as if an investigation of the company's procedures might ensue, Oakes Ames, a Congressman from Massachusetts, went about soliciting key members of Congress to buy stock in the Credit Mobilier, the idea being to discourage scrutiny by Congress, if possible. From earliest years James was obsessed about financial security. A frequent topic of his letters, personal prosperity was a goal at which James was constantly aiming. Thus, the weeks were spent in Chicago with the oil land investments, the purchase of property in Chicago and Iowa and so on. When James and Lucretia returned from Europe in the fall of 1867, James was evidently approached by Oakes Ames with the proposition that he invest in the Credit Mobilier company. Ames would sell him ten shares of stock, hold them for him, and pay for the stock out of dividends, so that James had nothing to pay. James, needing cash after his European sojourn, was tempted and evidently succumbed.*

He received a "profit" of $329 from his stock. Later, James said he had "borrowed" the money from Ames.

The scandal broke five years later, in September 1872, just as James and Lucretia returned from Kansas to Washington. James insisted, when summoned to a hearing of the investigative committee under the chairmanship of Luke Poland of Vermont, that he had never bought any stock from Oakes Ames, and that he had never received money from stock, though the testimony indicated that the $329 probably was not a loan.

Finding himself implicated in such a dismal scandal was a devastating experience for James. He needed all the support he could get from his friends, and especially from his wife, for he was soundly excoriated by the people of his district, as well as humorously chafed by commentators across the country. At the same time, just before the adjournment of Congress in the spring of 1873 James, as Chairman of the Appropriations Committee, voted in favor of an omnibus bill which included a motion to give members of Congress an increase from $5000 to $7500, to be retroactive to the beginning of the congressional session two years earlier! In the explosion which followed, Garfield was angrily criticized by his district even though he had not favored the item but had had to vote for it since it was part of the larger bill.

Often during these years James toyed with the idea of quitting public life for a law partnership. In 1874, however, he made the final decision to remain in politics. In 1875 he embarked on his much longed for trip to the West Coast; the chapter ends with the correspondence between James and Lucretia during that trip to California.

In September 1872, the New York Sun carried the story that Oakes Ames of Massachusetts had "bribed" members of Congress to keep them from investigating the Credit Mobilier company, a holding company for the Union Pacific Railroad. Among those named who had bought stock from Ames was James.

Solon, Ohio. September 29, 1872.

My Darling:

I can find nothing definite about my trip of today. I shall go towards it as fast as I can, and if I fail, let the blame rest wherever it will. I will telegraph for my letters this morning and have them sent to Fairfield, Huron County or to Urbana.

I hope the carbuncle of my sorrow broke this morning. The humiliating fact is that it should have broken in your presence. Darling, bear with me, forgive me and love me. I need you more than I can say. Write me at Urbana, Ohio, where I shall be on Friday.

Ever Your Own,

James.

Hiram, September 25, 1872

My Darling:

We returned to Hiram last evening and find everything in good order. Charlotte is quiet but received a letter yesterday from "her boy," as Mary says. I shall say nothing to her in regard to it unless she introduces the subject. We find Father very poorly, with some fever and a bad cough, but I hope he will be better in a few days. I am glad, darling, that the cloud began to lift before you started away. The whole thing is very aggravating, and I am very sorry for your suffering over it, but hope it was largely unnecessary. I find in the National Republican a full and explicit denial from Oakes Ames of all the Sun's statements implying any guilt on the part of himself or any member of Congress, and inclose it to you. I don't think it (the Sun's falsehood) can hurt you nearly so much as you have been fearing. I hope you can get home on Sunday if not sooner, for I feel the need of you so much. I am more nearly sick this morning than I have been since leaving Washington. My throat is very sore and I am sick all over. Mary thinks she can go to Washington, and when you come home we must decide whether it will be better for her to go with us or later. Can you not in your travels keep up a little inquiry for a good nurse for the children. I am going to write to Miss Ransom, and hope a little light may dawn on our family affairs before long. I am growing to feel a real hatred to a political campaign. It seems to me they do nothing for us at least but to worry and harass and wear out your very life. I am as ever yours in truest love, Crete.

Lucretia returned to Washington from Hiram. She is now near term for the birth of their next boy.

Washington, Oct. 30, 1872

My Darling:

I am thoroughly cross and discouraged tonight, and if you ever see your house finished you will have to come home and scare these miserable men into finishing by your presence. I don't know that I ever felt more out of patience than at this present moment. Not only is there no prospect of the job ever being finished, but the mantels I believe are ruined with the daubs of paint with which they are smeared. Frank has spent several hours today on the three on the second floor, and they are not only not clean but are roughened, and the polish all off. One of the painters says he will polish and put them in good condition when he finishes painting, but I shall only believe it when I see it done. There, I have said my say and scolded my scold, and I presume tomorrow morning will bring the ends of the world together, and everything will be finished up before I know it. . . . I presume I am well, but am really too angry to know. I don't wonder that most women rebel against the destiny which made them women. It is only such a good and loving and faithful and prompt and thorough and blessed husband that you are that keeps my heart from the rampant rebellion of the most rabid woman's rights female. Darling, good night. . . . Your Crete.

Toledo, Ohio. Oct. 31, 1872

My Darling:

Was ever a woman written to as you are since I left you? But it helps me bridge over the distance that separates us. Shortly after writing you at the Burnett House [Cincinnati], I went to Mozart Hall and spoke till ten minutes after nine, and then drove to the Depot of the Dayton and Mich R.R. and at 9:40 was on my way north. I reached this city a few minutes ago . . . and finding I could not leave for Bryan until eleven o'clock. . . . I came away to this new and very fine Hotel to get breakfast. I can enjoy my coffee better after I have told you that I love you and am constantly thinking of you and hoping you are well and happy.

A cette heure je le crois, ma soeur, Marie, est a Baltimore, en route vais Washington. J'espere qu'elle arrivera chez vous avant ce que vous etes malade. S'il est possible tenez vous l'enfant qui nous attendons dans son petit voiture vivant pendant une autre semaine, car je desire beaucoup d'assister a l'occasion tres interessante quand le petit homme mettra le pied a terre le premiere fois. Mais s'il ne peut attendre jusque ce que j'arrive, donnez lui mes complements avec mon salutation paternel. A sa mere je donne tout mon coeur et tout mon ame.

Maintenant, je vais a dejuner parmi des etrangers.

Pour Jamais, Je suis Jamis.[1]

On January 14, James was called to give testimony before the Poland Committee. He was able to clear himself. But on January 22 Ames again gave testimony, this time implicating James in a much more serious way. James, however, was not recalled. He did not return to rebut this second Ames accusation.

House of Representatives
Washington, Jan. 25, 1873.

My Darling:

Prof Agassiz[2] has just given me his photograph, which I enclose. I want to retain his noble face in our home and keep a new memorial of a sweet pure life. And now most precious one, I will try to take a new lease of courage and faith from your love and will endeavor to meet whatever comes to my lot with a fortitude more manly and high than I have exhibited during the past few days. It is by no means clear how the storm will leave me, for the wind may veer and must howl in other quarters very heavily before the gale is over. I have had many words of cheer and kind greeting since I reached the House this morning. Be brave for me, my Darling, and keep the dear home flock in good heart and hope. Would you like to go out with me this evening for an hour or two (say at eight) to attend the Celebration of Burns' birthday?

Think of it. A carriage will be sent for us to find whether we will go.

With all there is of me I am

Your own James.

East Cleveland, March 9, 1873.

My Darling:

I reached Cleveland last evening via Leetonia, Warren etc.

. . . On my way through the District and since I came here, I have heard the thousand echoes which the Credit Mobilier explosion has made among the people. To my surprise, I find that just now there is more agitation in regard to my vote on the increase of salaries of members of Congress than there is in reference to Cred. Mob. I cannot tell whether it is the hour of breaking up or not. I shall try to meet manfully whatever comes to my lot; but it is hard to bear the small talk of little carpers who know nothing of the case, except that they think they smell a stink. I awoke this morning in the gray of dawn and lay there in the Dr.'s upper chamber, hearing the angry lake winds slamming the shutters, and howling cheerlessly as if they knew the cheerless outlook of my life, and knew they were echoing the storm which has been raging around my path for the past three months. I cannot tell you how much I heed and need you—my courage, my hope, my love, my all-in-one. Be brave for me, Darling, and whatever life has in store for me I pray the All-Father that He will keep you and thus save me from the bottom of the gulf.

Dr. Robison has promised to write a prescription for a plaster, which he says will greatly relieve the spasms of coughing of our little ones. Dr. Streator, at whose house I write, says give them all the good coffee they will drink. He says it is very good to help them through the whooping cough.

I wrote a brief letter to your Mother, and also one to sister Mary on my way through. I hope to hear from you soon. And you know that [I] am wholly your own James.

Washington, March 9, 1873

My Darling:

Yesterday was so full of work and care that I did not get time to write a word to you, but there is quiet in the atmosphere this morning and out of it I can slip away to you for a little while. It is warm and springlike, and the gentle influence begins to lift my spirit into the hope that there is sunshine yet for our souls as well as for the poor frozen Earth that has been so stormed over this long winter. Darling, you must for the sake of our boys come up out [of] the darkness which you have allowed to gather around you.[3] When I look at our four boys with all the responsibilities of life yet before them, I tremble with fear with the thought that you may falter in life's struggle before you have given them the aid which their fierce individualities—inherited from you—need from your loving strong guiding nature. If you fail them, my fears for them will become terrors. I hope you can come home cheered and encouraged, and, darling, I will do all I can to help you.

I intended to write to cousin Carrie, but I don't know that it is necessary. You can see her and talk with her about the girl better than I can write. If we are to go to Ohio this summer, I suppose it will scarcely be necessary for a girl to come here now; but if we are not going, and the girl is willing to come alone, I think she had better come now. If she could find a girl who is a good cook to come, that would be of some account to us. I wanted to talk with you before you left, but we were in no mood for it, and had no opportunity.

If I have anything more to say, I will write tomorrow for Burke to carry to you. The children are growing worse with whooping cough, and are having a hard time. We all send love to you, and shall expect to see you without fail on Saturday if not before.

Hopefully and fondly all yours. Crete.

P.S. Love to all our friends.

Washington, April 18, 1873

My Darling:

I have finished *Middlemarch*[4] today. I grew intensely interested in it. It touches upon the passions and struggles which have so invested and entered into our lives for the last few months, that it grew in places to seem almost personal, and I can scarcely judge of the merit of it as a piece of literature, so absorbed did I become in the entanglements of its characters, and so in sympathy with all their trials.

Tonight in closing up my forty first year I can scarcely realize I am so old. I do not feel old, and our love is so fresh and full of rosy light that I cannot believe we are more than lovers yet. Even our big stormy boys who have teased and worried my patience almost to exhaustion today cannot make me feel that our love is old, and it never shall be. The dew of immortal youth is on it. The boys have both written to you this evening, and I hope you will not fail to answer them. Write to Mother too. She says if you want to hear from her, you must write to her. . . . Mr. Rose[5] is going with his wife to New York tomorrow. He was in doubt about going lest you might want him, but I told him to go by all means, that you would be very sorry to have him remain at home merely because he had not heard from you.

Darling, I hope the sky is clearing and your heart growing lighter. Think of me sometimes tomorrow. . . . All yours, Crete.

Cleveland, April 19, 1873

My Darling:

I write in honor of the birthday of the dearest and best woman in the world. I did not get off to Hiram on the morning train, and shall stay here until afternoon. I am sure I shall hear from you, when I get to Hiram tonight; but you can hardly know how desolate these eight days have been made by my not hearing from you. I know, however, that your heart is warm and true, and waiting and longing for me. This gives hope to life, and makes me work for the future and you.

I thank the Giver of life, and all the happy fates, that brought you into being forty-one years ago today. When I think of the separate paths in which we wandered so long, before knowing each other, I bless each little bush and tree that veered those paths until they met and brought us together. How many chances there were that might have prevented us from meeting! How infinitely greater were the chances that, having met, we might never have known each others' souls! I hope you are writing me today, to tell me you are glad you were born to be given to me.

It is a grief to me that I cannot call up your face to my mind's eye, and see it as it is while I sit here in this roar of men who do not know what love is as we know it. I have tried many years to do this, but your dear face has always evaded me. I can bring you up within fifty or a hundred yards, and no nearer. You beckon me to come the rest of the way; and if I start, you recede asking me to follow to the place where your precious body lives and breathes.

I hope this new birthday has not dimmed the eye of your love, nor made your relish for love-letters less keen. I have been your fellow student, your teacher, your friend, your lover; and I hope I am now your husband-lover more tenderly cherished than ever before. At no moment of my life, have I loved to think of you, dream of you, long for you, so much as now. Darling, can your soul say the same to me? I am sure it can; and in that confidence I live and work.

Do write me dearest in special answer to this letter, which is not a rhapsody, but the sober deliberate, unshakeable conviction and result of twenty years of acquaintance. Were I now alone and with an unwedded hand and heart, but knowing your nature as I now know it, I would woo only you and use all the powers of honor and effort to win you and make you mine, as against the world. Tell me if you would listen to my suit and say me yes, as you said it nineteen years ago in the lower chapel at Hiram?

How strange it is that marriage can be considered a bond, a shackle! To me it is liberty, love, life. As clouds gather upon all other phases of life, eternal sunshine settles upon our love and summer, with all its balm, reigns around the garlanded life that our marriage has brought. Speak to me, Precious One, and tell how it is and what it is to you. Into this circle come our dear little ones, and

in them, hard and difficult as the task sometimes is, we are fulfilling the high
ends and aims of life. I want them sometime to know what our love is. Can't
you teach them a few letters of its alphabet? Do, if you can. I cannot write this
morning except of love and you. The little poem of Anacreon,[6] which you read
to me in Greek so many years ago, is truer today than then. To Crete. Ever and
Always Your own James.

James had asked Crete if she might not be willing to go to Ohio to stay for the summer.
She would of course have to stay in her family home, since they were renting their own
to the Hinsdales. What with ailing parents and Martha, her brother John's widow
and Martha's three children, Lucretia understandably did not relish the idea of moving
with her own four children into a house which she would be expected to manage.

Washington, April 24, 1873

My Precious:

I received your dear letter of the 20th last evening and intended to write to
you after the children were in bed, but it was a rainy evening and the children
were so wild that I was both tired and impatient before they were asleep and I
was afraid I should say something unkind of the little scamps if I tried to write;
but the morning brings rest and patience with their teasing. I try to think that
their bellowing, striking and kicking are the child ways of working out the
strength and activity which you have given them and which you have worked
up into the grandeur of your manhood, and I hope that is what ails them, but I
sometimes get to feel that they are the worst children ever born. When I feel
this way the thought of going to Father's to take charge of the house and manage the children, with Martha's three with them, as they would necessarily be,
is really appalling. And it does not seem at any time as though I could undertake it. With such a family of little children it is quite hard enough to keep my
own house in a place where I can have help. I have not the least faith that we
can get any reliable help in Auburn [Ohio].

If there's a housekeeper there to be hired, she will expect to be the most
important member of the family. I might get along with that in my own house;
but not in Mother's. Darling, I know it is a real trial to you to know what to do
with us; but for the sake of the boys' school I think we ought to stay here until
it closes. I am really discouraged with Hal this morning. He has no ambition it

seems to me for anything but to go away and I think it has been a mistake for them to expect to go away until the school closes. I am growing more and more alarmed for the influence our kind of life is having on the children. They certainly ought to have some fixed school habits, if no others, and they cannot have them when their school term is merely an uncertain period in the middle of a school year. They ought to begin with the year and finish it, and their holiday be the vacation. We will discuss this more when you come home. I hope it will not be very long before you can come, although I know it will be better for you to stay until you have done all you can to put the District right.[7] I think it strange you had received only one letter before the 20th. I had certainly sent three of four and some of them long enough before to have reached you. I have written some of the[m] every day and have never let more than one day pass without writing; but I hope you know how much I love you, whether or not you hear from me. Love to all.

Ever your Crete.

Hiram, April 27, 1873.

My Darling:

At last the back of our winter seem to be broken. This is the first day for a week that we have not had snow. The day has been pleasant, and the sun and wind have commenced the work on the roads. After church and dinner, I went into the woods pasture (which was woods fifteen years ago) and tried to find the spot where you sat beside me in the autumn of 1858, and agreed to be my wife. The chill and gloom of those days have all melted into warm, glorious sunshine, and the remembrance of them makes our wedded life all the dearer and sweeter for the contrast. I have been at church again this evening, have taken a bowl of mush and milk in the kitchen with your father and Burke. He has now gone and I am alone in the wide house with your love as my only companion. Why can it not be that you can be with me to make this silence sing, and all the wheels of life rejoice as they revolve? How very long it has been since you and I have staid in a house alone! I hope it is not selfish to wish that now and then we might be a pair of hermits. You can hardly know how wide, and large, empty and cold the chamber is where I sleep. Life was made for two, not one. I read today a passage from "Merivale's History of Romans under the Empire" which gave me a thought on this subject. In speaking of the first plan of Rome, which covered only the Palatine Hill, he says: "The Pelasgic fortress was enclosed by Romulus within the limits of the new city, which, after the Etruscan fashion, he traced with a plough drawn by a bull and a heifer, the furrow being carefully made to fall inward, and the heifer yoked to the near side to signify that strength and courage were required without, obedience and fertility within the city."[8]

This is a rough figure, but I wish I gave to the team as much strength and courage as you do sweetness and light and life. But it is hard to work in the yoke alone. I am reading "Hare's Walks in Rome,"[9] and every page reminds me of our precious week among the ruins, the mighty glories of Rome. The time must come when we can again, with a new access of culture and power to enjoy it, wander in the forum and on the Capitoline, and let the sweet air of Italy breathe upon us. This hope, and every other that promises pleasure for you with me as your companion shall ever aid me in turning the furrow on your side of the plough.

I shall sleep sweetly tonight in the sure hope of a letter from you tomorrow, and in the hope that it will bring me a day's march nearer to your arms. And here I am at the foot of the page, with nothing said that is any adequate symbol or sign of the strength and power with which my heart goes out after you. But going or staying, it is all yours and I am Your Own James.

After his fence mending in Ohio, following the Washington scandals, James spent much of the summer in Washington, with Crete in Ohio. That fall they were back in Washington, but in November James journeyed to New Castle, Pennsylvania, on trial business.

Washington, Nov. 5, 1873

My Darling:

I cannot tell how much such a letter as I have just received from you today cheers and encourages me. The certain knowledge of my shortcomings makes me know that the half you have said is but one of your illusions concerning me; still to know that I am something to you and to the family more than any other person can be makes me alive with new hope and courage. I am glad to be able to say that before I had received your letter I had by stout resistance nearly overcome the whole train of despondencies that had beset me, so that I did feel a little more worthy your praise than I did on Monday evening, and now I will say what is far more the truth than anything you have said about me—that you are the strength and light of our home, and our need of you is always so great.

Now a word about our boys. They are growing contented and happy in their new school and say they do not want to change. Miss Marvedell[10] thinks she has found a person who can instruct them in reading, and I believe that with the other instruction they will receive there, they will do far better than in the Public or any ordinary private school. Mother and I visited the school today and although it was the last hour, it was surprising to see the spirit of work in the whole school. Jim seems as docile as a lamb there, and he is really a better boy at home since you have been away this time than I have ever known him to be. He and Hal both are much more easily managed than usual. I have taken one short step myself in the way of intellectual culture. I go down into the parlor and shut myself in from eleven o'clock to half past and read, and short as the time is you have no idea how it is revolutionizing my whole day. It is a solid half hour of time set like a pivot on the firm rock and the whole day revolves smoothly around it. I hope to be able after a little to take an hour at least, but the one little half hour is an outpost gained which gives me hope that I may yet be able to storm the citadel and put order where chaos has reigned.

Darling, it is you who inspires me to everything that has any good in it, and it is due to you and the book you were reading to me that I have commenced this new work. I hope you can come home before our anniversary arrives.

With loving hope and trust.

Yours Forever, Crete.

In the autumn of 1874, thoroughly sick of politics, James gave careful consideration to an offer made to him to join a partnership in law in Cleveland. He went so far as to contemplate the purchase or rental of property in Cleveland for the next year. It was his friend Dobson Cox, however, who dissuaded him. He told James that it was too late to leave politics; that he doubted he could ever "recover the habits of . . . private office work" and that he would possibly become "melancholy and restless in private business." Thus, in the end, James remained in public life.

Forest City House, Cleveland, October 13, 1874.

Most Precious One:

What jealousy seems always to dwell in true love. I, sorry, troubled, grieved, and fearful, because Friday came and went and brought me no letter from you. You, fearing lest I were sick or offended, because the mail did not bring you my letter so soon as it ought! I am glad and thankful that this fearfulness, this shadow of unreal danger falls into the vision of each. It would never come except to the eyes of love. And still I ought to have written you sooner. But I was in a continual whirl from the time I left you until I arrived at Hiram, on Thursday. I came here last night to get the news of the election, and to consider the question of our future work and life in Cleveland. Before this, you have read of our great victory and you know how sincerely I am rejoicing at the triumph of truth over error. I have worked very hard since you left me, and have done some of the best speaking of my life. Weary as I am today, I look forward with pleasure at the prospect of relief from the burdens of public life. And yet I have found shadows across the path of my proposed partnership. I am afraid that Mr Estep's habits will be a serious drawback to the success of the plan.[11] In every other respect, he appears to be just the man who would meet my lacks and help me to be successful. I am thinking fast, for I must reach a conclusion before I leave for Washington. I am going to ride out with Dr. Streator to see that house which you and I drove by. I do so wish you were here to counsel together on this deeply important question. Dr Robison offers me the half front of Celtrie's lot, being 75 feet front by 800 feet deep for $15,000, nothing to be paid down, and no payment except 6 per cent interest until I please to pay the principal. This would give us a good orchard and room for a fine garden. It would be nearly an acre and a half of ground. Now, I must say I very much desire a home of our own, rather than a rented house. I will look the field over very carefully; but will determine nothing until I see you. If we could settle upon the kind of house we want, and make the arrangement this fall, we could have a house of our own to go to when we leave Washington the next time. Think of this before we meet, and we will talk it over when I come. I want you to know that I have carried out fully the programme I proposed last year: 1st to defeat my enemies (which I have done this fall). It now remains to show people that I can lay down an important office for the sake of myself and family. All this has been made possible because I had a dear precious wife who is more to me than fame in any form. I do so much wish you were with me today, that we might go over the whole case together. I was grieved to hear that the boys were not behaving as well as they ought. Please tell them for me that as well as I love them, I shall be severe with them, if they do not obey mamma promptly and thoroughly. I will go to Toledo tomorrow and, as I now see it, I think I can leave here about Tuesday next. . . . Do let me hear from you as often as possible. Love to all the dear ones, and know that I am as Always and forever, Your own James.

In the spring of 1875 Lucretia, Edward and Mollie spent some time in Hiram so that Crete could look after her mother, who was thought to be dying. James remained in Washington with the four boys.

Hiram, March 29, 1875.

My Darling:

I sent you off a hurried slip this morning by Joe to mail at Cleveland so that it could reach you the sooner, but the morning's mail has brought me your dear precious letter from home, and I will commence this as a conclusion, or rather continuation—for nothing which bears the trace of love can ever be concluded with us—of this morning's note. It is very sweet to know that you feel that I am missed at home. I felt that your arrival there would so satisfy them all that I would scarcely be missed, and if you had dared to tell me, would that not have been the truth? No. I am wrong. The little boys would miss Mamma a great deal, I am sure. I know they all love me, and, I often feel, a great deal better than I deserve to be loved. They are all dear precious boys and my mother-heart is very proud of them. Proud of them for what they are, but in a dearer sense proud of them for that of your life which lives within them. Do you know baby is the largest one of the seven at his age? Harry had always borne the palm, but he only weighed 16 lbs when four months old. We ought to give him a *name*. I fully realize all the doubts you expressed concerning Mother's condition. She puzzles me continually. Her symptoms are all better, still she must have a continual fever, or else she would not suffer so with heat, nor have such rapid pulse. I shall not be surprised if, when her fever leaves her entirely, she drop away very suddenly. This slow fever will, I fear, burn out all the vitality she has left.

The snow is all gone and the sunshine is full of that balmy dreaminess which only comes to a spring day in the country, and which sends the blood with a faintly conscious thrill through the veins. The few years we have been

away from our Northern Springs were pushing the earlier years into forgetful-
ness, and I am glad to revive the old impressions, and live over the times that
have been, and verify "the thing which hath been shall be." Darling, you will
think often of me while this temporary separation is dragging itself slowly away,
and we will meet, as we parted, loving each other with the young lovers' love,
and holding the continual presence as sweetly sacred as the truly wedded
ever must.

Write to me every day. You will have some new adventure or circumstance
to tell me of each day. With me the days do but repeat themselves, and I will
have but one new thing to write, to tell of the love ever new. My heart and
thoughts are with you and with the dear children every hour. All send love.
Mollie read your letter to me and whispered to herself looking up shyly at me,
"My precious one." I hope our love will be a sacred inheritance to our children.

Ever and forever yours, Crete.

In the spring of 1875 Henry Ward Beecher, the great New England preacher, was
called to trial by Theodore Tilton, who charged him with adultery with Mrs. Tilton,
demanding damages of $100,000. James attended one of the trial sessions.

New York, April 5, 1875.
My Darling:
I reached here this morning, and have spent most of the day in Brooklyn,
attending the Beecher Trial. I did not reach the Courtroom until a quarter past
eleven. The trial was in progress, and the room very greatly crowded. I sent in
my card to Judge Fullerton (Knox's partner, and the leading counsel for
Tilton) and he came out to the door, and took me in to a seat by his own table
directly in front of the Judge and The Witness Stand. I had become so much
interested in the development of the case, and specially in Mr Beecher's testimony, that I was anxious to see the parties, and get the scene more vividly
impressed in my mind. I had an excellent opportunity to let the whole formu-
late itself fully, so that I shall always carry the picture with me. In the Judge's
stand sat a large number of the leading judges and lawyers of N.Y.: among
them David Dudley Field whom you know. At the two tables fronting the
Judge's Desk were the counsel, Tilton and Moulton sandwiched between

Tilton's lawyers. The witness stand is an elevated seat at the corner of the Judge's desk and immediately to the right and front of the witness is the Jury Box. Outside the railing which encloses the Court, Jury and Lawyers are the seats for the audience. I was greatly moved by the appearance of Mrs Beecher. Her hair is almost perfectly white, her face is pale and bears evident marks of feeble health; but her eye is lighted with the unmistakable gleams of faithful love for her husband, in this supreme crisis of his fate. When recess came Ingersoll (our Williams friend) introduced me to her. I asked after her health, and she said she was standing the strain far better than she expected to; that she only desired to have it hold out till the struggle was over, and then she did [not] care: she knew her husband would [be] triumphant because he was true. Her daughter sat beside her, and looks strikingly like the father. I had time to study the face of Moulton, who is to me the most mysterious and sphynx-like character in the tragedy. I am half persuaded to adopt Tracy's description of him, a few lines of which I copy from Tracy's opening speech. After describing Da Vinci's picture of the last supper, he says: "In the most striking portrait of that group of Disciples you will recognize the startling likeness between the red-matted hair, the low forehead, the sharp, angular face, the cold and remorseless eye of Judas Iscariot, and the same features in his legitimate successor, 'the mutual friend.' There on that consecrated wall, the portrait of Francis D. Moulton has stood, waiting for his birth 400 years and will stand for twice four hundred years after this resurrected Judas shall have sunk into eternal infamy."

This picture is somewhat exaggerated, but there are points of resemblance between Moulton and DaVinci's Judas. Beecher bore himself grandly and beautifully on the stand. I could see the indignation work on his face as the questions of accusation were read to him. There was a strange blending of solemnity, feeling, power, pathos and humor on his remarkable face. He held in his hand a small bunch of wild violets, of which he occasionally exhaled the odor. His replies were frank, direct, full, careful, characteristic, and he carried the spectators with him, by what seemed to be an irresistable tide of trust and sympathy. It does not seem possible that he can fail to carry the Jury, though there is one man who seems to have an almost idiotic stare, and who, I am sure, has no comprehension of the case in any way. At the recess I spoke with him, and then accepted Mr Evart's invitation to dine with him and his brother lawyers on the defense. If I can possibly find the time, I mean to come on here, and hear Evart's closing speech.

I dined here with Gen McDowell and then went with him to Booth's Theatre to hear Henry the V, by an English Company.

Your dear letter of the 1st I found awaiting me here this evening. I am somewhat in doubt what to do. I very much want to go to Ohio and come home with you, but I fear my 6th St. Presbyterian Church case will come up in the Supreme Court before I could get round.[12] I will telegraph to Washington in the morning and find out and then will at once determine. Much as I want to see you, I want you to stay with Mother as long as you can. Gen McDowell is very much determined that I shall stay with him two or three days. Indeed he has engaged me to dine Tuesday evening at Mr. Pattens. I will wait till I hear from home, and then if I find I cannot go to Ohio, I will stay here until Wednesday evening and go home to Washington. Come to us when you think you can be spared. I have agreed to go to Lexington, Mass, April 19th to attend the Centennial anniversary of that battle. I want you to go with me, to celebrate your own birth. Darling, please do accept my company for that occasion. The week's work in committee has been very hard, and the issue is close and doubtful. I think I have done them some good, but I have remembered your admonition and have not made so long speeches as usual. The probabilities are that I cannot go to Ohio, and I write this with that expectation. I am not able to tell you how hungry I am for the sight of your blessed face. Give my love to little Whack [Mollie] and tell her I thought of her when I saw Beecher's daughter. I hope she will love her Papa most as well as her mamma, but not quite. Remember me affectionately to all the family. The family here send you love.

As ever and always, Your ownest James.

James did not go to Lexington for the centennial celebrations of the Revolution. Instead, he went to California on his only trip to the West Coast. Lucretia, as usual, stayed home with the children.

Washington, April 18, 1875

My Darling:

"He asked water and she gave him milk; she brought forth butter in a lordly dish."[13]

This morning I came into the library and found your Bible lying open on your desk, left by the boys after studying their Sunday school lessons, and I said to myself I will read the first verse my eye falls on for my darling, and the text with which I began this letter was the one, and I hailed it as an omen that the grand, large-hearted, queenly Occident would receive you kindly.

When you left me last night, my heart was full of sobs and I could scarcely choke them down. I went through the rooms putting out the lights so that no one should see how full of tears were my eyes. I almost wondered at myself that I had had the courage to say to you go without me. I undressed and went to bed as soon as I could and fell asleep thinking how long it would be before I should hear your voice or look into your eyes again, and feeling almost as though I must fly after you and call you back again. Suddenly I started up with an impression that the doorbell rang. I waited a moment and surely it did ring again. I sprang out and opened the windows. There was the driver with your dear note. I told him to slip it under the door and I ran down and got it. I felt the moment I heard the bell that it announced a message from you, and it seemed to bridge the chasm of silence which falls between the voice, the embrace, and the communion which the letters establish, where we take up our loved ones into the interior life and give to Memory, and hope ourselves to be comforted. This morning we slept late and Hal got up cross-grained and did not get straight until after Sunday school. Since then the day has passed comfortably. I have allowed Jim to print more than half the time to keep him quiet, and he is learning to run the machine quite rapidly. I am not sure that it will not be a help to him in learning to spell. It is like winter again. I did not get to church but have spent a large part of the day in your Library with Harry and Jimmy. This evening I read to them a couple of chapters of "Roughing It,"[14] and told the children that it was the story of a journey made through the same country you were going to travel over. I hope you will not be detained very much by the floods but from accounts now the Directors's car will not be able to pass through, and you may have a good many miles of staging it in the old fashioned way. The children are all in bed now, and I am alone by your table too lonely to dare think of it, but I hope I may turn your absence to some advantages.

Monday evening. April 19.

The forty-third birthday has passed very pleasantly. The children have all done very well, and I have attended to all the affairs you requested me to attend to today, and Emma sent a birthday surprise to the dinner table in the form of a beautiful cake. Irvin insists that he peaked through the keyhole and saw Emma making it, and kept the knowledge all to himself. If it were one of the other children it would be past belief, and it has somewhat the appearance of romance as it is. We half expect you to give up your trip and turn back to us, the papers represent the condition of the road so wretched. I shall scarcely know whether to be glad or sorry. I shall be afraid that you will be so disappointed and broken up for the Spring that you will almost [be] restless if not miserable at home. Still if you could be happy and contented with your California trip postponed, I would try to help you to some enjoyment here these coming weeks that we remain before we take our summer flight. Big goodnatured Hal sits at the type machine telling you of his trials over Mamma's prohibition to play in the "new house." Jimmie is curled up in your big chair wrapped in your double gown and says "many a little boy would be glad of such a nice warm place to sleep." Mollie is wrapped in another coat on the lounge. Irvin is in our bed to sleep with Mama tonight. Little bright Abe went off to bed after a rolicking play, and little nameless is asleep too. Mother says to tell you that not many waking moments have passed since you left that she has not thought of you.

How we all join in love to you you already know much better than words can tell.

If this ever reaches you, I fear you will cry enough, and ask me to be less diffuse hereafter. I hope you will send me back a letter from every post, so that I may be able to keep my thoughts near where you are during the journey. Always give me your programme as many days ahead as you can so that I may know about where you are each day.

With All-Loving love, Yours forever, Crete.

While James was in Chicago waiting for a break in the Union Pacific rails to be repaired, the wife of William Ralston, director of the Bank of California, invited James to ride in her private car. In this letter, too, reference is made to the presidential chances of James Blaine of Maine: he had been Speaker of the House and was a close friend of Garfield's. Now he was being spoken of as a strong Republican candidate for the election of 1876.

Chicago, April 21, 1875.

My Darling:

How very trying it is to stay here, perhaps five days, when I might have remained with you, and still have reached San Francisco as soon as by waiting here. The time is too long to spend here, and too short to go back to you, and return. Yesterday afternoon the Superintendant of the road telegraphed that our train had not better leave here before Saturday morning unless we had different orders soon. If I knew we should not leave before Saturday, I would go to Cleveland and spend a day or would go to Michigan and see brother Thomas. But the break in the Union Pacific Road may be repaired sooner than is now expected, and so I must stay here and lament that I cannot be with you, or on my westward way. I telegraphed you last evening, so that I might hear from you once, at least, before I leave here. Today I have had a long visit with Frank Palmer, late a member of my Committee, but now the Editor of the Inter-Ocean, and a still longer one with Joseph Medill, the Editor of the Chicago Tribune, with whom I discussed the question of the next Presidency, and especially Blaine's chances. He told me a curious thing which I never heard of before. He says that Halstead of the Cincinnati Commercial and Watterson of the Louisville Journal are strongly inclined to support Blaine, but that a circumstance occurred in his early life which is likely to be brought out against him, in case he is a candidate—to this effect. It is alleged that when he was schoolmaster in Kentucky, many years ago, he met a Yankee schoolmam, and their warm blood led them to anticipate the nuptial ceremony, that thereupon he took her to Pennsylvania, his home, and married her; that they went thence to Maine to begin life in a new place; and that there their first child was born about five or six months after their marriage. It is said that the Editor of the Cincinnati Enquirer has quietly been procuring affidavits of these facts, and will publish them in case Blaine is nominated. How does this story strike you? If it is true, should it have weight with the people in the Presidential Campaign? Please give me your thoughts on the subject.

I think I ought to write to Blaine on the subject; and yet I hesitate to do so. There may be nothing in it, and it is not a pleasant thing to write about if there is.

Last evening I met Mrs Ralston[15] and her party, which consists of an old lady named Mrs Petty, a young Miss Leland, daughter of Warren Leland, late of the Metropolitan Hotel, and two other young misses who go with her. The invitation is so very cordial, both from her and her husband, who has telegraphed on the subject, and also from the manager of the road that I think I will accept their offer. If we were to go at once, I should be glad for I am in danger of getting homesick by this delay.

I enclose a few pages of my Journal for Mr Rose to enter in the Diary. I may conclude to keep [it] in a book as I go, but for the present I will send it back in installments.

Now, Darling, please remember our talk about writing me the little and great particulars of your daily life. Take enough time from your daily duties to tell me what you are doing and thinking. Tell me of what you read, and let our minds and heartskeep track of each other. Life will be too short to tell all our love—so let us seize the hours as they fly and make them yield the sweets of love and life. As ever Your Own James. . . .

Washington, April 25, 1875

My Darling:

Another Sunday has come with sunshine but with quiet and loneliness to my heart. I have not written to you since Wednesday. Your delay in Chicago made the world stand still, and I felt no courage to write a cheerful letter, and I did not think a cheerless one would add anything to your happiness. Now even that you are speeding away from me I am happier, for it is hastening your return. It is now near eleven A.M. and I presume you must have reached Omaha and perhaps passed beyond it. I hope you will encounter no more delays, though I much fear you may from accounts of the snow still falling in the West. Yesterday morning I went out feeling that it was too warm for any wrapings. Before noon I was hurrying home through a fierce wind and by three o'clock it was cold enough for furs. It perplexes all the weather-wise to account for this strange season, or to tell what the summer may bring forth.

We have received all your letters up to the 21st inst. Last night brought the one of that date. It was a queer piece of gossip you gave me of Mr. Blaine. I scarcely believe it. But if it is true, it ought not to affect the voters very much unless it would have been considered more honorable by the majority to have abandoned the woman—seduced. My opinion of Mr. Blaine would be rather heightened than otherwise by the truth of such a story: for it would show him not entirely selfish and heartless. I can scarcely understand, though, how such a strong, positive, self-asserting intellectual nature as Mrs. Blaine's could have been tempted into any such unwisdom. I would sooner believe the story, which it seems to me I have sometime heard, that they were secretly married more to gratify some romantic fancy than for any other notion. It seems to me there is very little now to tempt a man to go into the contest for the Presidency. If it could be possible for any one man to so tower above all other in true manliness and statesmanship that the people should demand him for their head, such a one might accept the place with some gratification, and feel that he was in a true sense honored. Darling, it may be only a wife's fancy for the man she truly loves, and knows to be worthy of honor, but I have a very deep feeling that if there is such a one in the wide world, you are that one, and I somehow feel that both the real or intended and the accidental occurrences of your life, which seem almost *unkindly* sometimes to hold you aloof from so many political cir- cles, are all in a quiet way singling you out from the wrestling struggling throng. Carrie [Ransom] thought you were neglecting a great opportunity in giving up Lexington, and when you were held in Chicago it did seem as though an adverse fate had prevented you. But to me it seems rather the benign care of the far-seeing spirit guarding you from the temptations to throw yourself into the scramble for place and power, and preserving you for that time when you shall become

> "The pillar of a people's hope
> The centre of a world's desire."[16]

Evening

This P.M. Mr. Allison[17] called and delivered your packet of letters. I seemed almost to have touched your hand again so lately has he seen you. . . .

I am both glad and sorry that you are homesick and lonely, but I am sure you will grow interested in your journey as it progresses, and while you may miss me somewhat you will not be entirely inconsolable. The children have some of them been writing to you almost every day and I gather up all the scraps knowing how precious they will be to you although they do seem of lit- tle account. The boys do tolerably well, though I do not believe as well as when I was away from them. I asked Hal one day why it was that they were better boys when we were both away. His reply amounted to this, that there was no one to think for them then and nobody for them to tease, so it was easy for them to act like men. . . .

A card from Harry Rhodes last evening announced the birth of a daughter on the 23rd inst. Letters from home report Mother still gaining. Libbie[18] sung at Cleveland and writes she was very kindly and pleasantly received. She expresses a great deal of thanks to you for her brother's appointment. Now, my darling, remember how lonely and bereft I am here, and don't fail to send off as much as you have time to write each day. May only the good, the true and beau- tiful attend and bless you on your way, and bring you safe to my arms and keep you in the memory of all the love you have left here in your home for you. Ever and forever yours, Crete.

❧§§❧

San Francisco, May 5, 1875.

My Darling:

Today I have been made glad and happy by the arrival of your most precious letter of the 25th April. The time between it and its predecessor had
begun to lengthen out till a kind of faintness came to me with the lapsing hours.
But now is the "winter of my discontent made glorious summer" by the light
that came into my heart from the full envelope of messages from the children
and yourself. Tell each one of them for me that papa thanks them for their good
little letters, that he is so glad to know how they are doing in school, in music
and in play, and that he is so anxious to have them good children at home, so as
to make it easy and pleasant for mamma. I want them to keep writing, and even
if they should be so unfortunate as to be naughty once in a while, I want them
to tell me of it.

For myself I am almost ashamed to write to you for the old schoolbred reason that your letters are so graceful and perfect in matter and manner that I am
ashamed to have mine placed in the comparison. I know you will turn up your
little nose at this; but it is true, and if you could look at me this minute you
would see a little touch of that timidity which I had when I first started out to
school.

I was greatly interested in what you said of the Blaine gossip. I have not
been able to see how it would hurt him, unless it might be that the threat of
publication would dissuade him from being a candidate for Mrs. Blaine's sake.
I think it extremely doubtful if any Republican can be elected to the next
Presidency, and I agree with you that striving for the place is not a very safe
means to secure it. I at least, have been successful in keeping that maggot out of
my brain. . . .

Speaking of pictures, the people of this city are raving over a painting called
"Elaine" by a Jewish artist, a resident here whose name I do not at the moment
remember. It is a scene from Tennyson's Idyls of the King and represents the
barge bearing the dead body of "Elaine." I shall try to visit it and write you more
fully about it.

In that connection I ought to say that Californians claim that their atmosphere and sky are even superior to those of Italy. In this I cannot agree with
them, although the air is very clear, and the sky deeply and tenderly blue. The
effects of constant breezes from so vast an ocean blowing across a narrow plain

and slope against so high and cold a range of mountains does, indeed, produce many of the meteorological elements that are found in Italy. But I think the climate here is not so mild, though it is perhaps an even—But I intended to devote this letter more particularly to the people of this place, and their spirit, so far as I have seen it exhibited. Remember that the discovery of gold in 1848 by the law of natural selection called out from each community of the East the most daring and enterprising spirits and these settled California.

Thursday, May 6.

My Darling:

Since my arrival I have been whirled away through so many scenes that I have fallen behind in my account of them; and I will now try to bring up part of the arrears. In my last or perhaps next the last, I stated that I went to Belmont. If you look on a recent map of California, you will see a rail road running south from San Francisco along the shore of the bay. A ridge of high hills, a part of the Coast Range, hides the ocean and the road winds along among beautiful slopes that touch the hills on the west and the bay on the east. Belmont is a little station twenty miles from the City, and half a mile back from it, nestled among the hills, is the country residence of Mr. Ralston.[19] He has there about 400 acres of hill, valley and ravine decorated with every variety of fruit and ornamental tree [growing in] the midst of it. Excepting Chatsworth,[20] the finest country house I ever saw. He frequently entertains fifty guests with the most familiar and open-handed generosity. In his stable I counted 25 magnificent horses, and his grounds are a marvel of beauty. He is not yet 50 years old, was born near Mansfield, Ohio, and came here a poor boy in 1850. He has the reputation, and I should say justly, of being the most powerful business intellect on this coast. The amount of work he performs daily is something enormous. He rises at six; works incessantly and with the utmost rapidity, is the President and Soul of the Bank of California, an institution whose operations are larger than all others in the City combined. He is the chief mover in several of the great rail roads here, is the owner and manager of a very large real estate, and is personally superintending the building of the Palace Hotel, which is much the largest hotel in the world. His wealth is away up in the millions, and he manages the whole with such keen, prompt decisive effectiveness that I look upon him as one of the very most remarkable men I have ever met. His only recreation is at Belmont. He leaves the City at 2 P.M. each Saturday, spends the night at home, drives or rides on Sunday, and in the evening returns to the City to resume his week's work.

He received me with the greatest kindness and treated me as though we were old acquaintances. He has one iron habit which probably makes his career possible. He goes to bed not later than 9:30 P.M. no matter how many guests may be visiting him. His wife is a woman of strong sense and fine qualities and between them they have the faculty of making their friends feel the utmost freedom at their home. Everything is rich, generous and what is more striking in sincere good taste. The kitchen is in keeping with the rest of the house, and is kept in the most perfect order, by their Chinese servants. Billiards, games, music, pictures and statuary make the house brilliant with attraction. As Mr. Ralston bade us good night at half past nine, he said there would be a cup of coffee ready at seven in the morning and at half past seven carriages would start for a drive. At that time he took the reins and with 13 people in his four horse carriage we drove 12 miles back after visiting some places of rare beauty. All doors were open to us, and we came back laden with the richest flowers that bloom in these scenic tropical gardens. We returned at 11 A.M. and at 11:30 sat down to breakfast with 25 at the table. I led Mrs. R. to breakfast and read her that beautiful first page of your letter of the 19th and told her that she and her husband had fulfilled the prophecy of the text you quoted. At 2 P.M. we drove ten miles more towards the City, stopping at several beautiful places, and at 4:30 took the cars for the City. Among the guests at Ralstons was J. T. Young's wife, a son of Brigham Young. I had a long talk with her in reference to the Mormon faith, and especially in reference to polygamy, which I will tell you of when we meet. You will understand better the nature of this society when I tell you that the energy of its people and the wonderful resources of the country have made an unusual number of rich men here. It is said that there are more than 200 millionaires in this city, and there are perhaps a dozen or twenty men who are worth from 10 to 40 millions each. They did not make their money slowly by those small methods which make men narrow and penurious, but they did it partly by great boldness in enterprise and partly by the lucky accidents which attend a mining country. Hence they are generous and broadminded. I find it necessary to brace myself against the inclination to rebel against the fate that placed me in such a narrow groove in reference to business and property. But after all, I come joyfully back to this solid fact, that with your love I am richer than they all are. Bless you, Darling.

On Monday Sargent[21] went with me to the Mint, and we spent nearly four hours in going through that great building and examining the processes by which the silver and gold of this state are turned into the coin of commerce.

On Tuesday Mr Hart took me through the great steamship "The City of Peking," the second largest steamer in the world, and at 2 P.M. we started on a four hour trip through the Chinese quarters, which I must spare you until another letter. In that I will try to write something that will be of interest to our dear little ones. I am very well except that the hemorrhoids have visited me again with savage fury, notwithstanding my buckeye.[22] I have however gained one pound in weight since I left Chicago. If you know how I longed for your letters, you would not hesitate to make your letters long and frequent.

Ever all your own James.

Washington, May 9th, 1875

My Darling:

It is a warm summery Sunday, and has come so suddenly on that we almost begin to faint before the swift coming summer heat. Your telegram on your first arrival is the last intelligence we have of you, and we at home begin to feel that a long silence has fallen between us. I know it is scarcely time for a letter to have reached us, still I shall feel the shadows coming if a letter does not appear tomorrow. I was at church today and heard a young man pour out his wisdom in a long discourse on this text: "Without the shedding of blood there is no remission." When will our "coming preacher" be found in other pulpits than those of Beecher and Everett and a few like them? Why cannot our young men at least see that the world is ready for something better than a harvest of doctrines. I just finished last evening Mrs. Stowe's last story, "We and Our Neighbors."[23] It is full of the best religious thoughts of today, and in one place she says something like this: Why call the world more wicked and sinful than formerly? Is there not a more sweetly spiritual life prevailing, a stronger spirit of labor for others' good than at any other period of the world's history? And it seems to me what we want to hear from our teachers is not a talk about ordinances and doctrines but words of cheer and guidance in the work of growing to be more like Christ and of helping others in that work.

Darling, I must make a confession to you which I am afraid will surprise you. Last night when undressed and ready to turn out the light, involuntarily I turned and kissed a good night to you. Now the confession is that not once before since you went away have I done that nor have I even thought of it. I cannot understand it, except that the stern work of adjusting myself to the command of myself and of these boys is so unlike the tenderness and thoughtfulness with which you invest my whole life when with us, that for a time everything but the loss of you was forgotten. It made me feel almost that you had turned homeward to find my spirit taking up again one of our love-habits, and I fell asleep with wandering away into all the tenderness of your arms. . . .

Just now Hal, Jim, Irvin, Kitty, Mabel and Mollie started out for a walk. Hal begins to show the boy. When I suggested that they all go together, he laughed in an embarrassed sort of way and said maybe the girls don't want us to go. I said, O, yes, Don't you, girls? Kittie said "Yes." So they started, but when I looked after them, the boys were tagging on behind. I expect they soon caught up when out of sight. Irvin went to church but after a few moments he began to grow restless, and looking up said in his queer way, "when will they bring round the bread." I don't want to begin to tease, but somehow I feel as though I must ask if you are thinking anything when you will be home again. I will start this packet away to you, hoping it will bring me something to answer. You never can know how much I want to be with you, but, darling, we will go sometime there together, I hope. With all-loving and ever abiding love, Yours Crete.

Mariposa, Cal. May 13, 1875

My Darling:

The party . . . consists of Gen Burns[24] and wife and two daughters; Mr Hardenbaugh[25] and wife; Mr Wells[26] and wife; Mrs Burton of N.Y. and little son; Mr McFarland of San Francisco;[27] a young gentleman from Boston whose name I do not remember, and your husband without his wife. We left San Francisco wharf at 4 P.M. yesterday and took the Central Pacific R.R. to Lathrop and thence by branch Road to Merced, 165 miles from San Francisco. We arrived at Merced at half past ten last night and stopped at a very large, fine hotel capable of holding 500 guests. This morning we took breakfast at half past five, and at six o'clock our party were loaded on a stage, five on top and the rest inside and were galloping away across the San Joaquin Valley (pronounced WAKEEN). It is a valley of immense breadth, with the low-lying peaks of the coast range on the west and the grander heights of the Sierras on the east. Our route lay to the northeast, or nearly east, and we galloped to the first relay, a distance of 6 and a half miles, in 35 minutes. During the next hour the route became rougher, and by nine o'clock we had reached the old adobe Mexican town of Honitas (Ho-nee-tos) at the base of the foot hills and among the old placer mines. . . . At noon we reached this place and we are to stop thirty minutes. I can take dinner and fill two or three pages for you before the stage horn will blow. This place is in the center of the great Mariposa track, which Fremont took up soon after the Conquest of California. Across the street from where I now write, Fremont erected an adobe house in 1848. His fortune was then in the ascendent, and his name was gathering that glamour of romance over it, which made him the standard bearer of the young and hopeful Republican Party in 1856. He laid out this town, built its first house, brought his Jessie here to share with him the stirring and roseate hopes and aspirations of that golden dream of 1848–9, which did not culminate until the "Path Finder" failed to be elected as President in 1856. Before 1856 this was a bustling mining town of 3000. The fortunes of mining, like those of Fremont,[28] have drifted away in other directions, and Mariposa is now a decayed village of 800 inhabitants. The horn is blowing and I must close. I am sorry to tell you that for the last hour I have been suffering torture from a return of my malady [piles], so that nothing but my love for you could enable me to sit at a table and write.

Thursday evening. May 13.

My Darling. For an hour and a half after I finished the above I was faint with pain and I really thought I should be compelled to leave the stage and lie down, but as we ascended the mountain the air grew cooler and my pain nearly ceased. . . . Mariposa is at the foot of the Sierras, and on leaving it we commenced to wind up the long slopes of the mountains, which rose in majesty away to the north, south and front of our line of travel. For five hours we climbed zig-zag up the sides of the Sierras, and at six P.M. were on the summit from which we looked back upon the San Joaquin Valley and the blue line of the coast range far beyond. From the summit, we plunged down at an exhilarating rate. At 7:15 P.M. we reached a fine homelike group of cottages where we are to spend the night. It is called Clarks's[29] and is 26 miles from Mariposa and 68 miles from Merced. . . . The cottages here are full to overflowing; and, in addition to those who have staid over from yesterday, two stage loads besides our own came from Merced today. I am too weary to write and must try to get some sleep and rest for the further journey tomorrow. . . . Ever and forever Your Own James.

Yosemite, May 15, 1875.

My Darling:

My last was written at Clarke's and addressed to the children. . . . While I was writing that letter my malady returned again with a good deal of pain, and I left a blank page for that reason. I passed an uncomfortable night but awoke in the morning feeling pretty well. Our party had been increased by two, as I mentioned in my last, and the remainder of the stage journey to Yosemite is so rough that the stages are smaller, holding only nine persons, so that it would require two stages for our party. We were awakened at half past five and breakfast was to be ready at six so that we could start at half past six. As the day, yesterday, was one of adventure and some peril, I state its history somewhat minutely. When I came out of my room it was beginning to snow, and by halfpast six one of the heaviest snowstorms I ever saw was raging. The stages were delayed till after seven and by that time several of the older members of the party said it would be dangerous to make the attempt to go through as there was no house between Clarke's and Yosemite, and we might be snowed in on the mountains. Several of the party resolved not to go and one of the stages was taken back to the barn; but the other had to go back to the end of the stage route towards Yosemite.

While the matter was being debated, the old Scotchman quietly took his seat in the stage, and Miss Palmer of Steubenville, who had gone with us to the Big Trees also took her seat. I thought it would hardly be manly to let her go off alone and so I entered the stage. At this, Gen Burns and his family concluded to go, and also Mr McFarland. These eight took seats, the curtains were buttoned down, and a little before eight o'clock we started off in three inches of snow, and the air full of the largest flakes I ever saw. I was not without some doubt whether we were not committing an act of foolhardiness, but the novelty of the thing, a wild snow storm on the 15th of May, made it attractive. We commenced slowly to climb the mountain and in an hour and a half there were eight inches of snow on the track and the pine trees were loaded under its weight. It really began to look as though we were to be blocked. By half past ten we had made not quite ten miles, and there we were met by a horseman from the end of the stage route, who had been sent to order the stages back that may have started from Clarke's, and the first we knew, our driver had wheeled around and was headed for the return. It was offensive to us to have him thus turn us back without our consent, and we remonstrated. He was stubborn and we threatened to put him off the seat and take the reins ourselves. I looked the case over as well as I could and concluded it would be nearly as bad to go forward 15 miles as to go back ten, and so I told the driver and the agent we would be responsible for results if they would obey our orders, and that we had resolved to go forward. They finally gave in and the agent galloped away to order saddle horses up from Yosemite to the end of the stage line, which was in the mountains five miles from Yosemite and 20 miles from Clarke's. We then started on, and in half an hour we were surprised and delighted but somewhat embarrassed by the arrival of three of our party and a guide on horseback. When they saw the snow storm cease, and the sun break out, they were unwilling to remain behind and tried to get the other stage to take them to follow us. But the driver said it was too late. Then they got saddle horses and a guide to follow us. When they overtook us, it was found there was not room in the stage for the additional three (who were Mr Manning of Boston, Mr Wells and his wife—a gallant little woman, born in Greenville, Pa. . . . and resembling you). She was drenched with the melted snow, and so all insisted that she must get into the stage. Miss Palmer, the Ohio lady, offered to take her horse and I took her husband's horse. Manning kept his own, and so we three with the guide rode on. In a short time we had reached the summit of the mountain and the sun made the snow covered trees a most glorious sight. It was strange to feel the warm, almost summer rays of the sun and see them flashing back from the snow till you were nearly snowblind. Soon the snow began to melt and drop in heavy masses from the overhanging trees. From the summit we descended again for two or three miles, only to climb another equally high mountain ridge. While crossing the latter another snowstorm came which raged grandly for half an hour and was succeeded by a glorious sunburst. At a quarter past two we reached the end of the stage road, where was a Chinese encampment. We were, perhaps, an hour ahead of the stage, having galloped rapidly whenever the nature of the road would permit it (for I found Miss Palmer an excellent rider) and then, from the brow of the second mountain I have named, we commenced the long descent to the valley into which the waters of the Yosemite empty. Our path was a mere bridle path, very steep, which zig-zaged down more than 2000 feet and over a distance of three miles before we reached the foot. Just before we reached the foot, we met the agent with a train of saddle horses going to bring our stage companions down, when they reached the end of their stage journey. After reaching the river Merced we rode into the Valley two miles more to this hotel [Black's Hotel], which was so full that it was only by appealing to the gallantry of the gentlemen guests that I obtained rooms for the ladies of our party, who were to arrive later. We three and guide reached the hotel at four and a quarter, having encountered all possible vicissitudes of weather, the last chapter being a thunderstorm and heavy showers, as we entered the jaws of the valley, and closing with a splendid burst of sunshine against the great Yosemite fall, just as we reached our hotel, where the meadows were bright green with no flake of snow upon them. We had ridden on horseback fifteen miles. A little before six P.M. our comrades arrived some on horseback and some in the stage that had gone out to the jaws of the valley to take such as were over-wearied with the horseback descent. In this latter number was the old Scotchman, who said that the donkey he rode to the Big Trees the day before had "well nigh broken a' his bones."

So after all we saved the day, had the satisfaction of carrying our point, and were not a little praised for a plucky, though somewhat lucky and imperious crowd. I am glad to tell you that all day I have almost wholly escaped any pain. After getting supper I took a hot bath, and there being no room at the hotel, a single bed was made up for me in a bath room and I slept soundly and well close beside the bath tub. I am writing this on the little washstand while one of my knees rests against the bed and the other on the bathtub. I will not on this sheet attempt to say a word about the Valley itself, except this: that it [is] one of the very few things I have ever seen that is far beyond all I ever heard said or sung about it. I know I can give no adequate account of it, and I must study its awfully grand lessons before I can begin to interpret them into written words. Think of me, Darling, as being confronted by a volume so full of glorious meaning that I must first study its glossary before I can read its pages. I do really feel it is almost a crime for me to study it without having your dear hand in mine. With all my soul, Ever and All Your Own James.

Washington, May 23rd, 1875

My Darling:

Another Sunday has come warm, dry and dusty. I hope it is your good fortune to be the guest of the Ralston's again to enjoy the freshness at least of the country. I imagine from your letters, however, that you do not have that excessive all-day heat that we have here even in San Francisco, and we begin to appreciate through the want of it here the delight of the cool night breezes. It gives me great pleasure to know you are so kindly received wherever you go. The old world is not so blind yet that it does not know its king. Now don't laugh, and say that is altogether too Mrs. Tiltonian, for it is Thomas Carlyle speaking and not the poor little abused woman of Brooklyn. Have you seen Judge Porter's argument yet? Em Reed has been reading it to me, or else perhaps I had not. I have not the patience to read anything more of the trial, and would not listen even to anything more, if it were not on Beecher's side. To me Mr. Beecher is a true and honorable man, and I will not listen to anything to the contrary. Argument on both sides might be continued till doomsday and no one be one whit nearer the truth than he is now. Not one thing has been proven against Mr. Beecher, and if faith is worth anything in this world it is of worth when given to men and women who for any reason have become the victims of persecution. The frank avowal of religious and social opinions which Mr. Beecher has always made instead of convicting him in my eyes on account of their liberality make guilt seem to me the more impossible. To his nature concealment was not possible. Openly and boldly he said all he had to say and did all that he would do. Had he been one of the straightlaced orthodox preachers I should be much more easily convinced that he might secretly sin. As it is, my innermost consciousness tells me that he is innocent, and I will not listen to any argument to the contrary. I am no judge of the strength of Judge Porter's argument, for he says so exactly what I believe that it is truth to me, however weak or however strong.[30]

Yesterday we had for the first time green peas and strawberries, and today it is genuinely hot. Will you be with us three weeks from today? Oh, how much I hope so. Darling, I believe your absence has perhaps been of some use to me in self subjection. But you must live and save your life to help me with these boys. I am really afraid that on the whole Jim will sum up a more impudent and reckless boy than when you went away, and Irvin is learning of him as fast as a child can learn. Don't think I am disheartened. I am not, and I believe we shall bring them through all right, but we have got to learn all the wisdom that head and heart can learn, and then learn how to use it wisely. But we can make it a sweet soul cheering work in our loving sympathy and through the conflict win crowns, and teach them in turn to win. I am alone in the Library at this moment, but all the family are with me in sending love to you. With dearest truest love, Your Crete.

Glenbrook House, Lake Tahoe, Cal.

June 1, 1875

My Darling:

It is a curious fact that since I left Chicago I have not been left alone at any point in my journey until tonight, and since I cannot have you with me it is a luxury to be left alone. Even now I have been alone only since seven o'clock this evening. At Carson City I found that the Chief Clerk of the Mint was a Washington boy who used to know me in 1868–9. His history will interest you, as it has me. His parents are Germans, and they live close by us in Washington. His father is a Mr. Hoffer, a bellhanger, and his shop is on NY Av. near 12th st. This boy ran away from school when he was not quite thirteen years old, and hired out as a telegraph messenger boy on 15th St. opposite the Treasury. He worked away until he learned telegraphy. He was then for a while an operator at the Capitol. Being a bright, active boy, he at the same time kept books for some one in the city, after his day's work was done as an operator. His activity attracted the attention of the superintendent of the Carson Mint, who happened to be visiting Washington, and he offered him a clerkship if he would come out here. Hoffer was then (1869) sixteen years old. He came here and worked as a copyer at $1400 per year. At the same time he got work outside the mint which gave him about $50 per month. He has gradually risen to the second place in the Mint—$2500 per year—and by his industry and shrewdness has become a member of a firm of stockbrokers and is now worth not less than $25000. He is but 23 years old, has a nice wife, and a little baby just one day older than our baby, and is thoroughly respected by the people of Carson City. When I get home I must see his father and let both father and mother know how well their boy is doing. Ask Hal and Jim what they think of this, and what they propose to do about it. So much by way of preface. The Superintendent of the Mint being away, young Hoffer[31] showed me through it, and was very intelligent about all its operations. He remembered me and asked me to take breakfast with him. So this morning about eight o'clock he called at my hotel and took me around to his house, a pleasant little cottage, and I took breakfast with him and his wife. Then we visited the Mint again and saw it in operation. I will tell the boys, when I get home, all about how gold and silver coins are made. Then he got a fine pair of horses and a carriage and drove me to this place, and stayed with me till nearly seven o'clock this evening, when he left me and drove back to Carson City. That, as I have already said, leaves me here alone for the first time since I arrived at Chicago on my way west.

The trip today has been very full of interest to me. The distance from Carson to this place is 16 miles by the wagon road, which leads up a wild and rugged canyon, by a steep zig-zag road, a part of the old stage route to California. Stages still run here; and I saw, on top of one of them, the celebrated Hank Monk who drove Horace Greeley from Carson to Placerville about eleven years ago. Please go to my bookshelf and get Mark Twain's "Roughing It," and read the story to the boys.[32] I think it is told in that volume. On my way here, I saw a most remarkable example of the enterprise and resource of our American people, when placed in new and difficult situations. Remember that the soul and center of Nevada life is the mines, that they are of most extraordinary richness, and that they are located among the most desolate mountains, where no tree grows and scarcely a touch of vegetable life exists. The great problem is how to extract the precious metal from the earth and as incident to that how to feed, clothe and warm the men who do that work, and also how to supply the enormous mass of timber and wood needed for the mines and mills. When I tell you that the single mine I was in yesterday uses 50,000,000 feet of timber per month and that every quartz mill consumes 25 cords of wood per day, you will see the importance of finding means of getting these articles to the mines. In the beginning it was about ten miles to the nearest timber, and the mines had not been long worked until it was twenty and thirty. The Rail Road was built from Reno to Va City and for a time aided to solve the wood and timber problem. But soon the wood near the R.R. was exhausted. Still there were millions of acres of beautiful forest, but it stood on tops and in the wild canyons of the high Sierras, at points so distant and so inaccessible as to make it cost perhaps $100 a cord to cut it and haul it to the mines. The measureless richness of the mines became an overwhelming motive for finding a solution of the problem. Necessity presses upon the human mind with tremendous force. They smite upon each other like flint upon steel, and the fire must be lighted. It was lighted in this case, and the solution of the problem was so novel, so effective, so American that I know you will be interested in it. Whose brain conceived it I do not know, but it was done here on these heights a few years ago. I wonder that no one has written about it. I imagine I see the hardy lumberman, standing near some peak of these high Sierras three or four thousand feet above the great mines and twenty-five miles away from the possible reach of a rail road. Around him on all sides is the boundless forest of pine, cedar and fir. Down the canyons below him, roar the torrents, fed forever by mountain lakes and perpetual snow. The thought flashed upon him to harness these torrents and make them drag the forest to the plain below. The result was this: he nailed two planks together thus, V , making a triangular trough, about two feet on a side. This he set on trestle work, or in a ditch dug in the side of the mountain and extended down steep canyons, across deep gorges, to the rail road station, and at the top and at various points lower down turned in a part of the waters of the mountain. This gave something between a canal and a cataract, with the controllability of the one and the speed of the other. This new thing he called his "Flume," and into it he tumbled his wood, his timber and his lumber, which went swimming down the current with the speed of fish. I have today ridden fifteen miles along such a flume and have seen the wood and the heavy timber, some of it 30 feet long and six inches square, darting past at the rate of 15 miles an hour with a dash of foam at the bow of each heavy stick gleaming above it like a banner of triumph. The flume along which I rode is twenty-two miles long and has as many miles more of branches that come in from the several canyons of the mountains. This flume costs about $3500 per mile, is easily kept in repair, and by means of it, Carson City is supplied with wood at seven dollars a cord. I fear this may not be as interesting to any body else as it is to me; but I assure you I have seen nothing in this wonderful country that has impressed me so much as this simple, strange, rude, but perfect contrivance by which a vast industrial problem has been solved. It is to me a new illustration of the immortality of the mind. The canyons and the mountain sides echo the dust of hundreds of saw mills and the chopper's axe breaks the old silence of the forest, to feed these flumes with freight. I must go to rest by the shore of this lovely lake of which I will tell you after I have crossed it tomorrow. But even here, by its deep blue water, I am 7600 feet above the sea. From these heights, I send you a heartfull of love and Good night.

Ever Your Own James.

❧ NOTES ❧

1. Perhaps James felt it was inappropriate to write about such a thing as childbirth in English, or, more likely, he decided to write in French because he "was going to have lunch with foreigners." He wrote: "At this hour I believe that my sister, Mary, is in Baltimore enroute for Washington. I hope that she will arrive at your house before you are sick [in childbirth].

If it is possible, keep the child that we are expecting in his little live carriage for another week since I want very much to be present for the very interesting occasion when the little man will set foot on earth for the first time. But if he cannot wait until I arrive, give him my compliments with my paternal salutations. To his mother I give all of my heart and all of my soul. Now I am going to have lunch with foreigners. Forever I am Jamie."

2. Professor Agassiz (1807–1873) was a highly regarded Harvard scientist on the board of regents for the Smithsonian Institute.

3. Just after Garfield had become President in 1881, Calvin Chaffee wrote to Senator Henry Dawes as follows: "Do you remember my going to your room one night and finding Garfield there—during the Credit Mobilier investigation—how thoroughly demoralized he was—how pitiful his condition was—how glad he was to get aid from any and every one? I do—and I sometimes wonder if he remembers such things—and who it was that induced Judge Poland not to recall him to the stand" (Margaret Leech and Harry J. Brown, *The Garfield Orbit: The Life of President James A. Garfield* [New York: Harper and Row, 1978], 176).

4. George Eliot's *Middlemarch* was published in 1871–72.

5. Mr. Rose was James' secretary.

6. The Anacreon poem Crete had translated in 1853 reads:

> *I wish to honor Atreus' sons,*
> *Of Cadmus wish to sing:*
> *But love alone my lyre resounds*
> *Upon its chords. Of late*
> *Its strings I changed, to change the*
> *Harp entire, and then began*
> *To sing the toils of Hercules.*
> *The lyre replied but love.*
> *Heroes, henceforth, farewell for us:*
> *For only love we sing.*

7. James was staying at the Rudolph house in Hiram while he traveled around his District trying to explain why he had voted in favor of the "salary grab" and what his involvement was in the Credit Mobilier. "I find this town," he wrote in his Diary, "in which and for which I have done so many years of hard work and poorly requited work, is in a state of ferment, with worlds of mean slings about me for the salary vote. Perhaps Sidney Smith was right when he said, 'Gratitude is a lively appreciation of benefits expected.' But here is discipline for my soul—and perhaps for the people of Hiram. . . .

I wonder what my boys will think of [this controversy] twenty years
hence. I wonder what I will, if I am alive. Perhaps all this trouble may look
very small and be laughed over. Perhaps not. For it may mark the decline
and fall of my political power. Let either fate befall I shall hope to make culture and sweetness out of it. I now take up my other woe, the Credit
Mobilier. When and where to publish it is the question with me. I must
wait until the salary storm is somewhat abated" (Harry J. Brown and
Frederick D. Williams, eds., *The Diary of James A. Garfield*, [East Lansing:
Michigan State University Press, 1967], 2: 170–71).

8. Charles Merivale, *History of the Romans under the Empire*, was published in
   six volumes between 1850 and 1862. The passage referred to by James is
   from book 4, chapter 40.

9. August John Cuthbert Hare (1834–1903) wrote *Walks in Rome*.

10. Emma Jacobina Christiana Marwedel (1818–1893) was a pioneer kinder-
    garten leader and early leader in the advancement of working women. She
    came to Washington from Germany in 1871 and established a private
    school applying the theories of Friedrich Froebel. Garfield was particularly
    interested in her approach to primary education. Marwedel left
    Washington after five years, however, carrying her kindergarten idea to
    California.

11. Harmon Austin had evidently told James that Estep was "an intemperate
    and licentious man." Thus, the "shadows across the path of my proposed
    partnership" and one probable reason for breaking off negotiations.

12. In building a new station on Sixth Street, the Baltimore and Potomac
    Railroad Company placed tracks along the street from Virginia Avenue to
    the station. The Presbyterian Church took the Rail Company to court
    charging the laying of track in front of their building had adversely affected
    their work. The Sixth Avenue Church was awarded damages, so the
    Railroad Company took the matter to the Supreme Court; but the earlier
    judgment was upheld.

13. This passages is from Judges 5:25.

14. This is Mark Twain's *Roughing It* (1872).

15. William C. Ralston, whose wife invited James to ride in the directors' car,
    was president of the Bank of California. Soon after this, James visited the
    Ralstons in California.

16. These verses are from Tennyson's *In Memoriam*, section 64.

17. "Mr. Allison" refers to W. B. Allison of Iowa, a member of the House.

18. Libbie was Joe's wife, Lucretia's sister-in-law.
19. Ralston, who so dazzled Garfield, died in August 1875 by drowning; some thought it was suicide.
20. Chatsworth is the estate of the Duke of Devonshire in Derbyshire, England, visited by Lucretia and James in 1867.
21. Aaron Sargent was a Republican senator from California.
22. James had an intestinal ulcer which was cured when he returned home by an operation. A sentimental Ohio boy, he always carried a buckeye in his pocket.
23. Harriet Beecher Stowe's *We and Our Neighbors* was published in 1875.
24. General Burns was an Ohio graduate of West Point living in San Francisco; he was chief commissariat for the Division of the Pacific.
25. Mr. Hardenbaugh was Hardenbergh of New York, a Union officer in the Civil War.
26. George R. Wells was a San Francisco lawyer residing in the Grand Hotel, where James met him.
27. Edward C. Macfarlane (Macfarland) also lived at the Grand Hotel.
28. John Charles Fremont, the "Path Finder," had been a soldier, an explorer, and a politician. He was the Republican presidential candidate in 1856.
29. Galen Clark (1814–1910) was the official guardian of the Yosemite Grant before the government gave the Valley to the state of California.
30. Beecher's trial ended inconclusively; the jury could not agree as to whether or not Theodore Tilton's charges were true. Beecher himself told two of his attorneys, who had apologized for consulting with him about the trial on a Sunday: "We have it on good authority that it is lawful to pull an ass out of the pit on the Sabbath day. Well, there never was a bigger ass, or a deeper pit." Beecher, whatever the truth of the situation, had undoubtedly been careless in the management of his private affairs.
31. Theodore Hofer later became chief clerk in the U.S. Mint at Carson City, Nevada.
32. Hank Munk was a stage coach driver, made famous by a Mark Twain anecdote in *Roughing It.* Garfield wrote in his diary, "I suppose I have been told the story of driving Greeley to Carson City at least a hundred times."

CHAPTER 10

Spring 1876–June 1879

DURING THE SUMMER OF 1875, *Crete spent a few weeks at Ocean Grove, New Jersey, while James remained in Washington. In the fall, it was the usual thing: James in Ohio campaigning and Lucretia in Washington with the family. In the spring of 1876, James went on a speaking tour to New England. Summer once again found Crete on the Jersey coast and in Philadelphia at the centennial exhibition while James went campaigning into Maine. That fall, when James was back in Ohio "on the stump," little Ned, the last child born (who had only recently been named Edward) fell ill with the whooping cough. He died in October 1876, and was buried with his sister Trot in the Hiram cemetery.*

What to do with his family in the summers had become a problem for James. Washington was hot, they had sold their house in Hiram—Lucretia had never really liked it—and the Rudolph house, where the Garfield family had been staying, was complicated to manage. Obviously, a summer home was needed. Accordingly, James bought a 180-acre farm near Mentor, Ohio, close to Lake Erie. The farm house, a nine-room structure, was "in a sad state of dilapidation." It would have to be renovated. Still, the location was pleasant, and it was in Garfield's district, near "Erie's billows." James hoped his boys might learn something about the land during their summers there. Dr. Robison helped with the transaction. He himself had a farm just up the road. Garfield called his farm Lawnfield.

The election of 1876 was one of the closest in our history. It appeared at first that Tilden had won, but the returns of Louisiana, South Carolina and Florida were in doubt, so much so that President Grant asked James, along with other Republicans, to form a bipartisan committee with Democrats to oversee the counting of the ballots in

*those states. James left Washington on November 14 and returned on December 2 with
the news that the Republican candidate, Rutherford B. Hayes, was the winner.*

*The years began to pass quickly. James made an extended trip to Alabama on trial
business in the late spring of 1877, while Crete was busy making renovations in the
farm property. In the autumn Crete went to St. Louis with her mother to visit her sister,
Nellie, while James was campaigning in Ohio. In 1879 Crete's mother lay ill once
again, and Lucretia had to be with her in Hiram. She was able to go to the farm in
Mentor in late May, where she heard some vicious gossip about James and a "notorious woman," about which she immediately wrote to James, who was in Washington.
It is an indication of the total change in their relationship that Crete took no credence
in the story whatsoever, but sent off a stinging letter to the presumed perpetrator of the
story.*

*The chapter ends in June 1879 with Lucretia in Mentor writing to James and the
two older boys in Washington. Of the more than two-hundred letters exchanged during
this period, twenty-eight are here included.*

*In the spring of 1876 James went on a speaking tour into New England, Lucretia
remaining at home in Washington.*

Hanover, New Hampshire.
March 7, 1876.

My Darling:

I spent Sunday in New York with Wm M. Evarts,[1] who came for me soon
after I had taken breakfast, and drove me for two hours in Central Park.[2] Of
course, it is not a favorable season to see the Park; but the weather was fine, and
it was a pleasure to listen to the brilliant talk of the great lawyer. We got out of
the carriage to see Quincy Ward's Statue of Shakespeare, which is really very
fine; and a sitting statue of Walter Scott, copied from the one which you and I
saw in Edinburgh. From the Park we drove back to Mr. Evarts' house in the
City, where we took a sort of lunch dinner; and talked incessantly until half past
five o'clock. He gave me a minute account of his two journeys to Europe during
the war, which he undertook for Mr. Seward to prevent complication and perhaps war with England and France. And then he gave me the interior history of
the part he took in the great argument before the International Tribunal at
Geneva. His wife and two of their daughters were at the table; but we did not
remain long with them, nor did we join them after dinner. It was really a great

treat to listen to Mr. Evarts, and to measure my mind by his. I suspect that no amount of brilliancy in a man can make his egotism altogether agreeable; for pleasant as it was to listen to Evarts, I could not forget that he was making himself and his own achievements the centre of nearly seven hours of talk. Is that *my* way, when I talk to people? Don't fail to tell me so if it is. At six P.M. we went to the Brevoort House, where Evarts had arranged to give me a dinner in company with some other gentlemen; but I was able to sit with them but half an hour; and at seven I took the train for Springfield, Mass. where I arrived [at] half past midnight, and stopped at the Massasoit House, where I spent a night twenty-one years ago. I ought to have mentioned that I went to Booth's Theatre and saw Shakespeare's Julius Caesar superbly mounted, and wonderfully well performed, especially Davenport's part as Brutus. In the morning I found Fry,[3] who had preceded me to Springfield, and we spent the forenoon reading and visiting. I found my classmate Bowles and two other Williams men. At half past two Fry and I went to the Depot and while we were waiting for our train to back down into the Depot, we had the mortification to see it move off and leave us sachels in hand, and no means of transportation. I found the Superintendent, a genial old man,[4] who fired up an engine and taking us aboard and managing it himself, ran us nine miles in ten minutes, and enabled us to overtake the last train at Holyoke. Being wearied by want of sleep, and much reading, I fell asleep and on awaking found we had passed South Vernon Junction, and looking across the snow I saw the train for Keene steaming away to the north east while I was being dragged up the Connecticut Valley on the Vermont side. On reaching Brattleboro, I left the train and hired a livery man to drive me across the mountain to Keene, twenty miles away. We left at six P.M. in a sleigh and passed over a beautiful road, after crossing the Connecticut on the ice, and, among the deep woods of birch and maple and pines and under the bright moon, we swept with exhilarating speed, and in just two hours I was in Keene and beginning a speech to two thousand people. . . .

At eleven thirty I took the train and came to White River Junction and thence to this place, the seat of Dartmouth College, now in its 107th year. I am to speak here tonight, tomorrow night at Claremont, Thursday P.M. at Milford. Thursday evening Nashua, Friday evening at Farmington, and Saturday evening at Exeter. Whence I hope to go to you as fast as steam can carry me. I am beset with calls from professors and students and have written this amidst constant interruption. I was greatly in hopes to hear from you at Keene, but shall still hope to hear soon. Love to all. Ever and Always Your Own James. . . .

Washington, March 7, 1876

My Precious Darling:

I have just received your dispatch from Keene and infer from its nature that you have not received the letters I sent you on Sunday. I thought I should surely get another letter from you before this; but if you are half as busy as I am I have no heart to blame you. Abram has gotten over his symptoms of croup but is nearly sick and the crossest little scamp you ever saw. Mollie and Neddie too are half sick with colds, and Jimmie has a bad face—swollen and I am afraid gathering pus. Lacy[5] is on hand too with her pitiful importunities. Their flour barrel is empty, her husband's boots are so nearly off his feet that he cannot come to the city even to ask for work. To gratify her I did go to Mr. Smith and ask him if there was a vacant messengership in his office. I thought you would not object to that. Of course, there was no such vacancy, and this morning I gave her a note of introduction to Mr. Stowell. What a pitiful thing the struggle of life is to the average human creature. Surely I ought to thank our kind Father every hour that I am so blessed in the place given to me through your love and protection. I am told by several persons that the rumor on the street and in some of the papers is that the War Secretaryship is to be tendered to you. Mr. Smith asked me about it when I saw him last night and said he hoped you would not accept it if it were offered, chiefly I think because he feels you are more needed in Congress, but partly because he feels that you could do yourself little justice to help finish out an administration which has become so odious. This perhaps would be a selfish reason for there was surely now more need that honest men in some way become the leaders. I doubt however whether the President would want you, for unless he has grown much less self-reliant than formerly he does not want anyone near him so capable to advise, and whose advice he would be so compelled to heed. I send you the letters now on hand but I doubt whether you will receive anything later than this. My letters are always so slow to reach you. I hope you can send a few lines each day. It helps so much to rest me from the weariness of living without you. All join in love to you, our dearest one. Tell me what kind of a speech you are able to make with the air so black with revelations and rumors of revelations blacker still. I think you must feel as though you were suffocating as we all feel here today with this hot stifling wind blowing our very breath away.

With all love, Your Crete.

While James traveled to Maine to campaign, Lucretia visited the Philadelphia
Exhibition. This first great centenary celebration of U.S. Independence had been established by an act of Congress in March 1871 as "an international exhibition of arts,
manufactures, and products of the soil and mine, in the city of Philadelphia, and state
of Pennsylvania." The Exhibition opened 10 May 1876. James and Lucretia were
there for the opening ceremonies. James wrote in his diary that he had no doubt of two
things: "first, that the Exposition will not be a financial success; second, that it will be
great success in the way of education and stimulus to the people who participate."[6] He
vowed to return with children. Lucretia visited it twice more, the second time being in
September 1876.

Philadelphia, Sept. 1, 1876

My Darling:

Notwithstanding all your statements concerning the amount of paper
brought here, these slips are the whole that I can find. I awoke this morning
with a headache and decided to stay at home and let the girls and children go to
the Exposition. Hal and Jim decided, too, to spend the day otherwise, and
Abram wouldn't go, so Mollie and Irvin are the only two with the girls. It was
so lonely to come home last night without you. Darling, how am I to be reconciled to all these absences which each year you stay in political life is to bring?
They have always been hard enough to bear, but each year they become more
unendurable. I ought to be reconciled to anything this Fall, the Good Father is
helping you to so vindicate yourself and to lift off the weight of adversity which
has been so overburdening. And I am trying to let this fact make me happy—
triumphantly happy, in spite of the heavy hours. I must warn you, though, to
treat yourself tenderly and not let the great swirling clamorous public sweep
you into its whirlpool and overwhelm you with its demands. If you are worth so
much to the Country now, is it not chiefly because you will be of so much value
when the elections are won? Save yourself for that, and for me. All join me in
love to you—our dearest and best. Ever all yours, Crete.

P.S. Remember me with kindest regards to Mr. and Mrs. Blaine and family. . . .

Augusta, Me. Sept.4, 1876

My Darling:

After writing you my hurried note of Saturday, I spoke to an immense audi-ence and then spent the night and yesterday at Blaines in company of the Ingersolls, of whom I have many things to tell you when we meet. I go this morning to Bangor where I speak tonight and I go north along the border and within the province of New Brunswick to Aroostook Co. Let the boys follow me on the map and find Houlton and Fort Fairfield. I shall return through Bangor, so after you receive this write me one more letter and direct to Bangor, Maine.

I have had a new revelation of what love is from our great William [Shakespeare]. Turn to the Sonnets and read the cxvi, and when we meet we will read it together. I am now disposed to believe that no human composition has ever equalled that as an analysis of love. I will not attempt to comment upon [it], except to speak of one couplet or two:

> *"Love's not Time's fool, though rosy lips and cheeks*
> *Within his bending sickle's compass come;*
> *Love alters not with his brief hours and weeks*
> *But bears it out even to the edge of doom."*

Think, Darling, of that immense figure of Time with his vast sickle, reaching out for all that is mortal. He can grasp within his sickle's compass "rosy cheeks and lips," but love itself is beyond his utmost reach and bears it out even to the edge of doom. How that answers the fear you have sometimes expressed that our love would wane when the light of life began to burn low. In this connec-tion I have caught another thought: that true love, immortal love, is unselfish and *hence* immortal. If I love you for my own sake, that love might perish by changes in me. If my love is planted in you; if I love you for *your* sake, then it lives out of and beyond self, and depends not upon my changing moods but upon the immortal being in whom it is planted. Thus it rises above *impediments*, above intervening obstacles, outlasts Time, "looks upon tempests, and is never shaken." Follow this thought out, my Darling, and tell me about it when you write, or when we meet.

It is too soon to say on what train we will meet, but I will now expect to leave Boston next Sunday evening, and I think I can meet you on the train which takes you from Washington Monday morning, or at latest Monday noon. But I will write or telegraph you when I learn all about it, so that I can make no mistakes. I want you to stay in Ohio not less than three weeks. If possible, I hope you will stay until the election and then let me go back to Washington with you. I beg you not to tire yourself out at the Centennial as much as you did with me. I look confidently for a letter from you when the mail comes today, so that I can read it on the cars on my way to Bangor.

Love to the precious little ones and to you a love that lies beyond the sickle's compass. Ever and all our own James. . . .

Hiram, September 15, 1876

My Darling:

I did feel it was too bad to let you go away alone last night; but I knew I could see you so little and then must come dragging back alone this morning, and I was too selfish. Then too I saw that Nellie would feel a little bit hurt. Darling, I don't believe anybody quite knows or can understand how dear to each other we are, and I have a kind of fear that people will set down to silliness our fondness. I hope you found Harmon in good feeling and got your arrangements all to satisfy you. It is very pleasant to be at home again, but I confess to a little homesick feeling to be here without you and the boys. This morning Will Howell's Life of Hayes[7] and Wheeler came in the mail and several letters. You did not tell me what to do with your letters, so I will keep them till you come. Now, Darling, take care of your health and write to me as often as you can. I will write to Mother and the boys today.

Ever and forever Your Own Crete . . .

Neddie died in Washington during the third week of October. James went home from his campaigning—he had been in New Jersey—to be with Crete during the crisis. Then the two went with the body back to Hiram to bury Edward next to his sister, Trot. James wrote in his diary for October 27: "At eleven A. M. the house [in Hiram] was filled with friends and neighbors, and Burke [Hinsdale] preached a strong sweet sermon. He read . . . the account in 2 Samuel 12th chapter, of the death of David's child. At the close of the services, we bore the precious body to the graveyard, and buried it beside the grave of our little daughter, which was made thirteen years ago. I did not know, since that great sorrow, that my heart could be so wrung again by a similar loss. I am trying to see through it the deep meaning and lesson of this death.

I can hardly think that this child died for itself, but for us. God help me to use the heavy lesson for the good of those of us who remain."[8]

Washington, Oct. 29, 1876

My Darling:

I am home again with the dear loved ones still left to us, and am so glad to be here; but I scarcely dare stop to think or even to stand still lest my heart sink into such utter loneliness for our dear little lost boy. The children are all well and as happy as children must and will be except while the pain of the blow lasts. I am sorry both for you and myself that you are so far away from me. Nothing but the need that you say all that there is need to be said, and in your own effective way that could reconcile me to your absence from me. There is a paper lying on the table here now with quotations from the Louisville Courier Journal and the Lancaster Intelligencer so mean and unfair that I almost despise Judge Black for having such supporters. I send them. But I suppose the poor old superannuated party must make some sort of a death gasp, and it would not be true to itself unless it make a very mean struggle.

Joe and Libbie and Mrs. Yates and her son came home with me, and if Mother and the children are well I think we will all—not the children, of course—go on together to Philadelphia on Tuesday morning. Darling, I cannot get over the stunned feeling which almost robs me of thought. Darling, I hope nothing will prevent you from coming immediately after the election. Mother sends the notice of Neddie. All join in love to you. Ever yours, Crete. . . .

Washington, Nov. 4, 1876.

My Darling:

Mother and I returned last night from Philadelphia where we have been since Tuesday morning. Mother endured the fatigue far better than I expected and enjoyed it all very much. I am very glad she has been there. It has con-tributed to her happiness a great deal and the recollection will give to her much delight. Your first note from Warren was forwarded to me at Phil. but I was so occupied every moment until I was too weary to do anything but go to bed that I did not write a word to you. Then I have a feeling that nothing will reach you there while you are so constantly changing places. Last night I found your sec-ond from Ravenna. I feel so sorry for you and so anxious about your health.

Darling, I feel that you need me and how my heart longs for you and to be with you to soothe and caress your head and heart. I hope the Good Father will keep you from illness and all harm and bring you safe to us again. I think I was never more lonely in all my life than while at Philadelphia. To be there again alone where I had so little time ago been with all our six children and with you, it seemed as though my heart would break. Nothing but the resolute determination to make Mother happy kept me there a moment, but it was good for me and I am very glad I had the courage to go through it with apparent happiness. . . .

The children are all well and the boys I think are doing better than ever before. I am quite of the opinion that it will be a good thing for them and especially for Mollie to have Miss Mays[9] stay with us this winter, and I may speak to her about it before you return. Mollie is so alone, and she is just coming to the age when it is of great importance to her to have gentle and ladylike influences to help her lose the hoydenish manners of a girl so constantly in the society of brothers only. With my heart full of love to you and full of hope for your safe return. Yours forever, Crete.

P. S. Give my love to Father and Mother and bring a tub of butter.

James left for New Orleans to canvass the 1876 election returns on November 11.

Washington, Nov.12, 1876.

My Darling:

The lengthening shadows tell us that one of the days of your absence is drawing to a close and would that I could hasten them, make them rush. How little we know of the future and how futile all our plans! This autumn promised us more of quiet and rest in our home before the winter's work should begin than that of almost any other year since our marriage. But how has it been broken and filled with sorrow and lonely hours. And yet I am not entirely miserable; and today there has come into my life and heart a feeling of exaltation—almost. A feeling that the Good Father is in some way preparing us for a larger grander life of work and love. It was hard to send you away last night into the midnight and the darkness, but at the same time I took hope and heart from the fact that it was only the sternest sense of duty that called you away, and going thus I felt you and all of us would be blest. There was so much that was sweet and perfect—perfect in its sweetness and sweet in its perfectness—in all our union and communion yesterday that I remember it as a new blossoming of our wedded love and hail it as a harbinger of the grandeur of perfect love unto which we shall attain. Darling, even when the darkness of the night was deepest over our lives and in spite of all its hopelessness, I would pray that our united lives and love should yet reveal a light and glory of wedded love never before known, and are we not quietly opening to the world mansions of untold wealth and filled with joys never thought of by the wildest dreamer? Darling, I believe many homes have been brightened and blessed by the love we have revealed to them, and it gladdens so much my life to know it.

The day has been tolerably quiet. Jim will break out occasionally, but always comes so penitently and asks to be forgiven that I have no heart to complain of him, though I have no assurance that he will not break out again in five minutes thereafter. Irvin's throat is about the same, but I thought best to have Miss Edson see him this morning.[10] He is running about as usual. Mollie has had a turn of sick headache since church but has been asleep and just came in here feeling better. I hope we shall all keep well while you are away, and that you may be kept safe from every harm. With all our love and prayers for success to your work, we remain in hopeful waiting for you. Ever and forever, more and more, all your own Crete.

St. Charles Hotel, New
Orleans, November 16, 1876

My Darling:

Soon after writing you yesterday, your most precious letter came to my hand and filled my heart full of thankfulness and joy to know how tenderly you were carrying me in your heart. I, too, have dwelt upon that last perfect day, made all the more perfect by the knowledge we each knew the other was grieving that it must end. Many a time during the day I thought how sweet it would be if we and the day could have been made immortal. We owe a debt of gratitude to our great Shakespeare for speaking for us as he has done in the sonnets; and I do feel that we have entered upon a larger world of love than any in which we had hitherto dwelt. And yet the vision of its calm glories is haunted by the fear that it is too perfect to last, not that I have the least fear that either of us will fail in the fuller and permanent enjoyment of this love; but that the supernal powers may envy our joy or mar it, for ours seems to be a love like that of which Poe speaks, "a love the winged seraphs above coveted her and me."[11]

You can hardly imagine how the intense interest of the great political question, which has brought us here, fills all minds and occupies all the thoughts of the people here, and throughout the country. I have literally been unable to sit down by myself three consecutive minutes since my arrival here. All the time since I began this letter there have been not less than twenty-five men in the room, and several times I have been interrupted to consult or be introduced. I almost despair of getting an opportunity to write you such a letter as is in my heart.

I do not yet see the outcome of the work here; but I believe that a fair count of the lawful vote of this state will give it to Hayes. Still, I am not sure how Florida has gone. It is almost impossible for us to get any trustworthy news here from the remote states. The associated press is in the hands of the democrats, and they send the most sensational reports and give their version of affairs. Give my love to Dear little Mollie and thank her for her good little letter to papa. The dear little girl was very sweet and good to papa during the evening that I left.

If I can get time I will write to her. I hope you have received my letter in reference to opening my mail and paying the premium on my life insurance policy which will be due on the 23rd. Harried by this crowd, I must ask your forgiveness for so poor a letter.

Ever and all your own James.

Washington, Nov. 18, 1876

My Darling:

Just a week ago you were starting away. It has been a long week, and it has been a short one—long in the time you have been away and short in the comparatively pleasant time we have had with the children. Today it has rained all day and the boys have been housed. Leslie Dungan has been with them and is with them still getting up games to amuse the children. You never saw two more polite gentlemanly boys than Hal and Jim were at dinner today. Jim—nor any of the rest for that matter—can be good all the time but it is a relief to have spells of quiet. Last evening after the Club broke up, they adjourned to the parlor and had music and singing and Jim recited the "Bugle Song" beautifully.

Little Neddie's bright face has been before me more vividly today than at any time since he went away from us. I cannot quite understand why so bright and promising a child should not have been permitted to stay with us. There was so much that was strong and beautiful in his little nature.

Sunday, November 19th

I found I could not get your letter off last night so left it to finish on your birth-day.[12] I am not quite reconciled that you must be absent, still if any good can come out of it I'll not complain.

We have had no word from you since you reached New Orleans, although this is the fifth day, if you reached there on Tuesday as you expected. I am read-ing Daniel Doronda.[13] I am sure you will be greatly interested in it. It is unlike any story I ever read except it is full of George Eliot's pictures, and I think some of the criticisms on it I have read are extremely stupid, showing that the critic had no appreciation of her characters and no conception of her thought. Darling, I don't know that I would ask for you that you may double the years you have lived, but may you many times double the *life* you have grown into and the wealth of your attainments, so that your last years ripened by culture and full of rich development may be your happiest and best. With abiding and ever growing love and trust, Your Own Crete.

New Orleans, Nov.20, 1876

My Darling:

Soon after I mailed my letter of yesterday, yours of the 16th came with its birthday benediction, and kept my heart warm till I slept. The day was quite cold, as is this. I am sitting in the hall of the Board of Canvassers, the State Senate House, with my overcoat on, and occasionally go to the stove to keep warm. Strange that in the land of flowers so cold a day should look down upon roses and orange groves. The weather seems to have imparted its fickleness to the people, who smile in the morning and murder at night. My old opinion of the Latin races is confirmed, that they have not the genius for self-government. I am sitting here as one of the five Republican witnesses to the count of the returns. To avoid a crowd and the turbulence and delay it would occasion, the Board have excluded all but those legally authorized to be present, and the five "distinguished northern visitors" from each political party. Every hour, I am learning most curious things about this curious people, and am getting a clearer

view of the strange muddle into which the war and the partisan struggles which
followed it have involved this State. The value of our visit here may be two-fold:
first to aid in reassuring and calming the public mind which is in a state of dangerous inflammation; and second to be prepared for the great discussion which
is almost certain to follow in the House if Hayes is declared elected, as I am now
almost sure he will be. The Board are now counting the votes of those Parishes
(counties) concerning which there is no contest. When these are counted,
they will take up the contested parishes, and hear testimony upon the charge of
intimidation and fraud. It is impossible to tell how long it will take to complete
the count; but the eyes of the whole nation are upon the work now going on in
this room; and the election of our President probably depends upon what is
done here. When you reflect that the interest and passion of 45,000,000 of
people are concentrated upon the work going on in this room, you can imagine
the stress and strain of the hour and how much steadiness of mind and nerve
are needed to bear one's self through it and keep his head level.

I shall have another man in my place tomorrow to enable me to accept the
invitation of Capt. Eads to go down to the mouth of the Mississippi to see the
great work going on there to deepen the channel of the river by means of jetties,
one of the greatest works of its kind ever attempted.[14] The boat leaves this
evening, and will not return until tomorrow night, so that I may not be able to
send you a letter during the day tomorrow. How much I want you with me, to
see this remarkable country. Besides needing you every hour for my own sake,
I want you here for your sake, that you may see all that I see; for I want you to
share all my experiences that are instructive and pleasant.

This morning a delegation from Mississippi called on me and made a
remarkable statement of the outrages and intimidation practiced in that state by
the rebel Democracy. If half they tell is correct, the election in that state was an
outrage on good government beyond endurance. And yet as that state is wholly
in the hands of the Democracy, and as they have carried all their electors and
Congressmen, there seems to be no means of correcting the wrong; and so that
state must be counted for Tilden, and its congressional vote must give the
House to the Democracy. I hope the disclosure of the facts will result in awak-
ening our people to the necessity of putting national elections under the control
of national officers, and bringing the result under national supervision. I have
new occasion to thank Mollie for the good letter in which she has, a second
time, remembered her absent papa. I wrote her and Harry a long letter, which I
hope they will have received before this reaches you. I am well and I want you

to dismiss all anxiety about my personal safety. These people are on their good behavior and no harm will happen to any of us who are visiting them. Ever and all your own James.

Gulf of Mexico. On board the steamer Rio Grande,
November 21, 1876.

Dear Friends at Home:

I hope it will interest you to follow me on my trip, which is now half completed, to the great work now in progress to deepen the mouths of the Mississippi by means of jetties. Eight or ten of our party accepted the invitation of Capt. Eads, the great engineer in charge of the work, and at eight o'clock last evening we went on board the little steamer "Julia" and started down the river. In about two hours the fog was so dense that it was not safe to run, and we tied up for the night, and slept soundly until morning. About eight this morning the fog lifted, and we went on down the great river. Vast plantations, producing cotton, sugar cane, or rice, lined the banks on either side; and great orange groves made the shores beautiful with green and gold. Great mills for manufacturing and refining sugar, with their tall white chimneys and taller columns of black smoke, were seen at almost every bend of the river. When we had steamed down seventy-five miles below the city, we came to Forts Jackson and Philip, which were captured by Admiral Farragut early in the War. If you will take my large book, Harpers History of the War, you will find a most interesting account of the bombardment of these forts, and the passage of Farragut's fleet under the fire of the forts, and the subsequent capture of New Orleans. Gen Beauregard was with us; and he gave us a full account of the battle. He also told me quite fully the history of the battle of Shiloh, in which we were both engaged. After the fall of Gen. A. S. Johnston, he commanded the rebel army and suffered defeat on the second day of the battle. It was curious to hear the story of the battle by the rebel commander.

After passing the forts, we soon came to the last of the plantations; for you will remember that the lower portion of the river is bounded by marsh and flat sandy land, formed by the deposits of earth brought down by the current. By looking at the map, you will see that the river has built out into the gulf a mass of land, but most of it is still too flat and too near the surface of the water to be tillable, though, in the course of a century, it may be.

Twenty-five miles below the forts we came to the point where the river divides into the three mouths, or passes, which form the delta. By looking over your maps, you will find that nearly all the rivers which empty into enclosed gulfs form deltas at their mouths. This is because the dead water in gulfs leaves but little tide, and the river current becomes so sluggish that the mud and sand are deposited near the mouth and form a great bar. When the river is high, it forces channels through the bar and thus forms the several mouths or passes to the salt water. Just above the delta the river broadens into a wide bay from which the three passes make their way to the sea. The eastern pass is called "pass a l'outre"; the western one, the south west, and the central one, the south pass. We descended the latter pass ten miles to the open gulf. Its banks were thick grown with wildcane, a kind of gigantic grass which grows to the height of ten or fifteen feet; and every few moments we saw alligators that had crawled up on the shore and were sunning themselves in the edge of the grass. Several of our party fired pistols at them, but the huge fellows, eight or ten feet long, lazily slid back into the river, apparently caring less for the bullets than for the noise. The shores of the pass were low and narrow; and on either side, the blue waters of the gulf stretched away east and west. About half a mile to the eastward we saw a vast flock of white pelicans, which (Irvin will remember we read to him about in Audubon) were wading in the shallow water near a low lying island. When we had gone down the South Pass about eight miles, we came to the beginning of the jetties. They are formed by making what they call "mattresses" composed of willows about 30 feet long, fastened together in the form of a bedmattress, each about 30 feet square and three feet thick. They float these out to the proper place and load them with stone and sink them to the bottom, where the willows soon fill up with earth and sand and thus make the foundation of a wall. Then they lay other mattresses upon these until the wall reaches the surface of the water. In this way they have formed two parallel walls, one thousand feet apart and two and a half miles long. These two lines of jetties are now built up to the surface of the water. When they began work a year and a half ago there was only about fourteen feet of water in the south pass. By building the jetties, the current of the pass is made more narrow at the mouth and therefore more rapid; and it has cut the channel down so fast that there are now nearly 20 feet of water the whole length of the pass.

We steamed out beyond the end of the jetties and floated on the open waters of the Gulf of Mexico, which, with its deep blue water, stretched away to the soft summer sky. Great white seagulls, long-necked cranes, brown pelicans and many bright winged birds were in sight; and away off on the shallow water, along side the jetties, long-legged wading birds were dipping their bills into the sand in search for food. At eight o'clock we were on board the steamer Rio Grande, and starting back to the city. This steamer was built on the Clyde at Glasgow, Scotland, was brought here by the rebels as a blockade runner, and was twice captured. It is a very swift running boat and we steamed up the river at the rate of fifteen miles an hour. You can hardly imagine the beauty of the sunset in this soft southern sky. I sat on deck and watched the gathering shades of twilight. The shadows of the willows and orange groves on the banks were reflected in the dark mirror of the river; and as the stars came out, one by one, the earth and sky were very beautiful. I looked long for the north star; the dip-per was below the horizon. You could have seen it at that hour, but I am so far south that many of our northern stars are out of sight. We took tea on board; talked of the war, and of the early days when LaSalle and other French men sailed along this great wild river before any white man lived upon its banks. Then of days of 1812 when Jackson defeated near New Orleans the great army of veterans who had fought under the Duke of Wellington. And so the talk went on, until near midnight we saw the bright semicircle of lights on the wharves of the great city. It was too late to go up to Judge Pardee's house; and so I took a room at the St. Charles and slept until seven this morning. The only event which marred the happiness of the day was the fact that on my return I found no letter from the dear ones at home. At eleven this morning I came to the State House to attend the session of the Returning Board; and have written this last sheet while the noise and bustle of the counting was going on.

God bless you all, my dearest and best of friends! I wanted you all with me to see and enjoy the trip to the Gulf. More still, I want to be with you in our own quiet home. When that will be I cannot tell, for the work here drags on very slowly and grows more important at each step. With my heart full of love to you all. I am all your own J.A.Garfield.

Louisville and Cincinnati train.
December 4, 1876.

My Darling:

I expected to have reached home in time to eat breakfast with you tomor-row morning. But it is thought very important for our party to see Mr. Hayes, and so we all go to Columbus this morning. We shall leave there tonight and reach Washington Tuesday evening. Judge Martin, who goes through tonight, will call and hand you this. Living in the hope of seeing you all soon, I am as ever Your James.

On 31 October 1876, James completed the purchase of a farm near Mentor, Ohio, about a half mile east of a farm owned by his old friend, Doc Robison. The following April the Garfields began work on the old farmhouse. "The general state of chaos opens before us a fine field for work and contrivance," James wrote in his diary.[15] That spring, James and Lucretia spent days shopping in Cleveland for what would now be their summer quarters in Ohio. They moved books and furniture from Hiram, built a library for the house, bought some farm animals, harrowed and planted the fields, and settled into a busy life of farming, reading and letter writing. Near the end of May James left in order to participate in a trial in Mobile, Alabama. Lucretia stayed on in Mentor.

Mentor, Ohio. May 30, 1877

My Darling:

Your note from Buffalo we did not get until yesterday, Tuesday 2 P.M. I had already started whatever mail there was by the early morning train to Washington hoping you may receive it before leaving this evening. Doctor [Robison] came down yesterday morning and put into better running shape the work that was dragging. Butler began to plough the "sorrel field" yesterday noon and is going on with it today. Bancroft drew off the stumps from the meadows and is today sowing plaster. I asked him yesterday if he had planted the sweet corn by his house. He said he told you that he would like all that garden for himself and that you said all right. Of course I couldn't contradict him, but I don't believe you ever told him he could have all that acre. I am thoroughly disgusted with a man with a family on the place. His wife is of no account in the world to us, and I'll warrant they will get a good support off the farm beside their wages. Doctor says a great deal of the corn will need to be planted over in the fields that you harried _____ so marvelously. Also that the ants and cut-worm are playing the mischief. Behold the farmer's vexations! But enough of complaints. We must take the bitter with the sweet, and be thankful that there is no bitterness in our love, that our heartaches are for each other when miles and days intervene with long loneliness and even that brings the "fuller gain of after bliss." Darling, write to me often, for your letters are the sunshine of your absence, even the poor meagre little postal card had one or two rays in it. We are all well and send love. Yours as ever, Crete.

Mobile, Ala. June 4, 1877

My Darling:

You are "the shadow of a great rock in a weary land." At the close of a day of heat and work and while sitting down to a long evening of work among the tangles of a most intricate case, your sweet letter of the 31st May comes to me all full of love and blessings, and at once I turn aside from the case to tell you how happy I am with the treasure. How it brightens the long pathway of dusty, hot miles between us to know that your dove has shaken her white wings over every hill and valley of the 1200 miles that separate us. It is the sweet compensation which absence brings. I am so glad I can now think of you as having help enough to lighten the burdens that were resting on the dear little shoulders when I came away. I think of you with the changes and betterments which have been made since I left you and rejoice in the thought that they are all made for you. Darling, do you ever stop to think that you are the centre and soul of all our circle? Do you remember the circular stone in the old Roman Forum in which centered the roads from Europe, Asia and Africa? "All roads lead to Rome" says the old proverb. In the Directory of my life all roads lead to Crete. Even when I am going away from you, I remember I am travelling on a circuit which ends in your arms, and so the car wheels sing of you as they hurry me on.

I have nearly recovered from the diarrhea of which I wrote you yesterday and have begun to feel my grip on the lawyers and the case. It was poorly prepared when I came, but I am gathering up the threads of the case into my hands. It was called today and, after a little preliminary skirmishing, was set down for tomorrow morning at ten o'clock. There are, in fact, three cases, and they may all be heard in one. I am strongly in hopes we shall see the end of them before the close of the week. Did I tell you, in my last, that Cowles telegraphs me that Schneider has declined the Swiss Mission, and he wants me to go to Washington again and get it for him? After all that has happened, I cannot refuse and so shall probably be compelled to go home via Washington, which will add two days to my absence. Surely the way of politics is hard.[16]

I shall look to you for the daily bread of my heart until I leave here. I will telegraph you when you need not write more, though I half incline not to do it, so
that some of your letters may follow me to Mentor. Thank the boys for me for
their better report of Thursday last.

Ever your James.

Mentor, June 5, 1877.

My Darling:

I don't know what does ail Jim. Yesterday he was one of the best boys in
the world, was happy, and acknowledged that it was because he was so good.
This morning without any apparent reason he is pouting and cross and so
crabbed about his Latin that it is enough to make one's soul cry out with the
pain he gives. I don't know how to manage him. I cannot conceive of any possible reason why he should be such a trial to my life, nor do I believe it possible
for you to know what a wearing worrying child he is. I cannot be patient with
him, any more than I could submit with patience to some extreme physical torture. What he will ever become I don't know, and I am almost afraid to think of
his future. Just now I hear him reciting his lesson with a pleasant, kind voice,
and so from morning till night I never know one moment what he may do the
next. I am sorry to write you such a blue letter, but I have told Jim that I will
write him down just as he is. It is horrible to be a man but the grinding misery
of being a woman between the upper and nether millstone of household cares
and training children is almost as bad. To be half civilized with some aspirations
for enlightenment, and obliged to spend the largest part of the time the victim
of young barbarians keeps one in a perpetual ferment. Now, I will stop, and
complain a while of *things* or of one thing. The drain seems to be out of order.
The water comes into the tank only in small jets and of course is fast being low-
ered. We have sent to Mr. Northcote, and he says he will come and see what is
the trouble.[17] Every thing else is going on splendidly. Today it is raining
superbly, for which we cannot be too thankful. I hope your work will not keep
you long. It is a glad pleasure to live with you in spite of all discomforts. Jim is
good-natured at this moment, and I will close in this burst of home sunshine.
Ever and forever yours, Crete.

Mentor, June 8, 1877.

My Darling:

Night before last two boxes of plants came from Washington, one of house plants which I inferred were for Mr. Steele, so I decided not to go to Cleveland yesterday, but Jim and I were up at five o'clock and at six started for Painesville with Mr. Steele's[18] box. His gardener gave us a quantity of his plants so that after I'd reached home at 9 A.M. and had spent an hour in arithmetic, I worked nearly all the time until dark arranging and setting out plants. Then went with the children to the strawberry festival. This morning I awoke so tired and lame that I concluded to stay at home today and go to C[levelan]d tomorrow. Your Library is not finished yet but the grainers say that we can put the books in as soon as next Thursday, so if we can have the greys [horses] on Monday we will go to Hiram.

Yesterday I received your first two precious letters from Mobile. Darling, I wonder if there is another man in the world who by every word and deed both when present and absent is able to make his wife so happy. I am conscious of a great deal of natural perversity for ever becoming impatient or disturbed. The consciousness of your blessed care and loving protection ought to keep me forever placid and happy. Our dear old Jim! we came so near to losing him yesterday that I hope I may be a little more patient with him than some of my former letters have indicated. Mr. Bancroft took him into the field with him to unload tile. Jim got tired and sat down on the wagon seat. There was an umbrella on the seat and as he sat down he thought it broke, and with one of his dashes he turned his back to the horses and threw open the umbrella to see what he had done. The horses caught sight of it, gave a leap, and started for the barn. They dashed over a stump, tearing it out by the roots, and rushed across the road straight up the hill east of the sandbank. Jim had caught up the reins by this time, and as he saw them plunging for the bank pulled the rein in time to save them from going over, but they dashed against the fence with such force as to break off a post and drive the fence back. The wheel then struck the roots of the old tree at the head of the lane, and as they turned into the lane, the wagon box with Jim and the tile were thrown whirling into the air and dashed to the ground. Mr. Bancroft says he looked on feeling perfectly sure that Jim was killed. But by the time the horses had reached the barnyard gates, Jim crawled up and says he saw them dash through the gates and bring up astride the old locust west of the house. The crash brought us all to our feet. Both horses were broken loose, the tongue of the wagon broken and the part left on the wagon plunged a foot into the turf. You may imagine our terror, knowing that Mr. Bancroft and Jim had been with them, and we made a general rush for the lane, but before we reached the barnyard their two heads appeared above the hill, to our great relief. As the horses broke loose at the locust tree one of the carpenters caught one and the other after running around the house dashed away to the stable where he was caught. Jim was scarcely scratched, although he says he can remember nothing after he felt the shock of striking the fence and then the roots of the tree, until he "woke up" as he says with the wagon box on his head, and looking up saw the horses just going through the gates. Today he has a headache and begins to feel lame. Surely the good angels must have been near him, and I am very thankful to the Good All Loving Father that he has saved him to us. My fear now is that the horses have been nearly ruined with the fright. They were the most terrified creatures I ever saw. I have been hoping all day to receive the telegram you promised to tell me that I need not send more letters to Mobile, and I think I will send this to Washington to meet you there. Can you bring a volume of Shakespeare? Also a little shawl of mine at Miss Ransom's?[19] I am afraid you will be disappointed that more has not been done when you return, but there is so much to be done, and then I think it needs someone to manage for the men. I often notice where a little headwork would help them to accomplish a good deal more without adding to the labor, but I haven't the courage to suggest to them my ideas. Men have so much contempt for a woman's ideas, especially men without culture. I will stop now after saying all are all very good now.

Ever yours, Crete.

Evening

Darling, I received Mr. Duncan's[20] dispatch this P.M. Am very glad that you turn your face homeward tomorrow. I send this letter to care of Mr. Touhay lest it may be forwarded to Mentor before you reach Washington. Present my very kindest regards to the Touhays.[21] How soon may we expect you home? I hope you may be here before another week has passed. Jimmie has been on the bed or lounge all day but is sleeping quietly now and I hope he will be quite recovered tomorrow morning. Do not worry about him for if he is not as well I will telegraph to you. With kisses and all hope that you may be brought safely home to us, I am as ever, yours, Crete.

*In September, Lucretia visited her sister Nellie and family in St. Louis, taking her
mother with her. James, of course, was on the stump in Ohio.*

Kenton, Ohio. Sept 17, 1877

My Darling:

After a very weary, sleepy and breakfastless ride of seven hours, I arrived at
Kenton a little after eleven. The town was astir with expectation to get a sight of
the President and his party who were to pass southward. A large concourse
waited at the Depot until his train came and went. I stood within thirty feet of
dear old Gen Rosecrans as he came out on the rear platform of the President's
car and spoke a few words to the crowd, but he did not see me. The President
was looking plump and even burly. Soon as the train was gone the great crowd
surged up to the public square, where a platform had been erected facing the
wind, and near the roar of wagons in the street. Just across the street behind me
three carpenters were furiously hammering on roof boards to protect a new
building from a storm of rain and wind that seemed to threaten. Under these
cheering circumstances I tried for an hour and a half to make 5000 people hear
me, and though I succeeded, it left me soaked with perspiration and choked with
hoarseness. I rested all day yesterday and am somewhat better this morning. I
ride ten miles to Dunkirk, a station on the Pitts & Ft W R.R. and go thence to
Van Wert, where I am to think of you as sweeping by me at only ten miles distance and away into the night. Somehow I can't help but feel that I am neglecting
you to let you go off without me. If I were only ill enough to cancel my appoint-
ments and go with you, I should be quite reconciled. The Committee have
changed my appointment for Ashland, or rather have withdrawn it. I am to
speak at Galion Friday, whence I reach Cleveland on the 7 A.M. train Saturday.
Let me hear from you at Galion, so that I may know what train you will arrive
on. I shall be in Columbus Thursday evening and Friday morning and your letters previous to the Galion letter should be sent to the care of Gen J. S.
Robinson,[22] Columbus. I shall probably speak in Painesville next Saturday, but
whether P.M. or evening I do not yet know. Give my love to Nell and Carn and
Archie and the Udulls, also to our dear Mother. And darling, do write to the love
lorn wandering man, whose highest joy be wholly and always Your James.

St. Louis, Sept. 19, 1877

My Darling:

Just as I had your letter of yesterday sealed I received the one you sent from Kenton. It was so sweet to find your dear words following me away over the wide prairies. Darling, how our love enriches and ennobles life. There is not much of life but love, and when it [is] so strong, so full of royal wealth, so kingly as ours has grown to be, then life is a kingly inheritance, and I blame myself that anything should ever annoy me when you give me so much to make life so full and ripe, so full of pure true enjoyment. Darling, I have been almost hoping that you would get sick enough to come on here for a day or two to go home with me, but it will be only two days more now before Saturday, and my heart is full of prayer that we be allowed then to meet in our dear little home with all the loved ones there well and happy. We are having a pleasant visit, and Mother is feeling so well that I am very glad I came. Today we drove out to Shaws Gardens and through Tower park. I am surprised to find St. Louis so beautiful a city. The parks remind me of the London parks more than anything I have seen in this country. Darling, I shall leave here if nothing prevents on Friday evening and shall reach Cleveland 2 P.M. Saturday and get home in time to meet you on your return from Painesville. With love in which all join, I remain the same as ever loving you always. Crete.

P.S. Nellie says tell you she "wants to see you awfully" and so wishes you could come now.

Back again in Washington for the work of politics, James and his family spent the season of 1877–1878 together as usual.

House of Representatives
April 22, 1878.

My Darling:

You and I are invited by Mr. Ford, Manager of the Washington and Balto. Theatres, to join a party of 40 or 50 ladies and gentlemen to go at 5:30 P.M. to Baltimore and hear Booth in Hamlet.[23] He will take us and bring us back tonight.

Will you go if I find it possible to get away?

Answer.

Always Your Own James.

Back campaigning in Ohio during the fall of 1878, James writes to Crete on the farm in Mentor.

Pomeroy, O. Sept.24, 1878.

My Darling:

How I want you here to see one of the loveliest homes I know! V. B. Horton, born in Windsor Vt., near where your mother was, is now 76 years of age. His wife, a Boston lady, is nearly as old. They settled here 50 years ago. In a short, deep, broad ravine which descends from the very high river bank, and two thirds of the way up toward the summit, stands their great roomy house from which on two sides descends a steeply sloping wooded lawn stretching to the water's edge. The broad river and bluff hills of [West] Va. lie in sight beyond. Behind the house the shelter of wooded hills, a cool retreat for summer, a warm nest for winter. Here their three daughters, Mrs. Pope, Mrs. Judge Force, Mrs. May (her husband a Harvard professor), and their two sons were born, and here all their children on summer pilgrimages to the birth shrine.

Mr. Horton studied law in his early manhood with Samuel Dana of Conn. who was a member of Congress 24 years, beginning with Washington's administration, and thus heard many an anecdote of that early period from one who was a conspicuous character in the events of our beginning as a nation. Mr. H. was three terms in Congress before the war, and is now a candidate against Gen Ewing. I hope he may be elected, for, among other reasons, I want you to know the noble old man, who is so fine an example of a patriarch and a gentleman of the old school.

I had a very enthusiastic meeting at Logan yesterday, came back to Athens and spent the night; and this morning was driven in a carriage 30 miles to this place. I have just spoken out of doors to 5000 people and must speak tonight at Middleport to an out doors audience. My voice has held up unusually well, and I am in hopes of bringing it home to you, not wholly destroyed. The day after tomorrow is bright with the promise of letters from you. I have written this with the worst pen I ever encountered.

All your own James.

Pomeroy, Sept. 25.

My Darling:

And now I want you for another reason. Mrs. Force, wife of Judge Force of Cincinnati, who is staying with her father and mother, is full of all the new knowledge about floors, wood, carpet, rugs, wallpaper and paint. I only say enough now to remind you of my wish to talk it over with you when we meet. The points to which my mind gravitates are these:

1. Adopt Rugs instead of carpets—both for beauty and economy.
2. For borders lay down wool carpets or stain the floor.
2. The question of paint vs. paper must be further discussed. Mrs. Force and the Hortons condemn paper on the ground that nearly all paper has arsenic as an ingredient in its color. We must look to this.
3. Remind me of a recipe which Mrs. Force is to give me about treating floors.

I spoke nearly two hours at Middleport last night to an immense audience and am nearly well in voice this morning. At 9:30 A.M. Mr. Horton and I leave by buggy for Porter, Gallia Co. within ten miles of the Yellow Fever. Tomorrow Chillicothe and your letters. Forever and everywhere Your Own James.

In the late spring of 1879, Crete was once again back at Hiram to help with her ailing mother.

Hiram, May 8, 1879.

My Darling:

I don't know what Grandma thinks of her daughter. Yesterday she lay looking at me very seriously for a long time. I wondered what she was thinking about, but she said nothing, and I did not ask. This morning Martha[24] told me something which may explain it. She said Mother broke out one day in this lamentation. "It is too bad that James has been defeated for Senator. He has worked so hard for it, and Crete is all mixed up in it." I don't know but she thinks I have grown to be a troublesome intriguing woman. Or is her mind wandering in prophecy? I confess it worries me a little. Are you to be hurt by me through the past? I hope not. Or perhaps it is only the wandering of a distempered imagination. Yesterday she asked Joe[25] if Gen Grant had gotten the nomination for the Presidency. Her condition is very singular. She is perfectly conscious, knows everyone who comes in to see her perfectly well, and remembers whatever we can get her to understand; but every now and then asks those strange questions, or makes remarks like the one above about me. She does not seem to suffer any pain and lies quiet nearly all the time. She has wasted almost to a skeleton, although she eats as much as any one in good health.

I have received two letters from Jimmy, sent over from Mentor. I hope his sprained ankle may not prove troublesome. It was very funny that Miss Ware should have been able to tell him so much of his history. Ask him if he does not think there must be something in the lines of the hand which does tell the story of life. Tell Hal that I conclude his surgical duties must be heavy since he does not find time to write, too. . . . I am hoping to get a letter from you today. I think of you and the boys as having a good time, and wish I could be with you. . . . I have seen Burke only for a moment, and Phebe not at all. I get letters from Mentor every day. They are getting on nicely. Mr. Tyler and his sister write that they will be very glad to take our house for the summer.[26] I think they had better have it. With all my heart of love for the dear boys and the wholest whole for you. Ever yours. Crete.

Hiram, May 14th, 1879.

My Darling:

Yours of Sunday with all the inclosures came last evening. Some of your letters come at noon and some in the evening. These come like a benediction. After all the care of the busy day is over, the children and Mother quietly asleep for the night, it is such a sweet rest to sit down with an unopened letter in my hand with the most perfect assurance that whatever else it may contain, there will be a great wave of love to fall over me and envelope me in its grand life giving power. Next to your own coming is the arrival of a letter from you, and next to nestling nearest your heart is the delight it gives me to write to you. Mother continues just the same for aught I can see. She is sitting up now on the east porch and seems very comfortable. The weather is very warm and dry, and Mother's chief suffering is from the heat. I had a letter yesterday from your Mother. I had written asking her if she would not like to come to Hiram before going to Mentor. But she writes not. That the warm weather so overcomes her that she only wants to get home. I intend now to go home on Saturday and will write to her to meet me at the depot at Solon and go with me. When I see Burke again I will read him what you have written about the present contest.

I think he is a little, or perhaps a good [deal] anxious to hear from you. I hope you will comb him down thoroughly. It compensates largely for my absence from you that you and the boys are getting into so much more intimate relations. They will never forget these days with you, and I believe they will lay the foundation for future companionship between you which will be broader than you might have ever otherwise gained. Draw them out in every way that the opportunity gives and get into their minds and hearts, and then put as much of your own mental and spiritual life into theirs as you can. I want them to realize to the fullest the kind of man they have for a Father and be inspired to emulate you in every way. Tell Jimmy that he must find out whether there is one or two t's in the past participle of *write* and that Ernest is spelled without an a. All the other words in his letter were spelled right—would you say "rightly"? On Sunday neither the chairs nor paper had arrived at Mentor. I sent a note to Herendon[27] and hope they will not be delayed longer. They write from the Mentor home that everything is going on nicely. Dr. [Robison] says however that he met with a misfortune on Sunday. His hat which had just been bought the day before had tumbled into the privy vault. Last summer he lost a coat there. I hope he will not continue to make deposits in like manner. The chance for dividends is too unpromising.

My love to dear old Hal and Jim, and for yourself the perfectest of all love, that which embraces all others. Ever Yours, Crete.

The gossip Crete mentions in the following letter, which seems to have originated with Mrs. Spencer, was particularly irksome to her since the Spencers had been close Washington friends for many years.

Mentor, May 18th, 1879

My Darling:

I was able to come home yesterday, and it is a great delight to be here again. I left mother in about the same condition. I suppose she must be gradually failing, but it is so slowly that it is scarcely perceptible. I must go back to Hiram tomorrow, and if Mother lives stay until Nellie comes. The farm and garden are looking well in spite of the dry weather, and everything is going on tolerably well. A few complaints have been lodged—Jerry and Miss Mays are indignant that Josie was taken into the field to work, and especially that Green was so sharp with her that he scared her. Today on his way from church Dr. Robison called me aside to say to me that Telegraph Operator Green told him at church today that Jerry was driving Josie around nights up and down the street, whipping and driving her in such a manner that some of the people talked of arresting him, and they wanted you informed. The Doctor and I agreed that it would be best for Norcote [Northcote] to take him in hand; for he works well about the house and garden, and we thought he would probably do better if he did not know that we about the house knew of his behavior. Norcote is to see that he never takes Josie out except by our order. It is evident Josie has not been treated properly. She does not seem nearly so gentle as she was last summer, and I am both hurt and angry over it. When shall we ever find anyone to trust? So much for the farm.

But I am much more hurt—no, angry—over a thing Anna Boynton told me yesterday. A Mrs. Keller—I think that is the name, a woman's Right woman—told a friend of Anna's that when Mrs. Spencer was in Cleveland she told her that General Garfield was a very licentious man, and gave as evidence that on one occasion you went to New York in company with a notorious woman telling me that you were going on business, that on your arrival there some friend of mine saw you with this woman and telegraphed to me and that I went on and confronted you. This has come so straight that there is no doubt about it. I don't know whether to write to Mrs. Spencer or wait until I see her, but whatever I do she shall know the opinion in which I hold her, or at least the opinion in which I hold her doings. Darling, we will put our trust in each other and God, and hold our lives so true and so pure that our own hearts shall approve, and then wherever our feet may be led our heads shall always be in the sunlight. Is there any hope that you can soon come home? The papers yesterday were foretelling a closing up of the session in the course of two or three weeks. But I am afraid they don't know. It has been three days now that I have had no letter from you, but I have not written, therefore cannot complain. I hope this silence will soon close up with a grand triette. The piano has arrived. I don't like its tone very well, but perhaps it may improve. With love in which Grandma who came with me joins, I am as ever your own Crete.

Washington, May 20, 1879

My Darling:

We were nearly famished for want of letters from home, until yours from Mentor came to me at the Capitol today, although we have been generously dealt with both by you and by the family at Mentor. Still we had no letters for two days, and that was so unusual that we felt it all the more. I am sorry you could not have staid with the children and I hope Nellie will soon come to Hiram to relieve you. You have said nothing to me about the state of your health, and I am constantly anxious lest you overwork yourself, which is very perilous at your time of life. Please tell me specially your situation and condition of health, and I beg you to be very careful of your health, which is so precious in our sight. . . . I will write Northcott to discharge Jerry, or any one else, who uses Josie without orders. Men seem to think they can impose upon me in my absence as much as the social scavengers do here.

What you hear of Mrs. Spencer is simply infamous, and if she said it, she ought never again to be recognized by us. I am in doubt whether I will call on her and state the case as you have written it, or suggest that you write. Only think of it. She has been here twice to see me in reference to getting a commit-tee and when she came day before yesterday she talked of her family affairs as if I were one of her most intimate and trusted friends.

Indeed, she said things of her family which I am quite sure you would never speak of to any man but me. If she said what Miss Keller reports, she must have known she was making a lie out of whole cloth. I am quite sure I never went to New York with any woman but you, and the part of the story which refers to you is of course equally without foundation. It really seems as though the spirits of evil had combined to assail me. With the single exception of Mary Clemmer's article,[28] no one of them have ever ventured to carry the warfare beyond their own vicious circle. Perhaps it was not discreet, but Carrie [Ransom] called here this evening, and I told her the substance of what you wrote on that subject. She says several persons have told her that Mrs. Spencer is untruthful to the last degree. But Carrie says she has frequently heard her speak in my praise, and had never heard anything of this story. I charged her to say nothing about it. She thinks you had better write to Mrs. S. directly and that you can put the case better than you could in conversation. Do what you think best, but let me know your conclusion. If you want me to do so, I will write to her, or see her. Carrie says there's a Miss Keller who is, or was, a teacher in the Cleveland schools. It appears to me that Mrs. S. who knows the love that reigns in our home, is enraged at the spectacle and would be glad to destroy it, as part of her scheme of alienating all husbands and wives. The doc-trine she holds is a demon that would ruin every home if it could. When we meet I will tell you some of her talk when she was here last. If you conclude to write her, suppose you send me a draft of the letter that I may return it to you with any suggestions that may occur to me before you send it.

It is midnight, and I write this while waiting for Hal to return from the May ball. Jim has worked at his lessons faithfully, until ten minutes ago, when he went to bed. With a love that I do not believe the power of hate can shake, I am more than ever Your Own James.

Hiram, May 23rd, 1879

My Darling:

I received last night yours in answer to the one I wrote from the farm. It was the first I had had since Monday, and I was getting very hungry for words from you. Do you now intend to come to Ohio for the Cincinnati Convention on the 28th? If so, will the boys come home? Let me know so that I may meet you in Cleveland and go out home for a night. Mother seems a little stronger for the last day or two and a little more like herself in mind, although she is very flighty and says very queer things. I believe if she were dying she would say something to make us all laugh. Last night I went in to see her before going to bed. I suppose she thought I was Addie, and she looked up into my face and said, "Are you going to marry Schadel?"—a young man who comes to see Addie sometimes. I answered whom do you think I am, but she said "Well are you going to marry anybody?" I said I am married, and she replied, "O I am so glad, when were you married?" I answered, twenty years ago. She looked surprised and asked, "Whom did you marry?" I said, Why Mother don't you know? James Garfield. O yes, she said. Well, you have had a pretty stormy time of it. I answered, no: I have had a very good time. Well, yes, she said, "He shall have some succatash when he comes."

This is a specimen of the way she wanders around in her mind. I do not see now why she may not live on through the summer, and I hope as her strength comes back she may grow more natural, though I fear she is very much broken. Tell the boys they must not wait for me to answer all their letters. When I write to you, they get all the news, and my praise for the dear good boys they are, and I want them to write me frequently about all their doings. I want to hear Hal's report of the May ball, and Jim's of whatever he is interested in. I had a letter from Mentor last night, too. They are all well and getting on beautifully. They say Grandma seems very happy and contented, and it is a pleasure to them that she is there. When are we all to gather in our dear home again? a home so hedged about with your careful protection and so fed _____ and glorified with your great love! Darling, it is so wicked that anyone should dare to assail your loyalty and fidelity to home and wife. I have sent to Mrs. Spencer a letter of which the inclosed is a copy. You can do whatever you think best in regard to it. I have sent it to her without waiting for your opinion so that the charge could not be made that you had revised it, or that it was instigated by you. It makes me nearly sick to write such a letter, but I felt that I must. This reminds me that you have asked after my health. I am very well and I will guard my health if for nothing else [than] to be your defender, and to save you from anxiety. The second plaster is received, opened but not lost. What have you decided about the house? Is Mary McGrath still there? Tell the boys if they want to bring home their fancy ball costumes that they will find them in a box, either in their closet or on one of the shelves of the big closet. With love from all the family here to you all, I am with bravest love,

Yours forever, Crete.

Lucretia to Mrs. Spencer

My Dear Mrs. Spencer

I don't know how else to address you although my heart is full of bitterness toward you. A story has come to me so straight that I cannot doubt it, namely that while you were in Cleveland attending some convention, you said to a Miss Keller that General Garfield was a bad, licentious man and gave as proof that on a certain occasion he went to New York with a notorious woman, having told his wife that he was going on business. That a friend of Mrs. G's in New York met them on the street and telegraphed to her, and that she went on and confronted them. Now that whole story is nothing more nor less than an infamous lie. You may have heard it. The General has malignant enemies who not only turn to his disadvantage every act which they can torture into wrong, but who willfully say what they must know to be false.

But when you who have professed friendship for so many years could have given credence and currency to such a report and branded with licentiousness the reputation of a man whom you have been able to know so much about, I am utterly unable to explain to my own mind how it could have been unless in your infatuation over the Rights of Woman you allowed spite to triumph over reason and all friendship in your opinion of a man whose councils led him to disagree with you, and I must say to you that you could have given me no better proof of your unfitness to be in public life, no better illustration of the methods you would employ to gain your ends than you have given in coming with compliment and praise and with friendly kiss to ask favors of a man whom, if what you have said of him you believe to be true, you should have felt it contamination to approach, except to rebuke.

Pardon me if I am unjust. I can pass an avowed enemy by with silent disdain when they can gratify their hate only with calumny. But when one whom we have called friend strikes such a wicked blow I cannot let the bitterness in my heart be silent and keep up the appearance of friendship.

With sorrow and regret that I must say these things to you, I am as ever, Lucretia R. Garfield

Washington, May 26, 1879

My Darling:

After I had written you yesterday morning, I mentioned to the boys the possibility of my getting a chance to see you while in Ohio, but said I would not do so if they preferred to have me come directly back from Cincinnati. They both insisted that I should go to see you, and if possible go with you to Mentor. Just before the mail went out this morning, they hurried off a postal card to you asking you to have me come home by way of Mentor. The dear fellows are as tender of us both as though we were children and they were men.

I leave for Cincinnati by the 11 o'clock train tonight, and I am writing this half an hour before leaving for the cars. Townsend and Updegraff go with me.[29]

I write now to say that Mrs. Spencer came here early this morning in great grief over your letter. She broke down more than I ever saw her before. She said in the most positive manner that there was not a word of truth in the Cleveland charge against her; that she had never heard of the story, nor any semblance of it; that she did not know Miss Keller and that she had always and everywhere defended me against assaults. She said all this so positively and with so much feeling that I am compelled to believe her. She brought a letter to me from Henry, which I enclose. The whole affair puzzles me exceedingly, and I don't know what to make of it. I have received incidental proof, independent of Mrs. S., that she has on several occasions defended me when I have been assailed in her presence. I think we are bound to accept her statement of the case until we have other evidence, though of course you can judge of the Cleveland end of the story better than I can.

I will try to leave Cincinnati Wednesday night if you will let me, and meet you in Cleveland Thursday morning. We can go out home on the 11:15 train and see the little ones. I do hope it will be possible for us to do this. I will telegraph you in Cincinnati if there is any change in this programme. If you hear nothing to the contrary, please go to Cleveland on the Thursday morning train and I will meet you at the Atlantic Depot. The boys join me in love to you, most precious wife. Your Own James.

Mentor, June 17, 1879

My Darling:

You can scarcely imagine the sweet quiet pleasure the dear home is giving me. I came home yesterday to stay until they send for me, and were it not for my poor sick dying Mother I should be as perfectly happy as I can be away from you. Our yard and garden are a delight—so thrifty and tidy. Jerry[30] is a capital gardener and keeps everything about the yard as clean as a good housewife keeps her kitchen. The roads are not quite a success yet. The gravel doesn't pack. I think it needs something with it. But we will leave a few things for you to look after when you come. Is hope to be deferred again? and are you not to be here this week? The only thing that makes the prospect of delay endurable is that I do believe you and the boys are having a royally good time, and to you all a valuable experience especially to the boys. Tell the dear old fellows that Irv and Abe have started out on their own hook for the first time today, and I think their adventures will interest you all.

This morning Irvin came to me to borrow (?) five cents. On questioning him I found it was to buy a fishing line. I saw from his manner that the boy-spirit was bursting out, and a little freedom must be given rein to. Therefore, the five cents was loaned, and thereupon he started for Dr. Luce's store. At noon Abe with Miss Mays for escort went to the store for the same purpose. In the meantime Irv was digging bait. After putting on warmer clothes (for it is very cold) they were finally ready for a start. They watched the clock for Eddy Green to come from school, and when it was four o'clock away went the three young fishermen for Rose's brook. Irvin said he thought they would be home by *sundown*. When we were at supper we saw a little straw hat trotting up the road, and presently Abe appeared at the table with the trotting hat still on, very resolute but somewhat subdued. We all looked but kept silent, when the following monologue was delivered: "Say, I lost my fishing line but didn't lose my knife. Irv lost his line, too (pause) and his suspenders!" (Exclamations all around the table) "Yes, he took off his clothes to go in swimming"—"only to sit down in the water," as Irv explained when he arrived as cold as a frog—"and his suspenders got lost; and I got a fishhook in my toe and in my finger, but I got it out: my finger is awful sore." But where are your fish? we asked. "Eddy Green's hook caught on a great big one in the bottom of the brook but it was so big he couldn't pull it out, and mine did, too. Then Eddy said he didn't care anything about his line and he gave it to Irv to tie on his pants." I put the two adventurers down by a warm fire where they talked over their exploits until bed time, and no doubt now they are dreaming them over again.

Yesterday and today letters have come from each of you for which we are very thankful. Miss Mays wishes me to say that she is very pleased with yours to her, and that she shall always keep it. Jimmy asked in one of his last letters if Mary should take down the parlor curtains. I think so. The summer sun might not fade them, still I presume they had better be taken down, and also the dining room curtains. Don't forget to have the parlor furniture taken out and thoroughly whipped. Ask Mary McGrath to go to the tray of my largest trunk and take out two quilts, not quilted yet, and send them home by you. Two that Grandma pieced for Mollie and Neddie. I must not forget to tell you what a brave little "whack" you have got. She went to see a dentist when in Cleveland and he told her it would be necessary to take out four double teeth, one above and one below on each side. So she waited over at Cousin James Mason's until yesterday, and I went with her to have them out. She would not take any gas but sat down and with as little fuss as possible had them out. They had wide prongs and one of the upper teeth the Doctor had to take hold of the third time before he could get it out. That was the last tooth, and she did not make a sound when he took hold the third time. But when it was all over she sat down and had a good cry. She was so brave and resolute I think she deserves a handsome present of some kind, and I scarcely know what she would like most. You and the boys think about it, and I will find out if I can what would please her most, and you shall get it and bring it home when you come. If I want to use any money more than I have, shall I get it out of the bank or would you prefer to send it? I have already drawn $125.00 to pay the Southworth[31] bill $48.20, and to make some purchases for the house which I think you will approve, and I shall want a little more probably than I have left of it. . . . I had nearly forgotten to tell you that we had green peas for dinner today, and we can now have from this [time] on a supply from the garden of something nearly every day.

This I think is ahead of any of our neighbors, even the Doctor. Darling, I have not been writing quite as often as at first, but I think my letters make up for infrequency by length. I am so happy that the boys are doing so well. Kiss them for mamma and hug them tight. With kindest regards to all friends, I am as ever and forever Yours, Crete.

❧ NOTES ❧

1. William M. Evarts was the lawyer defending Beecher at his trial in 1875. He was sent to England in 1863–64 to put an end to the building and equipping of vessels for the Confederacy and also went as counsel with a group to arbitrate claims against Great Britain resulting from boats sunk during the Civil War.

2. Central Park was designed by Calvert Vaux and F. L. Olmsted in the late 1850s, so it was relatively new as a tourist attraction. This was probably James' first visit to the park.

3. "Frye of Maine" was a member of the House as well as a Senator and a great speaker and debater.

4. The "genial old man" was John Mulligan, superintendent of the Connecticut River Railroad.

5. Mrs. Lacy was a woman in whom Lucretia had taken an interest. James went to the Post Office Department in order to secure a clerkship for her.

6. Harry J. Brown and Frederick D. Williams, eds., *The Diary of James A. Garfield*, (East Lansing: Michigan State University Press, 1973), 3: 291.

7. Lucretia refers to William Dean Howells' *Sketch of the Life and Character of Rutherford B. Hayes (etc.)* (1876), a campaign biography.

8. Brown and Williams, *The Diary of James A. Garfield*, 3: 371.

9. Martha Mays, an English woman, had worked in the Treasury Department before she became governess for the Garfield children in 1876.

10. Miss Edson was a graduate of the Cleveland Homeopathic Medical College. She attended the Garfield family during these years and nursed the wounded Garfield in 1881.

11. This is from Poe's *Annabel Lee* (1849).

12. James was forty-five years old on 19 November 1876.

13. George Eliot's *Daniel Doronda*, the last of her novels, was published in 1876.

14. Captain Eads is James B. Eads, an engineer who built a bridge across the Mississippi at St. Louis in 1867–1874, and who then proposed a plan for opening the mouth of the Mississippi into the Gulf of Mexico. This project, the subject of the next letter, was completed in 1879.

15. Brown and Williams, *The Diary of James A. Garfield*, 3: 473.

16. Edwin Cowles, editor and owner of the *Cleveland Leader*, had been an ardent supporter of James, so James owed him some favors. James called on President Hayes to ask for the appointment, but the Swiss Mission had already been filled.

17. Thomas Northcote was a farmer who worked for Doc Robison. Northcote sometimes helped out at the Garfield farm.

18. Horace Steele was Collector of Customs in Cleveland.

19. The shawl was at Miss Ransom's in Washington because Lucretia had been sitting for a portrait there.

20. Mr. W. B. Duncan was one of the principals in the law case James was attending in Mobile.

21. The Touhays were house-sitting for the Garfields in Washington.

22. J. S. Robinson was a Union officer from Kenton in western Ohio.

23. Crete and James drove to the Sixth Street Depot to go to Baltimore but were a minute too late, so they returned home and did not see the celebrated actor in Shakespeare's *Hamlet*.

24. Martha was Lucretia's widowed sister.

25. Joe was Lucretia's brother.

26. John C. Tyler was a Mentor farm neighbor.

27. Herendon's was a store on the Public Square in Cleveland.

28. Mary Clemmer Ames was one of the first women correspondents in Washington. She wrote about politicians in a sternly moralistic tone, judging them on the basis of their personal behavior as well as on their political activities. She attacked Garfield once.

29. Amos Townsend (1821–1895), a Cleveland wholesale grocer, was in the House of Representatives, 1877–1883. Dr. Jonathan Updegraff had been a surgeon in the Union armies.

30. Jerry was a farm hand.

31. Southworth's was a Cleveland store.

CHAPTER 11

The Final Two Years,
September 1879–September 1881

In September 1879, after a summer on the Mentor farm, the two older boys, Hal and Jim, entered St. Paul's preparatory school in Concord, New Hampshire. This chapter begins with Lucretia's letter to James, who is unable to accompany them, telling of their reception at the school.

James, himself, is ready for new things, too. He decides to put his name up for the Senate, and in the winter, while he watches closely from Cleveland, he is easily elected by the Ohio Legislature to the United States Senate. As part of the political "understanding" between him and the former Ohio Senator, John Sherman (now Hayes' secretary of the treasury) it was agreed that James would support Sherman for the presidency at the Chicago Convention in June 1880.

Accordingly, James leads the Ohio delegation to Chicago in June. Though he felt strong pressure to support James Blaine of Maine, his good friend, as opposed to the Conkling group advancing General Grant for a third term, he loyally sticks by Sherman knowing full well he has little chance of being nominated. At that chaotic convention, the two leading candidates, Blaine and Grant were deadlocked in a rancorous conflict. More than thirty ballots were cast before delegates from Wisconsin threw in Garfield's name, when it had become obvious that James was the only candidate who could win the nomination.

In the meantime, Lucretia was back on the farm dealing with painters and carpenters, and writing James about the refurbishing of their home there. The contrast in their activities makes for an interesting exchange of letters.

James fought his last campaign in the fall against General Winfield Scott Hancock, a popular general from the Civil War. James barely won the presidency.

After the election he returned to Mentor to plan for his first term in office. In January 1881, Crete traveled secretly to New York to be fitted for her inaugural gowns. James was sworn in as president that March. He and Lucretia took up residence at the White House on March 4. But in May Lucretia fell seriously ill with what was probably malaria. After several weeks she was taken to Elberon, New Jersey, to convalesce. She remained there until June, but James corresponded with her only by telegram during that separation. His dispatches and her last letters come in late June, as they were planning a trip together through New England for James' 25th reunion at Williams College. James was shot on July 2 in the Washington railway station as he began this journey. He lay dying much of that long, hot summer, finally succumbing on September 19. He was not yet fifty years old, and he and Lucretia had been married less than twenty-three years.

Of the eighty or so letters exchanged during these last two years, thirty are here included.

In the fall of 1879, Lucretia took the two older boys, Hal and Jimmy, to St. Paul's prep school in Concord, New Hampshire. James could not be with her for this important occasion, though he planned to visit the boys at school later on. The son of Colonel Rockwell, James' intimate friend and Williams classmate, was also at St. Paul's.

Eagle Hotel, Concord, N.H.
September 3, 1879.

My Darling:

We arrived here on the 10.30 train this morning, came directly to the hotel where we found a room, due I think to the thoughtfulness of Col. Rockwell. He had not yet come, so after reading your precious letters the boys bathed and dressed in their Sunday best, and as soon as we had taken dinner we drove to St. Paul's. I will not try to describe the place to you since you are to come and see it, but I assure you we were not unfavorably disappointed. Dr. Coit received us graciously and soon put the boys at ease by sending them to their dormitory, the same that Don Rockwell occupies, and very soon they were sent into their examination. While that was going on Dr. Coit's brother took me to his own house, which is the infirmary. His wife was a Cleveland girl, and we spent a pleasant half hour together. I should think the boys would get sick very often. I then went back to hear the boys' report. I met Jim first as I was passing through one of the halls. He was bursting full of tears. We went aside into one of the rooms, and as soon as he could speak he said the teacher who examined him in Greek said he had better go into the third form. I questioned him and found that he had passed well enough in Latin and Arithmetic, even better in the latter than had Hal, and I think the proposition to put him in the third form was more on account of his age than his failure in examination, though Hal said he wasn't sure but they would think he ought to go in there, too. About that time Col. Rockwell and Don arrived, and I think from my talk with him that there will be no trouble in getting them both into the fourth form. Mr. Coit (the brother) said the fourth form were nearly all poor in Greek, that it was not a "Greek form," and Dr. Coit[1] told the Colonel that he would take Don and a few others who were poorest and coach them up himself for a few weeks; and I presume he will allow Hal and Jim to go in with them. I think the boys did not do justice to themselves. They said they were so scared that they could not think of anything, but Hal said, "I know I can keep up when I begin to study." I am not sure but it was the best thing for them that they did do so badly. It makes them see the necessity of working the harder, and I think when you come you can get it fixed all right. The Colonel and I came back to town and left the boys all there. Tomorrow morning we are going out at seven o'clock to attend the chapel exercises and see them again. What I shall do after that I don't know. . . . If I should go to Boston I will either write or telegraph to you on Friday. I could make myself as lonely as poor Jim thinks he will be if I would stop and think about it tonight with you and the boys so near and yet all out of my reach. I shall try to put in the time somehow, however, until you come. . . .

Loving and longing and waiting for you, I am as ever yours, Crete.

Fall 1879 finds James on the campaign trail in Ohio. Lucretia is in Mentor.

Marietta, Ohio.
September 17, 1879.

My Darling:

After writing you yesterday I spoke an hour and a half to nearly 2500 people, was then driven 16 miles down the Muskingum to Beverly, where I spoke an hour and a half to 700 people in a hall, and was then driven 20 miles, arriving here half an hour after midnight. Thus during Monday and Tuesday I have ridden 102 miles in carriages and 35 miles by rail and spoken four times, am still alive and feeling remarkably well. You have a right to blame me for it; but really I could not help it. The only way you can keep me from such excesses is to go with me. I spent the last half of the night at the house of Mr Alderman, the Republican editor here, and shall stay here until noon when I go to Belpre, twelve miles down the Ohio, and opposite to Parkersburg, West Virginia. I will take the time to write to Hal before I leave. Every day I see new and striking manifestations of the cordial and enthusiastic feeling of the people towards me and I am sure my meetings are doing much good to the Republican cause. If I find the work makes inroads upon my health, I will shorten sail and do less.

But every day of absence makes me homesick for you. When I think of the bright sweet days we might spend on the farm together it makes me rebel against the fate that keeps me away. I look forward with pleasure to tomorrow when 150 miles from here I expect to meet a letter from you. I hope also to hear further from the dear boys and God grant that my anxieties about old Hal may be allayed. He is glad he "has to dig," the dear boy. How strange it is that I should dread for him the hardships that I have always welcomed for myself. And yet I know it is best he should bear them. And he was silent about Jim. Is it possible that Jim may get on so well as to need less of our sympathy than Hal? Perhaps, but hardly probable. Write me next to the Gibson House, Cincinnati, where I shall be one week from today, or better still, to London, Madison Co. where I shall be next Monday, if you can reach me in time. With all my heart full of love, I am as ever and forever, Your Own James.

Toledo, O. Oct 8, 1879.

My Darling:

The New London people held their 4000 crowd until 3:50 P.M. when I reached, and spoke an hour and a half. Exactly at 5 I stepped into a carriage and at 7:30 got out at Monroeville, 24 miles away. There I spoke nearly two hours, and spent the night with a Mr. Roby, the Republican candidate for State Senator.[2] Yesterday morning I went to Findlay passing through Fostoria where Charley [Wilber]'s father came on board and went with me to the meeting. He is 79 years old and his wife is 75. In view of the topic we examined on Sunday I studied the old man's face with deep interest. Charley is a striking repetition of his father's type of body and face, but with these striking differences: his father has light hair, blue eyes and light complexion, but his mother has given to Charley her brown hair, black eyes and brunette complexion. That is, the father gave Charley his type, chalked the outline, while the mother laid on the tints, mellowed the picture and doubtless attuned his spirit to a softer and higher harmony. It seemed a strong evidence of the doctrine we were discussing.

At five P.M. I took the train for Fremont, where I waited until eleven o'clock. Called on President [Hayes] who met me on his porch, and said, "Mrs. Hayes has been out gathering hickory nuts, and is now having her feet washed. She will be out soon." I spent half an hour with them, looking through their home, which is a great substantial building. It stands in the centre of a natural grove of 30 acres of great oak trees and was built by Hayes' bachelor uncle, who seemed to have a prophetic view of the use to which it would be put.

The President told me that he had heard several prominent people say that my speeches are making a remarkable impression on the public, much greater than any others in the field.

At Fremont I was invited to go to bed in the Director's car of Mr. Shoemaker of Cincinnati and so got a good night's rest,[3] awaking this morning at eight in the Toledo Depot. At eleven I go west to Stryker, speak at Pioneer tonight, Akron tomorrow, Alliance Friday, Cleveland Saturday and with you at 11:20 Saturday night.

Please send Jerry to Mentor Station. Perhaps you will meet me at Cleveland and go home with me. Love to all my Darlings and ever and forever, Your Own James.

Senator Zachariah Chandler had been Secretary of the Interior in 1876. James had described him as "a man of coarse fibre, with little culture; intemperate both in drink and in habits of mind. There runs through his character a strong infusion of the 'bummer.'" He died of alcoholism, as is clear from the following letters. James traveled eastward and to Washington, while Lucretia remained in Mentor.

Mentor, November 3, 1879.

My Darling:

I have just received your dispatch from Syracuse and conclude if an express package can reach you, a letter may. I did not get your letter from Buffalo until late Friday evening and having no hope that you would get a letter should I send one, did not send one. This morning's papers bring us the first intelligence of Senator Chandler's death. It is very sad both for his family and the Nation; but the valiant work he has been doing since he was last made Senator will perhaps be a more living influence than it could be were he still to be present on the floor of the Senate. His prophesies will rise up in his place and stalk before those Democratic Senators like Caesar's ghost. Darling, my hope for you is in your temperate habits. The work you do, however great, is done with natural healthful life, not by fires kindled by artificial stimulants which burn out body and soul, and after all give out only a lurid light.

I see from your dispatch that you probably go to Washington. When will you be at home? On Thursday the trees are to be sent. The largest maples at the nursery are no larger than those we have, and I conclude you would prefer to have larger. I very much wish you had ordered those you saw in Cleveland, and think you may perhaps decide to do so yet.

Mr. Riddle sent me a note last week in regard to Secretary Sherman. See Mr. Riddle[4] if you can. The tenor of the note was, if I understood it, that Mr. Sherman would not be candidate for Senator. Last night a heavy snow fell, but the sun is out today and will soon dispose of it; at least I hope so. Nothing is more dreary than a snow storm. I am glad the children do not feel as I do; for it would surely make poor Jim homesick. With love from us all. Yours forever and most lovingly. Crete.

Washington, Dec. 16, 1879.
House of Representatives.

My Darling:

I have made a discovery, which helps me over the dead point on which I stuck this morning. I found I have not drawn my mileage, and this puts me in immediate use of $220, which I had not counted on. So consider me not only, as always willing, but now able to meet all the little mahogonies. I enclose $40 with which you may pay the antique salesman and give him joy for his Christmas turkey.

As always your loyal lover James.

At the new year, James went out to Ohio to keep an eye on the Ohio Legislature, which would be voting for Ohio's Senator, a post he now coveted. He determined not to go to Columbus to work actively for it, since he was certain the election would fall to him in any case. Lucretia participated in the Washington New Year's festivities without James.

Washington, January 2, 1880

My Darling:

Although I sent no word of greeting to you yesterday, my heart was full of them. We had a busy day. Mrs. Hayes sent a messenger the evening before inviting me to come with any guests I might have at half past ten A.M. to witness the reception of the Diplomats. Grandma and I decided to go and spent an hour there. The glitter of the court costume was really quite dazzling to say the least of it. We then kept open house the remainder of the day. It was one of the brightest New Years I remember, and the gentlemen made the most of it. Lieut Corbin[5] was the first who called here, and he wished me to say to you that Grosvenor and Bickham[6] had both written that Matthews' friends are very confident.[7] He said it might mean nothing; but if you thought he could be of any service to your interests he would go to Columbus. That you should telegraph him if you want him to come. Of the sixty persons who called not more than a dozen I think failed to express their interest in your success in this senatorial contest. Nearly all thought there was no doubt of your election but their different opinions in regard to your going to or staying away from Columbus were amusing. Each one knew exactly what you ought to do, and the more inadequate he was to judge, the more positive was his opinion. The prevailing opinion however was that you ought to go.

Hal, Jim and Don [Rockwell] went out together and reported themselves as having had a splendid time. Grandma was unusually gracious, and Mollie I find is quite a little lady! So on the whole our day was as pleasant as it could be when you were so far away. Tonight the boys are going to a little dance at Pay Master Cutter's, consequently must have pumps. Mollie does not want to go, and I am just as well pleased to have her stay at home. If you stay away many days longer, you must provide for paying the gas bill which will be when discounted nearly nineteen dollars. Then the bill at Moses for curtains—c.$65; another at Singleton's of $10 or $12; and the one from Galt's. Darling, I hope it won't make you blue to hear me forever talking about bills.

Give my love to all the friends and remember me as always loving you.

Ever yours, Crete.

House of Representatives
April 29, 1880.

My Darling:

Dr. Baxter[8] has given me some prescriptions which I have sent to the drug store, cor. N.Y. Av. and 14th St. and which will be sent to you during the day with the bill for payment.

Baxter says I must now, and for ten days come rigidly down to beef steak (an inch thick cooked thoroughly but without grease), stale bread, toasted or untoasted, and milk—with a table spoonful of lime water to each glass.

Please make arrangements to put these savage orders into execution.

As ever and always, Your Own James.

Mentor, May 20, 1880.

My Darling:

I forgot to mention yesterday that your reaper had come. I was at the farm several hours yesterday but it was so warm and dusty that I did not go around very much. The garden is pretty well started and if it would rain would soon look well. The orchard is a pretty dreadful looking place not having been cleaned up and having on one side five large . . . piles of the old house debris as the Doctor does call it. But no one is to blame for the orchard. The only wonder is that everything is not looking worse when we consider the amount of work that has been done. The little alderney calf is a beautiful little creature, as wild as a fawn, and looks more like one than like a calf. Yesterday morning one of our cows died, the red cow with horns like old "Black face." They said she seemed perfectly well the night before. The Doctor found her horns entirely hollow but didn't know whether that was the whole trouble. The painters decided that they could paint the roof for about $20 less than the Doctor estimated by using yellow ochre for the first coat. I have decided to have the blinds painted green. The house is lighter than I thought it would be and a good tint for green blinds. No one suggested it but I remembered you had rather expressed a preference for green and so took the responsibility to change, and this change decreases the cost a little. I have decided to let Mr. Fridd have his way in regard to the front door glass. He wants to put in a perfectly clear plate instead of what he calls french plate. This last will cost only about ten dollars and the clear plate about twenty dollars, but notwithstanding the Doctor's opposition I think when you come to see the beautiful view from our hall, you will be glad of my decision. I have set a woman at cleaning of floors this morning before the painters go on with their work. The windows cannot be cleaned until the putty is harder. I shall not be able to do quite as much as I would be glad to do before you come. Still I hope to get in such shape that one can finish up very soon after you come. Mrs. Robison got off one of her sharp remarks on the Doctor at breakfast this morning. He was talking about running for President himself, when Mrs. R. said in her quiet way, "A man ought to be able to manage his own business before he undertakes to manage the nation." The Doctor rolled up his eyes, you understand how, and turning to me said: "Tell the General if that is Betsy's opinion of me, what must she think of the "dark horse"? I think of nothing more this morning. Love to the little "homekeeper" and "my baby." Always and forever lovingly, Your own Crete.

James arrived in Chicago for the Republican Convention four days early on May 29. He knew at the time that he was a dark horse, but he committed himself and the Ohio delegation to John Sherman, a favorite son candidate, who was thought to have no chance of winning the nomination.

> Grand Pacific Hotel
> Chicago, May 29, 1880

My Darling:

I arrived here at 8 o'clock, and find the city boiling over with politics. Everything is in the vague of vastness and uncertainty.

No definite thing appears on the face of this chaos except the fact that the unit rule will be the center of battle and to that I expect to address myself. Whatever fight is in me I will make on that point.

I enclose a slip from the Cleveland Leader which I found at Cowles last evening. I took tea at his house and he drove me to the train.

You know that my heart is with you in your struggle to bring order out of our house of your planning, and I would gladly exchange this turmoil for the smaller and sweeter turmoil of the farm.

Don't fail to write me every day. Each word from you will be a light in this wilderness.

Always and All your own James.

Mentor, May 29, 1880

Darling:

I have time for only a word. I am well and loving you every moment, and all is going on well. I hope you find the situation no worse than you expected—on the contrary, better.

I will write you more tomorrow.

Ever Your Own Crete.

Chicago, May 30, 1880.

My Darling:

The mail this morning brought me your brief note, the shortest I have ever received from you, and yet sweet and full of love. Since I wrote you the hurried note of yesterday, the turmoil has increased; though I begin to see the direction of the currents which are driving through waste of waters that surround us. I suppose more than a thousand people have talked to me today, and a still larger number have been introduced or recognized.

All the elements indicate a convention full of sharp and fierce antagonisms. The result is shrouded in all manner of doubt and uncertainty. I ran away for an hour and a half this morning and attended the Disciple Church on Indiana Avenue. Less than 75 people in attendance. There seems to be, just now, a dearth of religion and a plethora of politics in the city. Every hour I long to be away from this turmoil and with you in our dear home. Dozens of interruptions have broken up even this short note.

All your own James.

Mentor, May 30, 1880
Middle East Chamber

My Darling:

I sent off the poorest little note to you yesterday and would be ashamed had it not been the best I could do to fulfill my promise to you. With the many calls this way and that I barely managed to get the hall exactly measured and a diagram made out for Stirling before it was time to post it for yesterday's mail, but while waiting for Jerry to bring out the horse I scratched those few words to you and sent them off to redeem my promise. I drove Josie to the Post Office and then took in Mollie and Mamie Aldrich and went to Willoughby. The carpenters are pretty well through but the Doctor thought best to keep five of them a few days longer so as to get the odds and ends more quickly finished. The painters have finished all the painting inside except the last coat on the sitting room and on our room. Then there will remain only the oil finish for the hall and dining room. The blinds are nearly finished for the present, and yesterday a part were hung. They improve the appearance of the house more than you can imagine, as does also the painting of the sash. Yesterday we put up beds in the attic and the girls staid here last night. Mollie staid with Mamie Aldrich and Abe and I went to the Doctor's and will do so until we feel it is perfectly safe to stay here. Last night we had a long soaking rain which has done a world of good coming so soon on the heels of the last rain. I hope the dry weather is over. I shall watch the papers with great anxiety this week, and for your letters with not only anxiety but with a great longing. I forgot to buy ink yesterday, hence your pen cannot do duty.

With an ever abiding love and hope that you will be your wisest and best,

I remain always yours, Crete.

P.S.   Evening.

Since I have finished my letter, I have found ink. Also, we have had another tremendous rain. Are these rains portentous? They come with some storm and tempest, but with more abundant good. May they indeed foretell the good that shall follow the disturbance of the political elements. Pardon my platitudes, and love me just the same.

Crete.

Chicago, May 31, 1880.

My Darling:

Another day nearly over full of the extraordinary passion, suspicion and excitement of this convention. I have tried to keep my head cool and have sailed rather steadily over its rough seas, yet all the while longing for land, especially the little farm where my hopes and loves are centered.

I begin to feel quite confident that neither Grant nor Blaine can get the nomination, and I fear that the bitterness already engendered and yet to be will make it impossible for the Convention to restore harmony to the Party.

You can hardly imagine the embarrassment I have been in from the moment of my arrival here by the number of delegates from all quarters who are openly expressing the wish that I was the Ohio candidate. So much of this is said as to put me in constant danger of being suspected of ambitious designs; but I think I have been so prudent as thus far to disarm most of the suspicious ones. I shall do no act that will in the smallest degree be untrue to myself or my associates, and I do not think anything will come out of the deeps to me. But I am greatly surprised at the number of prominent delegates who want to bring out my name. Many are firmly of the belief that all the candidates will be dropped and that I will be taken up. I hope you do not think I am disturbed by this, or in the slightest degree elated. I shall do nothing and ask nothing, far better pleased to have nothing but the knowledge that many desire me. I . . .

June 1, 7 P.M.

I could not finish this last evening and I now close it by saying that the meeting of the National Committee of last night indicates a most serious row in the Convention. Swaim, Henry,[9] Nichol,[10] and a host of good fellows are here, too many to make it possible to write a connected letter.

As ever and Forever Your Own James.

P.S. Please send my love to the boys at St. Paul's.

Mentor, June 1, 1880

My Darling

I have just received your Sunday letter and will snatch from out my turmoil time enough to tell you where we are. The plumbers are here today putting in bathtub and sink. Yesterday the Doctor was at Cleveland and put himself behind a number of things which would have dragged on interminably and when the Doctor gets that position you know what follows. Two men worked all day yesterday cleaning out the cellar and there is a good deal yet to be cleared out, but Johnny Gone, if that is his name, is coming tomorrow with seven barrels of water lime to finish the cellar.

This morning it rained again heavily so that three of the painters who were on outside work are not here. I am sorry, for as the day is turning out, they could all have been at work. The carpenters who are making the dining-room cupboards have promised the Doctor that they will send them out on Saturday. The Doctor made them consent to his sending them back if they were not here on Saturday.

I do think we shouldn't have had our house before September if it had not been for the Doctor's push. So much for the house.

I have looked through the morning paper to learn the situation at Chicago. Your name is on the list for the vice-Presidency. I know you would not take it; so I am not made anxious over it. Governor Foster[11] is also mentioned. I presume he would take it, as it would just fit on to his expiring Governorship. The days will drag this week, and still go too fast for the amount of work we can accomplish before your return. With a heart full of love for you and implicit faith in your wisdom, I remain

Always Yours, Crete.

P.S. It rained again, so it is well the painters did not come.

The Convention opened on June 2.

Chicago, June 2, 1880

My Darling:

Your precious letter came and cheered me in this tempest, as no other light on all the coasts of the world could do. Monday night I did not get to bed until nearly one o'clock; and just as I was going to sleep a friend knocked at my door, and asked me to allow his brother (a stranger) sleep with me. My bed is only a three quarter size and with a stranger stretched along the wall, I could not sleep [and consequently was unable to get more than] a minute of rest or sleep. That made me wholly unfit for good work yesterday. I have arisen at 7 this morning to tell you the peril I am in. I have not made the first step in preparation for my speech nominating Sherman and I see no chance I can get to prepare. It was a frightful mistake that I did not write [it] before I came. It now seems inevitable that I shall fall far below what I ought to do. The belief that the nomination will come to me increases in many minds, but I do not believe it. If I were well out of this strait and with you, I should be happy. My love to everyone. Ever and forever Your Own James.

Mentor, June 2, 1880

My Darling:

We have just this morning received yours of yesterday and letters from our St. Paul boys. They are well and their letters full of their anniversary details, among which is the account of their dinner which made nearly all of them sick. Hal won the third prize in the Mile run, and he is working hard for the elocution prize. Since he can't get a first testimonial, he says he is going to work hard for the elocution. Jim thinks he may get a "first." He never counts on the margin _____, and I presume would not be surprised if he failed to get it. He says of Hal, "I heard some gentleman say as he went up to get his prize for the run, That is a fine appearing boy." I have no doubt he was more pleased to have that said of Hal than he would have been to have heard it of himself. I will leave the rest for you to read on your return. All eyes are turned to Chicago today, and we shall almost hold our breath until we know the result. I hope the factions may be harmonized, and whatever nomination is made that it may be unanimous. Give my love to Swaim and thank him for the paper. We are working away but it is as hard to wind off as it was for Lana Beam with her essay. I am afraid we shall still be staring through open windows in the Hall door when you return as the glass has not yet come. I think the Doctor is rather glad of it, but if we can stand it, he must. I am again rushing this letter through to get it to the noon mail, so pardon haste and know how well I always love you, and that I have no fear for you in whatever place you may be put. Yours forever, Crete.

Chicago, June 3, 1880. 6am
My Darling:

The great peril of the preliminary organization was passed over yesterday in safety, and we are getting out of early beds to approach the second danger, which lies very near the core of the passion which fills this vast assembly in every vein, viz. the discussion of the unit rule. After a long and earnest confer-ence in a sitting of three hours, the Committee on Rules of which I have been made chairman has resolved to declare the right of each [delegate to have his vote] counted, as he gives it. This will encounter the fury of the Grant men who insist that each vote from a State shall be counted as a majority of the del-egates from that state may determine. The fate of Grant and the personal suc-cess of Conkling happen to be involved in this, and hence we expect a fierce fight which I must probably bear the brunt of. Since I wrote you yesterday morning, the signs have multiplied that the Convention is strongly turning its attention to me. Large numbers of men are confident that will be the result. I should think there was something in it, but for the contest I am to have with Conkling. If I win that fight, it will be likely to embitter him and his followers against me. If I lose it [the Grant faction may win out. Thus I am] between two fires. I take to myself the lesson I lately wrote to Hal and say I will do my whole duty as I see it, and take the result as an indication of what is best. You can never know how much I need you during these days of storm. Every hour I want to go and state some case to your quick intuition. But I feel the presence of your spirit and it is helpful. Your precious daily words have not yet failed me. You have heard from our noble boys and I am longing to read their letters. Tell them when you write, how I am begirt and how I love them. I build up in my imagination every new thing done by my architect and her workmen, and think of her as waving her creative wand and banishing chaos while order and beauty come smiling out of the night.

Thank the good Doctor [Robison] for his constant and powerful help. Tell him I am happy in expecting no lightning to strike me, but am gratified that so many men here think it will.

When my name was called in the Convention yesterday, as a member of a committee, there was a great and unexpected demonstration. . . . [Ever and for-ever, Your Own James].

Chicago, June 4, 1880.

My Darling:

Your dear message written on the 2nd reached me yesterday just as I was leaving the hotel for the Convention, and I read it amidst the roar and glare of that remarkable assembly and place. Your words from the dear home and the sweet boys at school came to me like a beam of peaceful light shining across evening fields into a tempest tossed sea. Bless every one of you. How proud it makes me [to read of] the modesty of Jim, after his fine achievements in scholarship—"The nightingale thought I have sung many songs. But never a one so gay." The good Jim is happier at Hal's praises than his own.

Our work here still drags its slow length along through more passion than there was at Chickamauga. I have seen nothing like it in politics. It would take me a week to give you in writing any adequate description of the sweep and swirl of great forces and impulses concentered here. As to myself, I have only time to say that without any act or word of mine to induce it, there has been growing hourly a current of opinion which were Ohio and I honorably free might nominate me. . . . [Ever and forever your own James].

Mentor, June 4, 1880.

My Darling:

From yesterday's proceedings at Chicago I infer you will not be able to start for home before Friday night or Saturday morning, consequently send one more note. We (I mean the painters and carpenters) are putting the finishing touches on fast now. All is looking well, and unless you think you cannot at all afford it I wish you would get a new bedroom set for Mother's room. And more I wish you could afford to get one of the *red* mahogany sets. Her room opening as it does off the sitting room ought to be nicely furnished, and the mahogany would not only be beautiful in that room but would be a set to *keep*. I only suggest all this. You know I don't want to be unreasonable though my tastes are expensive.

I begin to be half afraid that the convention will give you the nomination, and the place would be most unenviable with so many disappointed candidates. I don't want you to have the nomination merely because no one else can get it, I want you to have it when the whole country calls for you as the State of Ohio did last Fall. My ambition does not stop short of that.

Hoping to see you so soon, I remain still in haste yours as ever, Crete

Chicago, June 6, 1880.

My Darling:

The mental and physical strain of the week ending with two days and nights of Chickamauga were hardly less than that which Chicago has brought upon the men of this Convention. You have doubtless followed the course of events and will see before this reaches you the steps of progress. For any man to have kept his head upon his shoulders is no small matter. If I have succeeded better than most it is largely due to the fact that I see always before me your calm sweet face, counseling wisdom, prudence and truth. On the work of last night as on all since I came, I hope I have your approval. There have been times in the convention when it seemed that it could not be in America, but in the Sections of Paris in the ecstasy of the Revolution, and again it was old Ephesus where the claquers of the silver smiths cast dust in the air and by the space of two hours cried "Great is Diana of the Ephesians." I shall never be able to give you any adequate idea of the scene which preceded the vote on the Illinois con-tested seat, and the similar scenes of last [evening when] the different [candi-dates] were put in [opposition]. I will not try now. I persevered to the end in writing a speech. I marshalled a few ideas in line and left room in their ranks for any things that might come from the suggestions of the hour and in this I think I was fortunate, for Conkling's extraordinary speech gave me the idea of carry-ing the mind of the convention in a different direction. In that I think I had some success. At least it was success of a better kind than his. Of all these things we will talk later. I think the good opinion of the Convention towards me is not lessening.

Your suggestion of a mahogany set for Mother's room is so good of itself that were I less able than I am to bear the expense I should approve. Do it. Esthetics join with filial duty in its favor. It is needless to tell you how anxious I am to be with you and I shall be happy if I am let alone by this convention. Your sentence on that subject is a very crystal of wisdom and pride.

Loving you with all my power to love, I send kisses to all the dear children and am always your James.

On June 8, Garfield was nominated the Republican candidate for president on the 36th ballot. Mary Clemmer Ames, one of the earliest women correspondents, described the scene: "The culminating moment came. Other names seemed to sail out of sight like thistledown in the wind, till one (how glowing and living it was) was caught by the galleries, and shout after shout arose with the accumulative force of ascending breakers, till the vast amphitheater was deluged with sounding and resounding acclaim. And he? There he stood, strong, Saxon, debonair, yet trembling like an aspen. It seemed too much, this sudden storm of applause and enthusiasm for him, the new idol."[12]

TO: MRS. J.A. GARFIELD
MENTOR, OHIO.

DEAR WIFE. IF THE RESULT MEETS YOUR APPROVAL, I SHALL BE
CONTENT. LOVE TO ALL THE HOUSEHOLD.

SIGNED: J.A. GARFIELD

From Chicago James went directly to Washington.

Mentor, June 15, 1880.

My Darling:

I made a successful afternoon of work yesterday and reached home to find all safe and quiet. It rained all night and is raining this morning, so the painters can not go on with the roof. They got on enough paint yesterday to show that it will improve the appearance of the house immensely. I suppose you are now in Washington but I hope not overwhelmed. I will give a list of things to be brought home as I think of them and you can add to it as you please. First get from the cedar chest in the big closet on the third floor my India shawl. This you can bring in your trunk. Also I think the Limoge pitcher and the square jardiniere. These are I think on one of the shelves in our closet. Have Daniel[13] pack them carefully among your clothes; I would like too, if you can bring them easily, the fruit dish and the glass berry dish and the dessert plates of the china set. We shall find it very convenient many times to have the coffee urn. But do as you think best in regard to these larger articles. Then of the furniture the dining-room table and the longest mahogany side table if you think best. It would make a good hall table and release one already there for the boys' chamber. The Hungarian chairs and the two ottomans in the parlor or sitting room are perhaps all you had better bring now. I do not think of anything else, unless it is the fender. That can be wrapped well and sent by express. But if you see anything else you think we might need, bring whatever you please. Mr. and Mrs. Hayes' pictures would go in the bottom of your trunk.

The mail has just come. Not so large as yesterday. One to me from Henry James[14] is very characteristic. Another from an "Evangelist" with his circular and inclosing an extract from some paper in which I am made to give your temperance principles. He asks me to write him *immediately* and tell him whether I am truthfully reported. I think he will wait. Two others ask for Photographs from which to make an oil copy. I will wait 'til you come. The events of the past week grow to seem more and more unreal. But I suppose I shall grow accustomed to it all after a while. I ought to be now, for I have had to travel fast and think faster ever since I have known you, to keep even within seeing distance.

I shall hope to see you at home by the end of the week. Love and thanks to all the Roses for their kind congratulations. And always to the Major. Ever and same and always Yours, Crete.

Washington, July 8, 1880.

My own Darling:

I slept in this house last night without you, and I found it necessary to resist the sense of gloominess and loneliness which filled the places where you were wont to be. But the dear house is so full of fresh memories of you that nothing but the place where you are can be sweeter. I found everything in good order here, except that the cockroaches have appeared in the basement, and I engaged Mr. Summer to begin a campaign against them. His wife has been detained by the illness of a relative and will not be here for two or three weeks. The [servant] girls are here and well. We do not have the range heated up but take our meals away. Of course, the girls are anxious to know what is to be done with them and I hope you will soon determine whether you want Nancy or not. We had a fine shower last night and cool air which made sleep agreeable, though when the sun rose our old flies, the very ones that were so unkind to you, came and woke me and would let me sleep no more. It is singularly quiet while I write. No Jim or Hal to wage war with "Charlie Blair" or "Goosie Birch." I shall hurry over the days that are to keep me from you and them. Tell me if the goods I sent you from Cleveland reached and please you?

And now, Darling, do not fail to give me a few minutes of every day to cheer my loneness and bridge over the time till we meet and with all my love for you and the dear little ones, I am your own James.

Though much of his campaign took place at Mentor on the front porch of Lawnfield, James did make some "whistle stop" train trips.

Buffalo, August 4, 1880

My Darling:

The demonstrations of yesterday and last night have hushed me into something like awe—perhaps superstition. Word of my coming was not given along the line until late Sunday, or in some cases late Monday. Yet the crowds have far exceeded those which met me on my return from Chicago and Washington. Here we passed through an almost continuously dense mass of 2 and 1/2 miles of people, from the Depot to the Hotel and the building and its grounds packed with so many thousands that all attempt to estimate the mass is wholly vain. Men of all shades of Republicanism and of every grade of prominence are joining us to make the journey to N.Y. Of course, it is too early to judge of the outcome, but the more sanguine ones among us say that the [enemy] will be burned in the fire of this human prairie.

The train calls and I kiss you and a world of love. Ever your J.A. Garfield.

James was elected president in November with a scant majority in the popular vote of less than ten-thousand. In preparing for the inauguration, Lucretia went secretly to New York City with Mrs. Sheldon for a companion. Whitelaw Reid, editor of the New York Tribune, *looked after her in New York, along with Mrs. Sheldon.*

New York, January 20, 1881

My Darling:

No word from home yet! Yesterday we made effective by making some decisions—final in regard to two suits at least. The prices seem extravagant, still I have not made very large inroad into the amount you sent. Mr. Reid says tell you that we have not been betrayed yet, and shall not unless Mrs. Sheldon forgets to address me as "Mrs. Greenfield" at some unguarded moment. The carriage is at the door again, so I must be excused for the delightful work again. I will write you again this evening and tell you some things you will be very glad to know.

With kisses and love to yourself and the little boys, Yours Forever, Crete.

Cleveland, January 21, 1881

My Darling:

Swaim and I came here on the late train last evening and spent the night with Gen. Sheldon. The loneliness of the two homes brought us together and then I wanted to see Mollie home this evening. The family here looked for a letter from Mrs. Sheldon this morning but were disappointed. I hope one may come before we leave. Yesterday we had a trial of our patience. A Kentucky woman, a Disciple who has lived less than two years in Cincinnati, came yesterday noon, armed with a couple of Disciple letters of recommendation and modestly wanted to be made P[ost] M[istress] of Cincinnati. She dismissed her driver before she came into the house and we apparently had her on our hands for five hours. Fortunately the express was an hour late, and we got her off at 2:30. She was greatly grieved not to have seen "Sister Garfield" and still more grieved that "Brother Garfield" would not give her the P.O. The little boys are doing very nicely. All well at home.

Loving you always. James.

New York, January 21, 1881

My Darling:

Today has brought two letters and I am very gratefully happy. But I am too both ashamed and alarmed that I should have misspelled *tailor*. I did the same thing again this morning. Mrs. Bayard Taylor is here and having her name in mind I spelled the other with a suspicion going through my mind that it was not right, but with the response to myself "what other way is there to spell it?" I believe I will never write to anyone but you, unless I am with you to look over my letters.

This has been a most fearful day. The falling rain has frozen on the trees and telegraph wires, so that the limbs of the first are lying almost in piles beside the street and the wires are broken down into a tangled web almost blocking the streets in places. We have spent nearly four hours at one store today gathering up odds and ends to a much better advantage than we could have done on a crowded day. I have gotten drawers for you at ten dollars a pair that were reduced from eighteen dollars because they were a little soiled, and have made another bargain which will quite astonish you, when you consider my weakness for paying big prices. Perhaps, however, Mrs. Sheldon deserves more of the credit than I; but I think a good deal was due to the bad day. Mr. Reid told me this morning that Morton had been very ugly in his talk about you, using the expression that seems to be so gratifying to the Conkling clique—"That Ohio man" cannot be relied on to stand by his pledges. And said that Mrs. Don Cameron[15] said with a toss of her head after Mrs. Morton's outburst of indignation over the New York Senatorial election, "Oh, Mr. Morton[16] will be taken care of if General Garfield does as he agrees to do." I think you had better turn the whole crew over to Brown to expend his strength on, that he saved up from the Chicago correspondent. You will never have anything from those men but their assured contempt until you fight them *dead*. You can put every one of them in his (their—which?) political graves if you are a mind to, and that is the only place where they can be kept peaceable.

I am afraid Hal is going to waste time on his music. Did he say anything concerning the new tutor? How I wish I could be with you on Sunday morning, but it is not possible if we accomplish the work we came to do. I will add a word in the morning. In the mean time kiss precious little Abe a thousand times for his Mamma and help Mollie and Irvin to get over Sunday pleasantly and kiss them too. With all love, Yours forever, Crete.

Morning. January 22.

I am afraid I was very unwise and perhaps wrong last evening. At dinner Mr. Reid said, Mrs. Garfield, so you know Emma Jaynes? That was a red flag, and without stopping to consider I answered, "She is the most villainous woman in Washington." "Well," he said, looking a little curious, "I am glad I asked you. She has lost her place and has been importuning me until I was almost growing tender-hearted." I found then that she had been furnishing the "social gossip" for the [New York] Tribune at the Washington end, and had lost her place for that work.[17] Afterward he asked me more about it, and I thought best to explain a little more fully. He immediately sent off a telegram to his Washington manager that he should sustain him in his decision. If I had suspected that the

Tribune had business relations with her, I would have been on my guard, for I
have no wish to do her harm by depriving her of work where she can do no mischief, as she probably would not by anything she would write.

The storm is over this morning. You will see from the papers how violent
it has been. I shall have my dresses fitted today and shall hope to get away as
soon as they can spare me. The dressmaker wishes me to wait for one dress to
be entirely finished; and I think that will be more satisfactory, so if there is no
reason to the contrary I shall stay for that.

With love to all, Yours forever, Crete.

New York, January 23, 1881

My Darling:

My head and heart are full of things to say to you this evening, and I wish
either that you were here or I with you. Mr. Blaine was here for dinner today
and said he was coming back tomorrow evening to lay before me a matter of
"State." Mr. Reid tells me that it is in regard to your going to Washington soon
to spend a few days. Blaine is afraid you are growing a little morbid shut in as
you are from the people you most want to see, and moreover that each visitor to
Mentor stirs up the jealousies of all the rest. Logan[18] was blustering around,
wondering why Allison should have been invited to Mentor,[19] and he not. Mr.
Blaine thinks you can go to Washington and with two or three capable persons
to stand guard you can give everyone a chance to see you who has any right, and
gratify them without saying anything yourself. I don't know how much wisdom
there is in all this, but I feel that it has done a great deal for me to get among
different influences. I wish it were possible for you to come here. I think by
tomorrow I shall be able to set the time for starting home. I am getting homesick to see you all, and I fancy Mrs. Sheldon feels just a little blue this evening,
though she will not confess to any such weakness. Did you go to Cleveland? By
the way, thinking of Major reminds me that I saw in the Tribune this morning
that there was some expectation in Washington that General Devans[20] was to
have the Judge Advocate's place until by some vacancy he could be put on the
Supreme Bench and then Maj. Swaim was to have the Judge Advocacy!
Mr. Grow[21] has been here this evening to consult with Mr. Reid on the course
he shall pursue in the Pennsylvania contest. He is determined to break the ring,
and Blaine says that Cameron is burying or rather drowning his mortification

in his cups. So there may be another break in the ring domination. Reid says the defeat of Paddock in Nebraska[22] is another failure of Conkling's power. That C. had written a letter expressly asking that Paddock should be reelected. "The Mills of God" are grinding.

With love to all and kisses to the few.

Yours forever, Crete.

New York, January 26, 1881

My Darling:

I did hope this evening to be able to say to you that we would start for Ohio tomorrow evening; but the dressmaker annouces to day that I must wait until Friday morning for the final trial of the two dresses I am having made here, consequently we must wait until Friday evening before we start. For a reason I will not give until I am home, I will go right past you on Saturday noon to Cleveland and return on the evening train. Perhaps you had better telegraph to Mollie to wait and come home with me, but say nothing of my arrival in Cleve'd. Mrs. Sheldon and I have another secret to keep. Yesterday I met Mrs. Eels, so had to *confide* to her the troublesome secret. Today I ran against Mrs. Grant, but she is too near-sighted to know anybody.

Mr. Reid says he wrote to you today so you have the political news from him.

Congratulate Major for me. I see the President has sent in his name to the Senate [for Judge Advocate General of the US Army.]

Kiss the precious little boys for their Mamma and tell them they will not be half so glad to see me as I shall be to see them again.

If you think of any last errands before we start home, telegraph, and be on the look out on Saturday. With love to all.

Yours forever, Crete.

The long letter following is Garfield's lament over Lucretia's continued absence during a time when he most needs to have her return home. The irony of Garfield's complaint after the many times he delayed his return when Lucretia needed him is too rich to resist noting.

Mentor. January 31, 1881.

My Precious Wife:

When you are here, I shall probably never be able to reproduce the experience of the past week, for the reason that the joy of your presence is so rich and
full a substitute for other sentiments that it dominates and to some extent oblit-
erates all others.

Even now in the crisis of the experience I have no hope of being able to
convey to your mind even an approximate picture of the effect which the last
few days of your absence have had upon me and on the problems I am trying
to solve.

I retired at 9:30 last night determined if possible to force myself to get
some sleep of which I have been able to get very little during the past week; but
the wrestle was vain until after midnight. Half an hour ago I awoke and after a
fruitless struggle to sleep again, I thought I could do no better than try to tell
you some of the things I have wrestled with. Thinking also that I may be in a
morbid state of mind as well as of body, I may be able to "purge my bosom of
the perilous stuff"[23] by writing. In the first place, I doubt if any husband or
lover (and I am both in intensity) was ever more foolishly desolate at being left
alone than I have been during the past half month. I kept up very well during
the first week, though the pathetic pleading of the little boys and the anxious
questionings of Mollie when she came home a week ago last Friday made me a
very small child among little children. When your letter of a week ago yesterday told me that you expected the next day to set your time for coming, I
thought it would be too late for another letter to reach you and so denied myself
the pleasure of writing, which next to seeing you is my greatest solace.
I counted the hours which would bring me a telegram that you had started. The
hours dragged on into days. The days lengthened to Thursday, when I
telegraphed Reid, and he answered you would leave Friday evening. The distress I felt at not seeing a word from your hand was sharpened by the reflection
that I might have written you every day and given you and myself that great
consolation. I watched each train thinking if it did not bring you, it might give
me the consolation of seeing the tailor that I thought you would send, that I
might ask him if you looked well and happy. But even the comfort of a stranger
with a measuring tape did not come to me. In the mean time very grave and
difficult complications were preparing for me in Washington. The bitterness

swelling up in New York minds over the supposed nomination of Blaine in the cabinet was fast coming to a head. A long letter from Morton told me that the most formidable pressure of the whole N.Y. force was to be brought to bear upon me to give him the Treasury, and on Thursday night, a telegram came from Gov. Cornell at Albany asking if he and friends could see me on Saturday afternoon and evening. I knew from your letters that you had probably had an important conference with Blaine, and that you had news from the vital center of N.Y. affairs. When Reid's telegram came that you would leave Friday evening, I said, Now I shall see her before the Cornell party comes, and I shall be armed to meet them, and I answered I would see them here Saturday afternoon and evening. On Friday Reid's telegram came that your departure was postponed until Saturday evening, and I saw I must meet these men in the dark, without the much needed help. I felt as though I could take real satisfaction in wringing the necks of all the dressmakers in N.Y. for thus disarming me in the face of the enemy. Saturday dragged its weary length along with a crowd of hungry office seekers and others who would have been glad to cut me up inch by inch in hopes of dissecting some secret from my nerves or brain. Cornell and Platt were delayed five hours by belated trains, but arrived here at seven Saturday evening and stayed until ten.[24] I wrestled with them as best I could. When they asked to see you, I would have given an arm to have had you here. Then one of them remarked they understood Mrs. G. was in N.Y. at a private house, and I knew then that Mr. Conkling knew you were the guest of his enemy and I cursed the dressmakers again that they had pushed you into the second week and betrayed your whereabouts. I covered the defeat as well as I could by remarking in as careless a tone as I could command that you were there shopping quietly to avoid the crowd. I kept Judd up till near midnight to watch the course of your train and be sure you were coming.[25] I had telegraphed to Mrs. Sheldon Saturday afternoon (in receipt of your letter of the 26th which was three days on the road) that Mollie was here and asked if I should have the train stop at Mentor Sunday. As no answer came (and none has yet come) I telegraphed Reid at 10 P.M. Saturday night to the same effect, but at midnight no answer had come, nor has one yet come. Sunday came but had brought me so little sleep I was nearly ill. Sunday morning brought Gen. Cox and Henry E. Knox[26] from opposite directions, one of them to go over the whole situation from the standpoint of an independent, and the other to detail the perils of the N.Y. situation. I gave the day to them with every nerve throbbing with a dull ache. Not hearing from you or Mrs. S. or Reid, early Sunday morning your letter of the 28th came, saying you hoped to leave Sunday evening but were not sure, but if you did you would go by to Cleveland for some secret reason, which I know must be a good one, but I know it is futile if it is intended to conceal the journey. I telegraphed the conductor of the train to tell Mrs. Sheldon that her train was to stop at Mentor (I had stopped it to let Gen. Cox go) and when it came, two hours late, I drove down hoping I might at least catch a glimpse of you as you should go by to Cleveland.

But the conductor gave me back my dispatch with the hurried word that no such person as Mrs. S. was on the train. I then fell back upon the hope that your letter of the 28th was later than Reid's telegram of the same date and that you might start on the Sunday evening train. Knox stayed until eight last night and drove to Painesville to take the late train east to make such explorations of N.Y. affairs as would if possible give me by Wednesday next the inside of movements there. Hoping to hear from Reid that you had left by the six P.M. train Sunday night, I waited in the office till nine and gave it up, thinking the dressmakers were an overmatch for all my resources of statesmanship. Just as I was undressing for bed, Swaim came up to say that Judd was receiving a long dispatch. I redressed and went down to find that Judd had been taken with vomiting and had gone to bed, but the dispatch of 75 words lay on the table. I thought that at last the long and mysterious silence was to be broken. But I found it was a telegram from Carrie Ransom, asking me to meet with the Classical Society of Washington on the 10th of February and read a paper on the comparative merits of Tacitus and Greene[27] and Macaulay as historians!! I shall answer her this morning that I can give no time to any history more ancient than A.D. 1881.

Monday, 8 A.M. January 31

I tried again to sleep without success. Mollie was brokenhearted yesterday afternoon when she found you had not come. I told her what you said and she filled up but did not cry. Papa, she said, "I cannot go away without seeing Mamma. Let me stay home until she comes." I answered, "If you say so, you may, but think of it till morning." After Knox had gone, she came to me and said, "I will go and I am trying to get my lessons." I went into the little hero's room and helped her for half an hour before she went to bed. Then she said, "You must rest and I will work." She saw the light in my room at six this morning and came in to know if I had slept. She kept up bravely and did not ask for news from you until time to drive to the station. Judd was still in bed and not yet well. So I drove her and Swaim to the station and had the operator there ask if there were any dispatches for me. He asked the Cleveland office, and soon the answer came, "No, Sir." She kissed me and stepped on the train saying "I think you will see her today"—the precious brave girl. I sent Swaim to Cleveland with her and he will wait there until evening to come home with you, if you arrive there.

Nine A. M. Monday.

The little boys took their breakfast and left for school accepting the inevitable without a word, though they have filled up to the lips and eyes at every mention of your name for the last three days. Judd has just brought me a dispatch from Reid that "Friends left last night at 6 in good spirits—They prefer to stop at Cleveland." This last sentence takes away another hope on which I have been building. A delegation of Congressmen from Washington is to be here this afternoon, full of the questions I must meet. I had hoped you would arrive here by the 12:57 train today so that I could know what you had learned before I met them. But the Cleveland mystery deprives me of that help and I shall watch the smoke of your train as it bears you across the farm and fight another battle in the dark.

Now, Darling, if I ever conclude to let you see this long wail, and if you ever get the time to read it, I beg you to be sure that there is not one shadow of feeling of blaming you. I know you have suffered anxiety and disappointment and could not know that your presence here during the last three days seemed more important to me than any days since our marriage. Perhaps also my great anxiety to see you had made your coming appear more important than it really was. But I have felt some relief in telling you the story. I will add that I thought to be able to present you a rough outline of my inaugural address on your arrival and last week I made a beginning, but after what I have written, you will not wonder that I gave it up with an intellectual loathing that makes me now feel I can never resume it.

Still, the thought that you are on the road; that you will really be here tonight fills all the house with light and makes me feel as though I would soon be able to live again. Out of my weariness I sing with Milton, "Strong Son of God, Immortal Love," as though it were written for us. And yet I would gladly blot out the remainder of this day until six o'clock.

Ever and Forever Your Own James.

James was inaugurated in March. He, Lucretia, his mother, Mollie, Irvin and Abe arrived from Mentor on March 1, staying no longer in their own home on New York Avenue but at the Riggs House hotel. On March 4 the inauguration took place at the Capitol, and after a luncheon with the Hayes', the Garfields took possession of the White House, where they expected to live for the next four years. In May, Lucretia's illness—probably malaria—caused her to leave James for some weeks in order to recuperate at the Jersey shore. Their correspondence during this separation was mostly by telegram.

WASHINGTON. THE WHITE HOUSE. JUNE 27, 1881.
TO: MRS. J.A. GARFIELD, ELBERON, N.J.

FOUND ALL WELL HERE. MRS. ROCKWELL WILL BE WITH YOU TUESDAY EVENING. LET ME KNOW BY WIRE HOW YOU HAVE BEEN ALL DAY.

SIGNED. J.A. GARFIELD.

WASHINGTON. EXECUTIVE MANSION. JUNE 29, 1881.
TO: MRS. J. A. GARFIELD, ELBERON, N.J.

THE REMNANT OF THIS HOUSEHOLD SEND AFFECTIONATE GREETINGS AND TO KNOW HOW YOU HAVE PASSED THE DAY AND NIGHT.

SIGNED. J.A. GARFIELD.

WASHINGTON. EXECUTIVE MANSION. JUNE 30, 1881.
TO: MRS. J.A. GARFIELD, ELBERON, N.J.

YOUR DISPATCH RECEIVED. SWAIM GOES TONIGHT AND WILL BE WITH YOU EARLY TOMORROW MORNING. WILL SEND THINGS. HOPE YOU ARE IMPROVING. SORRY I CANNOT GO MYSELF.

SIGNED. J.A. GARFIELD.

Elberon, N. J. June 30, 1881

My Darling:

I did not write yesterday because Mrs. Rockwell sent off a letter, and I a telegram. In answer to your note about moving to Soldiers' Home, I scarcely know what to say. If it were not for the boys, I should think it of little consequence to go there at all. We go to Ohio so soon after our return from New England, but since the boys must stay probably four or five weeks, perhaps we ought for their comfort to make the change, and if so I would think it best to have the change made while we are in New England. What an incoherent lot of stuff this is. It finally amounts to this—that we had better move, and that it should be done while we are away. The things to be moved are bed and table linen and only just what will be needed. The bed linen that has been left out will be enough to begin with and Mr. Crump will know about what table linen will be needed.[28] I understand the China and glass have not been provided. That can be attended to on our return. I had a splendid sleep last night, more natural than any since my illness and was more sleepy at eight this morning than when I went to bed, and am feeling very well this morning. You will see from Anna's [Boynton] telegram that she will probably go home with the children. Last evening we received the passes over the N.Y. Central, but it specified for "Mrs. Boynton, two children and nurse." What shall be done for Harber? He has both telegraphed and written that he can go any day, and I have answered that they should start on Friday. I hope you or Colonel Rockwell will be on hand to attend to starting the party. Miss Mars spent the night with us and joins us in love to you all.

For two nights I have taken a glass of port wine, and conclude that is one reason I have slept better, but I have only a little more wine and if you can bring me a little more that you can trust as pure port, I think it may be of advantage to me. Be sure and send the little boys' clothes, and Mary McGrath's, if she sent any of hers home, by Colonel Rockwell if he comes. By the way, I think you or the Colonel must come as early as to start this evening, so as to be here in time for all arrangements for the departure of the children.

With love to all, Yours Always, Crete.

FROM: EXECUTIVE MANSION, WASHINGTON, JUNE 30, 1881.
TO: MRS. J.A. GARFIELD, ELBERON, N.J.

IS THERE ANYTHING YOU WISH SWAIM TO BRING EXCEPT THE
CHILDREN'S CLOTHES? TELL ME SPECIFICALLY HOW YOU ARE.

SIGNED: J.A. GARFIELD.

FROM EXECUTIVE MANSION, WASHINGTON, JULY 1, 1881.
TO:MRS. J.A. GARFIELD, ELBERON, N.J.

HOW ARE YOU THIS MORNING? I HOPE THERE IS NO DOUBT THAT YOU
WILL BE WELL ENOUGH FOR THE NEW ENGLAND TRIP. DOES HARBER
GO TO OHIO WITH THE BOYS AND WHEN DOES HE LEAVE. ANSWER.

SIGNED: J.A. GARFIELD.

At the conclusion of these letters exchanged between Lucretia and James is a note scrib-
bled in Lucretia's hand, dated July 1881:

> *These are the last letters and telegrams received from My Darling during the five days*
> *I remained at Elberon previous to the fearful tragedy of July 2nd, 1881.*
>
> *Lucretia R. Garfield.*

Lucretia returned to Ohio, where she lived during the summers for the rest of her
life, spending winters in southern California. With a $50,000 grant from Congress,
James' Congressional pension of $5,000 a year, plus the income from a generous fund
raised by public subscription, she and her family were financially secure. She preserved
the enormous collection of James' papers, including these letters, in a fireproof library
added to her Lawnfield home. Gradually, the papers were turned over to the Library of
Congress, where the entire collection now exists. In March 1918, Lucretia died peace-
fully in California. Her remains were brought back to Ohio to lie beside James in the
Lake View Cemetery in Cleveland.

❀ NOTES ❀

1. Dr. Henry Coit was head of the St. Paul's school; he was an Episcopal clergyman who devoted his life to St. Paul's.

2. Henry M. Roby of Monroeville, Ohio, was defeated in his bid for State Senator.

3. Mr. Shoemaker of Cincinnati was president of the Cincinnati, Hamilton and Dayton Railroad.

4. Albert Gallatin Riddle, a lawyer from Cleveland, later moved to Washington. He was a good friend of James, and in fact, he wrote a biography of Garfield, published in 1880.

5. Lieut Corbin was a career army officer, a Clevelander, who later was secretary of the committee in charge of Garfield's inauguration.

6. Charles Grosvenor, speaker in the Ohio House of Representatives, was influential among Ohio Republicans. William D. Bickham was a correspondent and editor of various newspapers from Cincinnati.

7. Stanley Matthews was competing with Garfield for the post of senator from Ohio.

8. Dr. Jedediah H. Baxter was James' doctor in Washington.

9. Captain Henry was an old time friend of Garfield's from Hiram and Civil War days.

10. Thomas M. Nichol was an alternate delegate from Wisconsin and was instrumental in bringing Garfield's name to the floor of the convention as the compromise candidate, after both Grant's and Blaine's candidacies had failed.

11. Charles Foster had been elected governor of Ohio.

12. Quoted by Horatio Alger, *From Canal Boy to President, or the Boyhood and Manhood of J. A. Garfield* (New York, 1881).

13. Daniel Spriggs was a servant in the Garfield home.

14. Henry James (1843–1916), the American novelist, had already published *Roderick Hudson* (1875) in the *Atlantic Monthly*, as well as *The American* (1877), *Daisy Miller* (1879), and *Portrait of a Lady* (1880–81), which Lucretia had just finished reading.

15. Levi P. Morton (1824–1920) was a Republican in the Conkling faction. He later became vice president (1889–1893) and governor of New York (1895–1897).

16. Don Cameron was a senator from Pennsylvania. He and his wife were friends of the Garfields.

17. Emma Janes, a correspondent covering Congressional affairs for a Cleveland paper, had evidently passed on scandal in her dispatches.

18. John Logan, a senator from Illinois, was in the Conkling camp along with Levi Morton.

19. Allison, a senator from Iowa was an old friend to whom Garfield offered the post of Secretary of the Treasury, which he declined.

20. General Charles Devens had been Attorney General.

21. Galusha A. Grow (1823–1907) was a member of the House.

22. Algernon S. Paddock was a senator from Nebraska.

23. This is from Shakespeare's *Macbeth*.

24. Governor Alonzo Connell was in the Conkling faction, along with Thomas Platt.

25. Otis L. Judd was the telegrapher at Lawnfield and, later, at the White House.

26. Henry Knox of New York was a Williams classmate of James'.

27. John Richard Green (1837–1883) was an English historian, whose *Short History of the English People* was published in 1874.

28. William T. Crump was the White House steward.

Bibliography

Akers, W. J. *Cleveland Schools in the Nineteenth Century*. Cleveland: W. M. Boyne, 1901.

Alger, Horatio. *From Canal Boy to President, or the Boyhood and Manhood of J. A. Garfield*. New York, 1881.

Ames, Mary Clemmer. *Ten Years in Washington: Life and Scenes in the National Capital, as a Woman Sees Them*. Hartford: A. D. Worthington, 1880.

Appleton's Cyclopaedia of American Biography, vol. 5. New York: D. Appleton and Company, 1888.

Baehr, Harry W., Jr. *The New York Tribune Since the Civil War*. New York: Dodd, Mead and Co., 1936.

Beecher, Catharine E. *A Treatise on Domestic Economy*. New York: Source Book Press, 1970.

Berg, Barbara. *The Remembered Gate: Origins of American Feminism*. New York: Oxford Press, 1978.

Brown, Harry J. and Frederick D. Williams, eds. *The Diary of James A. Garfield*. 4 vols. East Lansing: Michigan State University Press, 1967–1981.

Brown, Herbert Ross. *The Sentimental Novel in America, 1789–1860*. Durham: Duke University Press, 1940.

Buckman, David Lear. *Old Steamboat Days on the Hudson River: The Stirring Times that Followed the Introduction of Steam Navigation*. New York: Grafton Press, 1909.

Coffin, Charles Carleton. *The Life of James A. Garfield*. Boston: James H. Earle, 1880.

D'Emilio, John and Estelle B. Freedman. *Intimate Matters: A History of Sexuality in America*. New York: Harper and Row, 1988.

Dye, Nancy Schrom and David Blake Smith. "Mother Love and Infant Death." *Journal of American History* 73 (September 1986): 329–53.

Emerson, Ralph Waldo. "Love." In *The Early Lectures of Ralph Waldo Emerson, 1835–1842*, vol. 3. Edited by R. E. Spiller and Wallace E. Williams. Cambridge: Harvard University Press, 1972.

Fuller, Corydon. *Reminiscences of James A. Garfield*. Cincinnati: Standard Publishing Co., 1887.

Henry, Frederick. *Captain Henry of Geauga County*. Cleveland: The Gates Press, 1942.

Howells, William Dean. *Years of My Youth*. New York: Harper Bros., 1916.

Leech, Margaret and Harry J. Brown. *The Garfield Orbit: The Life of President James A. Garfield*. New York: Harper and Row, 1978.

Havighurst, Walter, ed. *The Great Lakes Reader*. New York: Macmillan, 1966.

Hart, James D. *The Popular Book: A History of America's Literary Taste*. New York: Oxford University Press, 1950.

McKinsey, Elizabeth. *Niagara Falls: Icon of the American Sublime*. New York: The Cambridge Press, 1985.

Peskin, Allen. *Garfield*. Kent, Ohio: Kent State University Press, 1978.

Rose, Phyllis. *Parallel Lives: Five Victorian Marriages*. New York: Alfred A. Knopf, 1984.

Rothman, Ellen K. *Hands and Hearts: A History of Courtship in America*. New York: Basic Books, Inc., 1984.

Ryan, Mary P. *The Cradle of the Middle Class*. Cambridge, 1981.

Sears, John F. *Sacred Places: American Tourist Attractions in the Nineteenth Century*. New York: Oxford University Press, 1989.

Sklar, Kathryn Kish. *Catharine Beecher: A Study in American Domesticity*. New York: W. W. Norton, 1976.

Smith-Rosenberg, Carroll. *Disorderly Conduct: Vision of Gender in Victorian America*. New York: A. A. Knopf, 1985.

Smith, Theodore Clarke. *James Abram Garfield: The Life and Letters*. 2 vols. New Haven: Yale University Press, 1925.

Williams, Frederick D., ed. *The Wild Life of the Army: Civil War Letters of James A. Garfield*. East Lansing: Michigan State University Press, 1964.

Index

A

Adams, Charles Francis and family, 255-57

Agassiz, Professor Louis, 290, 321n.

Ames, Mary Clemmer, viii, 352, 359n., 376-77

Ames, Oakes, 286-88, 290

Antioch College, 26

Atwood, Lizzie (Pratt), 24, 41n., 75, 91-92, 95, 98-99, 201

Austin, Harmon, 108, 111, 118, 147-48, 149, 179-80, 199, 207, 250, 322n.

B

Beecher, Henry Ward, 210, 227n., 242, 300-2, 317, 323n.

Black, Jeremiah (Judge), 244, 264-65

Blaine, James G., 193, 304, 305-8, 329, 360, 371, 382

Booth, Almeda, xii, 10, 41n., 44, 46, 49, 58, 73, 74, 76, 77n., 79, 99, 122, 141, 147, 148, 149, 162, 166, 169, 170, 179, 191, 199, 200, 201, 202, 203, 207, 208, 210, 212, 213, 215, 222-24, 228n.

C

Calhoun, Lucia Gilbert, xi-xii, 199-200, 206, 207, 210-14, 227n., 229, 234-38, 242, 260n.

Campbell, Alexander, 11, 41n., 50, 89

Carlyle, Thomas, 4, 5, 8, 40n.

Chandler, Zachariah (Senator), 364-65

Chase, Salmon P., 156, 158, 177, 179, 181, 227n., 228

Cox, Jacob, 106-7, 109-10, 111, 113, 128, 159, 164, 203, 211, 298, 385-86

D

Dennison, William (Ohio Governor), 114, 115, 124, 230-31, 260n.

E

Eliot, George, 292, 321n., 335, 358n.

Emerson, Ralph Waldo, 30

Evarts, William M., 302, 325-26

Everest, Harvey W., 30, 42n., 139, 154n., 169, 191, 197n.

F

Fiske, Theophilus, 27-28
Flathead Indians, 262, 275, 278-84, 285n.
Ford, Wallace, 118, 207-9, 214, 246
Freese, Andrew, 83-84, 92, 116-17n.
Fremont, John Charles, 313, 323n.
Fuller, Corydon, 16-18, 40-41n., 112

G

Garfield, Edward ("Neddie"), 289, 330-31, 334-35
Garfield, Eliza Ballou ("Grandma"), 54, 71, 135, 173, 191, 201, 204, 208, 215, 217, 219, 228n., 262, 263, 267, 273, 366
Garfield, Eliza Arabella ("Trot"), 104, 192-96, 200, 201

H

Harber, Giles B., 257-58, 261n., 390
Hayden, Sutton, 8, 41n., 47, 71, 73, 74, 76, 79, 85
Hayes, Rutherford B. (President), 325, 345, 364
Henry, Charles ("Captain"), 117n., 198n., 371, 391n.
Hinsdale, Burke, 107, 117n., 139, 181, 207, 265-66, 349-50
Hofer, Theodore, 318-19, 323n.
Hopkins, Mark, 21, 22, 56, 66, 251, 274, 276
Horton, V. B., 347
Howells, William Dean, 269, 284n., 358n.
Hubbell, Mary, 12, 14, 35

J

James, Henry, 378, 391n.
Jaynes, Emma, 381-82, 392n.
Jones, Harry, 135, 149-50, 155n.

K

Knox, Henry, 385-86, 392n.

L

Lamb, Charles, 60
Learned, Maria, 43-44, 59, 63, 66-67, 78n., 168, 197n., 260
Lincoln, Abraham, 107, 109, 159, 162, 217-18
Longfellow, Henry W., 24, 36, 41n., 47-48, 67, 77n., 78n., 132, 154n.

M

Macauley, Thomas B., 5, 40n., 386
Marwedel, Emma J. C., 297, 322n.
Miller, Hugh, 33-34
Munnell, Thomas, 29, 42n., 58

N

Niagara Falls, 2-6, 32, 35, 232, 273

P

Pardee, Don (Major), 131, 136, 339
Plumb, Ralph (Captain), 136, 137, 138, 139, 140

R

Ralston, William C, 304, 305, 309-11, 322n., 323n.
Reid, Whitelaw, 379-87
Ransom, Caroline ("Carrie"), 266-67, 284n., 288, 307, 344, 352, 386
Rhodes, Harry, 72-73, 79n., 85, 88, 99, 118, 138, 139, 140, 150, 154n., 159, 166, 169, 172-74, 176, 179, 180, 181, 185, 198n., 220, 250, 307

Riddle, Albert Gallatin, 149-50, 155n., 365, 391n.
Robison, John P. ("Doc"), 32, 50, 137, 149, 155n., 160, 174, 291, 298, 340, 350, 368
Rockwell, Almon (Colonel), 361-62, 389
Rose, George U., 277, 285n., 292, 306, 321n.
Rosecrans, William S, 156-57, 182-84, 189, 192, 345
Rudolph, Nellie, 166-67, 221, 260n., 325, 346
Runkle, Mrs. Cornelius. See Calhoun, Lucia Gilbert
Ryder, Symonds ("Uncle Symonds"), 22, 39, 41n., 46-48, 58

S

Sault Sainte Marie (Michigan), 105, 117n.
Schenck, Robert, 230, 260n.
Selleck, Rebecca, 43-44, 59, 63, 64, 67, 68, 70, 78n., 80-81, 90, 164-65, 167-69, 180, 218, 236, 242, 247, 260n., 261n., 263
Sheldon, Lionel A., 123, 131, 379
Sherman, John (Senator), 360, 365, 373
Spencer, Mrs, Henry C., (Sara Andrews), 250, 261n., 272, 277, 284n., 350-56
Stowe, Harriet Beecher, 44, 47, 48, 311-12, 323n.
Swaim, David G. (Captain), 159, 197n., 254, 262, 263, 278-84, 371, 380, 382

T

Tennyson, Alfred, Lord, 59, 198n., 307, 309, 322n.
Turchin, John B. (Colonel), 144, 145, 150

V

Virgil, 4, 6, 8, 20, 26, 40n.

W

White, Henry Kirk, 70-71, 78n.
Wilber, Charles, 27, 30, 41n., 97, 363-64
Williams, Augustus, 126, 129, 141, 148-49, 154n.
Williams College, 19, 22, 30-31, 46, 66, 276
Willis, N. P., 5, 40n., 65, 97, 117n.